Shanghai in Transition

When the Communist Party took control of Shanghai in 1949, the city was one of the world's most cosmopolitan, 'modern' cities. In the ensuing decades, Shanghai's economy, infrastructure and links with the world all atrophied. Lack of change in the city's physical structure was paralleled by a similar fixity and immutability in people's everyday lives, careers and expectations.

However, since the 1990s, far-reaching economic reforms have been implemented which are designed to recreate Shanghai as a cosmopolitan, world financial and trade centre. An influx of domestic and foreign capital is transforming the city's physical structure at a frantic pace. This book focuses on the lives of local residents and their perceptions of their changing city, and presents an evocative series of ethnographic perspectives of the city's shifting sociological landscape in this period of transition.

Jos Gamble examines the flow of domestic and international migrants, capital and mass media across Shanghai's boundaries and the consequences of these on a transitional economy. The book introduces the changing senses of what it means to be Shanghainese, and the ways in which consumption is producing, facilitating and marking out new divisions within society.

Jos Gamble is an anthropologist and Lecturer in Asia Pacific Business at the School of Management, Royal Holloway, University of London.

Shanghai in Transition

Changing perspectives and social contours of a Chinese metropolis

Jos Gamble

RoutledgeCurzon
Taylor & Francis Group
LONDON AND NEW YORK

First published 2003
by RoutledgeCurzon
2 Park Square, Milton Park, Abingdon, Oxfordshire OX14 4RN

Simultaneously published in the USA and Canada
by RoutledgeCurzon
711 Third Avenue, New York, NY 10017

First issued in paperback 2014

RoutledgeCurzon is an imprint of the Taylor and Francis Group, an informa business

Typeset in Times by
Integra Software Services Pvt. Ltd, Pondicherry, India

British Library Cataloguing in Publication Data
A catalogue record for this book is available from the British Library

Library of Congress Cataloging in Publication Data
Gamble, Jos, 1959–
Shanghai in transition: changing perspectives and social contours of a Chinese metropolis / Jos Gamble.
p. cm.
Includes bibliographical references and index.
1. Shanghai (China)—Economic conditions. 2. Shanghai (China)—Social conditions. I. Title.

HC428.S47 G36 2002
330.951′132—dc21

2002067990

ISBN 13: 978-0-7007-1571-8 (hbk)
ISBN 13: 978-0-415-86162-5 (pbk)

To the memory of my father, William Jack Gamble

I will take the liberty of saying, that the stranger, who discovers nothing amiable among the Chinese people, never gave them an opportunity of seeing that he has any ingredient of that sort in his own composition, and that he, who has not gained their goodwill and their applause, has assuredly not taken much pains to deserve them.

(G.T. Lay, *Chinese Repository* 1843: 136)

Contents

Maps

Preface: ethnography of a city

In the 1990s far-reaching economic reforms were implemented in China which were designed to re-create Shanghai as a cosmopolitan, world financial, and commercial centre. Policy-makers and citizens have been engaged in the difficult and potentially hazardous task of 'crossing the stream' from a 'socialist state planned economy' to a 'socialist market economy', a transition which often involves adopting policies dramatically opposed to those which went before. This book aims to furnish new perspectives and insights on the parameters of that transition, and especially upon how social boundaries and identities are becoming reconfigured.

Shanghai is a veritable cornucopia for research. Until the late 1940s, it had an ambivalent reputation as a cosmopolitan, semi-colonial entrepôt based upon *laissez-faire* capitalism. Under Communist Party rule it then became the centre of a socialist state-planned economy with a greatly diminished international role. The rhetoric of the Maoist period, especially during the Cultural Revolution, divided Chinese society into a limited range of unambiguous categories, stressed equality and egalitarianism, and actively sought to 'cut off all tails of capitalism'. By contrast, current policies – 'socialism with Chinese characteristics' – accept, indeed, encourage, that some may get rich first. They criticise egalitarianism, and permit the emergence of new modes of livelihood. Since the mid-1980s the Chinese government's attitude toward Shanghai and other large coastal cities has undergone a striking and radical change. After three decades of official rhetoric which emphasised the need to reduce the economic dominance of cities such as Shanghai, and the neglect of their infrastructure which accompanied this, the government began to promote these cities as models of development.

Since 1990, and spurred on especially in 1992, measures have been implemented which are intended to re-create Shanghai as an international financial and commercial centre. Since that time Shanghai has embarked upon one of the most adventurous and frenetic building programmes the world has ever known. In early 1998, Shanghai had around 23,000 building sites and some 20 per cent of the world's cranes were currently in the city. An increasingly important private sector has re-emerged and private markets, restaurants, and bars have proliferated. Shanghai now retains more of the profits made in the city, and vast sums of domestic and foreign capital have flowed into the city. The first reform era joint venture was established in 1980. By the end of 1996, over 16,000 foreign-funded enterprises in the city employed nearly 600,000 people and produced 34 per cent of the city's industrial output. By early 2000, over half the world's largest 500 companies had established operations in Shanghai. The stock market has returned and Shanghai has regained some of its pre-1949 cosmopolitanism. The Pudong New Area in the south-east of the city has been earmarked as a 'new Manhattan' and is being redeveloped at tremendous cost. A local writer, a strong supporter of reform, commented to me that the changes in Shanghai since 1991–2 were 'of an extent that a person such as myself could never have imagined.'

Shanghai is undergoing fundamental and rapid, even frantic, socio-economic change. Increasing choice, mobility, and fluidity are unpicking and fraying the once encloistered texture of everyday life. Boundaries, both spatial and social, are being dismantled, fractured, undermined and reconfigured. This work explores the increasing diversity, flux, and uncertainty in China's largest city as experienced by a range of informants and commentators at the micro-level. The main topics explored are representations of the changes under way in Shanghai; the perceived consequences of Shanghai's half-open 'door' to intra-national and global cultural flows; the differential markings of spaces and place-related identities within the city; consumption and consumerism; and the emergent discourse of share dealers. I build upwards from 'street level' perspectives and stress ways in which the quotidian lives of Shanghai citizens are co-implicated with wider historical, political, and economic phenomena. Where possible I draw broad brush strokes, but always with attention to the craquelure – those cracks and fissures which comprise them, but which may have their own, different, stories to tell.

In contrast to Maoist China, a welter of statistics now emerges from the country. The Party-state is particularly keen to flaunt its achievements. In the years 1993–9, China's Gross Domestic Product (GDP) grew at an average of just under 10 per cent per annum. Figures for Shanghai are even more impressive – in these same years, the city's GDP grew by an annual average rate of around 12.7 per cent. Even faced with the winds of the Asian financial crisis, Shanghai's GDP grew at 9.8 per cent in 1998 and 9.4 per cent in 1999, compared with a national rate of 7.8 per cent and 7.1 per cent, respectively.

Inevitably I have incorporated a range of statistical data into this study. However, there are limitations to such bald statistics, even assuming their accuracy.[1] Statistical data, with its seductive averages, tells us little or nothing about the situation of individuals' lives. Statistics provide little indication of the, often contradictory, perceptions, values, and experiences of actual people. In this study there is an especial and deliberate emphasis upon the voices of local residents, their constructions of their own lives, of others, and of their city. The great benefit of qualitative, ethnographic research is that it can provide much richer insights and more nuanced portrayals of lives as they are daily lived, experienced, and reflected upon. The intention is to provide a sociological topography of the world as viewed from the perspective of Shanghainese residents.

WHY SHANGHAI?

> [Shanghai is]...the chief seat of commerce, the home of progress, in short the nerve-centre of China, whose influence reaches out to the remotest corners of the land.
>
> (Mary Gamewell, *The Gateway to China: Pictures of Shanghai* 1916: 19)

As Lucian Pye wrote in the early 1980s, 'serious analysis of nearly all important aspects of life in China must, eventually, confront Shanghai and its special place in the Chinese scheme of things' (1981: xi). With the gathering pace of change in the years since this comment, and in view of Shanghai's renewed global attraction, study of the city is even more warranted. Shanghai has vast potential, not only in terms of its own industrial base and human resources but also because of its propitious location. The three adjacent provinces alone have a population of around 170 million providing a vast potential workforce and market for the city's goods and services. The city is also being promoted as the 'Dragon head' of the entire Yangtze basin area. Shanghai is exerting an increasingly powerful centrifugal influence globally as well as nationally. It is indicative that a mid-1990s BBC television documentary should focus upon Shanghai as one of the 'cities of the future' (BBC2, 29 November 1995). It has been a particularly timely point at which to conduct an ethnographic study of Shanghai.

Anthropology is still popularly seen as the study of the remote, the 'exotic'. Since the 1960s, however, anthropologists have begun to pay more attention to urban contexts although relatively little attention has been given to cities. With a worldwide trend towards urbanisation, it would seem incumbent upon anthropologists to address and examine the diversity of the urban experience (cf. Harvey 1989). It seems particularly appropriate to explore the specificities of urban dwelling and city life in China since town and city dwelling are increasingly the experience of Chinese people themselves. In 1980, the population of urban China was around 140 million (Kirkby 1985: 59) and accounted for about 15 per cent of the total population (202). Between 1980 and 1995 the number of cities with a population over one million more than doubled, from 15 to 32 (*Economist* 8 March 1997: 22). By 1995, the urban population was around 29 per cent. Kam Wing Chan anticipates that in the coming two decades, the urban percentage of China's population will almost double (1994: 153). Shanghai's population is also expected to rise: in 1998 the city's population was 13.075 million, it is expected to reach 16 million in 2020 (*SS* 22 February 2000: 4).

Shanghai has a total area of 6,340 square kilometres.[2] Administratively, Shanghai is one of China's four municipalities (the others are Tianjin, Beijing, and Chongqing) with a status equivalent to a province. The municipality is divided into three parts: (1) the central city with its ten urban districts of Huangpu, Nanshi, Luwan, Jing'an, Xuhui, Changning, Putuo, Hongkou, Zhabei, and Yangpu; (2) the four suburban districts of Baoshan, Minhang, Jiading, and Pudong New Area; and (3) the six suburban counties of Songjiang, Qingpu, Jinshan, Fengxian, Nanhui, and Chongming. These three zones constitute a

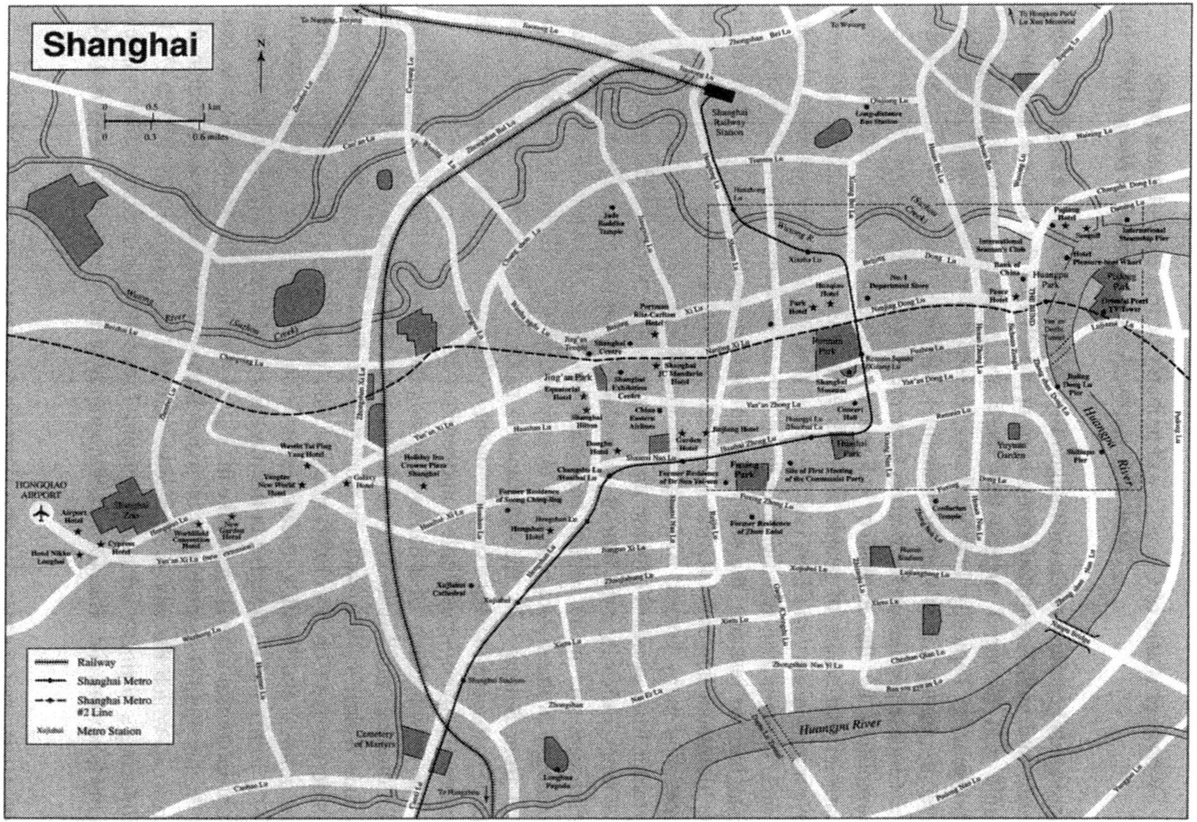

Map 1 Shanghai municipality.

three-tier household registration system – with 'city', 'town', and 'rural' zones. My main concern here is with the city zone and its ten districts. These districts, with a total area of 280 square kilometres, and a population in 1996 of 6,339,300 million, are further divided into neighbourhoods and street units.

> Whatever is said of China . . . will probably be true only of some parts.
> (Rev. E.J. Hardy, *John Chinaman at Home* 1907: 10)

Sinologists generally refer, unambiguously, to 'the Chinese' as a single, homogeneous, and undifferentiated group – an approach that the Chinese government would also favour. I suggest that there are good reasons to dismantle this homogeneity. Typically, both local sociologists and sinologists have highlighted diversity among China's ethnic minorities. However, even among the majority Han Chinese population themselves there are many cultural differences, a feature exemplified by the extensive indigenous discourses which essentialise the character and nature of people from different parts of China. Such discourses have a long history in China (see Eberhard 1965), and are ubiquitous in modern China. There is also significant linguistic diversity within China. In the case of Shanghai, for instance, the city's population is diaglossic. Whilst *putonghua* is the 'dominant language' (Grillo 1989), Shanghai dialect is the language of 'the street' and many homes. Although considered a dialect, Shanghainese is more different from standard Chinese than is Spanish from Italian. Shanghainese has five tones, rather than the four of *putonghua*, it also has extensive pronunciation differences and many lexical and grammatical divergences from *putonghua*; a dialogue in the dialect would be largely incomprehensible to an ordinary resident from Beijing.[3] By focusing upon a particular city and its distinctiveness I hope to discern to what extent we ought to dissolve notions of 'China' and 'the Chinese' as overly-monolithic homogeneous categories.

The growing body of urban anthropological studies of China generally deals with discrete, small-scale units or defined segments of society. Examples of this include Walder's (1986) study on work units, Rofel's (1992) study in a silk factory, Henderson and Cohen's (1984) study of a hospital, Rai's (1991) study on university politics, and Honig's researches on Subei people in Honig (1986, 1989a,b, 1990, 1992). I have deviated in the direction of Hannerz's suggestion that urban anthropological analysis may take the city as a whole as the unit of focus instead of 'rather limited assemblages of social relationships . . . lesser units within the city . . . in which the city itself recedes into the background' (1980: 296–7). In producing a distinctly urban ethnography I take the city of Shanghai as a whole as my fieldwork site. This, then, is ethnography *of* a city, not ethnography *in* a city.

SOURCES OF DATA – RESEARCH STRATEGIES AND TACTICS

A strategic feature of my research was to accumulate and utilise data derived from an eclectic array of research-gathering techniques and strategies. The empirical data used in this study was collected during several periods of research conducted in Shanghai between 1992–2000, totalling almost two years. The initial anthropological study was conducted in 15 months during 1992–3 and two months in 1994. This data has been supplemented during subsequent research visits to Shanghai: two months in 1997, one month in 1998, two months in 1999, and three weeks in 2000. I had previously acquired familiarity with the city during visits in 1984 and 1985, and two years residence from 1988–90 as a student of Chinese. The voices of local people, noted from diverse contexts ranging from structured, tape-recorded interviews to chance overheard remarks, are the main research data utilised in this study. China remains a country relatively under-studied by anthropologists which accentuates the originality and, I hope, significance of my street-level research.

Robert Weller writes of the People's Republic of China that '[r]arely has any state developed such powerful institutions to impose and foster unified interpretations' (1994: 188). Thus there is a countervalent value to be derived from qualitative research in China. I found that the institutions Weller refers to are now less powerful than he suggests, and that unofficial viewpoints are now more readily held, and certainly more readily voiced. Moreover, in a state which strictly polices the mass media and prohibits any collective action that might undermine its own dominance, I was able to observe many instances of what James Scott describes as 'weapons of the weak' (1990: 27). In Shanghai people say that 'the higher authorities have a policy, those below have a counter-strategy.' I encountered many instances of 'everyday forms of resistance' such as ridicule, truculence, irony, petty acts of non-compliance, foot dragging, dissimulation, and 'disbelief in elite homilies' (ibid.: 350).

Interviews provided access not only to respondents' conscious opinions and statements but also to the linguistic terms and categories through which they constructed their worlds and their own understanding of their activities. Interviews were of differing degrees of formality, ranging from encounters in officials' offices to friendly chats in people's homes. Some interviews were tape-recorded and transcribed later. In most instances I took notes at the time and supplemented them from memory later. On only one occasion did a respondent ask me not to record his words, saying that it would make him 'nervous'. For the most part, interviews were semi-structured; that is, I would begin with a set of prepared questions but follow up lines of enquiry alluded to or hinted at by 'informants'. My concern was that informants should not just follow an agenda and answer a list of questions based solely upon my presuppositions. Rather, I sought to ask open-ended questions which would allow respondents the opportunity to set the agenda, and me to be sensitive to *their* concerns and *their* interests in my supplementary questions.

Since the late 1970s, Western research in China has been steadily increasing. Initially, such exchanges 'required the cooperation of official gatekeepers in China' (Madsen 1993: 173). Norma Diamond records how during her 1979–80 research in Taitou 'all the interviews were arranged for me by the brigade leadership who always had to be advised in advance about the topics to be covered in the interview' (1983: 125). Families in Shanghai told me that my visits to their homes would have been impossible during the Maoist era. Many informants said that even until the mid-1980s it was dangerous to have any contact with foreigners; a visit by a foreigner would be followed by a visit from the police. The less politically charged atmosphere in Shanghai during the 1990s allowed for a far more relaxed and spontaneous interchange between foreigners and Chinese.

I was under no form of supervision, and my interviews were all arranged through informal contacts. Since local people were not permitted to enter my university room the majority of interviews took place in people's homes. Shanghai homes are crowded and in a typical interview situation several people would be in the same room. An advantage of this was that in such circumstances I was often in situations where my presence could become peripheral, even irrelevant, my 'foreignness' would be forgotten or, at least, recede into the background, and people engaged in the same activities and conversations as if I were not there. In these 'home encounters' I was a participant in 'real situations' which lacked the artificiality of more formal one-to-one interviews. I would stress again Shanghai's crowded situation – privacy, and being apart from other people, is not the norm.

Qualitative anthropological research involves learning 'how to be a person' (*zenme zuoren*), a key Chinese conceptualisation, in a different cultural environment. In all one's daily activities one is engaging in research, and I found that unobtrusive methods such as conversations, chats on buses and at parties, interaction in and observation of everyday situations provided significant research data. At times this was similar to the type of 'guerrilla interviewing' engaged in by Thomas Gold (1989), which he describes as 'unchaperoned, spontaneous but structured participant observation and interviews as opportunities present themselves' in which notes are written up afterwards (180). Conversations, and even overheard remarks, in shops, street markets, restaurants, buses, or elsewhere all provided insights and useful material. It was, for instance, whilst cycling and travelling by bus in Shanghai that I first became aware of the depth of feeling against migrant workers. It was at these times that local residents, my fellow commuters, often vocalised their disdain for the 'outsiders' who, as they saw it, crowded the buses and clogged-up the streets.

I sought to meet as diverse a range of local people as possible. My informants included a magazine editor, factory workers, laid-off workers, neighbourhood residents' committee cadres, dramatists, journalists, private entrepreneurs, school teachers, university lecturers and professors, university students, former senior military personnel, joint-venture employees, share dealers, and a former KMT official. This listing could, of course, be divided in other ways; for example, it includes Communist Party and non-Party members, former Red Guards and the victims of Red Guard assaults, teenagers and the retired, a couple of millionaires and those with less than one hundred *yuan* a month to live on.

A particularly interesting aspect of the way informants represented their views was the use of the term *laobaixing*. When I asked people about events in Shanghai they often spoke about 'the *laobaixing*' (the common people, the ordinary people – literally 'the old one hundred names'). At times it was evident that informants were verbalising their own feelings or experiences in terms of 'the *laobaixing*', although this distinction was not always clear. To retain this ambiguity, and to highlight the frequency of deployment of this term, the Chinese usage is retained throughout this study. I posed the question, 'Who are the *laobaixing*?' to various people. A standard response was that *laobaixing* includes everybody apart from high officials. A retired school teacher pointed out that 'during the Cultural Revolution the *laobaixing* were called "the masses" '. With the recent stress upon material incentives and consumerism old terms may be re-cycled and re-invested with meanings. The response of an engineer in his twenties was illustrative of this, for he described the *laobaixing* as 'those who use their ability and their own and blood and sweat to make money' whilst non-*laobaixing* were 'those who use power to make money.'

In contrast to many Chinese villages which are still largely dominated by face-to-face interactions among people who are connected, Shanghai is a highly literate, complex, media-saturated society. People's understandings of themselves and the world around them are influenced and informed not only by social and peer group pressures, but also by education, plays, and electronic and print media. Since these sources contribute to, and are constitutive of, people's cultural capital – their commonsensical notions and everyday discourses, it was important to make myself as familiar as possible with all these spheres.

The official media provide a source of representations of how the Party-state believes things should be, and such media are intended to have a propaganda function. In 1985, the then Communist Party General Secretary Hu Yaobang stated that 'journalism should make itself a successful mouthpiece of the party' (1986: 182). Moreover, he indicated that newspapers should devote at least 80 per cent of their space to reports on success and achievements. An editorial in *Renmin Ribao* of 1 July 1990 stressed: 'Mass media must adhere to the principle of the Party spirit, and be politically identified with the Party Central Committee'. The Party produces and sanctions media items which they intend viewers to 'read' in one way. However, I found that actual viewers sometimes made interpretations which did not accord with the Party's. Some local people were ironic readers of such messages. I was frequently told 'when you see the television news, the reality is the opposite of what is actually said.'

Local television is of particular importance. During the 1980s, urban Chinese joined the world's television viewers and the potential 'audience' in China now exceeds 650 million people. By 1986, television penetration in Shanghai had already reached 95 per cent (Lull and Sun 1988: 197). Watching television has become *the* most popular leisure time activity and it has undoubtedly 'influenced the audience's thinking on topics that range from sports and consumer activities to the most profound political, economic, and cultural issues' (Lull 1991: 172–3). Often the vocabulary people used to describe events and phenomena matched that used in media representations. Observing what the local population are regularly observing must be a part of any contemporary anthropologist's research. Media representations constitute valuable ethnographic data in their own right.

They are also useful as a basis for formulating hypotheses and addressing issues less amenable to more direct questioning.

Local newspapers were a valuable source of information. There are dozens of publications in Shanghai. Three locally published Chinese language newspapers were particularly useful – *Jiefang Ribao* (Liberation Daily), *Wenhui Bao* (Wenhui Daily), and *Xinmin Wanbao* (New People's Evening News). Typically, my informants portrayed *Jiefang Ribao* and, to a lesser extent, *Wenhui Bao* as 'the Party newspaper' and the popular *Xinmin Wanbao* as 'read by the common people (*laobaixing*).' As one informant commented, 'work units provide *Jiefang Ribao* or *Wenhui Bao*, *Xinmin Wanbao* the *laobaixing* read at home.' Two English language papers were also useful; the locally published *Shanghai Star*, and the national *China Daily*.

MAKING CONTACT

A local sociologist remarked to me that it is very difficult for both Chinese and foreigners to conduct research in China because 'there are many walls and curtains.' The ways in which I was able to meet people, and the kinds of networks I used to negotiate these boundaries, are indicative of the nature of interpersonal relations in Chinese society. Apart from the Party-state bureaucracy and work units there are few organisations in urban China. Shanghai lacks most of the myriad advisory and information services and voluntary associations which are found in Western cities. In many senses this resembles Sun Yat-sen's description of China as 'a plate of loose sand'. There is also a preponderance of walls and boundaries in Shanghai, a factor closely related to the cellular or 'honeycomb pattern' (Shue 1988: 50) of social organisation. It was widely believed that 'going through the back door' by using personal connections (*guanxi*) was the only effective way to surmount or negotiate these boundaries.

'*Nakunin, nakunin*' – the dialect term for 'foreigner' is invariably the first word of Shanghai dialect an overseas visitor learns in the city. When strolling in the city, I often heard this term used in the gossip around me. Parents would point me out to their children, and young children would tug at their parents, point, and tell them '*nakunin, nakunin*'. This was not only a linguistic initiation, but also an introduction to a different cultural environment. It revealed a key organising factor in Chinese society – *nei-wai you bie* – the distinction made between inside and outside. In this instance, the distinction was between China, 'inside country' (*guonei*), and 'outside countries' (*guowai* or *waiguo*). This distinction is drawn so clearly that I could never become 'Chinese' but must learn how to be a 'foreigner' (*waiguoren* – literally an 'outside-country person') in Shanghai.[4]

A combination of fear and nationalism tends to make Chinese people particularly circumspect in interactions with foreigners; these factors make them reluctant to mention shortcomings of Chinese society. Older informants, made cautious by the political winds of the past, tended to be the most wary of making comments which could bring them trouble. Nationalistic feelings, what local people described as 'national face', made some informants consider that discussing China's shortcomings with foreigners was *jia chou bu ke wai yang* – 'domestic shame which should not be made public.' A combination of 'face' and fear meant, for instance, that I had difficulty in trying to meet workers who had been made redundant. One contact knew several redundant workers, but none were willing to speak to me. He explained that 'they are very angry. They have nothing good to say about this society and are afraid of getting into trouble if they speak to you.'

People I encountered not only had their own ideas about what foreigners should not be told, but also differing ideas about what they could understand. In conversations which touched upon diverse aspects of Chinese society I was frequently told 'you foreigners cannot understand'. Using the notion of ethnography as a performance, it often seemed that there was a construction of the audience – in this instance myself as a foreign researcher – as a paedocracy (cf. Hartley 1987). That is, many informants believed Chinese society to be inherently too complex for foreigners to understand – a notion which serves as a kind of boundary maintenance device.

Being a foreign researcher in China does, however, have some distinct advantages. A foreigner is likely to be outside a person's regular circle of acquaintances – it may be 'safer' to speak to an outsider. One respondent, for instance, told me that he felt able to discuss certain topics with me that he could only mention, if then, to very close friends. An example of this was the notion that Zhou Enlai – still a popular 'hero' – was as much to blame for the Cultural Revolution as Mao Zedong. As a foreigner, I could be told this since I had no pre-formed 'barrier' against such ideas.

Foreigners in China are often described as 'foreign friends' and treated as 'exalted guests' (Butler 1983: 119). This politeness which is, in itself, a kind of distancing mechanism, has lessened since the 1980s as foreigners have become a more commonplace sight. However, as a 'foreigner' I often still received more cooperation than a Chinese stranger would. As a Chinese speaker, though, I tended to lose the category of 'guest' and some of the politeness accorded to this category of person. If tickets for a journey or the theatre were sold out, Chinese friends believed it would be most efficacious if I, rather than they, made a request for help. They would also advise me to speak English; on such occasions, prestige appeared to be attached to *not* being able to speak Chinese.

The foreigner/Chinese distinction is just one example of the inside/outside dichotomies which permeate Chinese society. At its most intimate level is the family, described in the Shanghai dialect as *ala ziga nin* (*women ziji ren*) – 'our own people/one of us' and everybody else. To be 'one of us' is to be bound by reciprocal rights and duties of mutual aid and support. The traditional legal system assumed a co-implication of family members – all those related to an offender could be punished, an ethos which persisted in the class labelling of families during the Maoist period. During Mao Zedong's time a crucial distinction was between 'the people' and 'enemies of the people'. This dichotomy can also be drawn between Communist Party and non-Party members, an increasingly hazy distinction – especially at the level of ordinary Party members – but still important nonetheless. It can also be 'we Shanghainese' in contrast to non-Shanghainese.

The borders of these inside/outside boundaries are of variable fixity and porousness. For example, the boundary of 'our own people' possesses considerable elasticity (see also King 1991: 67). It may, for instance, include a close friend who is regarded *as if* they are a family member. Similarly, even in chance encounters I was not solely related to as a foreigner.[5] Within the plurality of often overlapping dichotomies my knowledge of Chinese language, Shanghai dialect, and local customs, and friendships with local people enabled me to straddle the shifting insider–outsider boundary. This cultural capital made me an outsider with inside knowledge. People would describe me, variously, as 'half Chinese', 'like a Shanghainese' or 'almost Chinese'.

Western theorists of modernisation such as Anthony Giddens (1990, 1991) have suggested that one consequence of modernisation and urbanisation is that a reliance upon face-to-face, particularistic relationships will be replaced by a stress upon universalistic, credentialised relationships. Indigenous discourses in Shanghai and my own experience as a researcher in that city sharply contradict such an assertion. An overwhelming impression was that particularistic ties were considered an essential requirement to creating opportunities and attaining positive outcomes in diverse aspects of everyday life. Indeed, Shanghainese often described this as an increasingly prominent feature of modern life in Shanghai.

Contact-making in China is highly personalised, there are highly elaborated indigenous notions of networking and people have a high degree of what Hannerz calls 'network awareness' (1980: 196). I relied heavily upon an 'informal network', and built upon contacts (*guanxi*) made between 1988–90. Gold restricts *guanxi* to instrumentalism and describes it as a 'power relationship' (1985: 660). However, my understanding is that whilst *guanxi* may be used by people for instrumental aims and may contain relations of this kind – the patron–client relationship is a type of *guanxi* – nonetheless the term has a wider range of referants than this. *Guanxi* may be translated as relationships, particularistic ties, connections, or connectedness. The meaning of *guanxi* is context-related. It may have negative, neutral, or positive connotations; it may involve a power relationship or describe one of equality. Since no single English term encompasses the range of meanings of *guanxi*, I leave this term untranslated.

Informants characterised human relationships as like 'circles' (*quanzi*) with an inner circle consisting of household and relatives. Radiating outwards are classmates, teachers, friends, work colleagues, relationships of mutual benefit, and, perhaps, those of the same native place. Friendship played an important part in many people's lives, and becoming a 'friend' was also a vital element of my research. A popular expression advises: 'at home depend on relatives, outside depend upon the help of friends.'

In Shanghai the term 'friend' covers a range of different types of relationship from the highly instrumental to those resembling 'pure relationships'. The most unbreakable are *zhixin pengyou* – intimate friends, literally 'friendships in which one knows the heart.' The notion of *yiqi* (personal loyalty) is considered integral to sincere friendship. With *yiqi* there is an injunction to provide help when asked; the ideal is that one should be prepared to cut out one's own ribs (*liang lei cha dao*) for the sake of a friend. Complex layers of mutual indebtedness for favours, and help received and given create, promote, and strengthen *yiqi*.

Shifting state policies have affected friendship. During political campaigns, the risk of betrayal was especially high, and its potential consequences devastating. In such an environment people were extremely wary of creating too many 'moral hostages to fortune'. With the diminished political pressures of the reform era greater possibilities of association have emerged, including opportunities to expand the range of achieved as opposed to ascribed relationships. Among those engaged in commercial activities who seek to extend their range of contacts there is a strong incentive to increase 'friendships' of the more instrumental kind. Friendships of the latter type include *jiurou pengyou* – 'wine-and-meat' friends. Amongst such fair-weather friends the value of *yiqi* may be invoked by the parties concerned but were probably absent in practice.[6]

Shanghainese often use fictive kinship terms to describe relationships of friendship. For instance, male or female friends of roughly the same age may be called *xiao xiongdi* ('little brothers'). A similar term which suggests a closer relationship is *tse ku* (*chu ke*) *xiongdi* – 'brothers who have emerged from the same nest.' The use of such terms can be regarded as an attempt by metaphorical extension to make non-familial relationships become as dependable as (the ideal of) close kin ties. The manager of a stock exchange who told me that his aim was to make the company like a 'warm home' clearly had in mind the harmony and reliability of the ideal family. The ultimate imaginary family is the nation – the 'nation family' (*guojia*). In recognition of the city's vital economic contribution to this 'nation-family', Shanghai is sometimes referred to as 'elder brother' (*lao da*).

Friendship is often built upon a base of *tong*, 'sameness' or co-identification, such as with classmates and work colleagues. Friendships created during the formative years of education are a particularly important basis of *tong*. Classmates often form bonds of mutual understanding and trust which last a lifetime. My oldest informant, a man in his nineties, described the way that he and fellow university classmates had maintained contact, including regular monthly meals, for seven decades. Strictly speaking *tongxue* are those who have studied together. However, the elasticity of such concepts meant that I could be introduced as their '*tongxue*' by people of a similar age who had attended the same university as myself, although we had never studied together.

The teacher–student relationship was also important in my research. A traditional Chinese saying states: 'if somebody is your teacher for a day, they are your father for the rest of your life.' Relations between teachers and favoured students still contain elements of this traditional pattern. For instance, former pupils may visit teachers on festive occasions and amongst past and present pupils of one teacher there may be bonds of sentiment.

A distinct disadvantage of conducting research in a society where particularistic values dominate is that without personal contacts it can be extremely difficult to penetrate 'circles' of relationships. An advantage of this is that once accepted by one link in an interpersonal circle of trust one often gains access to a wide number of people. People will help others on the strength of sometimes very tenuous links. In instances where one 'depends upon the face' (on 'face' see Hu 1944) of a mutual acquaintance, contacts could be built upon in ways which would be unusual in England. My networking – described by one informant as a 'chain reaction' – stretched across a gamut of different bases of trust which may cross back and forth across the generations. As an example, I once met the parents of a Chinese classmate. My classmate's father subsequently introduced me to a work colleague who felt indebted to him for having helped him secure his present job. The work colleague then introduced me to a colleague from his previous job and to a schoolmate of his son. Via this schoolmate I met his girlfriend and another schoolmate . . .

An interview with a local government official indicates the differential information obtained once a basis of trust has been created. In interactions with officials one often encounters 'officialese' where the most interesting aspects are those which remain unsaid. On this occasion a young man introduced me to his father, a local government cadre who had recently applied to join the Communist Party. He explained that his prime motivation was to improve his career prospects, but swiftly added that during the course of his application he would, of course, convey an impression of pure altruism. To demonstrate his facility in providing what would be required, he proceeded to recite paragraphs of the prevailing dogma. If, as a stranger, I had met this man in his official capacity I would undoubtedly have heard only the latter official-speak.

Acknowledgements

This book could never have been written without the help of many hundreds of people. Let me, first of all, express my sincerest thanks to all those Shanghai citizens whose kindness, forbearance, and generosity enabled me to produce this study. To retain anonymity, no names have been used, but those who provided me with the most help are well aware of my debt and gratitude to them.

I have benefited immeasurably from the good fortune of having two excellent academic mentors. I offer my heartfelt thanks to Professor Tao Muyuan, my friend and teacher; his depth of knowledge and upstanding character are an endless source of admiration. Stuart Thompson, the supervisor for my graduate studies at the School of Oriental and African Studies of the University of London, played an essential part in the production of this text. His consistent encouragement, constructive advice, patience, and friendship have been invaluable.

The good humour, mutual support, and helpful advice of fellow research students at SOAS have been crucial. In particular, I thank Andrea Cornwall, Chen Wen-Te, Kevin Latham, and Jeff Roberts. I have benefited too from the insights of academic staff at SOAS, especially Elisabeth Croll, Kit Davis, Richard Fardon, Mark Hobart, David Parkin, and Andrew Turton. I would also like to thank Nick Tapp for his advice and extensive comments on the text. During my years studying Chinese and living in Shanghai I have been fortunate to make many friends; I especially thank the following for their kindness and support: Ann, Christine, David, Ding and Maggie, Doug and Tomoko, Fiona, Hui, Inge, Jaap and Lindy, Jenny, Jerry and Joan, John, John and Sandrine, Judy, Jun, Martin, Mei Lun, SoFoon, Stefan, Wang, and the Zheng family. Last, but not least, this is an ideal opportunity to thank my mother and father, and my brothers Adrian and Simon for their loyalty and support. For a host of reasons I dedicate this book to the memory of my father, not least among these for showing me by example the importance of loyalty, tolerance, and kindness.

I have received financial support from a number of sources. Most of the funding for the research conducted during 1992–4, was provided by the Economic and Social Research Council of the United Kingdom. I received additional support from the Central Research Fund of London University and the Radcliffe–Brown Trust Fund. I express my gratitude to all of these organisations. This is also an ideal opportunity to thank the British Council and the Leverhulme Trust who each funded me for one year in Shanghai between 1988 and 1990. It was during these two years that my fascination with the city developed, and this place and its people first became a vital and essential part of my life.

I thank Sage Publications for their permission to reprint pp. 181–215 of *Modern China* (23/2) [Gamble, J. © 1997 Sage Publications Inc.]. These pages have been reproduced in 'Share dealers, trading places and new options in contemporary Shanghai'.

Notes on the text

OFFICIAL EXCHANGE RATES, US DOLLAR AND CHINESE YUAN (*RENMINBI*)

1980	1 dollar	1.50 yuan
1985	1 dollar	2.94 yuan
1990	1 dollar	4.78 yuan
1991	1 dollar	5.32 yuan
1992	1 dollar	5.51 yuan
1993	1 dollar	5.76 yuan
1994	1 dollar	8.62 yuan
1995	1 dollar	8.35 yuan
1996	1 dollar	8.31 yuan
1997	1 dollar	8.29 yuan
1998	1 dollar	8.28 yuan
1999	1 dollar	8.28 yuan
2000	1 dollar	8.28 yuan

ROMANISATION

Most names and words are written in Mandarin, romanised according to the *pinyin* system. In a few instances, I have stuck with the much more familiar transliterations – such as KMT and Canton – rather than the *pinyin* version. A glossary of characters is provided. The transliteration for Shanghai dialect terms is based upon the phonetic system used in Thomas Creamer's (1991) *A Chinese-English Dictionary of the Wu Dialect*. Shanghai dialect terms can be located in the Glossary under their Mandarin equivalent.

ABBREVIATIONS

BR	*Beijing Review*
CD	*China Daily*
CDBW	*China Daily Business Weekly*

CR		*Chinese Repository*
DW	Duzhe Wenzhai	*Readers' Digest*
FBIS		*Foreign Broadcast Information Service*
FEER		*Far Eastern Economic Review*
FT		*Financial Times*
JFRB	Jiefang Ribao	*Liberation Daily*
KMT	Kuomintang	*Nationalist Party*
MZWYB	Meizhou Wenyi Bao	*Arts News Weekly*
MZWYJMB	Meizhou Wenyi Jiemu Bao	*Weekly Arts Programme*
NFZM	Nanfang Zhoumo	*Southern Weekend*
SS		*Shanghai Star*
SWB		*BBC Summary of World Broadcasts – Asia Pacific*
SWHYSB	Shanghai Wenhua Yishu Bao	*Shanghai Culture and Arts Newspaper*
SWYB	Shanghai Wenyi Bao	*Shanghai Arts Newspaper*
SYB	Shanghai Yibao	*Shanghai Translations*
WHB	Wenhui Bao	*Wenhui Daily*
WHDYSB	Wenhui Dianying Shibao	*Wenhui Film Newspaper*
WHYSB	Wenhui Yishu Bao	*Wenhui Arts Newspaper*
XMWB	Xinmin Wanbao	*New People's Evening News*

Introduction

HISTORICAL BACKGROUND TO SHANGHAI[1]

This brief outline provides some background information on Shanghai and highlights the main aspects of historical and contemporary significance. These aspects include Shanghai's: 'forgotten' pre-Opium War history as an entrepôt; its post-Opium War development as a cosmopolitan, semi-colonial city and a major industrial, financial, cultural, and political centre; its distinctive organisational structure under Communist Party rule; limited early post-Mao reforms; and the rapid socio-economic changes initiated during the 1990s and especially since 1992.

Pre-colonial Shanghai

At a conference in Shanghai, a paper by one Shanghai academic commenced an examination of the city's importance with the words: 'Over 150 years since the founding of Shanghai in the middle of the 19th century. . . ' (Xu 1993: 3). However, there has been a town on the site of contemporary Shanghai for over 2,200 years. Shanghai was an important coastal port in the Song and Yuan dynasties. By the thirteenth-century the city was a regional trade centre, and it was given its present name in AD 1280. A city wall, three and three quarter miles long and 18–20 feet high, was built in 1554 as protection against Japanese pirates. The transfer of the Ming capital from Nanjing to Beijing in 1421 and imperial prohibitions on sea trade brought some three centuries of decline for Shanghai. However, the city's fortunes began to improve when the Kangxi emperor lifted these restrictions in 1684. In the early 1830s foreign visitors described Shanghai as a prosperous trading city with its port handling a volume of shipping equal to or exceeding that of London.

Substantial British trade with China began in the early eighteenth century. For over 80 years, from 1760, European residence was restricted to a 24-acre site in Canton with trade conducted under stringent regulations applied by the Chinese authorities. In 1832, Mr Lindsay was sent from Canton to Shanghai to request that the city be opened up to foreign trade. He was unsuccessful in this but sent the East India Company a report with 'his glowing impressions of Shanghai's wealth and prospects' (De Jesus 1909: 9). Reverend Charles Gutzlaff, who also visited Shanghai in 1832, recorded in his journal that 'Shang-hae appears to be the greatest emporium of the empire. We found there more than a thousand junks moored opposite the city, and others were arriving whenever the weather permitted' (Gutzlaff 1833: 30). A visitor to Shanghai in 1843 described it as a 'mercantile emporium' with trade between ports within China and also international trade with, for example, Manila, Siam, Malacca, and Bali (*CR* 1846: 15(9), 466–9).

In June 1842, during the Opium War, Shanghai was occupied by British troops. Estimates put the population in 1843 at between 270,000 (Fortune 1853: Vol. I, 91) and 300,000 (*CR* 1846: 15(9), 467). Lt Forbes, who was with the British force which captured Shanghai, provides a glowing account of the city within its walls, its 'very large suburbs' and 'extensive trade' (1848: 10–54). He also described the expanse of country around Shanghai, 'its rich cultivation, and numerous canals, teeming with wealth, beauty, and ague' (15). Under the Treaty of Nanking, signed on 29 August 1842, the city was one of five treaty ports opened to British residence and trade (the other four were Canton, Xiamen, Fuzhou, and Ningbo, with Hong

Map 2 The main treaty ports of China.

Source: E.R. Hughes *The Invasion of China By The Western World.* London: Adam & Charles Black (1937: 3).

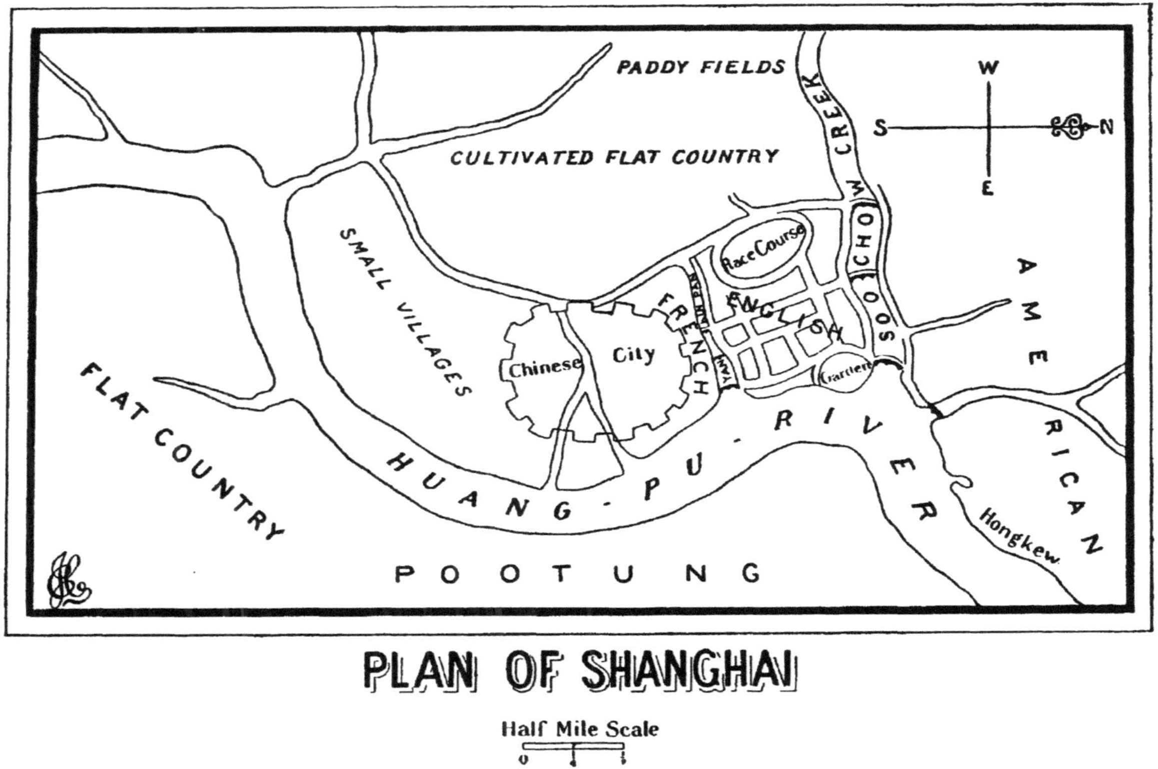

Map 3 Late nineteenth-century sketch map of Shanghai.

Source: Charles J.H. Halcombe *The Mystic Flowery Land: A Personal Narrative*. London: Luzac & Co. (1896: 9).

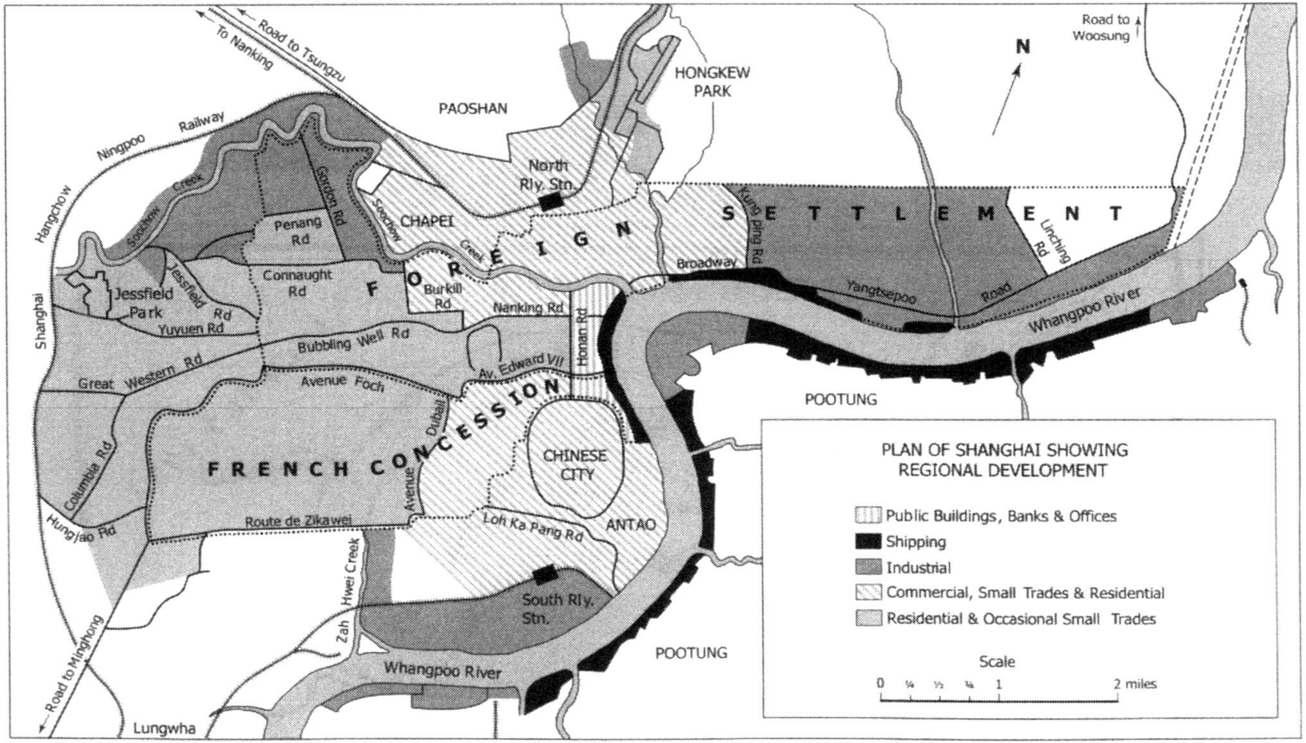

Map 4 Plan showing development of Shanghai by 1940.

Source: F.C. Jones *Shanghai and Tientsin*. Oxford: Oxford University Press (1940: 110–11).

Kong being ceded to Britain). The treaty gave British citizens rights of extraterritoriality, a privilege ultimately granted to the citizens of some 17 countries.

Semi-colonial Shanghai

In the West it often seems that the abiding resonances of pre-1949 Shanghai are of sing-song houses, gambling, prostitution, opium Dens, and kidnapping. This is the Shanghai of novels such as *Shanghai: City for Sale* (Hauser 1940) and *Shanghai, The Paradise of Adventurers* (Miller 1937). Miller wrote that 'Shanghai laughs, drinks and... loves outrageously, impudently' (1937: 22). Such images persist in post-1949 studies. For instance, Murphey writes that '[m]orality was irrelevant or meaningless in Shanghai' (1953: 9). In her semi-fictionalised account, *Gangsters in Paradise* (1984), Pan Ling mentions the 'showiness' of Shanghai (4), that it was 'an outlaw's dream' (12), the 'opium emporium of China' (28), and 'a city that catered to all sexual tastes' (13). These depictions, however, tell only a very partial story of this East Asian metropolis.

By 1847 'an out-line European town' had already begun to emerge on the Concession site, with some 100 foreign residents, three or four Protestant missions, and 25 commercial houses (*CR* 1847: 16(8), 406). In 1849 the French and in 1854 the Americans were granted land. The British and American zones amalgamated in 1863 to form the International Settlement. The foreign community set up their own Municipal Council in 1854, although White describes the ensuing 50-year period as one of 'maximum modernisation with minimum administration' (1981: 31). Shanghai rapidly grew from a prosperous domestic port into one of the truly great cities of the world. By the mid-1930s, Shanghai had become the major industrial, commercial, and financial centre of China and was the seventh largest city in the world.

Writers such as Edward Said (1978) and Ronald Inden (1990) have highlighted regularities in Western Orientalists' representations of so-called 'Oriental' peoples; a feature they attribute to the existence of unequal power relationships.[2] Post-Opium War representations of China by many British writers can be firmly placed within the wider discourse of Orientalism. China was portrayed as a country frozen in time, isolated from the beneficent influences of the West, its population in a somnambulant torpor. Once Shanghai came under the aegis of British domination it was readily absorbed into this Orientalist discourse. In marked contrast to earlier descriptions of Shanghai as a flourishing commercial emporium writers such as Archdeacon A.E. Moule described the city before 1842 as having been 'formerly somewhat obscure, difficult of access, and unimportant' (1911: 213). Similarly, O.M. Green concluded that 'Shanghai was never a city of importance nor of great trade until the foreigner settled there' (1942: 60). A common assertion is that Shanghai's development was 'all due to European initiative' (Bigham 1901: 103) and 'a splendid example of what British energy, wealth, and organising power can do' (Bishop 1899: 24). Contrasts were increasingly drawn between the native walled city and the foreign settlement – sometimes referred to as the 'model settlement' (cf. Dyce 1906). The foreign concession was described as 'an object-lesson of modern civilisation among the benighted millions of China'

(De Jesus 1909: i). In the early 1960s, David-Houston dedicated his history of Shanghai, *Yellow Creek*, to 'The men from the West who Built Asia's Greatest City' (1962). He comments that by 1870, 'in the face of sullen obstruction from the Chinese authorities, Shanghai had emerged from the slime and was already, in terms of trade, the fifth port in the world' (91).

By the 1920s and 1930s Shanghai had become one of the most 'modern' cities in Asia with major trading companies, factories, universities, department stores, modern public utilities, and banks.[3] The city developed an extensive 'civil society' composed of both non-governmental private economic activities and 'political society'. These included an extensive range of both Chinese and foreign corporate groups, voluntary associations, newspapers, and publishing houses. Shanghai was the leading cultural centre in China. China's film industry began in the city and in 1906 the first cinema was opened. Writers such as Xu Zhimo, Mao Dun, and Lu Xun all gravitated to Shanghai and during the 1930s there was a flourishing school of literature in Shanghai. Shanghai was also an important point of cultural contact. Western thought had considerable impact both through its direct agents, such as missionaries and educators (for example, St John's University set up in 1879), and also more diffuse cultural influences such as Western literature and films – in 1935, 18 of Shanghai's 37 cinemas showed only foreign films (Ch'en 1979: 220).

Many Western observers saw Shanghai as increasingly part of the 'modern' world (e.g. Hughes 1937: 268–74; Lang 1946: 93, 99, 120). Hughes described Chinese families in Shanghai as 'increasingly cut off from their ancestral village' and considered that the middle classes 'have through education come to a modern rationalist position, and see the ideals of old China as a lost cause' (268). With approval, he noted that 'Miss Shanghai' now wears short skirts, has permed hair and participates in 'sex romance' (269–71). Gaulton also comments on the emulation of the West and describes how 'Shanghai's middle and upper classes cultivated a distinctively Europeanised cultural style' (1981: 40).

Alongside commerce and industry, diverse underworld activities flourished in the city. Overseas visitors described it as the 'Sodom of China' (Gamewell 1916: 172) or 'the Paris of the China' a city where 'many young men [are] ruined by its attractions' (Hardy 1907: 70). One estimate puts the number of prostitutes in Shanghai in 1935 at 100,000, making it 'the largest single employer of female labour' (Hershatter 1992: 145). With a predominantly migrant population and three separate policing authorities Shanghai became the centre of organised crime in China (see Martin 1992). In Perry's estimation gangsters were 'the effective rulers of early twentieth-century Shanghai' (1993: 89).

As China's largest and most dynamic city and with relative freedom of expression Shanghai was home for many radical movements. Most notably, the Communist Party was founded in the city's French Concession in 1921. The city was also the site of many demonstrations against colonial rule (see Wasserstrom 1991). In addition, in the period between 1919–49, Shanghai had 'one of the most aggressive labour movements in world history' with strikes and labour disputes reaching a peak in 1926–7, 1946, and late 1949 (Perry 1994: 1; see also Perry 1993).

On 25 March 1927, the Nationalist forces of Chiang Kai-shek entered Shanghai. On 12 April, Chiang launched an attack on Communist Party members and supporters with the intention of eradicating Communist influence in the city. This aim was largely achieved and the Communist Party was forced to seek a rural power base. Chiang had 'grandiose plans to turn Shanghai into a modern urban settlement' and aimed to make it a fully 'modern' metropolis (Wasserstrom 1991: 151). However, civil war and war against the Japanese meant that such plans made little progress and were, effectively, shelved until resuscitated in the 1990s. In 1932, there was Sino-Japanese conflict in and around Shanghai. At the start of the 1937–45 Anti-Japanese War, in October 1937, Shanghai's Zhabei district was practically destroyed by Japanese bombers. The International Settlement was overwhelmed by Japanese forces following the attack on Pearl Harbour in December 1941.

In 1945, the Nationalist government regained control of Shanghai. Initially, many Shanghainese welcomed the KMT, but then by 1949 they 'had squandered this initial goodwill' (Wasserstrom 1991: 155). The period from 1945–9 has gone down in Shanghai history as marked by inflation, official corruption, and civil strife. However, the city's new government in 1949 came not as a result of these pressures, but as the result of battles fought elsewhere. On 25 May, with scarcely a shot fired, Shanghai fell to a largely peasant army.

Shanghai under Mao

Shanghai presented the victorious Communist Party with some extremely difficult problems. As a semi-colonial, cosmopolitan city it represented both a threat and an affront to the new government, but it also contained a substantial proportion of the nation's productive capacity and skilled work force. After the purge of 1927, the Communist Party even lacked effective propagandists who spoke the dialect to help consolidate its power in the city (Gaulton 1981: 50).

The new authorities established (or revived) highly effective means of organisational control and surveillance. In their comprehensive and systematic study of late-Maoist urban China, Parish and Whyte summarised the Cultural Revolution/Maoist model of urbanisation as having the following distinctive structural features (1984: 358):

- Strict migration controls and minimal urbanisation.
- A penetrating residential work unit organisational system.
- A highly developed bureaucratic allocation system.
- An emphasis on production rather than consumption.
- A relatively egalitarian distribution system.
- A rejection of schools as a basic mechanism for sorting talent.
- Much stress on citizen involvement in areas such as public health and social control.
- Rigid taboos on all forms of dress, expression, ritual life, and communication that did not conform to the official ideology.

These structural features had distinctive social consequences, most notably a high level of stability in jobs and residence, minimal differentiation of consumption patterns and life-styles, extreme bureaucratisation, and the creation of a sharp urban–rural divide. This pattern made the cities of that period (1949–78) distinct from the past in China and from urban areas elsewhere.

For over three decades after the Communist Party took power in 1949, Shanghai lay at the heart of China's centrally planned socialist economy. The Party adopted a strict Marxist-Leninist approach which engaged with strands of Chinese traditional morality suspicious of the market. The city's previous role as an entrepôt and an international financial and commercial centre was subordinated to a primary role as a domestic industrial producer. In 1952, the tertiary sector accounted for 41.7 per cent of Shanghai's industrial product but after 1956 this proportion declined, falling to just 18.2 per cent in 1970 (Jacobs and Hong 1994: 226).

Between Autumn 1950 and December 1957, the proportion of Shanghai's industrial workers employed in privately owned factories was reduced from 75 per cent to zero (Perry 1994: 7–8). By 1951 almost all foreigners had left and foreign and Chinese capitalist enterprises were gradually taken over, a process completed by nationalisations in 1956. Workers were employed in state or collective work units called *danwei*.[4] In 1978, 99.9 per cent of workers were employed directly or indirectly by the state, of whom 78.5 per cent worked in state *danwei* (Davis 1990: 89).

From the early 1950s until the late 1970s citizens were divided into a limited range of categories such as workers, peasants, soldiers, intellectuals or 'bad elements'. These labels effectively defined and limited the opportunities available to people. Individuals' lives were encapsulated within bureaucratically organised and policed structures. This severely limited the extent of 'civil society' which 'operates according to a logic and an organisational structure that is different from that of the centralised state and its administrative, military and legal arms' (Yang 1989b: 35). Organisational changes were backed up by the Party's moves 'to introduce and popularise a set of symbols, including a new political vocabulary, which it expected the people to use to structure their response' (Gaulton 1981: 48). Expressions of allegiance to and compliance with the prevailing ideology were frequently demanded of citizens.

In 1949, Shanghai suffered a loss of capital and expertise to Hong Kong.[5] Between 1949–79 the status of the city was further undermined through various measures including: government policies designed to reverse the concentration of the nation's productive capacity in coastal cities and to relocate the economic 'centre of gravity' to inland provinces; the centralisation of political power in Beijing; the government's policy of autarky; China's diplomatic isolation vis-à-vis the West and relative closure to foreign trade; and the lack of significant investment in Shanghai – the main exceptions to this policy were the founding of the vast Jinshan Oil and Chemical Plant and Baoshan Steel Plant, both located in suburban Shanghai, in the 1970s.

The siphoning off and leeching of the city's resources, both in terms of material resources and skilled manpower, was particularly significant. Between 1950–83,

Shanghai gave 86.8 per cent of its tax revenues to the central government and retained just 13.2 per cent (Jacobs and Hong 1994: 231). Despite the controls placed upon Shanghai, there was still significant economic growth in the city and it remained China's pre-eminent industrial centre. During the period 1953–78, the city's economic growth averaged 8.8 per cent per annum, above the national average.

Post-Mao Shanghai[6]

In 1979, Ye Jianying, a Communist Party Vice-Chairman, announced that the 'basic goal of revolution is to liberate and develop the social productive forces.' Rather than the former emphasis on class struggle, egalitarianism, and autarky the Chinese government began to stress the 'Four Modernisations' (in industry, agriculture, defence, and science and technology) – a policy first proposed by Premier Zhou Enlai in 1964. Some people and places were to be allowed to 'get rich first', daily life was to be depoliticised and a pragmatic approach adopted to economic affairs.

Initially, most reforms were instituted in the countryside. Between the late 1970s and the early 1980s, there was a rapid decollectivisation of agriculture and the introduction of the household responsibility system. In 1987, Gordon White wrote that policy and institutional changes implemented in rural areas since 1978 were 'transforming fundamentally the character of rural society' (264). At this time there were only relatively modest changes in urban China, such as the re-legalisation of small-scale private enterprises.[7] The main exceptions to this were in the experimental Special Economic Zones of Fujian and, especially, Guangdong province, places demarcated to present an 'Open Door' to Western capital and technology.

In 1984–5, the state began to implement a more concerted range of urban economic reforms and to vigorously advocate *gaige kaifang* ('reform and the Open Door'). In April 1984, Shanghai, along with 14 other coastal cities, was 'opened' to foreign investment. In October 1984, the Central Committee of the Communist Party endorsed the development of a 'socialist commodity economy' and urban economic reform. Central state control over the economy such as price controls and the allocation of labour diminished. Significant powers to make economic decisions were delegated to regional authorities and enterprise managers. These reforms began to introduce new dimensions of choice, indeed, the very concept of 'choice', into the lives of many Shanghainese. However, the scope, scale, and impact of these reforms was limited; they constituted no more than a tinkering at the margins of the socialist state planned economy. There was no fundamental economic restructuring but, rather, new forms and types of employment were grafted onto the existing system. This situation accorded with the prescripts of Chen Yun, a long-standing member of the Politburo and a Vice-Premier of the State Council. In the early 1980s, Chen 'declared that the relationship between the planned economy and the . . . market was like a bird and a cage. The plan was the cage and the bird the market. If the cage was too small, the bird would suffocate. If there was no cage, the bird would fly away' (cited in Bachman 1985: 152).

During the years 1978–90, economic growth in Shanghai averaged 7.5 per cent, below the national average of around 10 per cent. Throughout the 1980s Shanghai's relative pre-eminence in the Chinese economy declined. In 1978, Shanghai accounted for 12 per cent of China's gross industrial output and about 30 per cent of the nation's exports. By 1994, these proportions had fallen to 5.5 per cent and 7.5 per cent respectively. In 1978, Shanghai was the biggest contributor to national income, contributing 8 per cent of total revenues, by 1990 it was ranked tenth, providing only 4 per cent (ibid.). Despite Shanghai's relative decline, and despite the limited extent of urban reforms, by the mid-1980s most Shanghainese enjoyed rising prosperity. A World Bank (1990: 129) report estimated average per capita incomes for different provinces in 1986: Shanghai was highest of all at 3,471 *yuan*, next was Beijing with 2,130 *yuan*, the national average was 746 *yuan*, and Anhui just 599 *yuan*. However, as Jacobs and Hong point out 'Shanghai had been sacrificed at the beginning of the reform programme' (1994: 232). Shanghainese increasingly felt that their city's pre-eminence was being eclipsed by the Special Economic Zones of southern China.

In 1988, inflation became a serious problem for the first time since the Communist take-over. This was a prime underlying cause of the demonstrations which erupted across China in Spring 1989. In Shanghai, as in most Chinese cities, there were large-scale demonstrations together with overt demands for greater democracy and an end to corruption by officials.[8] After its clampdown on demonstrators in Beijing on 4 June, the Party-state sought to reassert its authority through the use of terror and an intensive propaganda campaign. During the period between mid-1989 and 1991 attempts were made to slacken the pace of economic reform, and this was a period of stagnation in Shanghai.

Shanghai in the 1990s and the early twenty-first century

> Shanghai of the future must be a metropolis equal to New York or London, said Mayor Huang Ju as he outlined revisions to the city's development plan designed to create an 'oriental Manhattan'... He was addressing the City Planning Meeting, the third since 1949... marking the city government's efforts to revive the past glories of Shanghai and make the city an international metropolis in the 21st century.
>
> 'City of Future' *Shanghai Star* (2 July 1993 front-page headline)

I was resident in Shanghai as a student of China from September 1988 to September 1990. In the year after 4 June 1989, the atmosphere often felt very constricted and depressing. Local people described this time to me as *men* – depressing (also 'tightly closed, sealed') – the written character depicts a heart enclosed within a gate. Two years later, when I next returned to Shanghai in September 1992, I expected there to have been little change in this gloomy scenario. It therefore came as a surprise to find a palpably different atmosphere, with a dramatic improvement in the morale of many Shanghainese citizens, and to discover that a main topic of conversation was stocks and shares! Many people had become busier, and all around me there was evidence of increased business and 'busy-ness'. Friends who had previously been in state work units and seemed able to take days off at will now worked for joint ventures with strict working hours, or were undertaking a second or third job and attending evening classes.

Following the Tiananmen crackdown, the state continued to promote the 'Open Door' policy. On 9 June 1989, during his congratulatory speech to the army commanders who had suppressed the demonstrations in Beijing, Deng Xiaoping stated that '[w]hat is important is that we should never change China back into a closed country' (cited in Rai 1991: 123). From 1990 the central government began to promote Shanghai and Pudong. However, changes of a qualitatively different order did not take place in Shanghai until after Chinese New Year in 1992. Deng Xiaoping chose this auspicious national holiday to make a highly publicised 'inspection tour of the south' in an attempt to 're-energise the reform process' (Shambaugh 1993: 488). During this tour, which included stops in Shanghai and Shenzhen, Deng was widely reported to have said that Shanghai should 'seize the opportunity', have 'more courage' and 'take faster steps' in reform. He even indicated his regret that he had not included Shanghai as one of the original Special Economic Zones established in 1979. A local sociology lecturer told me that Deng's comments 'represented the aspirations of the *laobaixing*', it was exactly what they wanted to hear. These enigmatic comments provided the crucial impetus to a quantitatively and qualitatively greater scope and pace of reform in Shanghai.

In measures announced in March 1992, Shanghai Municipality was given more authority to make decisions regarding investment approval. In addition, the central government granted Shanghai permission to issue stocks and shares and to permit trading in Shanghai of stocks issued elsewhere in China. Foreign stores were allowed in Pudong and income taxes on Shanghai enterprises lowered from 55 per cent to 33 per cent (Jacobs and Hong 1994: 234). In addition to these preferential policies the centre gave Shanghai an explicit regional leadership role as the 'Dragon Head' of the entire Yangzi River Valley. At a national level, the new policy direction was underlined in October 1992 at the 14th Communist Party Congress with its call for the development of a 'socialist market economy', and its declaration that 'the most clear-cut characteristic of the new historical period is reform and opening up.'

In 1990, Pudong, on the east side of Shanghai's Huangpu River, was earmarked as 'a focal point of the country's opening and reform drive in the 1990s' (*CDBW* 26 September–2 October 1993: 4). Pudong New District has a population of 1.38 million and an area of 518 square kilometres – about five-sixths the size of Singapore. During his January 1993 Spring Festival visit to Shanghai, Deng Xiaoping was quoted as saying that Shanghai should 'make some change in one year, and a great change in three years' (*XMWB* 23 January 1993: 1). A widely stated objective is that by 2010 Shanghai will 'achieve an international scale and breadth of economic development' and be 'a modern city of the first order in world terms' (Zhao 1993: 2). This agenda appears, belatedly, to bear out Pye's anticipation that with the 'Four Modernisations' policy Shanghai would 'again assert itself as the country's most advanced and dynamic city' (1981: xv). In 1999, Zhu Rongji, a former mayor of Shanghai and now China's premier, emphasised that 'Shanghai will be China's New York' (*Economist* 14 August 1999: 64).

Much foreign and domestic capital has flowed into Shanghai. Major infrastructure projects completed in the first half of the 1990s included two suspension bridges built to link Pudong with central Shanghai, the first 16-kilometre phase of an underground railway – opened in December 1994, and the completion of a 48-kilometre elevated Inner Ring Road. Since the mid-1990s, the pace of construction in Shanghai has been even more frenetic. The first phase construction of Pudong International Airport was completed in late 1999 – once fully completed in 2005, this airport will have a handling capacity of 80 million passengers per annum, compared to around 15 million at the existing Hongqiao airport. The Second Metro Line linking Puxi and Pudong opened in June 2000. The aim is that by 2005, Shanghai will have eleven metro lines and ten light rail lines. In August 1999, the 88-storey Jin Mao Tower opened in Pudong, at 420 metres it became the tallest building in China and the third tallest in the world. By 2000, Lujiazui Financial and Trading Zone, one of Pudong's four special economic development zones, had over 100 high-rises. New sectors are constantly being opened up to foreign capital. In 1997, selected foreign banks were allowed, provided that they based themselves in Pudong, to participate in *renminbi* business. Approval has been given to several foreign insurance companies to operate in Shanghai. Between 1990–2000, Pudong attracted 5,942 foreign enterprises with total investment reaching US$30 billion – 98 of the world's top 500 multinationals, including major investments by General Motors and Intel, have established operations in Pudong (*SS* 18 April 2000: 1).

The city's economic structure has altered significantly since the early 1980s. From 1980 to 1996, the state-owned sector's proportion of the city's total industrial output dropped from 87.2 per cent to 33.3 per cent, while the collective-owned sector rose from 11.6 per cent to 18.2 per cent, and the co-operative, private and foreign-funded sector's skyrocketed from 1.1 per cent to 48.5 per cent (Shanghai 1997: 20–1). Since the early 1980s the declining importance of the tertiary sector trend has been reversed. By 1990, it accounted for 30 per cent of Shanghai's GDP, and by the end of 1996 it contributed 42 per cent (SWB/FEW/2872 20 March 1997), the objective is that this will rise to 60 per cent by 2010. The key enterprises in the city are: steel, automobiles, petrochemicals, energy, telecommunications and computer products. Living standards for many Shanghainese have risen and this has fostered a consumer boom.

Shanghai's sociological 'landscape' is being radically altered by the newly adopted economic policies and the trends associated with them. There has already been a reversal or dilution to varying degrees of the distinctive structural features of Maoist cities outlined by Parish and Whyte. The radical transformations which Gordon White described as having taken place in rural China in the early 1980s are now being matched by equally fundamental changes in urban China. The 'more complex, ambiguous, competitive and potentially conflictual rural process' White (1987: 250) discerned now also has its parallel in urban China.

Since June 1989, the Party-state has successfully controlled public displays of dissent in urban China. However, the reforms are allowing an increasing diversity of lifestyles and modes of livelihood with a proliferation of categories of people who increasingly operate in a realm beyond, though constrained by, that controlled by the state. The new 'space' between the government and the populace has allowed a relative pluralisation and blurring of social categories and representations. In this study I investigate these changes and the new diversity, flux, contradictions, and ambiguities which I found in China's largest metropolis. A refrain echoed by one of my most insightful informants focused on how 'complicated' (*fuza*) Shanghai was becoming, and his inability to understand current socio-economic trends. During a discussion, even in a single sentence, informants often provided seemingly mutually incompatible portrayals of events taking place in the city. Rather than gloss over discrepancies and incoherencies, I emphasise this sense of flux and indeterminacy.

STRUCTURE OF THE BOOK

Each chapter in this book is intended to stand alone as a single 'perspective' on Shanghai, in the sense used by David Parkin (1987: 64) with his suggestion of ethnography as analogous to impressionist painting. Each of these perspectives comprises a vignette of brush strokes of differing thickness and intensity. In the shifting sands of 'Shanghai beach' (*Shanghai tan* – a name sometimes used for the city), I often found that the discourses and practices of people's quotidian existences presented quite different, and frequently mutually contradictory, contours to those of over-arching meta-narratives whether of Marxist-Leninist Mao Zedong Thought or sociological notions of global homogenisation, or the accounts 'from a height' of changes in contemporary China presented by economists and political scientists. My intention here is that each perspective should be meaning-full in its own right and provide substantial new and nuanced information on Shanghai and its people. Each of these five separate vignettes may then combine, collage-like, to form, a whole greater, perhaps, than the sum of its parts.

Chapter 1 explores the changes, or lack of change, local residents described as having taken place in Shanghai during the post-Mao era. I highlight the sustained and systematic metaphors which saturate these representations and pursue my investigation by following some of the trails of these indigenous terms. Maoist era Shanghai was typically described as having been 'stuck in a frame' and as having 'solidified'; lack of change in the city's physical structure was frequently presented as paralleled by and indicative of a similar fixity and immutability in people's daily lives, careers, and expectations. People were stuck with ascribed, and largely immutable, class labels, jobs they had probably not chosen; and egalitarian levels of consumption were strongly encouraged and, at times, enforced. For some, at least, the 'Open Door' has been like the opening of a sluice gate with all manner of phenomena and new 'tides' engulfing the city.

The second and third chapters are both drawn along a spatial dimension. Chapter 2 focuses on the consequences of the increasing porousness of Shanghai's boundaries to global and intra-national flows. Before the 1980s, Shanghai could be depicted as vertically integrated, cellular, and relatively closed to both global and intra-national flows. Informants told me that with this 'closed door' Shanghai's populace 'did not know what the outside world was like, for only the higher levels had access to foreign media.' This pattern has altered significantly since the mid-1980s with Shanghai's increasing reintegration into the global economy, a greater stress upon horizontal linkages, and extensive global and intra-national flows. I examine the consequences of various flows for 'Chinese' and 'Shanghainese' identities in Shanghai.

Chapter 3 focuses upon the way places and spaces within the city itself are differentially marked and trends which are affecting work places and home 'styles'. I provide further strands of complexity to senses of being 'Shanghainese' by exploring the differential attribution of qualities and identities which residents made of places and people in, or from, different parts of Shanghai. I also investigate aspects of the rapidly altering cityscape. Many physical boundaries are being dismantled or transformed and new 'walls' created with trends for work units to lose their all-encompassing functions, and became less enclosed and bounded, as, concurrently, homes become increasingly privatised and cloissonéed. I also suggest ways in which communication technologies and electronic media can both facilitate 'connections' but also create new boundaries and types of exclusion.

The two remaining chapters examine topics which were of particular moment and especially obtrusive as phenomena during my research period in Shanghai. The rise of popular consumerism and the rapid emergence of a share market since the early 1990s have been topics of definite importance. In view of informants' frequent discussion of them, and their obvious and far-reaching effects upon the fabric of the city, both of these topics demand attention. They are also of interest since they both appear to constitute developments in Chinese society which are radically opposed to policies pursued during the Maoist period. Each of these chapters highlights the new dimensions of choice and uncertainty in the lives of many Shanghainese and gives evidence of newly emergent social contours such as the shift from predominantly ascribed statuses to greater scope for 'aspirational identities'.

Chapter 4 explores changing patterns and representations of consumerism and consumption, themes which are constitutive of and central to an understanding of the socio-economic changes which are under way in contemporary Shanghai. Terminology from the literal consumption of food serves, through metaphors and analogies, to describe many aspects of life. Striking instances of this are depictions of the state as a consumer of Shanghai's wealth, and of individuals' consumption of the state or the 'common people's' wealth. The state's legitimacy, especially after 4 June 1989, military power aside, resides largely in its ability to bring economic improvements for the majority of citizens. I highlight ways in which consumption is producing, facilitating, and marking out new divisions in society.

Shanghai's re-internationalisation, the growth of advertising, media images, and the stress upon consumption which have been so marked in the reform era have all provided local people with many alternative images and products from which to fashion identities. Often, imported cultural phenomena become invested with new meanings. In Shanghai, for instance, the imported cultural festival of Christmas is becoming important, but with quite distinctive 'Shanghainese characteristics'.

Chapter 5 focuses upon the social impact of the introduction and rapid growth of the recently reopened share market, one of the 'crazes' in 1990s Shanghai which touched and influenced the lives of millions. The share discourse provides a microcosm of the forces and trends unleashed by the Open Door and reform policies including inflated expectations, hopes, dangers, risks, and unpredictability. The share market has hastened and facilitated a redefinition of the individual's relationship to society, contributed to 'widening the margins', and to the rapid social differentiation in the city. The Shanghai share market has played a significant role in the creation of a substantial number of *nouveaux riches* and, thereby, has contributed to and fuelled the sense of injustice many Shanghainese felt over rising wealth inequalities. The share market has also encouraged and provided an environment for civil society to emerge. Access to information is vital for traders and various formal and many more informal interest groups have begun to coalesce around the share market.

The final chapter makes no attempt to 'conclude', this would be out of keeping with the book's spirit of providing readers with multiple shades and perspectives. Rather, it recapitulates the main findings of the previous chapters, and then reflects upon a number of underlying, submerged themes of the book. Chief amongst these themes are notions of inside and outside and chronological dichotomies. Attention is also devoted to the concept of the 'common people' (*laobaixing*); a category that surfaced daily in my interactions with people in Shanghai. Throughout this book I pay particular attention to the way people speak, and the idioms and everyday metaphors they use. By the time the reader reaches this final chapter, my hope is to have provided each of them with thought-provoking, tangible, multi-faceted perspectives of Shanghai, and to have conveyed some senses of the breadth and richness of the ideas, thoughts, feelings, concerns and emotions of its citizens.

1 Opening the door, crossing the stream: representations and metaphors of reform in contemporary Shanghai

One informant's memorable description of *gaige kaifang* was to liken it to the opening of a sluice gate (*dakai shuizha*), adding that 'like when a sluice is opened, a great wave bursts forth.' Following this metaphor and that of the 'Open Door' involves an investigation of representations of when, why, and by whom this sluice or door was opened, what 'flow' this has permitted and with what consequences. In this chapter, I explore the changes (or lack of change) local residents I encountered described as having taken place in Shanghai during the post-Mao era. In particular, I highlight the sustained and systematic indigenous metaphors which saturate these representations and pursue my investigation by following some of the trails of these indigenous terms.

A phrase which has dominated official rhetoric in Shanghai since the early 1990s is *gaige kaifang* ('reform' and the 'Open Door'). These are the policies designed to make China a 'modernised' nation and Shanghai a thriving international commercial and financial centre. I examine ways in which the term *gaige kaifang* was understood and draw attention to the key 'watery' and socio-spatial metaphors of which the 'Open Door' is itself an example. I outline the new 'roads' and the 'flows' which have been permitted by the opening of the sluice. As implied by this term, a stream of pent-up energy appears to have been released with many new opportunities and choices, but also unprecedented risks and uncertainties, and I examine some of the dangerous currents and murky depths of *gaige kaifang*. This chapter concludes by delineating some of the ways in which *gaige kaifang* is said to have changed people's thinking, with changes in behaviour and attitudes, a renewed stress upon education, and the reproduction of inequalities through differing educational opportunities.

GAIGE KAIFANG

> In 1984 I came to Guangdong. At that time the rural reforms had been under way for several years, the urban reforms had just begun, and the first steps had been taken in the 'special economic zones'. Eight years have since passed. On this visit I find that Shenzhen and Zhuhai 'special economic zones' and several other places have developed extremely rapidly, and much more rapidly than I had expected. After seeing this, my confidence has

increased. Revolution is the liberation of productive forces; reform is also the liberation of productive forces . . . Unless we maintain socialism, unless we institute reform and the Open Door, unless we develop the economy, and unless we improve the lives of the people, we will be headed up a blind alley . . .

Why has our country been able to be so stable since '4 June'? It is because we have carried out reform and the Open Door policy, promoted economic development, and the lives of the people have been improved . . . Have greater courage in reform and the Open Door, dare to experiment, and do not be like a woman with bound feet . . . If great strides are not taken in reform and the Open Door, if we lack courage to be path-breakers, it is because we fear that there are too many capitalist things, that it is taking the capitalist road. On the crucial question of whether something is called 'capitalism' or 'socialism', the main criteria for making this judgement should be whether it is of benefit to developing the productive capacity of socialist society, whether it is helpful with regard to increasing the sum total of a socialist state's national strength, and whether it is beneficial with regard to increasing the people's living standards . . .

Taking the socialist road, is none other than step by step bringing about common prosperity. The proposed blueprint for common prosperity is that: those areas with the conditions can develop first, other areas will develop more slowly. The areas which develop first will spur on the less advanced areas, and ultimately all will achieve common prosperity.

Now, several nearby countries and regions' economies are developing faster than ours. If we do not develop, or develop too slowly, as soon as the common people compare [China's economy with those of these other regions] there will be problems . . . The opportunity of the moment must be seized, now there is a good opportunity. I am worried that this opportunity will be lost. If it is not seized, the opportunity before us will disappear, in an instant the time will have passed by . . . Shanghai now definitely has the conditions to go faster [in development] . . . Looking back, my one great mistake was not to include Shanghai when we set up the four 'special economic zones'.

(Comments made by Deng Xiaoping between 18 January–21 February 1992 during his 'southern inspection tour', reported as the headline article in Shanghai's *Xinmin Wanbao* on 6 November 1993)

Deng Xiaoping described *gaige kaifang* as 'crossing the river, feeling the boulders' (*mozhe shitou guohe*). In much the same way my piloting of the reader through the shoals and currents of this chapter has a broad and ambitious remit. Where present I mark out clear trends which emerge in local residents' discourses on contemporary Shanghai, and attempt to convey a sense of the potential range and parameters of discourses. As a caveat to this I note the following divergent views on the impact of *gaige kaifang* on the city:

- '*Kaifang* was like a tidal wave. Its impact was far greater than the leaders ever expected.'

- 'In recent years many things have changed in a way one could not have believed possible.'
- 'Talk in the foreign press about China's turn for the better is nonsense. China's economic prosperity is fake. Foreigners see only the tall buildings, numerous restaurants, and good clothing in Shanghai but the social and economic system has not changed.'
- 'The Communist Party hangs the sheep's meat of socialism but sells the dog meat of dictatorship.[1] There has been no change at all. It is just like a conjuring trick.'

To muddy waters further, I should add that these are the comments of a single person. With further explication it would be possible to unravel some of the apparent inconsistencies. Beyond this I suggest that these apparently mutually contradictory views are not simply illogical but highlight the degree of flux and tensions inherent in the changes under way in Shanghai. Responses and reactions to the changes are still being 'composed', there is an ongoing process of adjustment, of finding one's bearings.

Understanding *Gaige Kaifang*

Since the early 1990s, the term *gaige kaifang* has been ubiquitous and repeated like a mantra in all forms of state propaganda – often used a dozen or more times on the daily six o'clock television news. *Gaige kaifang*, the dominant paradigm for China's social and economic policies, is claimed as the means to achieve the 'Four Modernisations' advocated as national policy since the late 1970s and intended to make China a rich and prosperous nation. Attempts at urban reform were begun during the mid-1980s, but the degree of change in Shanghai was minimal until after Deng Xiaoping's southern tour in Spring 1992. This visit coincided with central government plans to change Shanghai from being the centre of the planned socialist economy to a thriving international financial and commercial city at the centre of a 'socialist market economy'.

A sociology lecturer in Shanghai when asked the meaning of *gaige kaifang* remarked 'nobody knows', and added that Deng Xiaoping's own depiction of China as 'crossing the stream, feeling the boulders' suggested his own lack of a clear definition. This expression also suggests some sort of necessary feedback process, a dialectic, if 'progress' is to be maintained. Even in official use the term *gaige* ('reform') tends to be applied indiscriminately to any type of administrative change or innovation in sectors ranging from housing to labour policies, enterprise management, and politics. *Kaifang* – the 'Open Door' policy – may be viewed as one of the reforms. It refers primarily to allowing an inflow of foreign capital, technology, expertise, and goods and to promoting export of the latter. Local residents often used these key slogans, and especially *kaifang*, in a range of different ways, and sometimes in radically different senses, to those they encountered daily through broadcast and other media.

When I asked a young employee in a joint venture company what he understood by the term '*gaige*' he replied immediately 'make money'. I next asked his understanding of '*kaifang*', his response was the same. This interpretation is the most baldly materialistic I was given and is a view criticised in the Chinese media as money worship. When referred to as a policy the term *kaifang* is translated as the 'Open Door', although this is not its literal meaning, a significant distinction which I discuss further below. Amongst its dictionary definitions *kaifang* has the meaning 'lift a ban', and I heard it used to refer, for instance, to allowing the installation of telephones in private homes in the early 1980s, and the sale of nude photographs later in the decade. In one instance, which stretched this dictionary definition, and is presumably not what Party leaders have in mind, a retired nurse commented that 'with *kaifang* the *laobaixing* can complain and even curse them [the Communist Party] – this is now *kaifang*.'

In everyday use *kaifang* indicates a sense of being 'modern' and open-minded, it often conveys a sense of being receptive to 'Western ideas'. Somebody who is *kaifang* is less bound by 'traditional' practices, whether this be parental involvement in choosing a marriage partner or acceptance of cremation in funeral rites. Young people often describe themselves as *kaifang* and older people as conservative. On one occasion, when I followed local courtesy and took a gift of oranges to an interviewee's home, he remarked that this was unnecessary because his home was *kaifang*. This use of *kaifang* conveyed a sense of 'modernity', an oppositional stance to social mores. Through being *kaifang*, this man sought to avoid embroilment in the round of reciprocity which the acceptance of gifts creates.

People who are prepared to talk openly and frankly with a Western observer such as myself could be described as *kaifang*. At a more general level, Shanghainese often described their city and its people as *kaifang*, especially when contrasted to other parts of China such as Beijing. This sense of *kaifang* draws upon an historical imagination of Shanghai as a city which was 'open' to the West before 1949, and whose people retain an openness to the outside world and a willingness and ability to accept new ideas. The contemporary rhetoric of the 'Open Door' also constitutes an important parallel to the events of the early 1840s. All Chinese schoolchildren are taught how then 'the Chinese door was forced open by British cannons', with only minimal resistance from a weak and enfeebled Qing government; they are encouraged to consider this a source of national shame and humiliation. By contrast, the Chinese authorities now stress that they open this door themselves from the inside, on their own terms.

Metaphor

> China generally is not at all like the willow-pattern plate. I do not know if I really had expected it to be blue and white; but it was a disappointment to find it so very brown and muddy.
>
> (Mrs Archibald Little, *Intimate China* 1899: 5)

Metaphor, the way in which 'we conceptualise one mental domain in terms of another' (Lakoff 1993: 203), is a fundamental and pervasive feature of language. Metaphor is not mere linguistic decoration, but 'a ubiquitous feature of our thinking and our discourse, the basis of the conceptual systems by means of which we act within our worlds' (Taylor 1984: 5). Thus, as an anthropologist seeking to explore and explain the cultural values and understandings of another society, it is of great value to explore indigenous metaphors.

In some instances, English and Chinese share similar systematic metaphorical concepts. An obvious example are orientational metaphors in which, for example, up is good, bad is down, high-status is up, low-status is down, virtue is up, depravity is down (Lakoff and Johnson 1980: 14–21). Similarly, there is a shared metaphor of politics as drama. In Chinese, for instance, *shangtai* – 'appear on the stage' also means to 'assume power', conversely, *xiatai* means both to 'step down from a stage' and to 'leave office'. Chinese people would also recognise Shakespeare's analogy of life as a drama. They too may describe life as lived on a stage with people acting out diverse roles. Of particular interest, however, are systematic metaphors which differ from those of English. These may provide us with insights into differing ways of perceiving, understanding, and ultimately, behaving.

Metaphors of reform

> The dregs of the old civilisation are like the sand and mud accumulated in the Yellow River; they have built up in the blood vessels of our people. We need a great tidal wave to flush them away. This great tidal wave has already arrived. It is industrial civilisation. It is summoning us!
>
> (Extract from *River Elegy*, Su and Wang 1991: 116)[2]

From the early 1950s military vocabulary permeated daily life, and especially in the Cultural Revolution. At that time, military clothing was the most fashionable, Shanghai's 'Peace Cinema' was renamed 'Combat Cinema' and words such as *fangong* ('counterattack') and *douzheng* ('struggle, combat') were widely used in civilian affairs. In the reform era the use of military language has diminished, those born before or during the 1950s are the most likely to pepper their conversation with such vocabulary. This would appear to be part of a paradigmatic shift in metaphor. The language of the reform era draws more readily upon analogies of natural forces, of irrigation and cultivation rather than warfare.[3]

Changes in metaphor are matched by a radical shift from the 'revolutionary gaze' – epitomised in Cultural Revolution statues of Mao Zedong, eyes focused on the distance and arm outstretched – to the promise of rewards now. A university student commented to me that in the past 'horizons were very limited, now there is much more scope.' This comment suggests that while Mao looked toward the fulfilment of his distant dream ordinary people were 'looking at the sky from the bottom of a well' (*zuo jing guan tian*), that is, they had a very narrow and restricted view. In the imagery of state rhetoric the revolutionary gaze and arm reaching for the future has been replaced by Deng's admonition for Shanghai people to 'grasp' the opportunities they see before them. The shift to materialism and pragmatism is encapsulated in a pun on the Communist Party's call for people to 'look to the future' (*wang qian kan*), which, by changing a single character, becomes 'look towards money'. The implication is that people are more concerned to make money in the present than to place their faith in an uncertain future.

The key metaphors which seeped through everyday discourse and appeared to structure the discourse on change in Shanghai were of two main kinds, the first socio-spatial, the second 'watery' metaphors. The term 'open door' is a significant generative metaphor in its own right. Although this is not a literal translation of *kaifang*, in everyday conversation people did talk about the opening of China's 'door' or 'window' in just this way.

From the etymology of *kaifang* one gains an insight into what it may involve beyond the usual translation 'Open Door'. *Kai* has a range of meanings including 'open' – as in *kaisuo* 'open a lock'; 'open out, come loose'; 'thaw'; and 'lift' (a ban or restriction, etc.). *Fang* also has various meanings such as 'let go, set free, release; let out, expand; blossom, open'. This etymology indicates unleashing, untying, loosening, and opening. The portrayal of *gaige kaifang* noted earlier as like the opening of a sluice gate becomes all the more apposite.

Another set of socio-spatial metaphors refers to roads and routes. At a macro level the route metaphor is used to describe the 'road' taken in national policy. China is officially described as 'taking the socialist road'. In the late 1950s China failed in an attempt to make a 'Great Leap Forward' towards communism. In the Cultural Revolution ideologues foregrounded a bitter struggle between the 'two roads' of capitalism and socialism. Contemporary propaganda slogans now declare that: 'Reform and the Open Door are the essential means (literally 'road') to liberate and develop socialist production!' The 'socialist market economy' is the latest version of the 'socialist road' designed to bring progress (*jinbu* – literally 'steps forward'). In 1993, the then Shanghai Party Secretary, and now Vice-Premier, Wu Bangguo, commented on Deng Xiaoping saying, '[t]his Spring Festival . . . he encouraged us to liberate our thinking, seek truth from facts . . . have a little more courage, take rather faster steps. He said, now Pudong's development can only advance and cannot retreat, moreover you have no way back' (*JFRB* 3 July 1993: 1). Many Shanghainese I spoke with felt that the city had embarked upon a radically different route from that advocated by Mao Zedong and that the economy was 'galloping ahead' (*tengfei*).

At a more mundane level, opportunities and people may be described using a transport metaphor of 'roads' (*lu* or *luzi*). The popular local phrase 'one more friend is one more "path"' (*duo yige pengyou, duo yitiao lu*), also underlies the potentially instrumental nature of friendship. A *lu* is a road or route via which some aim may be attained. Somebody 'without a road' (*meiyou lu*) has few choices, whilst somebody whose roads are 'wide' (*cu*) and 'clear' (*tong*) stands a good chance of attaining their goal. If one meets with some obstacle it may be necessary to take a less direct route and use the backdoor (*zou houmen*). The backdoor may be opened (*kai houmen*) by a connection (*guanxi*). If this connection is reliable (*ying* – literally 'hard') this may be easy, if not it may be necessary to 'surface the road' (*pulu*) using gifts or money. One informant defined *pulu* as 'putting money on the road like a carpet.' *Pulu* was used in similar circumstances to the English colloquial expression 'grease somebody's palm'. A redundant worker told me that it was difficult for someone such as her to set up a stall as 'whatever you do, you have to "spread the path", for example, to obtain a trader's license. Everything requires money. If you don't "surface the road", the road is impassable.'

In contemporary Shanghai, those made redundant are told to 'find their own way [literally "road"] out' (*ziji zhao chulu*) of unemployment. *Guanxi* is the key to such roads. If one lacks *guanxi* one must 'walk the roads' (*zou zou luzi*), that is, try to find *menlu* – literally 'the entrance to roads' – another term for social connections. Significantly, one entrepreneurial young informant described her mobile phone to me as a 'road' (*lu*) and an 'opportunity'. Since Shanghai was given the 'green light' (*lü deng*) for economic development by the Politburo in the early 1990s, new 'roads' have opened up. There are increasing opportunities not only for those who take the 'right way' (*zhenglu*), but also those who seek to prosper by 'crooked roads' (*wai luzi*) such as bribery, fraud, and corruption.

Flying over southern China, one is reminded of the importance of water to people's livelihoods. Rivers, canals, and streams are abundant and everywhere there is evidence of human endeavour to bound and channel this vital but potentially destructive force. For millennia the main form of long-distance transportation was by inland waterway or coastal boats. It is not surprising, therefore, that the Chinese language should be drenched with the symbolism of water, the sea, rivers, tides, and waves. The Chinese term for each of these phenomena has a range of meanings and exists within a much wider semantic field (sea?) than the English equivalents. For instance, meanings of the term for 'flow' – *liu* – include 'moving from place to place; spread, circulate; degenerate; banish; class, grade.' The course of a person's life and the past can be likened to a river, for example, in the term *huisu wangshi* ('recall past events') – *huisu* means both 'to recall' and to 'go against the stream'.

'Watery' metaphors seemed to be important generative metaphors of people's portrayals of the impact of *gaige kaifang*, the policies adopted after the passing of the 'great helmsmen', Mao Zedong. This is all the more apt in Shanghai, which was originally a small fishing village, and whose name means 'above the sea'. Nautical allusions were used by Deng Xiaoping, who remarked that 'the economy should develop faster, and it cannot be expected to sail in quiet and plain waters all the time . . . It is like a boat sailing against the current which must keep forging ahead or will fall behind' (*CD* 12 November 1993: 4). In portrayals of the rapid (rapids?) changes brought about by *gaige kaifang* references to the 'sea', 'tides', and 'waves' were common in the local media and the everyday conversations of Shanghainese I encountered.

In the Chinese television documentary series *River Elegy*, its writers (Su and Wang 1991), strong supporters of the 'Open Door' policy, contrasted the turbulent, muddy Yellow River and the clear blue water of the Pacific. Commenting on the symbolism of *River Elegy*, Richard Bodman remarks, '[t]he overall message is clear: just as the Yellow River must flow into the sea and its murky yellow waters merge with the clear blue ocean, so too must China abandon isolation, open up to the world, eliminate the "sediment" of its traditional culture, and seek for more "transparency" in the workings of society and government' (1991: 16). This contrast is especially clear in the sixth part of the series, 'Blueness', written by Xie Xuanjun and Yuan Zhiming who promote a theory of 'human civilisation split into two great divisions, of land-based civilisation and sea-faring civilisation' (Su and Wang 1991: 204). They contrast the insularity and conservatism of the 'yellow culture' of 'Orientals with a deep tradition of despotism' (220) with 'blueness' which represents the values of modern western civilisation, transparency,[4] democracy, individualism, vitality, and acceptance of a broad variety of different cultures and new ideas. The authors note that '[b]arely a century has passed since the ancient spirit of the Yellow River has clearly seen the face of the sea and recognised its vastness and strength' (212). They believe that 'only when the sea-breeze of "blueness" faintly turns to rain and once again moistens this stretch of parched yellow soil, only then will this awesome vitality... be able to bring new life to the vast yellow soil plateau' (213).[5]

Another metaphor is the official description of Shanghai as the 'dragon-head', with the city leading the way in China's economic growth. This metaphor, which owes more to geomancy than socialism, had not spread far beyond media reports.

OPENING THE SLUICE: REPRESENTATIONS OF THE PLACE OF *GAIGE KAIFANG* IN MODERN CHINESE HISTORY

> For approximately twenty-odd years in the middle of this century, China once again faced a good opportunity for economic development. And yet locking our country's door and blindfolding ourselves we set off to 'surpass England and America', never ceasing to engage in one great political movement after another... so that in the end our national economy was on the brink of collapse.
>
> (Extract from *River Elegy,* Su and Wang 1991: 171)

The majority of Shanghai residents I encountered portrayed the reform policies as constituting a radical departure from previous policies. One intellectual described *kaifang* to me as the opposite of Mao's policies of self-reliance (*zili gengsheng*) and closing the country to international intercourse (*biguan zi shou*). The fact that it was actually at Mao's instigation that China 'opened' its door by renewing contacts with the US and taking China into the United Nations in the early 1970s seems largely to be glossed over. A Party member in his sixties described Mao's approach to me as 'closing the door to become a big king' – Chinese rulers could purvey an image of China as a model of socialist success without fear of contradiction by comparisons with alternative images. He believed that '*gaige kaifang* is a change of 180 degrees from Mao's time. So Deng Xiaoping is quite right when he says that we must "change our thinking" (*huan naozi* – literally "change brains").' As an instance of this he noted that 'where there was once "dictatorship of the proletariat" now many stores are run by Hong Kong bosses.' Like most informants and Western analysts he considered the Third Plenum of the Eleventh Central Committee of the Communist Party in December 1978 as the crucial turning point. A man in his fifties told me that since this Plenum, China had 'extricated itself from the "leftist road".' He commented that 'previously people were locked-in [he indicated the meaning by miming a locking motion]. There was no freedom. Now it is *kaifang* and liberation (*jiefang*).' The term *jiefang* is usually reserved to describe the Communist Party's take-over of power in 1949.[6]

In promoting its latest version of the 'socialist road' the Communist Party faces considerable difficulties. On the one hand, many of the policies this involves appear to be diametrically opposed to those of the preceding era, yet to criticise and repudiate *all* of those policies would undermine its legitimacy. There is a limit to how much blame for 'leftist' policies, such as egalitarianism, can be heaped onto the 'Gang of Four'. In such circumstances, there is a premium upon vagueness and opacity. Current policies – the 'socialist market economy' – are described as 'socialism with Chinese characteristics'. However, a common view of people I spoke with was summed-up by one informant who noted that 'although current slogans all talk about socialism and Marxism the *laobaixing* are very clear that the "socialist market economy" is actually capitalism. The higher levels cannot say this because they would have to repudiate all they've been doing for the last forty years.'

It was not unusual to hear people subvert the Party's rhetoric and to speak of 'capitalism with Chinese characteristics'. At times Party rhetoric itself indicates the distinct change of tack with calls for people to 'liberate their thinking' and 'change their minds'. There is also a distinct contrast between the Cultural Revolution rhetoric of slogans such as 'we would rather have the grass of socialism, than the jewels of capitalism' and Deng Xiaoping's pragmatic approach summed up in his most famous aphorism: 'It doesn't matter if the cat is black or white so long as it catches mice.'[7] In the early 1990s, Deng reiterated this view, now not even bothering to use metaphor, in his widely publicised remark that: 'It does not matter if something is called "socialism" or "capitalism", so long as it increases the prosperity of the common people.'

Some informants depicted policy changes in Shanghai as constituting not only a sharp 'about-turn', but a return to policies promoted by the KMT before 1949. A company manager who held this view added that 'all Shanghai lacks is the horse race track.' Even this, he expected, would return sooner or later.[8] A young designer felt that with *gaige kaifang* 'the policies of Chiang Kai-shek are now followed by Deng Xiaoping. The Communist Party criticised the KMT for selling land to foreigners and called it "betraying the country". Now the Communist Party does the same thing.' Despite Deng's endorsement of this policy it still provoked considerable resentment. A university student commented that 'many *laobaixing* feel strongly that renting land to foreigners is "betraying the country" and similar to the days of the foreign concessions.' A young lecturer complained that 'leasing land to foreigners is selling the property of Shanghai's children and grandchildren.' However, he considered that the state now has few powers to prevent land being leased in this way since localism has become much stronger with *gaige kaifang*. The sense of returning to the past was accentuated by the revival of pre-1949 terms such as *dzi ka/qianke* (broker), *yezonghui* (night-club), and *maiban* (comprador). Terms of address have also completed a full circle and reverted to those used before 1949. The terms 'Mr' (*xiansheng*), 'Mrs' (*taitai*), and 'Miss' (*xiaojie*) are being revived, whilst use of *tongzhi*, comrade, is mainly limited to political contexts and older intellectuals.

Shanghainese often expressed regret that several decades had been wasted. One man who expressed this lament told me:

> I saw the corruption of the KMT before 1949, and the good things done by the Communist Party in the early 1950s. Now China has undergone all kinds of shifts and changes to return to a situation worse than when the whole thing started forty years ago. If China had developed in the way it was before 1949 things would be much better now.

Many informants had sympathy for such views, expressing a sense of waste and squandered opportunities with two 'lost' generations. Often comparison was drawn between Shanghai and the 'Four Little Dragons' and Japan. From being the most developed of these places in 1949, Shanghai had slipped to being the most backward. It was striking that many people evaluated returning to the past in positive terms. It is a telling comment when, after decades of educating the populace on the evils of pre-1949 Shanghai, people such as a young lecturer expressed the hope and expectation that 'in the future Shanghai will be like it was in the 1940s, a lively international city.'

A retired school teacher who had been an underground Party member in Shanghai during the 1940s broadly accepted the official line. However, he commented that 'from the eyes of the past what is happening now is all capitalism.' He remarked that 'before even growing flowers or keeping a goldfish was criticised as a bourgeois lifestyle. Now everyone goes in for share dealing and the son [Rong Yiren] of a Shanghai capitalist is vice-president!'[9] He noted that in the 1950s hooliganism, prostitution, and gambling had been eradicated, but had now all returned. With a tone of incredulity and some bitterness he added 'for three decades China struggled for the sake of socialism, now we go in for capitalism. Now Deng Xiaoping says it doesn't matter if something is called socialism or capitalism. Some feel their decades fighting for the revolution were all for nothing.'

One intellectual I spoke with located *gaige kaifang* policies within a broader historical framework. For him, *gaige kaifang* constituted a new direction, not only in terms of the Maoist past, but also when compared to 'traditional' China. He noted that in imperial times the Chinese economy did not develop because Confucian values stressed agriculture and looked down upon business. Observing that 'now everyone wants to go into business', he considered this a highly significant change in people's way of thinking that had occurred with *gaige kaifang*. In other words, he considered *gaige kaifang* to be bringing about more fundamental changes in 'Chinese culture' than had occurred during the Maoist era. In his estimation, Maoist policies and the commercialism of the reform era have coalesced to produce a 'deformed' (*jixing*) society.

Why *Gaige Kaifang*?

In the same way as the terms '*gaige*' and '*kaifang*' were understood in varying ways, so divergent explanations were proposed for the motive behind the state's adoption of these policies. Some informants accepted, or at least claimed to accept, the Party line. Put simply, this version is that the Communist Party recognised 'certain mistakes' had been made in the past and now promoted new, improved policies designed to increase the living standards and well-being of the populace. A more cynical interpretation was that these policies had been adopted solely in an attempt to maintain the Party's rule. A factory worker expressed the view that 'previously the government used power to control the *laobaixing*, now it uses money.' In his estimation, Deng Xiaoping's intention with *gaige kaifang* is that 'his children will have advantages.' Similarly, an intellectual believed that 'the Party had no other way out. The closed door policy was no good, it had to change. The point of *gaige kaifang* is to save the skin of the Communist Party, without *gaige kaifang* the Communist Party would have collapsed. *Gaige kaifang* is advantageous for the ruling class, but not the *laobaixing*.'

It often appears that far from being state-directed, policies promoted as 'reforms' by the state are a *post hoc* legitimation of popular practices, responses to situations the state cannot control. A young female clerical worker, employed in a local library, who remarked to me on the pace of change in Shanghai added that 'things which were illegal two or three months ago are now promoted.' She cited the instance of local cadres setting up street stalls, which had undergone just such a process. Press reports initially told people not to set up these stalls. A couple of months later these activities were being encouraged. Similarly, in November 1993, it was announced that individuals would be allowed to trade foreign currency. A *China Daily Business Weekly* report cited a local official as saying that 'it will be a severe attack' on the city's black market in foreign exchange and underground foreign exchange trading companies (7–13 November 1993: 3). This was an 'attack' only insofar as it legalised and formalised these activities. The stock market also shows state policy as following on behind popular practices (see Chapter 5).[10] Initially most stock trading was carried on in black market or semi-legal deals. Only later did the state permit the establishment of the Shanghai Stock Exchange. It may be that the state turned a blind eye to such practices, regarding them as experiments which it could suppress if need be. However, the impression given is of the state being reactive and led by events.

OPENING THE FLOODGATES: CHANGES BROUGHT ABOUT BY *GAIGE KAIFANG*

> Thirty or forty years ago [Shanghai] was a huge mud flat, that the high tides continually invaded, so that the lower rooms of existing houses were often flooded and made useless for habitation. Low grounds, where stagnant pools and green, slimy water abounded, existed everywhere.
>
> (Rev. John MacGowan, *Pictures of Southern China* 1897: 69)

Before the flood

Informants routinely characterised everyday life in pre-reform Shanghai and for much of the 1980s as presenting few 'roads' or opportunities – the city had become stuck in a rut, with little scope for individual choice and agency.[11] Shanghainese felt that the highly bureaucratic planned economy had been gradually stifling the city. A factory worker described Shanghai before the early 1990s, and especially before 1978, as *ninggu*, 'coagulated' or 'congealed', whilst a teacher reckoned it had been 'held fast in a frame'. A Shanghainese social science researcher commented to me that under the socialist planned economy 'people's food, clothing, accommodation, household registration, decision to have children, schooling, job assignments, type of work done, and salary were all decided by the state.' He added that 'there was no other alternative' and that 'what each person could do and obtain was more or less the same'. Western analysts, too, depict early 1970s urban China as characterised by residential stability and 'extreme bureaucratisation and equality' (Parish and Whyte 1984: 6). *Gaige kaifang* is designed to unblock restrictions, open up new channels and 'enliven' (*bianhuo*) the 'dead' (*si*) economy. By the mid-1990s, it had begun to make changes in each of the sectors mentioned by the sociologist, new channels have formed or seepage has permeated established courses.

Information

In pre-reform Shanghai, information flow was highly restricted and access to it 'highly stratified' (Parish and Whyte 1984: 299). During the 1950s, media were centralised and the arts generally were officially intended to serve politics and the Communist Party. Broadcasting was regarded primarily as a political tool – troops of the People's Liberation Army were stationed outside media centres and broadcasters read from censored statements. Parish and Whyte found that '[m]ost residents simply remained in the dark about what was really going on in their country' (1984: 295). A high level of surveillance and fear of repercussions ensured that few complaints were voiced.

An early 'flow' was the grumbling, complaining, and muttering of the populace, a simmering discontent which bubbled to the surface towards the end of the Cultural Revolution. Such weapons of the weak (cf. Scott 1990) like 'water constantly dripping wears holes in stone' (*di shui chuan shi*). These murmurings became magnified after the death of Mao and, in particular, once criticism of the Gang of Four was allowed and it was admitted that Mao had shortcomings, much suppressed anger came out. A university lecturer recalled that at this time 'the cursing of the whole nation burst forth like a tidal wave'. It appears that the sea-wall of Communist Party power could not resist the 'tide' of popular grumbling and complaining at the end of the Cultural Revolution. I frequently heard people voice grievances and make complaints in semi-public contexts such as crowded buses or restaurants. Many of these could formerly only have been voiced, if at all, to the most trusted of intimates. As an accountant in a state *danwei* expressed it, 'before one could not complain, one dare not speak. Now I have liberation (*jiefang*). The wall of the past has gone.' It is notable that here the term *jiefang* is used not to describe a social release but an individual emancipation. In losing its moral authority the Communist Party seems to have lost some of its ability to control the populace – it had no other choice but to permit this freedom to speak. As with the changes in economic policy noted above, it seems that this new freedom did not flow from any liberal sentiments on the regime's part but, rather, derived from a loss of state control over popular practices.

During the reform period there has been a significant depoliticisation of everyday life. This includes a reduction of controls over the media which has allowed a proliferation of magazines, music, television, and radio programmes with a much greater range of styles and themes. During 1992–3, for example, live television and radio phone-in programmes became extremely popular (*liuxing* – 'flow' and 'prevail/be current'). Topics I heard discussed included consumer rights, sexual fulfilment, and redundancy. A local theatre director remarked to me that such changes were a significant departure from the past when there was 'only the voice of the government'. For a few days in May 1989 'the dike of censorship itself seemed to have been washed away' (Faison 1990: 147). In particular, between 13–19 May the media's detailed and sympathetic reporting on the hunger strikers in Beijing gave an indication of what a free and 'open' Chinese media would look like. Following through the watery, irrigation metaphor and bearing in mind that the Chinese term for broadcasting '*bo*' also means 'sow, seed' one may see *gaige kaifang* as bringing life to many new shoots.

The proliferation of media is bound up with the commercialisation of the economy and the 'emergence of a cultural market' (Kraus 1995: 177). Considerations of profit and loss must now be balanced against 'political correctness'. Rather than simply promote Party messages the popular media, which is increasingly dependent upon advertising revenues, must produce items that appeal to consumer tastes. Within the freer media environment it is harder for the state to prevent the appearance of critical items. Censorship controls, which are still severe, prevent blatant criticisms of the regime, but there is greater leeway for newspaper articles and television programmes to *da ca bian qiu*, an expression derived from ping-pong which describes when a ball glances off the edge of the table.

The flow of information in China in the form of talk and a comparative liberalisation of the media has been greatly fostered by the opening of China's national door. A retired school teacher told me that in the Maoist era there 'was a news blockade and foreign broadcasts were jammed, so we did not know what the outside world was like. Only the higher levels had access to foreign media.' Another informant told me 'Mao Zedong had a closed door policy. Deng Xiaoping threw open the window and let the wind in. People could see what the West was like.' The English term 'wind' is an inadequate and partial translation of the Chinese term *feng* which has a diverse range of meanings and connotations in a wide variety of contexts. It can, for example, mean 'style, practice, custom; scene, view; news, information'. A 38-year old saleswoman made a direct link between changing values and ideas and the 'opening' of China's 'door'. She told me that 'previously people's thinking was conservative and closed up. Mao Zedong did not allow us to see the outside world, we were blind. When the door opened, we saw the discrepancy [with the West] and could not bear it.'

Through the 'open door' has flowed information and 'strange tales from over the seas' (*haiwai qitan*). Local people are now free to tune in to the *BBC World Service* and the *Voice of America* and other foreign broadcasts which drift in on the air-waves. Television enables viewers to gaze upon other people and places from their living rooms and provides the main channel for images of other countries. Having been told for years that China was outstripping the capitalist West, and hearing only of the sufferings of those in capitalist countries, people were surprised and often dismayed by what they saw. A Party member told me that 'it came as a shock when suddenly we saw that the West was far more advanced than we had ever imagined.' Comparison with Western nations was bad enough, but Shanghainese were even more dismayed to find that Asia's once most modern city had been eclipsed by 'upstarts' such as Hong Kong, Singapore, and Taiwan.[12] Shanghainese felt that their city had stood still, and even deteriorated, whilst these places had raced ahead and developed successful modern economies.

At the same time as *gaige kaifang* has enabled Shanghainese to compare their living standards to those of foreigners depicted on the media, so the 'open door' has also allowed the outside world to gaze upon China. This dialectic was evident during the 1989 demonstrations when many students carried banners in English obviously designed for consumption abroad (see page 101).

Those who expect Shanghai to develop rapidly and successfully point to factors such as its well-trained workforce, favourable geographic location, and the state's support for its development – one view was that the government wants to develop Shanghai at the expense of Hong Kong. A young businessman told me that he expects Shanghai will reach a similar level to New York and was confident that, at the very minimum, it will surpass Hong Kong within ten years. A retired teacher commented, 'Napoleon called China a sleeping lion, it is now awakening. Once fully awake, the world will not be able to look down on this race.' He added that 'now America gives China special economic status, but in five years time it will be the other way round.' His expectation, voiced ironically using the somnambulant metaphor so favoured in many Orientalist views of

China, is that the outside world will be able to gaze upon a newly assertive, rich, and powerful China.

Flow of capital

In the late 1980s, a standing joke in Shanghai was that when those who left the city three decades before returned to visit, they could easily find their way around because everything was exactly the same. Shanghainese complained about the lack of infrastructural work carried out in the city in the decades after 1949. Until the 1980s, Shanghai lacked any new architecture comparable to the early twentieth-century colonial structures on the Bund.

Gaige kaifang has brought significant changes in the city's outward appearance. The opening of the five-star luxury high-rise Hilton hotel in 1988, was widely viewed as the first sign of progress – a literal and a metonymical landmark. Informants generally viewed the presence of such buildings as material evidence of Shanghai's new found global ambition and increasing prosperity, even if they themselves could never afford to visit such places. The modern architecture of the Hongqiao development zone near the airport was another obvious sign of change. More recently, the development of Pudong, the construction of the Nanpu and Yangpu bridges – now attractions on all tourist itineraries – numerous hotels, share dealing centres, commercial entertainment centres, new roads, and metro lines are all visible markers of change. In 1993, the 460-metre high Shanghai Radio and Television Tower on the east side of the Huangpu River was completed. It is in keeping with the sustained watery metaphors noted in this chapter that this 'new symbol of Shanghai' should be described as 'The Oriental Pearl' (*CD* 15 November 1993: 5).

These changes are due in part to a greater retention of profits made in the city. In 1985 the amount of tax revenues retained in the city increased from 13.2 per cent to 23.2 per cent (Jacobs and Hong 1994: 231). There has also been a significant inflow of domestic and foreign capital. A *Wenhui Bao* article stated that '[n]ineties Shanghai, has opened wide its great door, and welcomes investors from every country to come and invest' (*WHB* 26 May 1993: 1). During the 1980s, Shanghai attracted a total of $3.3 billion in foreign investment. A similar figure was attracted in 1992 alone. In 1996, contractual overseas investment in Shanghai totalled $11.1 billion (SWB/FEW/0477 WG/5 12 March 1997).

Shanghai enterprises have begun to establish operations in other Chinese provinces. As foreign retail stores now set up in Shanghai, local businesses are starting to go nation-wide. Shanghai's No.1 Department Store Company, for example, has opened stores in Changchun, Chongqing, Hefei, Xian, and Tai *yuan*. By the end of 1996, Shanghai retailers had set up 369 retailing establishments in 68 cities, and manufacturing companies had established 1,001 manufacturing facilities in other provinces and cities, with some 4.76 billion *yuan* ($573 m) investment (*SS* 9 May 1997: 6). During 1996 alone, over 100 Shanghai companies set up manufacturing facilities in other cities and provinces.

Flow of people

International

The tide of news and information was soon followed by products and people. Foreign-made products – from Japanese consumer electronics to American toothbrushes and British cosmetics – which began to trickle and then pour into Shanghai were tangible evidence of China's new direction. A former KMT official observed 'things have changed 180 degrees. In the Cultural Revolution, I dared not have any foreign things visible in my home. American things were described as especially bad, now even the smallest shop likes to stick up a sign saying "China–US Joint Venture".'

Opening China's door has allowed a flow of people into and out of the country. In the 1980s many Shanghainese felt frustrated by the limited prospects within China. A Confucian saying describes an option when one's path is blocked: 'If the way is not accepted, get on a boat and take to the seas' (*dao bu xing, cheng cha fu yu hai*). A 'going abroad craze' (*chuguore*) began with 'large numbers of talented people turbulently flowing out of the national door' (*JFRB* 29 October 1993: 3). Better-educated young Shanghainese sought scholarships in Western Europe, Australia, and, above all, America. During the late 1980s and early 1990s, for instance, a majority of post-graduate students at Shanghai's elite Fudan University were actively seeking to study abroad. There is considerable evidence of a 'brain drain'. Many of Shanghai's most able younger intellectuals have gone abroad. Those with fewer qualifications often hoped to go abroad to work, and many went to Japan. One commentator described this behaviour to me as an example of the way 'water runs to low places, people move toward high places'. Significant numbers of citizens have also been sent abroad by the Chinese government for study and training. Some Shanghainese seek to marry foreigners to go abroad, a few simply using them as a 'springboard' to leave China. Sometimes the wish is to obtain a foreign passport since, as a wealthy young businesswoman told me, 'it is difficult to predict what will happen in China. Having a foreign passport is a kind of insurance.'

It is claimed that, since 1992, the 'going abroad craze' had been 'cooling' with fewer people leaving and 'an irresistible tide returning to China' (ibid.). This change was trumpeted as attributable to and evidence of the 'excellent opportunities' brought by the 'continuing deepening of *gaige kaifang*' in Shanghai. By the second half of the 1990s, there was, if not 'an irresistible tide', at least a steady trickle of returning migrants, about 15,000 students were said to have returned to Shanghai and begun work by autumn 1997 (*SS* 26 August 1997: 4). In addition, amongst young people I encountered, the desire to emigrate did appear to have diminished. Not only are there now more opportunities at home, but enthusiasm to go and live abroad has also been dampened by reports of the difficulties faced by earlier migrants and stricter immigration controls by recipient countries. At the same time, overseas tourism has become a possibility for Shanghai's newly rich. In the mid-1990s Thailand was a popular destination.

Official delegations also have greater opportunities to go abroad. In London in 1994, for instance, I met a party of share exchange officials from Shanghai who were visiting a London securities firm. A popular view was that such 'perks' were one of the ways in which the 'open door' provided new scope for corruption and official largesse.

Businessmen, teachers, students, and tourists have increasingly flooded into the city. Between 1990–7, passenger volume at the city's Hongqiao International Airport increased by more than 20 per cent per annum (*SS* 19 March 1999: 1). In 1996, for instance, 9,050 international flights landed in Shanghai, bringing in 1.45 million passengers (*SS* 6 June 1997: 4). In the same year, there were 6,234 registered foreign residents in Shanghai (*SS* 7 January 2000: 1). A saleswoman commented to me that 'now many foreign businessmen come to Shanghai. Shanghai is returning to how it was in the 1940s, a *shi li yangchang* ('a metropolis infested with foreign adventurers – usually referring to pre-liberation Shanghai' CED 1988: 800). There is now an international feel.'

Intra-national flow

During the reform era the city boundaries have become much more permeable. One notable effect is that 'a "Southern wind" has already blown into Shanghai' (*XMWB* 5 November 1993: 14). This 'wind' takes the form of cultural influences from Guangdong and Hong Kong including music, food, and linguistic expressions. Another particularly significant flow is that of migrant workers from other parts of China. This has been made possible by the end of rationing and the reduced effectiveness of the household registration system. An article in *Wenhui Bao* reported that '[w]ith the increased dynamic development of Pudong and Shanghai's current great strides towards being an internationalised great metropolis . . . there is a rush of great fervour (*rechao* – literally a "hot wave") towards "Shanghai beach"' (*WHB* 26 May 1993: 1). By 1994, Shanghai's floating population was reported to total around 3.3 million (White 1994: 86), city planners expect this figure to reach 5–6 million by 2010 (*SS* 2 July 1993: 1).

A *Xinmin Wanbao* article described migrant workers as a '"guerilla force" . . . stealthily entering [Shanghai's] factories' (22 July 1993: 12). This article noted that around 100,000 female textile factory workers had been made redundant in Shanghai and that they were being replaced by a 'tide of non-Shanghainese migrant workers' (*waidi mingong chao*) which 'blindly flows and surges into this city.' The willingness of these workers to do dirty and unpleasant jobs for low wages is described as presenting a 'threat' and a 'challenge' to redundant Shanghai women workers getting work again. Changes have also taken place to increase the 'talent pool' in Shanghai. In 1999, a *Shanghai Star* article titled 'Talent pool to be channelled into city', described how professionals who found a job in Shanghai would now be allowed to settle in the city with permanent residence status (*SS* 13 August 1999: 3).

Flow within Shanghai

In addition to an increasing topographical flow of people there is also flow within Shanghai in terms of greater social mobility and the opening up of new routes and channels. An early indication of the start of *gaige kaifang* was the announcement that class struggle was over and that economic construction was the central policy. In the late 1970s, the cessation of 'class' labelling, which was dominant as a distinctive classificatory and organising feature of social life from the early 1950s, began to loosen up the social system. In education, for instance, the old system under which many students' fate was fixed by the class label of their parents was replaced by more meritocratic criteria.

At the end of 1978, employment opportunities were still almost entirely restricted to state and collective enterprises. Workers had a high degree of job security, but could also 'be stuck forever in a very unpleasant work situation' (Parish and Whyte 1984: 33). A key shift marking a more tolerant attitude towards the 'tails of capitalism' was the re-legalisation in the late 1970s of small-scale private entrepreneurs (*getihu*). The services they provide, such as bicycle repairs and fruit stalls, alongside allowing peasants to sell their produce in the city, brought significant and qualitative changes to inhabitants' daily lives. However, it was felt by many informants that initially *gaige kaifang* only brought new opportunities to *getihu* (small-scale entrepreneurs).[13] In the 1980s state employees generally remained 'stuck', both residentially and occupationally (Davis 1990: 87).

During the 1990s significant changes in the economic base occurred which have allowed an increased range of choice for far greater numbers of people. The increased possibility to choose and change jobs are important new elements of choice. From 1991, what is officially called the 'mobility of talent' (*rencai liudong* – literally 'flow of talent') and popularly referred to as *tiaocao* (literally 'jump from one trough to another') became quite common. A state *danwei* employee contrasted the possibility to *tiaocao* with the situation 'in Mao's time' when one could not change jobs but was just a 'revolutionary screw' – a term which highlights both limited labour mobility and lack of individual choice. Even the term 'labour market', now used by officials, would have been anathema until recently, implying, as it does, that labour is a commodity. Instead of being channelled into a job, graduating students can now find their own jobs. Policy changes have increased the range of choice by allowing part or wholly foreign-funded enterprises and private companies – the number of the latter in Shanghai totalled some 62,000 by the end of May 1997, a 26-fold increase over 1991 (*SS* 22 July 1997: 1). Occupational mobility has also increased, with job advertisements and, for instance, a removal of restrictions on moves from collective to state enterprises. In the past such moves could usually only be made via the 'backdoor'.

An informant who described pre-reform Shanghai as having been 'solidified' considered that as a result of *gaige kaifang* 'the social structure is more dynamic, for example, somebody without *wenhua* can get rich.'[14] A young businessman noted that previously manual and service work had been regarded as low-status, but that now, for example, a hairdresser may be seen as 'high-class' and a bar worker have a high income which gives him status. It is ironic that in the Maoist era, when state rhetoric advocated narrowing the gap between mental and manual labour, this distinction appears to have been reinforced. During the reform era, when such rhetoric has been jettisoned, comments such as this suggest progress in this direction, although my own impression is that this trend is limited. For instance, many people still expressed negative attitudes towards *getihu*. On one occasion, however, an intellectual who had just outlined the usual negative stereotype added that 'people usually say *getihu* have lots of money and are slippery types. But in practice, many are not wealthy and they face many problems such as arbitrary taxes and corrupt officials.'

As a result of increased job mobility and the 'flow of talent', educational establishments and professions such as medicine have lost staff to commercial companies which can pay higher salaries. A *Guangming Daily* article described this 'brain drain' as caused by the move to the market economy and observed, for instance, that the 'once pre-eminent Fudan University is beginning to stagnate' (translated in *CD* 17 July 1993: 4). The article concluded that the way to resolve this problem is to 'let the market completely redistribute talented workers, putting them into jobs that give them the best opportunities to use their abilities.' Following through the irrigation metaphor, one may see this as a notion that the waters unleashed by the sluice will naturally find their own level and not be wasted by being poured down the drain.

Employees in state *danwei* are increasingly able to 'side-channel' their energies. A report in *China Daily* stated that '[t]he rigid personnel system in the State sector still limits labour mobility and restrains talent flow [but] moonlighters can try whatever they think they are good at... Shanghai has about 5 million moonlighters... working in their free time as peddlers, waiters, private tutors, editors, PR staff members and consultants' (*CD* 8 March 1993: 4). If the staggering figure of 5 million moonlighters is correct, and certainly many people I met were moonlighting, then most Shanghainese workers are engaged in this activity. Moreover, the list given does not even include those who deal in shares in the city's newly re-established share market (see Chapter 5). At least 1–2 million Shanghainese have 'thrown themselves into the share sea' (*touru le guhai*) (*NFZM* 18 June 1993: 1). After a visit to Shanghai in 1843, Robert Fortune described the city as 'essentially a mercantile city, and all the residents engaged in active business' (1853, Vol.1: 104). At times I felt that Shanghai could once again be described in this way.

Viewed from one perspective increased job mobility is a new opportunity. However, many people change jobs or take on additional jobs because their salaries are insufficient and promotion prospects limited. Furthermore, a policy shift allowing employees from collective enterprises to move to state *danwei* implicitly acknowledged the declining status of state *danwei*. State *danwei* employees told me that the sense of superiority they once felt had steadily evaporated since the mid-1980s. The main impediments to leaving a state *danwei* are the loss of welfare benefits and job security. Reduced funding of state enterprises and the introduction of a contract system for new employees has eroded these

Cartoon 1.1 'The True and the False'. The dozing figure is at his *danwei* job. The second figure carries a suitcase labelled 'second job'.

Source: *XMWB* 8 December 1993.

Cartoon 1.2 'Deformed'. The bucket in the left hand is labelled 'own job', the one in the right hand 'second job'.

Source: *XMWB* 29 April 1993.

entitlements or, at least, engendered the belief that they will deteriorate. On one occasion, during a conversation with a state factory worker at his home, a television news report mentioned that some state fruit stores had closed because they could not compete with *getihu*. The worker commented that 'the state cannot outdo *getihu*.'[15] This passing remark is a telling comment on the state's declining economic role.

Interstices

Before the reform period organisational and information structures were predominantly vertical, hierarchical, and relatively discrete. Exceptions to this were *lianluoyuan*, (liaison personnel) who operated on behalf of state *danwei* as middlemen between wholesale and retail units. Individuals could also use personal connections, although the scope for this was limited. Since the 1990s there has been much greater opportunity for connections to be made horizontally. Indeed, one informant suggested that *danwei* leaders, and by extension the Communist Party itself, were increasingly just 'signboards'.

Where previously the reach of the state touched directly upon each individual, now the former links between the Party-state and work units and citizens have become less direct and space has now opened up for new forms of association. The state's role in enterprise management has reduced, a change recognised in 1993, with a subtle but significant change in terminology. The term *guoying qiye*, 'state-run enterprises', would be replaced by *guo you qiye*, meaning state-held, but not necessarily state-run, enterprises.

Since the late 1980s, various types of intermediary organisations have emerged such as trade associations, commercial federations and scholarly institutes. Shanghai's commercialising economy provides scope for many types of brokers and middlemen, and there has been a flood of advice and 'how-to' books have emerged with titles such as *The Managing Strategy of Broker* (*sic*) (*Jingjiren Jingying Fanglüe*). Recently *dzi ka* (*qianke*), a pre-1949 term for broker, has been revived although it remains a rather derogatory term. One woman I spoke with, who said that she could be called a *dzi ka*, described herself as a 'cultural' or 'propaganda' broker. These activities included facilitating what she described as 'soft advertising', that is, publicising products in the guise of news items or other features such as interviews. She placed these items in the local media using a *guanxi* 'net' composed of 'familiar people' (*shuren*) including former classmates, and 'friends of friends'. In addition, she added, money provides a 'permit' to ensure the placing of such items. Overseas Chinese entrepreneurs often utilise or construct social ties with individuals to facilitate the process of investment in mainland China and to act as brokers (see Smart 1993). These people fulfil the same type of role as compradors in pre-1949 China.

There is greater space for civil society, particularly of a diffusely organised kind. The world of share dealers, which I explore in Chapter 5, is a significant example of this. Share dealers rely upon contacts and information for their trading activities. Amongst wealthy dealers and share exchange managers I encountered, lunch at expensive restaurants appeared to be a frequent event. To these were invited colleagues and friends often employed in government departments and other financial institutions. These meetings were clearly aimed at maintaining and creating 'connections' and 'oiling the hinges'. More generally, Shanghai's burgeoning restaurant scene is a symbol of the city's revived role as a commercial 'window' – these are the places where business deals are done.

Setting sail

A term which became fashionable after 1991–2 is *xiahai* (literally – go down to the sea). It refers to cadres and intellectuals – people with *wenhua* – who engage in business. Originally *xiahai* was the expression used to describe an amateur intellectual enthusiast of Peking opera (a *piaoyou*) who became a professional actor – this was called *piaoyou xiahai*. This dramatic analogy accords closely with the view of one informant that *gaige kaifang* provides a 'stage' on which individuals have the opportunity to give free reign to their talents. *Xiahai* had a derogatory connotation since actors were looked down upon by intellectuals. Some informants were unaware of this derivation of *xiahai* and provided imaginative etymologies. One teacher speculated that *xiahai* originally referred to pirates setting out on a raid. On a subsequent visit to his home he again raised the topic of *xiahai*. It was worse, he noted, than he had realised. From conversations with friends he had 'discovered' that *xiahai* originally meant for a girl to enter a brothel and become a prostitute.

Although these etymologies indicate that *xiahai* possesses at least a resonance of illicit behaviour most informants denied that *xiahai* retains a derogatory meaning. However one intellectual, well aware of the literary origin of *xiahai*, linked this term to *xiashui* meaning, literally, 'to enter the water' and, more figuratively, 'to take to evil doing' – he explained that 'it is like when one is clean and then gets into water, which is dirty. Both *xiahai* and *xiashui* share the meaning of "to head for the place with money".' I protested that water is clean, but he drew attention to a popular saying which may describe a person who seeks self-improvement: *ren wang gaochu zou, shui xiang dichu liu* – humans aim for high places, water runs to low places. His interpretation was that water is 'ignoble and does not want face', it runs downwards towards the *xialiu* – the lower reaches (also 'low-down, mean, obscene, dirty') – where all the dirty things are to be found.

Various factors provoked people to *xiahai*. A key motive was financial. Some considered prospects at their *danwei* too limited. Peer group pressure and media examples of successful money-makers could also be a spur to 'set sail'. By decreeing that workers' bonuses must now be earned by commercial activities within *danwei*, the state appeared to encourage such entrepreneurship. Informants also described *xiahai* as providing an opportunity to use and develop personal talents, some characterising it as an opportunity to 'temper' (*duanlian*) themselves. This reference to *duanlian* is an interesting instance of the way in which people took 'imposed knowledge and symbolisms' and 'made something else out of them . . . [and] subverted them from within' (De Certeau 1984: 32). This term was popular in the Maoist era when people would 'steel themselves' in 'great revolutionary movements' (CED 1988: 169). Writing on rural Guangdong in the Cultural Revolution, Richard Madsen comments that *duanlian* was a term used by village leaders and activists and that it included the notion of 'asceticism – spiritual exercise consciously and deliberately undertaken' (1984: 29–30). In both Maoist and contemporary China this 'tempering' involves hardship, but the intended outcomes are radically different. In the former instance the goal was revolutionary purity, the current aim is material well-being.

Sinking

In contrast to those Shanghainese who have succeeded or at least tested the waters in the commercial 'sea' many faced another type of *xia* – *xiagang*. Substantial numbers of workers in unprofitable enterprises have been given 'early retirement' or laid-off and told to 'find their own way out' of this problem. Unlike *shiye* – 'unemployment', workers who 'step down from their posts' (*xiagang*) retain a connection with their work unit and welfare entitlements. They also receive a percentage of their salaries. It is illustrative of the degree of flux in Shanghai that on several occasions when I asked informants to explain this term they had not heard it yet, and I became the one to explain its meaning to them! Typically, those who *xiagang* were the less well-educated, and often middle-aged women from the 'lost generation' whose education had been disrupted during the Cultural Revolution (1966–76). In the early 1990s, precise statistics on the number of *xiagang* workers were difficult to obtain – the state closely guards such information. However, occasional news items mentioned factories laying-off workers and my informants generally knew of people who had been laid-off. Since the later 1990s, this problem has been discussed more openly; a 1997 report stated that between 1992–6 some 1.3 million factory workers had been laid-off, of whom 1.1 million had been re-employed (*SS* 27 May 1997: 1).[16] One informant described the extent of *xiagang* as analogous to a bowl with a crack in it through which its contents leak out – the 'bowl' here being Shanghai's socio-economic structure. This would seem to be an apposite analogy for the fate of the 'iron rice bowl' in Shanghai.

The situation of *xiagang* workers, who in 1997 received around 400 *yuan* ($48) pcm, was extremely difficult especially if both spouses were laid-off. Many sought work in the service sector, setting up a street stall being a common 'road out'. The better qualified sought work in joint ventures. Some units set up subsidiary enterprises such as restaurants and redeploy workers in these. *Xiagang* workers who cannot find alternative work often return to their original jobs since *danwei* retain ultimate responsibility for them.

Although *xiagang* poses a great threat for many workers, some consider it a welcome opportunity to leave a job they dislike. Drivers, in particular, often welcome *xiagang* since their skills are in great demand. One factory worker told me that he was happy to *xiagang* since he would get half his wages, retain welfare entitlements, and be able to take on a part-time job which paid more than his original salary. In another case, a worker in a state *danwei* planned to volunteer to *xiagang* for several months in order to try out a job in a trading company. In this way *xiagang* provided a crucial security net.

The situation of the unemployed is especially dire. In 1997, they received just 270 *yuan* ($33) pcm unemployment benefit. The number of *xiagang* and unemployed in Shanghai in 1997 was estimated at 7–8 per cent of Shanghai's

4.7 million workforce. Unofficial estimates suggest that twice as many people could be out of work (*FT Survey* 1997: VII). These figures could rise still further if more bankruptcies are permitted or if there is any downturn in economic growth.[17]

Backwaters and stagnant pools

One state worker commented that '*gaige kaifang* provides a stage on which people can give full play to their talents.' However, she added that this was of little benefit to those who lacked talents and that this 'stage' could often only be entered via the backdoor. Another young state worker told me, 'there have been some big changes in Shanghai, but for those with no opportunities (*meiyou lu* – literally 'without roads'), and without a way to make money, their situation may be deteriorating.' Desirable jobs include state trading and financial companies, and foreign-invested enterprises in which most of the best opportunities are open only to the young and well-educated. Structural limits to occupational mobility remain. In particular, the provision of housing and welfare benefits is still largely tied to *danwei* membership. In addition, some workers who move jobs and, for instance, trainee teachers who do not take up job assignments, have to pay compensation.

State *danwei* workers I encountered often appeared to be marooned in enterprises where little had changed. One informant described them as 'like machines whose motor has stopped, and which continue to move only through residual momentum.' Similarly, a local government cadre told me that 'despite the constant talk about *gaige kaifang*, it's still just the same old situation.' It seems that the stereotypical state *danwei* where workers 'have a cup of tea, smoke a cigarette, and read the newspaper' still survive. Indeed, when I asked this cadre if he was busy at work he responded 'not at all, now it's *gaige kaifang*. The government is relaxed now, it doesn't want us to do much.' He added that '*gaige kaifang* brings some problems' including plans for cuts in local government bureaucracy. He considered his future prospects 'difficult to predict' but was not worried since 'there is always food to eat, the state will always arrange something – they won't make you unemployed.' This man was in the process of applying for Communist Party membership. He expected that this would 'make everything rather better'. For example, he would get a higher salary, an increased bonus, and more chance of promotion. Few younger informants considered this strategy – indeed, this man remarked that his own daughter considered his joining the Party as 'stupid'.

Many state workers had a lackadaisical attitude toward their jobs, they may *chugong bu chuli* – go to work, but not expend energy. A factory worker in his early thirties told me that in his job he just *hun* – wastes time – all day. Workers' efforts and energies are often channelled into a second job or sideline activities such as share dealing. In addition, the possibility of making money elsewhere has introduced subtle changes into the workplace. For instance, a woman with various sideline occupations commented that she would not obey her *danwei* leader since her salary was too low. However, not all workers can engage in such activities. In 1994, a 38-year old electrician on a salary of 280 *yuan* who described his *danwei* as 'still an iron rice bowl' told me that he had neither the time nor the energy for a second job – each day he spent four hours crossing the city by bus commuting from his home to his *danwei*.

Rising tides – living standards and consumerism

For many, probably a majority of Shanghai residents, the most important consequence, and indeed the very connotation of *gaige kaifang* was that living standards have risen. By 1997, average incomes had trebled since 1990 (*FT Survey* 1997: VII). By 1999, the yearly average income of local workers was 30,800 *yuan* ($3,600), almost three times the average of 10,663 *yuan* ($1,290) in 1996 (*SS* 12 September 2000: 10). As a proverb states: 'when the river rises the boat goes up' – particular things improve with the improvement of the general situation (*shui zhang chuan gao*). With rising disposable incomes, and a much greater range and quantity of consumer items there has been a 'consumer flood in the 1990s' (*WHDYSB* 5 June 1993: 7). I examine this important topic in-depth in Chapter 4. There are, however, many more dangerous currents, and I explore these in the following section.

FLOOD WATER, DANGEROUS CURRENTS, MURKY DEPTHS, AND WHIRLPOOLS

> Our coastal areas, silent for centuries, this Gold Coast of the Chinese people, with an appetite long held in check, are now the first to rush towards the Pacific. The Chinese people at this moment are more eager than ever before to enter the world market. And yet this people has been isolated for too long and is still unfamiliar with the [uncharted] seas of the commodity economy.
>
> (Extract from *River Elegy*, Su and Wang 1991: 173)

In official Chinese rhetoric the Cultural Revolution of 1966–76 was 'ten years of chaos'. Many people I encountered in Shanghai endorsed this view. However, I also heard people describe the present as 'chaotic'. Indeed some asserted that there was more 'chaos' in the 1990s than during the Cultural Revolution. I consider that following through the watery metaphors and attention to the differing meanings of the term *luan* can help to account for these seemingly irreconcilable representations.

The term *luan* has a wide range of meanings which include: 'in disorder, in confusion; upheaval, chaos, riot, unrest; confuse, mix up, jumble; confused (state of mind); indiscriminate, random, arbitrary; promiscuous sexual behaviour, promiscuity' (CED 1988: 447). When people described the Cultural Revolution as *luan* this may be a different kind of *luan* to that portrayed in 1990s Shanghai. For instance, Cultural Revolution *luan* referred primarily to political campaigns. In contemporary Shanghai the term was used, for example, of declining public morality, rising crime, the inadequate transportation system, and increasing prostitution. The demonstrations of May–June 1989 are also officially described as 'chaos'.

A magazine editor told me that *gaige kaifang* in Shanghai 'lacks order' and used a local saying to describe its unpredictable effects, 'when you step on a watermelon peel, where you fall is where you end up.' People often seemed to conceive of *gaige kaifang* as having a momentum of its own. Like water surging through a sluice, it may bring life-giving energy to parched earth, but it may also wash away seedlings and even the soil itself. In the television series, *River Elegy*, the sea is depicted as blue – pure, clean, and refreshing. However, I heard views which contested this image and portrayed the sea as dirty, dangerous, and murky. From my informants I was often presented with a description of Shanghai in which much is believed to be hidden from view and inchoate. In the next section, I examine several aspects which are felt to have been washed away or, at least, diluted in the flood, and then turn to some of the dangerous currents and murky depths of the reform era.

Washed away in the flood

The reform period has been marked by a dilution of the power and influence of the Communist Party. Trust in the Communist Party was undermined by earlier political campaigns. By the late Cultural Revolution the Communist Party had lost much of its moral authority (see Madsen 1984). Wholehearted expressions of support by the populace for Party slogans gradually gave way to ritual observance, feigned compliance, even irony, ridicule, contempt, and sheer boredom. Faith in the Party-state as an economic manager was further damaged by images flowing through the 'open door' which showed living standards elsewhere as much higher than citizens had previously been told. The events of 4 June 1989 finally eroded 'any vestigial notions that the Party was a moral force in Chinese society' (Saich 1992: 50). The Party's loss of moral legitimacy has been accompanied by the loss of the ideals it espoused. During my research in Shanghai those who actively argued in favour of socialist ideals were conspicuous by their absence.

Economic life is increasingly depoliticised, a shift symbolically manifested in China's bank notes. Gone are depictions of happy workers engaged in production – a nickname for the former ten *yuan* note was the 'great unity', so-called because it had a portrait of a worker, a peasant, and a soldier. In their place are romanticised portraits of ethnic minorities and, rather ironically in view of the 'Open Door' policy, the Great Wall. The Party's role in and influence over economic affairs has steadily declined. In June 1995, for instance, Hu Angang, senior fellow of the Beijing Academy of Science warned that 'China is risking collapse from fiscal weakness.' In 1994, central government revenues accounted for just 5.1 per cent of GDP. In Britain the equivalent figure was around 35 per cent (*FT* 16 June 1995: 6). At the micro-level, allowing graduates to find their own jobs has contributed to the declining influence of the Party by reducing the power of its members as bureaucratic gatekeepers.

Since the 1980s, there has been evidence of 'political society' re-emerging with a mushrooming of lobby and interest groups independent of Party control. A common way to express this depoliticisation and withdrawal of the Party from people's everyday lives is that China now has a 'small government and a large society' (*xiao zhengfu, da shehui*). My opportunity to conduct research was, as informants often noted, evidence of depoliticisation. Many of the previous forms of surveillance and indoctrination have become ineffective.

There has been significant depoliticisation within *danwei* (see You 1998: 31–108). Party cells are no longer active and political study is now minimal. Political study sessions had been compulsory and frequent in Shanghai *danwei* – during the peak of the Cultural Revolution as much as half the week could be devoted to such study. In many *danwei*-study sessions have been discontinued, or have become short perfunctory affairs. In educational units Friday afternoon is still reserved for political study. However, its effectiveness is clearly limited. On one occasion I asked a teacher to explain the meaning of several propaganda phrases used daily in the media. To my surprise she did not know. She explained that although her school still had political study it was very different to that in the past. She characterised these sessions as 'someone reads some document for a while, we then all begin to grumble about how long it took to get there on the bus and how much food prices have risen.' It would seem that, at least at times, the Communist Party speaks a language ordinary people literally do not understand. They are no longer taught it, nor is it required or enforced that they should know it. In joint ventures, foreign-owned companies, and for Shanghai's newly emergent economic status groups, such as share dealers and *getihu*, the Party has even less relevance.

Until the mid-1970s, at least, extra caution had to be exercised in comments made when a Party member was present. This is no longer the case with ordinary Party members. A retired man recalled that in the early 1950s Party members were said to be 'special material'. However, in his estimation, if one said this to a Party member now they would suspect sarcasm. In popular perceptions people now join the Party to gain some personal advantage and may be embarrassed about their membership. Party membership still brings certain advantages. Party members generally were described to me as being 'one level higher' than everybody else. For instance, they had more chance to obtain jobs in the media. Non-Party members complained that retired cadres received higher entitlements, such as higher pensions and living space allowances, than ordinary retired people. However, during the reform era alternative routes to success and status have emerged. Above all, a Party member in his early sixties told me, 'until the reform era social status was dependent upon the level of a person's official title, but now one's income is the main criterion, just like in the West.' Symptomatic of this trend is the party's failure to attract young people to join its ranks (You 1998: 98).

Neighbourhood Residents' Committees formerly acted as low-level surveillance units.[18] These Committees, set up in the early 1950s,[19] tended to be dominated by elderly women, often cadres' wives, and they were the people best placed to maintain surveillance over households' daily activities. These basic level organisations constituted the eyes, ears, and fingertips of the state. Families told me, for instance, that even in the early 1980s a 'suspicious' visitor would soon be followed by a visit from the police who would question them to discover who it was and what they had wanted.

In 1990s Shanghai, Residents' Committees lost their political role – although some informants felt that this could be reactivated if the state considered it necessary.[20] Instead, many Committees now run small-scale enterprises such as noodle stalls and hairsalons. In place of fear I found disinterest in their activities, especially amongst young people. Rather than concern about their surveillance activities elderly residents tended to complain that local Committees' entrepreneurial activities conflicted with their 'proper' functions, for instance, of maintaining standards of hygiene and organising evening security patrols – making money rather than serving the people had become their key concern.

Despite the depoliticisation outlined above actual political reform has been minimal. The limits to change are contained in the 'Four Basic Principles' enunciated by Deng Xiaoping in March 1979: to keep to the socialist road, to uphold the dictatorship of the proletariat, the continued leadership of the Communist Party, and adherence to Marxism, Leninism, and Mao Zedong thought. Many people had limited expectations of political reform. Apathy and a sense of helplessness were the main reactions to politics. Typically, informants expressed the view that the adoption of parliamentary democracy and a free press in China was not only highly unlikely, but would also be impractical and detrimental; they would promote chaos. Intellectuals tended to describe the *laobaixing* as neither wishing, nor being ready, for democracy since their *wenhua* level and 'moral quality' were too low. 'The result of direct elections would be chaos', one university lecturer told me. Similarly, a younger lecturer noted that 'in China now money can do everything. So even if there was a democratic system the big bosses would buy votes and those with the most money would form the government.'

Despite this general lack of political engagement some informants anticipated that the reforms will wash away the Communist Party within some 15 or 20 years. One informant expressed the hope that the tidal wave of *gaige kaifang* would 'flush away' the Communist Party altogether. He believed that this would involve a bloody confrontation whilst others expected a more gradual development. Such expectations were generally portrayed in economic determinist terms, perhaps a legacy of several decades of compulsory classes in Marxism. Informants spoke of a contradiction between continued economic change and lack of political reform; if the Party did not move aside this would break 'historical' or 'economic' laws. A man who had studied abroad in the 1920s felt that 'China is still a sleeping lion. One day it will wake up. However, it will need a great revolution for this to happen.' In his view this political reform will only come some decades, hence when a younger generation of political leaders who have studied in the West hold the reins of power.

Culture and morality

Most people considered that standards of living had risen in the post-Mao years and that there were fewer constraints on everyday life. However, these improvements were often described as having been accompanied by deterioration in standards of public and private morality; the 'social atmosphere' (*shehui fengqi*)[21] was considered to have been much better during Mao's time and people then more honest. Complaints were made that human relations had deteriorated and that traditional culture, values and morality had been washed away. Sexual mores and morals were felt to have declined, with a growth in divorce, pre-marital pregnancy, sexually transmitted diseases, extra-marital love affairs, and prostitution. Even informants strongly supportive of the Open Door policy and reform complained that moral values which had been sustained even during the Cultural Revolution had withered in the rush for money of the reform era.

Shanghainese complained about a lack of trust between strangers, and also the lack of universally accepted moral values. Taken together these constitute a distinct lack of civic sense. This lack of concern for others is encapsulated in the phrase: 'each person sweeps the snow from their own doorstep, no one bothers about the snow on another's roof.' The lack of unity and co-operation was matched by a sense that everyone was out for themselves and also jealous of the success of others. One academic, using the expression made famous by Sun Yat-sen, described China as like a plate of loose sand (*yi pan san sha* – in a state of disunity) with people just going after money. Another university lecturer remarked that in the past 'people were modest, now what counts is who can boast the most, now the self is much stronger.'

Indigenous explanations for the poor state of interpersonal relations included the crowded living environment of Shanghai. Others blamed 'China's history' or 'culture', portraying them as agents which act upon people. Some informants blamed deterioration in interpersonal relationships firmly on the policies and campaigns of the Communist Party, especially those of the Maoist period. One informant remarked that 'the Communist Party has harmed the thinking, personality, and emotions of people.' In place of the 'former honesty of Chinese people' he now saw only lies, boasting, and empty words. It was widely believed, as one informant expressed it, that 'Mao Zedong made it a society in which people attacked (literally "ate") each other (*ren chi ren*) in order to maintain control.' Turning a current Party slogan on its head, one academic remarked acidly, 'Deng Xiaoping calls for "stability and unity". But that is the last thing the Communist Party really wants. If the *laobaixing* unite, it will be unstable for the Communist Party!'

A common view was that current trends compounded damage done during past political campaigns. A woman in her late thirties remarked that 'the Cultural Revolution severely damaged interpersonal relations (her father committed suicide at this time). Now relationships between people are via money. People will only have contact with others if it is profitable to them.' A 38-year old clerk described personal relations in the 1990s as 'lacking human feeling and emotion', and as cold, selfish, and dominated by money. An intellectual expressed his concern that 'Deng Xiaoping's "black and white cats" have now found their way into interpersonal relationships. If it is advantageous to themselves people make friends with others regardless of whether they are "black" or "white cats".'[22]

A popular rhyme characterised the change in interpersonal relationships over three decades: 'In the 1950s, people helped each other. In the 1960s, they struggled against each other. In the 1970s, they cheated each other' (*wu shi niandai ren bang ren, liu shi niandai ren dou ren, qi shi niandai ren pian ren*). The depiction here of the 1950s, in particular, was accepted by almost all informants, of all ages, as axiomatic. The standard representation of the early years of Communist rule was of a 'golden period' in which standards of morality, politeness, and interpersonal relationships were particularly good. Many felt nostalgia for the comradely friendship (*tongzhi youyi*) of this time.[23]

The Cultural Revolution (1966–76) was considered to have had the most deleterious effect upon interpersonal relationships.[24] There was great pressure then on individuals to conform, and considerable fear that unorthodox views or behaviour would be reported. Faced with such risks it was necessary to exercise caution in all interactions. One informant told me that he took this to the point of not speaking at all. A retired teacher remarked that the legacy of class conflict is that 'people are now callous, aloof, and indifferent and will not deal warmly with each other.' He felt that political campaigns had 'deformed people's souls and damaged their moral quality.' In his view those who were honest and loyal towards friends suffered, whilst 'those without loyalty (*yiqi*), who were cold and secretive', were least likely to encounter problems. This experience led him to regard the highest practicable moral standard in contemporary China as: 'do not have a heart which harms others, but do not lack a heart which defends oneself against others' (*hai ren zhi xin bu ke you, fang ren zhi xin bu ke wu*).

The final verse of the rhyme proclaims that in the 1970s 'people cheated each other', although when I told informants this rhyme a common reaction was that this judgement was far more appropriate for the 1980s and 1990s. I asked the first person who told me this rhyme, a worker in a joint venture, to suggest supplementary verses for the 1980s and 1990s. He first added an extra line for the 1970s of 'people concealed things from each other'. For the 1980s he suggested 'each person looked after their own affairs'. For the 1990s he speculated that it may be 'people trample on each other' (*ren cai ren*). A female factory worker suggested 'people "consume" each other' (*ren chi ren*) for the 1990s.

In the reform era the state has paid less attention to communal activities. Moreover, in the state sector and political affairs there is a pervasive spirit of 'the more you do, the more mistakes you make' (*duo zuo, duo cuo*). People often seek solace in home life and disregard all matters that do not directly concern them. When asked about the ills of their society the usual response is '*meiyou banfa*', nothing can be done. One worker in a Neighbourhood Culture Centre outlined his philosophy of life: 'When asked to do something, I do my best to avoid agreeing to do it. If pressed I agree, but then don't do it. If I really have no choice, I just do the minimum possible.'

The main public events in recent years which contrast with such expressions of cynicism, the '*meiyou banfa* philosophy', were the demonstrations of 1989. Tu Wei-ming describes how '[f]or approximately fifty days, the city of Beijing exhibited a civic spirit, a sense of civility, thought to have been destroyed by the Cultural Revolution. There was a pervasive feeling of interconnectedness, mutual bonding, and collective responsibility in public places' (1992: 227). In Shanghai, this sense of shared feeling was replicated to an extent. However, many residents took no part in these events; on the evening after the Tiananmen crackdown I visited a *getihu* restaurant, and found the manager and a group of his friends enjoying a spontaneous party, apparently unconcerned by events in Beijing. When I told him the version of events I had gleaned from the *BBC World Service* his comment was 'the army has tanks and machine guns, the students don't, *meiyou banfa*.' He then returned to his revelries. Many older Shanghainese believed that young people were being tricked and duped by political manipulators in just the same way as their generation had been in the Cultural Revolution. Since 1991–2, the pervasive apathy which followed 4 June has increasingly been replaced by a belief that making money is one's primary concern.

Commercialism is felt to have entered many aspects of life, from cultural activities to the choice of marriage partners. University students eschew courses in history and philosophy for 'hot' subjects such as English, business, and accountancy. Intellectuals complain that 'serious literature' cannot get published whilst pulp fiction, including pirated foreign novels, with sex and violence, dominate the market. A local sociologist likened Shanghai's indigenous culture during *gaige kaifang* to that of American Indians during the period of European colonisation – it was being washed away. Older informants complained that the influx of 'foreign culture' such as karaoke bars, Michael Jackson records and disco dancing have edged out indigenous arts. Their only hope was that traditional arts which have gone abroad will be re-imported to China once the economy has developed.

State rhetoric urges citizens to 'seize the opportunity provided by the times'. Enterprising individuals have taken this advice and 'pushed the boat along with the current' (*shunshui tui zhou* – make use of an opportunity to gain one's end) – they attempt to make as much money as possible. Many complain that such people make money by improper means. Concerns are expressed about the way that everyone is now supposed to make money. For instance, many consider it inappropriate for doctors and teachers to engage in business. It is seen as detrimental, even immoral, for them to expend their time and energies on making money while neglecting their proper duties.

Many residents consider that Shanghai's commercialising economy is creating new opportunities. However, a common belief is that access to these opportunities is limited to those with power and who can 'pull' *guanxi* (to have power is also to have *guanxi*), especially if they also have ability. At the highest levels are those who operate within the *guanxi*-power nexus provided by military backing. Informants claimed that *guanxi* has flourished in the reform era. Recourse to *guanxi* is considered important or essential in diverse spheres including finding work, gaining promotion, obtaining housing, medical treatment, or a place on

Cartoon 1.3 'The Face of the Market'. Crammed in-between 'sea food hotpot' and 'karaoke' is the 'book shop'.

Source: *XMWB* 16 November 1993.

popular university courses and in any interaction with bureaucracy. A man in his sixties remarked to me that 'without knowing somebody, you cannot do anything.' The reverse also held: 'If you have connections, there is nothing you cannot do.' He concluded that 'in the West people say that time is money, in China *guanxi* is money.' The overriding ethos can be summed up by the English expression: 'It's not what you know, it's who you know.' It is often considered essential to create a relationship of mutual benefit (*li-hai guanxi*) with those who have access to resources such as housing. Subordinates may seek to ingratiate themselves by using flattery (*pai mapi* – literally 'pat the horse's backside'), or by giving gifts. A Shanghai saying notes: 'food is not ruined by too much salt, the giver of many gifts incurs no blame'.

Official statements decry *guanxi* as a 'hangover from feudalism'. However, extensive resort to the use of *guanxi* appears to have reappeared during the latter part of the Cultural Revolution as parents attempted to have their 'sent-down' children transferred back to Shanghai. This desperate wish on the part of tens of thousands of Shanghai households coincided with (and, perhaps, contributed to) a weakening of the structures of social control and surveillance. In the reform era, the flourishing of recourse to *guanxi* can also be related to changes in the economy since the death of Mao in 1976.

An arena where the potential for *guanxi* has proliferated is in job selection and career opportunities. Career mobility, especially for the young and well-educated, has expanded greatly during the reform era. Since the mid-1980s graduates from Shanghai educational establishments have been allowed to find their own jobs instead of being assigned to a *danwei*. Graduating students use *guanxi* to learn about opportunities and liaise with *danwei*. Although an employment market has developed with, for instance, job advertisements and job fairs, students believed that the best jobs went to those with connections. Under the old system, Party officials were responsible for making this choice which reduced the potential loci for *guanxi*.

Personal connections are considered vital for entrepreneurs seeking to take advantage of market opportunities. In a society where bases of trust between strangers are limited, it is inevitable that people turn to those they 'recognise'. In one instance I was acquainted with two young men who rented a shop counter and set up a small business selling clothing. Every step of this procedure involved personal connections, for example, locating a suitable site, obtaining supplies of merchandise, and finding shop assistants. One of the partners took long-term sick leave from his work unit. He explained that he 'recognised' a doctor who would sign the relevant sick note. Clearly one role of *guanxi* in this enterprise was to provide information about commercial opportunities. During the Maoist era information sources were strictly controlled. In the emerging socialist market economy, information has become increasingly valuable and sources of it elaborated far beyond the vertically organised state structure. Amongst Shanghai share dealers, for instance, information was frequently cited as the key to success and the main source of information were contacts. There was a strong incentive to build up extensive networks of persons whose knowledge could be trusted.

The change in personal relations was reflected in the way people described changes in the morality and behaviour of officials. An academic couple in their early fifties, both of whom experienced persecution during the Maoist era, still expressed nostalgia for some aspects of that time. Both felt that then 'leaders and cadres shared the hardships of the *laobaixing*. People's morality was good and they would help each other, cadres would "serve the people".' A dominant impression in contemporary Shanghai is that officials are primarily concerned with personal enrichment.[25] In the view of a retired mechanic, 'now Party members do what they want for themselves, their sons and grandsons, only then may they consider other people.' A recent addition to the saying *rudang zuoguan* – 'join the party to become an official' – is *zuoguan facai* – 'get rich by becoming an official'; securing an official position is simply a strategy to become rich.

Despite common perceptions that morality had declined and venality and corruption increased due to factors such as the political campaigns of the Maoist era and the marketisation of the economy, this can also be viewed as a return to a more traditional pattern. The perceived link between officials and personal enrichment is made abundantly clear in traditional sayings such as 'after just three years even an honest official will become rich.' Another traditional saying states: 'the *yamen* gate is open wide; with right but no money, do not go inside' (*yamen bazi dakai, you li wu qian mo jin lai*). In traditional, as in contemporary China, it seems that money and *guanxi* talks.

Certainty and security

The washing away of Party power and influence, of culture and morality, are key factors which have reduced certainty. A stagnant pond may not be especially desirable and being stuck in a rut may be monotonous, but at least they provide clearly defined boundaries and certainties. Certainty and stability is being drained away, leaving behind a residue of unpredictability, anxiety and short-termism. Many Shanghainese I encountered, and not just the elderly, looked back on the Maoist period, and especially the early 1950s, with nostalgia. It was represented to me as a time of good order, moral certainties and clear, shared national and community aims. For instance, Chinese society was perceived to have been divided into a limited range of clearly differentiated, morally good and bad classes. In Shanghai today, many lament the loss of these clear distinctions and are perturbed by the blurring of statuses as 'the whole population goes into business (*quanmin jingshang*)'. In the course of my research countless people advised me that 'now is the ideal time to do business in China' and expected me to *xiahai*. A university lecturer observed that 'things always go to extremes in China. In the past everyone had to study Lei Feng and Dazhai. Now everyone is encouraged to *xiahai*.'

With the 'market economy' food prices vary daily and store prices are no longer fixed, but differ from store to store. In the 1980s, inflation resurfaced as a significant problem. It was a major factor behind the 1989 demonstrations. The fear of unemployment has also returned to Shanghai, with over one million workers laid-off during the 1990s. Those in previously secure and well-provided large state enterprises now wonder what the future might bring as they see their job security and welfare benefits eroded. As elsewhere in China, crime is one of the big 'growth industries' (Dutton 1992: 200) of the reform era and my informants frequently expressed concern over rising crime.

A more general uncertainty concerns the future. Shanghainese express concern over increasing inequality, corruption, inflation, and crime – problems considered even more severe elsewhere in China. Such phenomena are attributed to a combination of the Party-state's weakened controls over the populace, for example, the

Cartoon 1.4 'Consumer'. The body is labelled 'real price' and the ever-emerging heads 'false price'.

Source: *XMWB* 18 December 1992.

increasingly ineffective household registration system, and as inevitable growths associated with a transitional stage between a planned socialist economy and the socialist market economy. In marked distinction to Western concern over lack of free speech and democracy in China, the problems which most worried my informants derived not from the Party-state being too powerful and intrusive, but rather its weakness and its failure to maintain the firm moral guidelines it espouses.

Uncertainty over China's future national path and Shanghai's prospects were often cited as factors underlying short-termism. A worker in a joint venture felt that 'people in Shanghai don't know what will happen in two or three years time, so they spend freely and have a good time whilst they can.' The stereotype of rich *getihu* was that they wantonly consumed their wealth in meals, women, and leisure activities rather than accumulating it to use in increasing production. Ventures such as restaurants were said to be particularly popular since they offered a rapid return on capital. Fear of a change in policy, such as the confiscation of private property in the 1950s, was one reason given for this short-termism.

Dangerous currents

> Law-abiding *laobaixing* who rely on a salary are not rich. There are no ordinary *laobaixing* in Shanghai's restaurants. All those who eat in them do so at the state's expense or are *getihu*. *Getihu* only make money because they evade tax, cheat people, exploit loopholes in state policy, and have connections with the police. Large scale corruption has the backing of high cadres. The KMT house was rotten. It had to be demolished and rebuilt from scratch. It has again reached this state.
>
> (Retired man's comment)

People I encountered in Shanghai generally supported *gaige kaifang* and acknowledged the improved standard of living associated with these policies. However, this did not preclude concern and complaints about problems which were considered to have emerged or become more serious during the reform era. These included increasing inequality, unfairness, corruption, and sleaze. These phenomena were considered detrimental to the *shehui fengqi* ('social atmosphere') of Shanghai. I begin the next section by examining popular perceptions of increasing unfairness and inequality, and then turn to corruption and sleaze – part of an 'unhealthy tendency' (*bu zheng zhi feng* – literally 'a dishonest or (morally) bad wind') which had filled the vacuum where public morality had been washed away.

Inequality

The Communist Party's former stress upon egalitarianism has been jettisoned and is now criticised. An article in *China Daily* observed 'the idea of equal shares for all has been shattered' (*CD* 15 July 1993: 4). Instead, some may 'get rich first' and income differentials diverge. Although average incomes rose during the 1990s, the gap between rich and poor increased dramatically and complaints about newly emerging inequalities were legion. In 1990, the annual per capita income in Shanghai was 2,050 *yuan* ($248) – the bottom 10 per cent had an average income of 1,278 *yuan* ($154) and the top 10 per cent 3,242 *yuan* ($391). By 1996, the average income of the bottom 10 per cent was 3,785 *yuan* ($456) and that of the top 10 per cent 14,953 *yuan* ($1,801) (*SS* 6 June 1997: 2).

Before the reform era most workers had just one source of income with relatively fixed, clear, and egalitarian rates of pay. This situation has changed radically. Within state enterprises basic salary differentials have not widened greatly – indeed there appears to have been convergence between collective and state *danwei*. However, enterprises now have increased powers to pay differential bonuses and these can differ considerably even within one sector. In early 1993, middle school teachers I met from different schools were paid from as little as 300 *yuan* pcm to over 1,000 *yuan*. In the latter instance, the school made considerable profits from leasing out its land as shop fronts – the resulting income of newly recruited teachers at this school was higher than that of head teachers in some Shanghai schools (see Page 122–4). In addition to high salaries and bonuses, this school's teachers also regularly received free products and foodstuffs, special bonuses on all public holidays, free restaurant meals, and subsidised trips.

Beyond the state sector, income differentials have widened even more dramatically. The manager of a factory which became a joint venture in 1992 told me that previously its managers earned just 5–6 per cent more than shopfloor workers. Within one year a middle manager's salary was roughly twice that of a worker's – whose salary doubled in the same period – at about 1,200 *yuan*. In early 1993, average salaries of a state factory worker were around 400–500 *yuan*, about 600–800 *yuan* for a joint venture employee, and 1,200 *yuan* in a solely foreign-owned enterprise.[26]

A particularly striking phenomenon of 1990s Shanghai was the emergence of a new wealthy stratum.[27] During my first stay in Shanghai from 1988–90, I was often uncomfortably aware of an unequal economic power relationship. It was automatically assumed that *all* foreigners were rich, and this assumption coloured interpersonal relationships between foreigners and Chinese infusing them with an unequal quality. By 1992–4, with the rapid emergence of *nouveaux riches* in Shanghai, the simple 'foreigner=wealth assumption' was only one equation among a far more disparate and confused range of possibilities. It was striking that in 2000, I was mistaken by a table of people in one bar as a waiter, something that would have been inconceivable a few years earlier.

The new wealthy stratum consists largely of people in the following categories: share dealers; private businessmen; small-scale private entrepreneurs; middlemen; those who have been abroad, made money and returned to Shanghai; families who had property confiscated during the Maoist era returned to them; labour contractors; popular media figures, singers and actors; and the sons and daughters of high Communist Party cadres. At the same time certain sections of society have become more vulnerable and may face declining incomes, including workers in factories with low efficiency, workers laid-off from enterprises, and the retired.

A visible sign of inequality is the plethora of recently opened or refurbished opulent restaurants – during 1992–3 some 3,600 restaurants opened within one year, an average of ten per day. Lavish restaurant eating was associated primarily with private entrepreneurs, the (mis)use of public funds, or, more generally, 'abnormal income'. A 70-year old man remarked on the way such restaurants have huge tables full of food. He believed that those who could afford this had got rich through profiteering and speculation, and added that 'our flesh is cut out by them'.

Rising inequality aroused considerable resentment. Several informants noted a saying of Mencius: 'do not fear if all are poor, fear only inequality' (*bu huan pin, zhi huan bu jun*). A retired teacher, a Party member, told me that Deng Xiaoping had tried to get rid of this belief. He added, 'Deng says that some should get rich first and the rest will become rich later. But the *laobaixing* do not believe this.' In the next section, I examine complaints of the unfairness which was widely felt to lie behind inequalities.

Unfairness

Alongside the increasing prosperity are complaints that those who rely upon salaries cannot afford many of the items in the shops. Still less can they benefit from the 'flood of consuming famous brand names' which are 'now gushing into Shanghai' (*WHB* 13 May 1993: 7), nor can they enjoy the proliferation of entertainments such as karaoke. A common refrain is that 'honest' *laobaixing* who stuck to the rules remain poorly off, whilst wealthy people have achieved their riches by irregular even crooked means. A local playwright in his late thirties told me that 'previously one could not exploit. Now, with *gaige kaifang*, if you have the ability you can exploit, only those without ability do not exploit.'

Some informants included morally positive factors in their assessment of who had derived advantages from *gaige kaifang*; they were those with talent and ability who work hard. More morally ambiguous cases mentioned were those with many contacts and the sharp-witted. Those who lacked connections felt themselves to be at a great disadvantage. A journalist complained to me that everybody was going into business, describing it as a 'retrograde step' since it does not contribute to society. However, his next remark was 'I would go into business if I could, but I lack connections.'

A more dominant theme was a stress upon negative factors best summed up by the expression: *ren wu huang, cai wu fa* – 'a person who does not commit some evil act, will not become rich.' A popular perception was that the rich were often those who had transgressed across moral space; they had 'crossed the sea by a trick' (*man tian guo hai* – practice deception). The wealthy were described as those with power and influence, speculators, the crooked, those with 'black hearts', and those able to exploit loopholes. Moreover, Shanghai's *nouveaux riches* were generally considered to make little contribution to society.

Intellectuals, in particular, complained that the wrong people (i.e. not themselves?) become wealthy. When I asked one academic about Shanghai's *nouveaux riches* he responded with the (rhetorical) question *sa nin fu la/shenme ren fu le*? – who is rich? He described remuneration levels as 'chaotic' with, for example, a receptionist 'without *wenhua*' in a big hotel earning 2,000 *yuan* a month – three times as much as a university professor – 'just because she has a pretty face.' Popular rhymes expressed feelings of unfairness, for example, 'those who deal with the outside of the head [i.e. hairdressers] earn more than those who deal with its inside [i.e. brain surgeons].'

Two groups often represented as unfairly wealthy were high-level cadres and their families, and *getihu*. Many people expressed resentment at the advantages and privileges enjoyed by high cadres. They were felt to have access to 'roads' denied to ordinary people. For instance, one informant noted that 'before there were no shares, now Deng Xiaoping's son can get ten thousand unlisted shares and sell them at a huge profit when they go on the market.'

Before the early 1990s, *getihu* were invariably described in morally negative terms as ex-criminals, crafty, low class people, with low *wenhua* and low moral quality who rip people off, fool around with women, gamble, and evade tax. Although such prejudice persists, the status of *getihu* has risen. A local sociologist attributed this changing attitude to the way in which '*gaige kaifang* has introduced a new standard and a new value, that of money – with money one can travel, go abroad, eat in big hotels and be a consumer of luxury items.' In the consumerist 1990s, money, rather than 'good class' or Party status became a key determinant of social status. Significantly, the social background of *getihu* appears to be changing; a joint venture employee told me that 'before only hooligans were *getihu*, now university intellectuals may be *getihu*.'

Murky depths

Some informants, although supportive of *gaige kaifang*, were sceptical about its apparent results describing them as 'superficial', a 'false appearance', or simply 'fake'. One interviewee advised me that 'in China, on the surface things are one way, but the reality is always very different.' I witnessed this at first hand during the 1993 East Asian Games. Dilapidated houses beside a main road had their facades painted over or were obscured by large, colourful advertising hoardings. At the same time as hiding these buildings from the tourist gaze, the occupants were denied light and visibility. The sense of being unable to trust the evidence of one's own eyes was vividly conveyed in an informant's description of Shanghai's economy as like a child's toy kaleidoscope – observed through the eyehole, the pieces of rotating coloured glass produce beautiful patterns. However, if this toy is broken, the fragments of glass look very ordinary. In this informant's view one must 'strip off the camouflage and expose what lies beneath.'

Several informants believed that Shanghai had a 'bubble economy' which may suddenly burst. One intellectual drew a parallel between *gaige kaifang* and the Great Leap Forward when reports were also all of increasing production and successes. He felt convinced that current reports presented an equally false appearance and would produce a similar result with economic collapse. In his view, China is like a watermelon which looks perfectly sound from the outside but is rotten inside. Another informant who felt that Shanghai's apparent economic success was superficial, remarked that much money goes on building large hotels and projects such as the Nanpu bridge. He considered such projects as designed to make Shanghai appear prosperous – especially to foreigners – and likened them to the way a person may *gue padü/guan paitou* – 'display a rich and arrogant manner to show off one's wealth or status' (Creamer 1991: 133). At the same time, the financial state of many state enterprises remains secret – published figures being specially doctored, and accurate figures kept for internal use only.

A popular perception is that many joint ventures are fake. Some are known to be fronts for the offspring of high cadres – including the so-called 'princes' party', the children of the highest level Communist Party leaders – to engage in real estate and other deals. In other instances 'suitcase companies', with no more to their name than business cards, wheel and deal 'buying empty and selling empty'. A similar problem is the proliferation of counterfeit goods such as fake foreign cigarettes and famous Chinese spirits. In popular mythology (and considerable evidence supports this), the offspring of high cadres are believed to control many highly profitable companies using their private connections to enrich themselves. Until the late 1990s at least (when it was ordered to give up its commercial enterprises), the military was also a major economic actor controlling many enterprises from hotels to clothing factories and discotheques. This involvement is often hidden from the public gaze, a distinct case of closed rather than 'open' doors. As one informant commented, 'who knows what the Chinese economy is really like?'

One informant described *gaige kaifang* as having produced great changes which were making the situation in Shanghai increasingly 'complicated and

摇身一变还是婆婆 张滨 画 (原载《中国青年报》)

Cartoon 1.5 'A sudden change of identity and it's still mother-in-law'. The two-headed figure has two identities, one as 'state bureau', the second as 'corporation'. The second figure is labelled 'enterprise' (In Shanghai, *popo*, 'mother-in-law', is a slang term for a boss.)

Source: *XMWB* 1 August 1993.

dark', quite the reverse of the bright, clear (*guangming*) future that many hope for. For instance, the increased autonomy of *danwei* heads allows them to recruit relatives and friends; previously the scope of such nepotism was limited since workers were assigned. Similarly, *danwei* heads now have increased power over remuneration levels and, along with increasing secrecy over payments, they can reward their favourites and not necessarily those who work well.

A factory worker outlined the situation at her *danwei*. Superficially the factory appeared to be prospering – the boss appeared on television, ate leisurely meals at expensive restaurants every day, and had a car bought by the *danwei*. However, she complained that she and half the workforce had been laid-off. She believed that many Shanghai *danwei* were like hers – 'mere skeletons'. City workers at her factory were laid-off, and production secretly transferred to the countryside, with the profits made going to the manager personally and not the enterprise. This woman remarked that 'the bosses just pull connections, eat, drink, and have a good time while the actual work is done by country bumpkins.'

Westerners who visit China have often been surprised by the close questioning they receive from local people over their incomes. However, what was once public knowledge is now entering an increasingly privatised zone. Before the reform era people had just one source of income, from their work unit, and salary levels were generally a matter of common knowledge. The former transparency and openness over incomes is now being replaced by secrecy and conjecture. Indeed, often individuals could no longer readily assess their own incomes. The incomes of those such as *getihu* and share dealers were particularly hard to ascertain – a small sprinkling of multi-millionaires was included in their ranks. However, in all sections of society, there has been a proliferation of sources of income apart from one's salary. This 'outside money' (*waikuai*) or 'grey income' (*huise shouru* – *hui* meaning both 'grey' and 'ambiguous') may come from, for example, share dealing, moonlighting, or money sent from relatives abroad. It could also include more illicitly obtained income, for example, from embezzlement.

Informants also spoke of *mohu gongzi* ('blurred or indistinct salary'). State enterprises' increased powers to pay differential bonuses and other payments are sometimes described as *mohu gongzi*. Such payments may be made in the traditional red packets (*hongbao*). The giving of *hongbao*, the contents of which are secret, engenders complaints about unfairness because the money may be given for personal motives and not based upon ability or performance at work. *Hongbao* are also frequently given to 'oil hinges', for instance, to get articles published in the press and to facilitate job transfers.

Dirty water, flotsam and jetsam

Corruption

Amongst the flotsam and jetsam deposited on 'Shanghai beach' was a widespread belief that morals are deteriorating and that there is increasing corruption and sleaze. Corruption was considered by many Shanghainese to be endemic.

It was, as even the official media acknowledged, an 'object of constant complaint' (*CD* 27 May 1993: 4). Frequent newspaper editorials and official pronouncements attacked corruption and those who take 'crooked roads'. However, people I encountered were sceptical of their efficacy, believing that corruption originated from, and was most serious amongst, powerful sectors of society which were beyond the reach of investigators. With the blurring borderline between state bureaucrat and private merchant (see Solinger 1992), it is widely believed that offspring and relatives of high officials are making vast profits from business activities. Many government departments, for example, have set up commercial companies – so called 'flipped-plate companies' (*fanpai gongsi*). One side of their name-cards has their official status, the other their company affiliation.[28] Commenting on this intersection between power and money one informant remarked succinctly that 'high officials have the most money because they have the most power.' Those with 'special power' have access to information and social connections (*menlu* – 'doors and roads'). Power can also replace money. For example, high officials can invite people to eat at the state's expense, have free trips abroad, and enjoy other benefits under the guise of 'work requirements'. During the 1989 protests such transgression of moral boundaries, *guandao* – official corruption – was a central target of demonstrators' anger. In the 1990s, the lack of differentiation between officials – including the military – and commerce increased.

Notions of what constituted corruption vary. For instance, on one occasion I asked a retired professor in his nineties about corruption. His response was 'do you know "*xiahai*"'? In his view, which he described as 'Confucian', intellectuals engaging in commerce was tantamount to corruption. For most informants *xiahai* may have problematic aspects, but it did not constitute corruption.

In everyday life scams, rip-offs, petty fraud, and double-dealing are considered increasingly common. For instance, informants would often ask if I had been '*tse/zhan*' at private markets or *getihu* restaurants. The dialect term *tse* is employed in a similar fashion to the English 'fleeced' or 'rip-off', although *tse* is 'to cut'. It is said of those skilled in *tse* that 'their knife is well sharpened'. Informants would tell me that, for example, 'restaurants *tse* the *laobaixing*' or 'schools *tse* parents' (through extra fees). Another complaint was that even professionals such as doctors and teachers now demand presents or *hongbao* – red envelopes with money in them – before carrying out their duties. In the media, the acceptance by journalists of gifts to promote commercial products had become so widespread that in 1993 a highly publicised campaign was launched against this practice. Lack of success in this campaign, presumably, led to a similar drive being launched in early 1997.

The lower reaches – sleaze

Pre-1949 Shanghai attained international notoriety as a sinful city, the location for large-scale prostitution, racketeering, and gambling, all organised by a criminal underworld which kept legal controls at bay by substantial pay-offs. Alongside a loosening of the puritanical sexual morality of the Maoist era many residents fear that such phenomena were returning to Shanghai. Older people especially believe that Shanghai is degenerating (*duoluo* – 'sinking'), with a proliferation of 'obscene, dirty, and low-down' (*xialiu* – also 'lower reaches of a river') phenomena.

Shanghai's rapidly proliferating entertainment venues such as nightclubs and karaoke bars are exemplars of these murky depths. In popular perceptions these are the venues for prostitution and 'rip-offs'. In one scandal, a restaurant was fined for adding a cocaine-related substance to its hotpot! Such locations are believed to be permitted to continue their business because they bribe local officials and the police. Regular news items detail police operations designed to 'sweep away' pornography, with female hostesses who accompany customers shown rounded up and herded into police vans. In August 2000, following inspection of over 29,000 entertainment places, a total of 2,782 were 'found by the police to have engaged in unlawful services in the past month'; eleven bars on Julu Road alone were closed down (*SS* 11 August 2000: 4). The intention is to keep Shanghai's streets not only physically, but also morally, clean. Often informants assumed that there was a murky and sinister intersection of power and corruption with state apparatus involved in such activities. With such strong backing, legal frameworks amount to little more than a 'paper tiger'. Many feared too that underworld gangs, such as prospered before 1949, would make a return, either as indigenous growths or transplanted from Hong Kong.

WHERE WATER FLOWS, A CHANNEL IS FORMED (*SHUIDAO QUCHENG*)

New roads in the mind – changes in attitude, behaviour and thought

> In the early 1980s the slogan was the 'Four Modernisations' and 'carry out modernisation'. Chinese traditional thought was like an iron door. It was no good just to tap against it. This conservative iron door had to be forced open. It cannot be closed up again.
>
> (Young businessman)

Gaige kaifang is frequently described as having changed the thoughts (*sixiang*) and thinking (*silu* – literally 'roads of thought') of local people and especially that of the young. The term *sixiang* has no direct English translation; it encompasses thought, thinking, ideas, and outlook. Economic reforms have increased the scope for individual choice, competitiveness, and uncertainty whilst the 'Open Door' policy has enabled people to see alternative ways of doing things. A typical comment, made by a university lecturer, was that 'now people think for themselves more. It is not like before when whatever Mao Zedong said went.' A corollary of such trends as increasing personal freedom and competition are complaints that people are now more selfish and interpersonal relationships colder.

A distinctive youth culture along with a generation gap has emerged in Shanghai. Informants felt that there were clear generational differences in attitudes and values.[29] The sudden inflow of images from the West after 1978 has played a crucial part in changing young people's attitudes and values by providing them with alternative perspectives and lifestyles. A teacher told me that he had first heard about the 'generation gap' in a television programme about America. From his relationship with his own young son he realised that China too has a generation gap – significantly the Chinese term *daigou* ('generation gap') is a direct translation from English. Parents sometimes considered the dating behaviour of the young immoral, found it hard to accept if their offspring changed jobs, and incomprehensible if they spent several hundred *yuan* on tickets for the concerts of Hong Kong pop singers. A teacher at a key middle school considered that the 'thinking' of children was now livelier. He explained that:

> In the past students' minds were closed because the country was closed. Now the thoughts of students are more *kaifang* because they have seen more. In the past they just listened to whatever the teacher said. Now children see television and many of their homes have foreign magazines and so on. We older generation cannot keep up.

A young university lecturer felt that since the early 1990s people's attitudes had become more positive, hopeful, and confident. In 1994, at the age of 28, he felt a difference between his outlook and that of current university students. He felt that 'now students stress themselves more, have a greater sense of self, and are more individualistic.' He added that 'they have more opportunities and fewer restrictions on them.' In my own research, I found that the legacy of political campaigns and the more rigid conformism of the past was often evident in the interactive style of different age groups. Since the death of Mao the presence of the state was no longer felt to be so omnipresent or all encompassing. Young people more readily spoke their minds, for instance on political matters, whilst older people tended to discuss such topics only in hushed voices.

When the water subsides the rocks emerge (*shuiluo shichu*)

The erosion of the iron rice bowl and the growth of competition presents new opportunities, challenges, pressures, uncertainties, and risks. One reaction is to bolster financial security through personal insurance policies. The insurance sector has blossomed since the second half of the 1990s; by mid-1997 there were already estimated to be some 20,000 life insurance agents in Shanghai (*SS* 17 June 1997: 6). Another significant reaction is a renewed stress upon education and the acquisition of skills in order to improve career prospects. A final-year university student remarked that 'every day *gaige kaifang* makes greater demands upon one. In the past it was "sixty marks forever", now even ninety marks is not enough. Many students take extra courses to enable them to adapt to the great tidal current of *gaige kaifang*.' Following the adoption of the 'Open Door' policy many English courses were set up, including preparation courses for TOEFL (Test of English as a Foreign Language), a prerequisite for many to fulfilling a dream to go abroad. Facility in English resembled a passport – it could open 'roads' (opportunities) which were blocked and inaccessible to those who lacked knowledge of it. Within Shanghai itself, proficiency in English has become an important requirement in many professions. Besides English, popular extra-curricular courses include computing, accountancy, Cantonese, and Japanese.

Parents are aware that their offspring will have to fit into a very different, far more competitive environment. Study is seen as a main route to a successful life. A shop assistant with a young son told me that education had become much more important. She felt that 'now *danwei* have contracts one must have education. If one does not study well, since there are so many people, they will not want you.' Parents are especially concerned to get their children into key middle schools. From a key middle school most pupils could expect to obtain a university place, from other schools only a small minority. Parents engage in various strategies to try and ensure that their children get into a key middle school. Some prepare the way for this by enrolling their children in unofficial 'key' nursery schools, arranging private tutors, and extra-curricular courses. Using language popularised in the reform era, a university student told me that one consequence of *gaige kaifang* is that parents were prepared to pay for their children's education; 'they invest a little money and hope to get a return later.' Moreover, since Shanghai families are restricted to one child, all their energies and financial resources are concentrated on this single offspring.

Newly emerged inequalities are being reproduced in educational opportunities. Even in the state education sector provision differs widely. At the key middle school mentioned above which rented out its land as shop fronts, these highly successful commercial ventures provided the school with an income several

租房政策和法规，加班加 一个外来暂住人员都持有

Cartoon 1.6 'Untitled'.

This 'suitcase' company's advertisement reads: 'Sales staff sought: Must have Masters degree or PhD'.

Source: *XMWB* 29 August 1999.

times higher than the city education department allocated it. This school had facilities far superior to schools in less central areas of Shanghai.

An even more striking instance of the way in which 'where water flows, a channel is formed' is the way Shanghai's new 'moneyed classes' are now able to enrol their children in one of the city's recently established private schools. At one private primary school, set up in early 1993, the largest proportion of pupils' parents were enterprise heads, often in companies involved in international trade. Other parents were joint venture company managers, high-ranking military personnel, teachers, media workers, or employed overseas. Contrary to the popular belief in *getihu* wealth, there was only one *getihu* parent. In its second term of operation the school required a one-off payment of 5,000–10,000 *yuan* per child, termly fees were 600 *yuan*, and even monthly fees for snacks and fruit totalled 400 *yuan*. Any official concern over such 'aristocrats' schools' (*guizu xuexiao*) was muted. A *China Daily* article described private schools simply as 'filling a gap in . . . demand' and as 'more flexible in adjusting to the demands of the employment market than their State-funded counterparts' (*CD* 18 May 1993: 3).

The rhetoric of individualism has re-emerged in the reform era. This is paralleled by a shift since the late 1970s from collective (*jiti*) toward individualistic (*gerenhua*) activities. During the Maoist period the state promoted 'revolutionary heroes', such as Lei Feng, who were 'characterised by selfless dedication to the cause of building a collective utopia under the leadership of the Chinese Communist Party' (Chu 1985: 268). In the early 1990s, attempts were made to revive the 'Lei Feng spirit'. Some informants expressed nostalgia for the ideal of selfless comradeship he embodied, more expressed cynicism suggesting, for instance, that China's altruistic hero had gone abroad, perhaps to make money.

Paul Pickowicz found many post-Cultural Revolution films 'exploring the complexities of "private" and "individual" life in the urban sphere' (1995: 197). In daily life the increased emphasis upon the self is evident in the promotion of fashion and cosmetics, and by the way leisure pursuits increasingly cater to individual tastes. Since the early 1980s, romantic love has become a topic of considerable moment. This includes numerous magazine articles, books, and even radio-in programmes on topics such as sexual fulfilment and the 'ideal partner'. In July 2000, there was said to be more than 2,000 shops selling sexual aids in Shanghai (*SS* 11 July 2000: 4). The rising divorce rate may be taken as further evidence of a growing desire to achieve self-fulfilment and to pursue individual desires. Between 1991 and 1996 the divorce rate in Shanghai doubled (*SS* 29 August 1997: 3). In 1999, 16,662 couples divorced in the city, 21.22 per cent more than in the previous year (*SS* 1 August 2000: 4). Rising divorce statistics and extra-marital affairs in Shanghai were cited as evidence of both an increasing individualism and selfishness.

The age cohort sent down to the countryside in the Cultural Revolution appear to have been pivotal in this shift. More than two decades later many still feel a sense of betrayal but also that this experience, far from their families, dependent upon their own resources and often in harsh conditions, had been a tempering through which they had learnt to rely upon their own abilities. I asked a couple in their late thirties who had taken part in political activities in the 1960s how they had then considered their actions. The husband replied, 'at that time people did not think at all. They had no mind. There was just one mind, that of Mao Zedong. People had no self.' His wife added, 'in the past people had too little self, now they have too much.' A joint venture employee in her mid-twenties considered her age cohort very different from her parent's. She felt that whilst the latter had 'solemnly followed the Communist Party. We are for ourselves. We have more personality, previously everybody had a single point of view allocated (*zhipei*) by the state, now we have our own.'[30]

Belief in one's own self was often associated with a profound pragmatism and 'this-worldliness'. Most of my informants expressed neither faith nor interest in metaphysical beliefs or explanations. However, during the reform era, the loss of trust in the Communist Party and socialism as expert systems, has been replaced by a tendency toward trust in economic laws (*jingji guilu*) and the market. A popular attitude is that deficiencies in the political system will be confronted by the inexorable development of the economy – a Marxian-type view the Communist Party itself appears not to share. It is notable that in this transition belief in progress remains, the mantle being passed from one set of expert systems to another.

'Everything before us, nothing before us'

> Society looks stable and flourishing, but we do not know what it will be like tomorrow.
>
> (Informant's comment)

Expectations for the future of Shanghai ranged from great optimism to fearful pessimism. Despite the economic reforms and depoliticisation described above, informants considered the lot of the *laobaixing* profoundly dependent upon China's national leaders. A typical response when asked what the future holds for Shanghai was that 'it all depends upon the higher authorities.' At the same time, in direct contrast to the notion of 'open' doors, informants stated that 'the *laobaixing* do not know the inner affairs of the state.' Expectations that the Communist Party will further reform politically were limited – this would be to 'ask a tiger for its skin' (*yu hu mou pi* – request somebody to act against their own interests). Informants appeared to believe that the populace could prosper under its own steam, but that 'struggle' amongst elite Party factions could prevent or destroy this. The Party, as it were, retained the ultimate power to misdirect and waste the energy flowing through the sluice.

The most optimistic scenario is for a prosperous and glorious future, with the policy of *gaige kaifang* regarded as irreversible, the only question being its pace. At the opposite extreme, pessimistic observers regard chaos as extremely likely, even inevitable. Increasing income inequality aroused particular concern, with informants noting that this had been a main cause behind the 1949 revolution. Similarly, corruption is considered endemic and to be insoluble for this reason.

In the view of one informant China appears stable, but 'change is like a woman giving birth – her stomach must undergo a period of pain before the child is born. The present system will definitely collapse and many will die in the process. Chaos is inevitable.' For him *gaige kaifang* is a transitional stage to non-Communist Party rule. The type of chaos he envisaged encompassed economic collapse, civil strife, increasing crime, warlordism, and even civil war. However, even those who predicted such worst-case scenarios considered the 'Open Door' policy to be secure, as evidence for this they pointed out that the military would resist a reversal of this policy because of its own extensive involvement in trade and commerce.

Since the 1980s there has been a 'dramatic revolution of rising expectations' (Goodman 1991: 15). Younger people often have especially high expectations; where parents expressed themselves relatively content with the pace and achievements of reform, their offspring often considered it too slow. The differential expectations and desires of the younger generation are themselves indicative of the changed socio-political environment in which they have been brought up. In Shanghai, many look forward to the 'comfortable' living standard Deng Xiaoping promised to them by the first decade of the twenty-first century. As notions of 'comfort' continue to inflate, this may become a chimeric target.

Although its power and authority has declined, the demise or modification of the Communist Party, widely predicted after 4 June 1989, has failed to materialise. A strong consensus of my informants was that the sluice gate which has been opened cannot be closed again. When irrigating fields great care must be exercised. Water is vital to promote vigorous growth but if not channelled properly it may be squandered, whilst too much water can also cause devastation. Both uncontrolled, surging waves and a proliferating, criss-crossing tangle of roads may create chaos – a great fear of many informants.

I have sketched some of the boulders, tides, and shifting currents in contemporary Shanghai. Since the early 1990s, the Party-state has nailed its colours to raising living standards, with a realisation that 'legitimacy, or simply acquiescence in its continued rule, can only be regained through economic success' (Saich 1992: 59). In Shanghai the Communist Party has, so far, generally been successful in this project. The policies of *gaige kaifang*, have, however, unleashed and fostered great expectations for the future. In the event of economic downturn, the dangerous currents I have outlined would surely provoke profound unrest and coalescence of the aggrieved. The dangers inherent were manifest in the demonstrations of May–June 1989, events described by some as a 'student movement' (*xuechao* – 'student wave').

Lakoff and Johnson argue that metaphors structure the actions we perform, for example, the 'argument is war' metaphor structures the actions we perform in arguing (1980: 4). They add that the systematicity of metaphorical concepts can hide other aspects of concepts (10). Leslie Hepple observes that the 'strategic silences of the metaphors we use are as important as the aspects that are thrust centre stage' (1992: 142). In the case of the metaphors explored above: What behaviour do they legitimate? What alternatives do they exclude?

An intriguing aspect of the 'watery metaphors' I have outlined is that although some provide instances of nature controlled and channelled by human agents, as in the sluice gate, many portray the consequences of human actions as though they are uncontrolled natural phenomenon, such as waves and tides. Thus to see immigration as a 'tide' or 'flood' seems to involve a denial of human agency. In such instances, there is a glossing over of the political, economic, and individual choices which lay behind migration; human actions become construed as vagaries of nature. The metaphors used to portray migration to Shanghai may legitimate discrimination against these people. They become seen not as people making rational choices, but rather as an inchoate potentially destructive onslaught to be defended against, restricted, and channelled. At times there is considerable resentment against migrants in Shanghai, while the metaphors used to describe them involve a denial of shared humanity, and may facilitate racist type views.

The socio-spatial metaphors of roads, routes, and doors, seem to present a rather different scenario. These are all phenomena which are constructed and subject to alteration by human design. Moreover, even the watery metaphors permit reformulating the content of expressions. Thus, the term *xiahai*, although sharing the downward inclining orientational metaphor of *xialiu* ('lower reaches', also 'low-down, mean, obscene, dirty') appears to have become a rather trendy, popular expression. By extension, is it possible that behaviour hitherto considered *xialiu* may be viewed in a more positive light?

William Taylor cautions that '[m]etaphors can be seductively reductionist' (1984: 11). However, the metaphors I have examined seem rich and fruitful enough to permit considerable growth, slippage, and overspill. They are readily susceptible to more than one interpretation and, therefore, symptomatic of moves on the political and economic fronts from rigid 'orthodoxy' to the condoning of alternative approaches and a degree of pluralism.

A Chinese proverb provides an appropriate analogy for the *gaige kaifang* project: 'water can support a boat, it can also turn it over' (*shui neng zai zhou, yi neng fu zhou*). It is evident from many comments in this chapter that there are felt to be distinct dangers in the profound and far-reaching socio-economic changes which have been embarked upon in Shanghai. However, as another proverb points out: 'when the water is too clear there are no fish' (*shui zhi qing ze wu yu*). In other words, any project designed to alter the economic structure of a major metropolis so as to improve the living standards of over 13 million citizens will inevitably involve risks and pursuing paths where the results are not always predictable. A final comment should, perhaps, be that of a lecturer in his mid-fifties who described a number of difficulties besetting Shanghai. However, he then expressed hope for Shanghai's future development and added that 'the most fearful thing is to be without hope. Now we have hope. This is progress.'

2 Global and intra-national cultural flows: renegotiating boundaries and identities in contemporary Shanghai

INTRODUCTION

> An interesting conversation was carried on during dinner between Sing-Hoo and the priests . . . They expressed their opinions freely upon the natives of different provinces, and spoke of them as if they belonged to different nations, just as we would do of the natives of France, Holland, or Denmark. The Canton men they did not like; the Tartars were good – the Emperor was a Tartar. All the outside nations were bad, particularly the Kwei-tszes, a name signifying Devil's children, which they charitably apply to the nations of the western world.
>
> (Robert Fortune, *Two Visits to the Tea Countries of China*, Volume II, 1853: 193–4)

Much Western and Chinese literature conveys the impression that there is a unitary and invariant Chinese identity, constant in both time and place. The intention in this chapter and the next is to disassemble crude stereotypes of the homogeneity of 'Chinese' identity through an examination of the layers of interweaving identities which may be asserted in the specific spatial location of Shanghai. With the 'Open Door' policy outlined in the previous chapter, Shanghai is rejoining the global economy and its boundaries to other parts of China have become far more permeable. This porousness has permitted a much greater flow of people, capital, technology, and images. It therefore seems an appropriate time and location to assess the impact of such processes upon identities. At a time when the Soviet Union has been disassembled, the former Yugoslavia is ridden with ethnic conflicts, and there has been discussion on the possibility that China will 'deconstruct' (cf. Goodman and Segal 1994), I assess the potency of, and potentiality for, a specifically Shanghainese identity.

SHANGHAI: POROUSNESS AND ENCLOSURE

Shanghai: from world city to Chinese city

Eighteenth-century Shanghai flourished as a cross-roads for trade and commerce. The Reverend Charles Gutzlaff who visited Shanghai in 1832 described it as 'the gate of central Asia, and especially of the central provinces of China' (1833: 30). After the Opium War and its establishment as a treaty port Shanghai rapidly increased its integration into the global economy. By the 1920s and 1930s, Shanghai had become one of the world's major cities.

As a thriving entrepôt Shanghai attracted 'sojourners from all over the globe' (Perry 1993: 12). The diverse range of Chinese migrants were joined by many foreign companies, workers, missionaries, tourists, and refugees creating a highly cosmopolitan city. By the late nineteenth-century, through regular mail steamers and the telegraph, Shanghai was 'thoroughly in touch with Europe and America' (Bishop 1899: 20). Its shops purveyed goods from every quarter of the globe and services were available to cater to every taste. Despite attempts by sections of the Chinese populace to wrest control from them through protests and strikes – especially in the 1920s – foreign nationals maintained jurisdiction over large parts of the city. They inscribed their domination upon its streets and avenues naming them after the places and heroes of their own countries, for example, Broadway, Edinburgh, and Edward VII Streets. The city was also a relatively free haven for diverse publications, cultural expression, and the exchange of ideas.

Chinese nationalism and an antipathy towards imperialist powers were important elements of the Communist Party's support. This was, perhaps, especially significant in semi-colonial Shanghai where incursions by foreigners had created a comprador class and many intellectuals espoused 'Western' thoughts. From the outset the new regime which took control of Shanghai in 1949 was hostile to or, at least, deeply suspicious of Western nations – sentiments returned in equal measure. In 1960, after the split with the Soviet Union – China's main ally and the model for many of its economic policies – the die was cast. This combination of external hostility and a belief in the need for autarky to preserve the existence of the state and its new government impelled China's rulers to adopt a policy of closing the country to international intercourse and of self-reliance. Shanghai was to be reinscribed as an unambiguously, wholly Chinese city, its gaze turning inward, rather than outward, from the Huangpu River.

In 1949, most of the foreign nationals and companies which had returned after the Second World War fled from Shanghai.[1] By the mid-1950s those who remained had their property confiscated and were compelled to leave or permitted to stay 'only on sufferance, confined to their enclosures and denied access to most of China except by special permission' (Jenner 1992: 91). People's experiences of interactions with foreigners could not be erased, nor the vast array of colonial architecture, much of it built to last for centuries. The race track, though, was replaced by People's Square, and other more ephemeral forms of Western cultural artefacts were gradually removed from the city; for example, cinemas were forced to cease their diet of American films.[2] Shanghai was still China's main industrial city, but the crossroads of Asia was now a *cul de sac*.

From the early 1950s until the early 1980s contact with foreigners and knowledge of the world beyond the borders of the People's Republic was extremely limited and strictly regulated. Media representations of other countries, for instance, were mostly limited to propaganda films imported from Eastern Europe.[3]

Distinctions between the 'inside' and 'outside' were sharply drawn, and the boundaries subject to surveillance and strict control. All people with foreign contacts, including overseas Chinese, faced suspicion and often persecution as potential spies.[4] Fear meant that contacts with relatives abroad trickled to a halt, and mention of them became taboo even within many families. In the words of one Shanghai academic 'there was no relationship with the outside world.'

Benedict Anderson's (1983) notion of an imagined community seems particularly applicable for this period.[5] Media of all types were closely controlled and a limited range of messages repeated across different types of media including books, newspapers, revolutionary operas, films, and the ubiquitous loud speakers. Alternatives to this monologic voice were available only to a selected few. Restricted-access publications were carefully graded and disseminated to Communist Party cadres according to their level in the Party hierarchy. At the lowest level of the vertically integrated structure controlled by ministries from Beijing, the urban workforce was 'enclosed' within work units – all-encompassing, cellular entities. Even following the United States' formal recognition of the People's Republic of China, and its accession to the United Nations in the early 1970s, China remained a largely closed country. The first major increase in porousness occurred – primarily involving Hong Kong – with the establishment of Shenzhen as a Special Economic Zone in 1979.

Shanghai's changing place in China – from traditional flow to revolutionary enclosure

> In essence, under Mao, an invisible wall kept out the peasantry and protected the urban population. In effect, the history of walled cities did not end with the demise of imperial China.
>
> (Kam Wing Chan 1994: 147)

Writers on 'traditional' Chinese cities (e.g. Mote 1977: 117–9; Skinner 1977a: 268–9) emphasise the existence of a rural–urban continuum and of native-place identifications in cities. Pre-twentieth century China is described as having had a 'vague and highly permeable boundary between city and countryside' (Parish and Whyte 1984: 26). This pattern was still evident to Olga Lang when she conducted research in Shanghai in the mid-1930s (1946: 86–7). Shanghai has attracted sojourners since at least the thirteenth century. From the second quarter of the eighteenth century in particular Shanghai developed as a 'broker city' (Johnson 1993b: 176). As a 'hot, noisy place' it attracted a large transient population and many migrants. Early Western visitors to Shanghai often remarked on the proportion of immigrants in the city population. The population in 1843 was described as 'a mixed, migratory one, perhaps not one half of those now resident having been born and bred in this city' (*CR* 1847: 16(11) 564). This diversity is recognised in Shanghai's street names – those running north-south have names of Chinese provinces, those running east-west names of Chinese cities. After 1842, Shanghai became an even more powerful magnet for both foreigners and Chinese, such that its population increased some tenfold within a hundred years. The number of foreign residents in the Settlement increased from just 50 in 1844 to 36,471 in 1930 (Feetham 1931: 49–53).

Native-place identity was an important organising factor in imperial China, especially for the extensive sojourner component of city populations which were typically organised along native-place lines and occupationally specialised by place of origin (Skinner 1977b: 538–46). On the basis of her research into the Ningbo community in Shanghai, Susan Jones considers that 'prior to the 1930's, native-place ties provided the primary channels through which family, class, and business interests were articulated in Chinese cities' (1974: 96). In Shanghai, native-place identities were maintained in many ways including by cuisine, native-place associations, adherence to local customs, use of dialect, separate educational arrangements, and spatially differentiated residence (see Goodman 1995: 22–7).[6] Workers in specific industries were often immigrants from particular areas, with hierarchy structured largely according to native-place identification. In the thriving underworld of pre-1949 Shanghai, native-place networks were 'the basic building bloc of gangster organisations' (Martin 1992: 268). Even the hierarchy of prostitution in Republican-era Shanghai was structured by regionalism (Hershatter 1989). Bryna Goodman (1992) writes that native-place organisations played an important role in the 1919 May Fourth Movement in Shanghai. In labour disputes, too, native-place and the 'politics of place... both opened possibilities and set the bounds to the development of collective action' (Perry 1993: 30).[7]

Migrants from Ningbo, Canton, and Jiangsu were prominent in Shanghai's commercial development. In the second half of the eighteenth-century Shanghai's flourishing trade and commerce attracted many Ningbo merchants, and they used ties of native-place in their gradual domination of the city's financial sector (see Jones 1974; Shiba 1977). The Cantonese in the city – some 60,000 in the 1880s – were most evident as compradors, and Bergère states that until the 1880s the terms 'Cantonese' and 'comprador' were synonymous in Shanghai (1989: 145, 38–41).[8] By the 1920s the comprador system was less important, though the Cantonese by then dominated the field of large modern shops and the cigarette industry.

Migrants from Jiangsu were involved especially in the cotton industry and in mechanised engineering. Those from southern Jiangsu formed the elite whilst those from northern Jiangsu (Subei) were predominantly an underclass and engaged in occupations seen as undesirable and inferior. Research on the history and contemporary situation of Subei people in Shanghai (e.g. Chu 1985; Honig 1989b, 1990; Wu and Lan 1985; Wu *et al.* 1985), provides evidence of the persisting importance of regional identifications and stereotypes in Shanghai.

The proportion of migrants remained high during the first half of the twentieth century. Shanghai's population grew dramatically from 1.3 million in 1910 to 2.6 million in 1927, of whom some 72–83 per cent were born outside Shanghai (Bergère 1989: 100). In 1987, Davis interviewed 100 Shanghai women born between 1925 and 1935, 68 per cent of these women and 78 per cent of their husbands had been born outside Shanghai (1990: 102). Despite the 'shallowness' of many families' residency in Shanghai local people have a strong sense of there being a distinctively Shanghainese identity.

Migration to Shanghai continued after 1949. In 1937, Shanghai's population was 3,480,018, in 1949 it was 4,447,015, and by 1953 it had risen to 6,204,417 (Pannell 1981: 99, 103). Between May 1956 and January 1957 alone there was an increase of 700,000 people, largely as the result of migration (White 1978: 188). Migration was gradually halted by various measures imposed during the 1950s which were designed as 'policing' measures and to promote local autarky, control the growth of large cities, and to redistribute resources to the interior. During the 'revolutionary period of comprehensive residence control' (White 1994: 63), these measures included migration restrictions and the rationing of many basic goods and above all, following the 1953 census, the introduction of the household registration (*hukou*) system.

The *hukou* system varied considerably over time both in its scope and the degree of enforcement. However, basic elements required that every person must be registered at birth and had to apply for permission to move elsewhere. An extensive rationing system also operated to control the movement of people. Once again, the extent of rationing fluctuated over time, following its first introduction in the mid-1950s. It was not until the mid-1960s that rationing reached its full form. At its most extensive, many basic commodities such as rice, meat, and cooking oil were rationed, as well as cloth, sugar, soap, and cigarettes. Since ration cards were for use solely in one specified city, movement to cities from the countryside, or from one city to another, was forestalled. With the notable exception of the brief period of 'revolutionary tourism' by Red Guards in the late 1960s, for most of the Maoist period travel within China was heavily restricted with a '*de facto* internal passport system' (Chan 1994: 91).

The various 'policing' controls effectively sealed Shanghai's 'frontiers' and 'an invisible wall separated the urban and rural populations' (Chan 1994: 97). This urban–rural divide gave 'hard edges' to cities such as Shanghai (Naughton 1995b: 73). Unlike most Asian cities, Shanghai did not sprawl into the countryside; instead there was an abrupt and visible difference between the city and the countryside which surrounded it. In rural China, 'local populations were more confined to their villages than ever before in Chinese history' (Croll 1994: 120). For the few rural residents able to come to Shanghai it was, one academic told me, 'as though they had got a green card.' Whilst the rhetoric of the Maoist period professed the goal of reducing the differences between urban and rural China, most analysts agree that post-1949 changes actually widened the gap substantially.

The traditional migration pattern was reversed, urban–rural interaction was primarily *from* urban *to* rural areas. From the 1950s onwards, there were various campaigns to relocate people out of Shanghai. Between 1955–72, there was a net outflow of 2.2 million people from Shanghai (White 1994: 66). Between 1968–71 alone, 890,000 Shanghai youth were sent to the countryside for periods of up to ten years, some indefinitely (Yan 1985: 109, White 1978: 53–97). Whilst Shanghai's central city area population increased by 1.68 million between 1949–59, between 1959–82 it rose by just 207,600; in 1949 its population was 4.19 million and in 1982, 6.08 million (Yan 1985: 107).

The imposition of strict urban–rural boundaries segregated the population into clear-cut urban and rural classes and cultures. For example, in an examination of funeral rituals Martin Whyte argues that 'peasants and urbanites, who formerly knew a common ritual vocabulary, are now increasingly aliens to each others' customs' (1988: 308). In these rituals he sees a 'sharp urban–rural gap that didn't exist before 1949' (304). I observed evidence of this urban–rural cultural bifurcation through attendance at weddings in the city zone of Shanghai and in the suburban counties of Shanghai. In the former, for instance, the families of the bride and groom ate together, but in the latter they ate separately. These differences were pointed out to me by informants who were, themselves, very clear about the existence of a sharp rural–urban disjunction.[9]

ORIENTALISING SHANGHAI: REPRESENTING OTHERS, DEFINING SELVES

> 'Beijingers love the country, Cantonese sell the country, Shanghainese leave the country' (*Beijingren aiguo, Guangzhouren maiguo, Shanghairen chuguo*).
>
> (Popular rhyme)

Notions of self/other

I find much of the literature on ethnicity and 'culture' overly deterministic, construing them as discrete essences, and holding forth the possibility of grasping and defining them. Ethnicity is, at best, an 'elusive concept' (Burgess 1978: 266). Even when analysts have suggested more fluid notions of ethnicity such as the creole metaphor (Drummond 1980) problems still remain. For instance, this notion seems to posit a false dichotomy between heterogeneous and homogeneous 'cultures'. Richard Fardon is rightly critical of the 'presupposition of a universal class of ethnic difference' (1987: 177). I prefer to avoid the term and talk instead of (potential) identities, and to examine the ways in which 'identities crystallise transiently and in terms of different registers of difference' (ibid.: 183).

Despite my caution and caveats as an analyst, it is important to note that my informants usually *did* essentialise and stereotype identities of both collective selves and others. People were willing and able to produce regional (also 'class' and gender) stereotypes and stereotypes of foreigners. For instance, if informants were asked to describe a 'typical Shanghainese', most responded without equivocation. For my part, I was often asked to describe a 'typical English person'. My failure and inability to produce an appropriate answer was generally regarded as evasive. Any consciousness that such stereotypes – which showed a remarkable degree of convergence – were problematic was generally absent amongst respondents of all educational levels.

Anthropologists such as Barth (1970) and Cohen (1985) have pointed out that identities often only become discursive at the boundaries where they encounter others. A common theme is that 'identity is always constructed by reference to others' (Cohen 1985: 95) and that 'the construction of the collective self... depends on its *differentiation* from the collective other' (Comaroff 1987: 308–9). Morley and Robins (1989) adopt a similar view, noting that 'difference is constitutive of identity' (14). They suggest two lines of investigation: 'how we define ourselves, by distinguishing ourselves from the Other' and 'who the significant Others are against whom (and in relation to whom) a given person or group is defined' (10).

From the mid-nineteenth century and into the early decades of this century there was a vogue amongst British writers for collecting instances of 'the curious topsy-turviness of things in China' (Darwent 1904: 66). Cumming found it 'really amusing to note in how many things Chinese customs are diametrically the reverse of ours' and provides a list of customs for the reader's amusement (1886: 125). Three decades later, in a chapter on 'Topsy-Turveydom', Reverend Hardy (1907: 90–4) provided an even more extensive list, prefacing his remarks with the observation that '[t]he Chinese are not only our antipodes with regard to position on the globe, but are also our opposites in almost every thought and act' (1907: 90–4). These extracts are, of course, all grist to the mill of notions of Orientalism as delineated by Edward Said (1978). They are clear instances of the way in which Western 'Selves' take it upon themselves to define non-Western 'Others'. However, it is important to bear in mind the extent to which non-Western peoples construct their own Others. For millennia Chinese discourses have maintained distinctive world views (see Graham 1983), with their own epistemology, which always culminates in 'Homo-Sinicus'. The perpetuation of the notion of China as the Middle Kingdom is, perhaps, symbolised in the way Chinese television news invariably commences with national events.

An attempt to 'read off' notions of self-identities by examining representations of others seems particularly appropriate in Shanghai since Shanghainese, both discursively, and in quotidian situations, so often drew sharp distinctions between themselves and other categories of Chinese. In nineteenth-century England, Malcolm Chapman describes representations of 'the Celt' as providing the definers with 'a figure of opposition, a mythical alter-ego which they used in pursuit of their own self-definition' (1982: 129). In a similar fashion, Shanghainese defined themselves in contrast to a universe peopled by various categories of non-Shanghainese. It is to Chinese and Shanghainese identities and to 'orientalising' Shanghai that I now turn.[10]

'Chineseness'

People I spoke to in Shanghai invariably had a strong sense of being 'Chinese'. In daily encounters my being a 'foreigner' would provoke self-designation by Shanghai citizens as 'Chinese'. The sense of being Chinese has a long history. For example, Elvin (1991) provides a fascinating insight into the 'inner world of

1830'. On the basis of literary evidence he concludes that 'the Chinese were already conscious, by this time, of being "Chinese"' (34). He also found distinct continuities between historical and contemporary senses of Chineseness.

Shanghai's semi-colonial status undoubtedly fostered the development of Chinese nationalism. Goodman comments that foreign displays of national power in the city 'had a crucial catalysing effect on Shanghai's Chinese residents' (1995: 28). With older residents I could still sense resonances of indignation from this time. These informants portrayed Chinese nationalism, and a strong sense of being 'Chinese', as having reached its apotheosis in 1949. The profound appeal of this new 'imagined community' was brought home to me by one man's memories of Mao Zedong's speech at Tiananmen in which he announced the creation of the People's Republic. He had watched this in a Shanghai cinema 44 years before and still recalled the great pride he had felt and the 'enormous power' of Mao's words 'The Chinese people have stood up!' I also met people who had returned to China in 1949 out of a sense of patriotic duty – many of whom became victims in the Cultural Revolution. Feelings of Chinese solidarity were described to me as enhanced during the Korean War with many Shanghainese volunteering to help in this crusade.

During the Maoist period state controls over the media and everyday life precluded the dissemination of alternative voices.[11] As informants told me, 'there was only one voice, only one kind of language – China only had one mouth.' The ubiquitous loudspeakers may serve as a dominant image of this period.[12] Political rhetoric stressed solidarity with, and support for, other Third World and socialist countries and was critical of 'bourgeois', 'capitalist', 'imperialist' countries and especially of America.[13] If identity is asserted in contrast to something, then the Maoist state offered relatively few alternative models. With the important exception of those dubbed 'enemies of the people' there was little reason to question what it meant to 'be Chinese'.

Sinologists such as Myron Cohen who have written on 'being Chinese' describe 'the ongoing crisis of identification' in the twentieth century (1991: 133). However, I found no such crisis over what constituted the basic attributes of 'Chineseness' – it may be that what Cohen and others are detailing is a crisis of the role of Chinese intellectuals. I found, rather, an exceptional degree of agreement and certainty over a 'bedrock definition of Chineseness' (Link 1993: 201). A fundamental and pervasive distinction was drawn between Chinese and foreigners (*waiguoren* – 'outside country people'). In numerous conversations my presence spurred an endless stream of comparisons between China and other countries. It was evident that 'much of what is distinctively Chinese is defined as different from "outside"' (Croll 1994: 220). A typical list of characteristics of 'Chineseness' includes physical features – in the words of a popular Chinese song, Chinese people have 'black hair, black eyes, and yellow skin'. Additionally, they have Chinese culture, that is, they speak Chinese language, eat Chinese food in a Chinese way, and have 'five thousand years of Chinese history'. These characteristics were felt, clearly, to distinguish Chinese from other peoples. For instance, as I note in the Preface, on the basis of spending several years in China, speaking

Chinese, consuming local food, and knowledge of local customs and affairs I was sometimes described as 'half Chinese' or 'like a Chinese person'. However, even if I could speak perfect Chinese, and been born in China, my facial features and skin colour would preclude me from being fully 'Chinese' in popular perceptions.

In popular representations 'foreigner' was a term used primarily to describe European, American, or Australasian Caucasians. Thus the Japanese, although strictly speaking 'foreign', did not fit the usual mental image of the archetypal 'foreigners'. There was particular ambiguity in the case of the Japanese both because of their physiological proximity to Chinese, and also since, as I was often told, 'all their culture came from China'. I heard various racist-type stories which depicted Japanese people as a kind of mutant or deformed Chinese. Most people I spoke with in Shanghai expressed a strong dislike and distrust of Japanese (emotions matched in intensity only by the desire to obtain Japanese consumer products). It was not uncommon to hear them referred to as *riben guizi* (Japanese devils). Informants generally attributed this antipathy to China's suffering at Japanese hands in the Anti-Japanese War (1937–45). Accounts of Japanese atrocities are kept alive in school textbooks, television programmes and films, exhibitions, and numerous press articles. In March 2000, for instance, a front page headline in the *Shanghai Star* reminded its readers 'Nanjing Massacre: "an undeniable fact"' (*SS* 7 March 2000: 1). Some informants expressed disgust at the Chinese government's (perceived) current weakness in its relations with Japan.

Assertions of a common Chineseness were made despite, for instance, manifest regional differences in cuisine and dialect. William Jenner (1992: 228) describes this as the 'myth of the oneness of the Han nation' which belies considerable ethnic diversity within China. Myth or not, my respondents invariably subscribed to this belief in 'Chineseness', a belief which could cut across legal citizenships. This can be explained in various ways. First, this degree of certainty is a function of the level of abstraction – in interactions solely between Chinese people great attention may be paid to regional differences. Second, the Chinese state has a vested interest in maintaining this 'myth'. Third, the written language is of key importance. Anderson stresses language's 'capacity for generating imagined communities, building in effect particular solidarities' (1983: 122). Even amongst the majority Han Chinese there are dialects so diverse – Shanghainese and Cantonese for instance – as to be completely mutually unintelligible. However, the notion of Chinese as a single language is underpinned by the cultural dominance of the written language. It is still largely the case that in China 'power does not speak – it writes' (Jenner 1992: 184). It is indicative of the privileging of the written word that the term for 'Chinese language' is *zhongwen* ('Chinese writing') whereas 'dialect' is *fangyan* ('the speech of the locality').

Even though the sense of belonging to an imagined community of Chinese people is very powerful, it co-exists with strong senses of regional identity. In Hong Kong, Barbara Ward (1985: 68–9) describes how Hong Kong fishermen may adopt various designations – for example, 'we Cantonese', 'we Chinese', 'we water people' – depending upon the context and matter under discussion. She notes that Cantonese boat people and Hakka farmers who have very different languages and customs both say 'we Chinese' in contrasting themselves to 'foreigners' (1985: 68–71). Similarly, Lawrence Crissman found that amongst overseas Chinese communities ethnicity was 'relative and situational' (1967: 189). In examining Chinese and Shanghainese identities I am, therefore, 'freezing' identities which are contingent, over-lapping, and in flux. I share Siu's approach that '"Chineseness" is not an immutable set of beliefs and practices, but a process which captures a wide range of emotions and states of being' (1993: 19). For these reasons I prefer to talk of 'being Chinese' and 'being Shanghainese', emphasising the potentialities for assertions of these identifications.

'Shanghainese' identities

> [T]hat the Chinese are identical in every province of the empire, a man needs not travel over many parts of China to see that this cannot be established by an appeal to reality.
>
> (G.T. Lay *Chinese Repository* 1843: 136)

As noted above native-place played a vital role in social organisation in pre-1949 Shanghai. This role was matched by strong attachments to native-place identification and persistent regional stereotypes, some of which are still of importance in Shanghai today.[14] Ethnic identification can be self-ascription or ascription by others. In the case of subordinate groups 'ethnic affiliation may originate in an *attribution* of collective identity to them on the part of others' (Comaroff 1987: 305). In such cases the 'identity imputed to a social group from the outside may be quite different from that same identity as subjectively experienced' (308). The prejudice against those from northern Jiangsu in Shanghai is an example of the way in which '[t]he boundaries of pariah groups are most strongly maintained by the excluding host population' (Barth 1970: 31). However, my key concern here is not with the stigmatised category, but with the defining population and what these stereotypes 'say' about the definers. My interest is with identifications as being 'Shanghainese'.

Bryna Goodman (1995: 146) downplays the importance of a specific urban identity as 'Shanghai people' until the establishment of a Chinese municipal government in 1927. However, Linda Johnson writes that a 'dichotomy between locals and outsiders can be seen emerging at Shanghai in the Kangxi era' (1993b: 163). In the late seventeenth and early eighteenth centuries the territory inside the city walls was 'largely reserved for official, religious and educational functions, residences, and retail shops… Native-place associations, by contrast, were usually located outside the city wall' (ibid.: 167). This spatial differentiation between (here Chinese) 'outsiders' and city residents is paralleled by the residence restrictions placed upon foreigners and rural migrants in contemporary Shanghai.

Shanghai's rapid development from the early nineteenth century onwards, and especially in the first decades of the twentieth century, provided fertile ground for the development of notions of Shanghainese sophistication and superiority over rural Chinese. Such ideas were well formed by 1949. Even in the weeks after the People's Liberation Army occupied Shanghai in May 1949, some city-dwellers could not resist spreading 'yokel stories' at the expense of the mainly peasant army (see Gaulton 1981: 43).

In contemporary Shanghai, citizens often identified themselves as 'Shanghainese'. In local media, Shanghainese identity was frequently asserted with a degree of certainty far greater than one generally finds of, say, English identity. On one occasion I asked a market trader if he was Shanghainese. He replied simply '*wo Shanghai*' – literally 'I Shanghai'. The way in which this self-ascription linguistically conflates personal identification and place suggests a high degree of topophilia. A similar instance of this conflation was the common reference by older informants to themselves as '*lao Shanghai*' ('old Shanghai').

Shanghai residents often drew attention to differences between themselves and other categories of Chinese people – many of these distinctions predate 1949. Various levels of intra-regional comparison were made. At the largest scale was a broad distinction between the cultural background and habits of those from north and south China. Shanghainese included themselves in the category 'southerners'.[15] Typically and stereotypically, 'southerners' were portrayed as good at business, sharp, and quick-witted, 'northerners' as comparatively slow-witted, honest, and traditional. Discourses on *yiqi* (personal loyalty) also invoked regional stereotypes; typically northerners are said to stress *yiqi*, whilst southern Chinese are 'devious.'

Residents also drew attention to differences between Shanghainese and Chinese from different towns or provinces of China. A particularly comprehensive list was provided by a Shanghai resident in his late sixties. He outlined six groups about whom Shanghainese have particularly strong feelings – those from Shandong, Shaoxing, Ningbo, Subei, Beijing, and Canton. From further interviews it became evident that the first three groups (and for many of my informants Subei too) were primarily of historical (i.e. pre-1949) interest. I examine representations of Beijingers and Cantonese in the next section since they appear more relevant to the current situation.

It is unnecessary to outline all the historical representations. A few brief comments on Subei people may serve as an example. My Shanghainese informants agreed that Shanghainese had looked down on Subei people – although some considered this prejudice purely an historical matter – because they had engaged in the lowest status jobs such as street sweepers, night soil collectors, and rickshaw pullers but, above all, because they were perceived as ignorant, poor, dirty, rough, and without *wenhua*.[16] From such representations of Subei people one can 'read off' the opposite factors as indicating what 'Shanghainese' are believed to be like. If Subei people are despised as ignorant, poor, dirty, and rough, then Shanghainese are cultured, wealthy, clean, and refined. However, I would argue that in the 1990s the category of migrant workers, which I discuss later, superseded Subei people as a far more visible and frequently discussed category of vilified others.

It is obviously difficult to assess the vitality of 'Shanghainese' identities during the Maoist period. However, there are grounds to assume that identification as

'Shanghainese' became more pertinent at that time. Goodman (1995: 146) argues that until the 1920s at least, for many citizens identification with their native-place was much more important than identification as 'Shanghainese'. During the Maoist period various policies undermined the role of native-place. In part the curtailment of migration and population movement reduced the need for native-place associations. The government also implemented policies, such as the nationalisation of their properties in the 1950s, which were specifically intended to diminish their influence. Later, in the Cultural Revolution, the ideology of native-place was criticised as feudal and icons of attachment to local place, such as family graves, were destroyed. As Shanghai's population became more 'fixed', and there was less scope to organise on the basis of native-place, it seems reasonable to assume that regional identities generally became less significant.

Informants also suggested that Shanghai residents' sense of superiority was enhanced during the Maoist period. The creation of strict urban–rural boundaries played a part in this since it entrenched urban privileges such as better educational opportunities, job security, and welfare benefits. In addition, with no foreign brand labels to compete with, across China products labelled 'Made in Shanghai' were the supreme cachet of quality and sophistication. At the same time the strict migration controls and limited possibilities for travel gave the city an allure made all the greater by its unavailability. Former rusticated youth were clearly aware of Shanghai's superiority and often spoke resentfully of having been 'assigned out of Shanghai'. A typical Shanghainese conception of rural China is abundantly clear in a scene redolent with symbolism in the play *Yesterday's Longan Tree* (*Zuotian de Guiyuan Shu*) by the Shanghai playwright Xu Pinli, who was herself sent to Yunnan. A group of 'rusticated' Shanghai youth are walking through a forest in Yunnan, approaching their destination in the countryside. One of them throws aside his case of books with the comment that they would not be needed any more.

Alongside the relatively privileged status of Shanghai residents there were also grounds for resentment over the city's treatment by the central government. After 1949 the new government was dependent upon Shanghai for funds. Until the reform era, with just 1.1 per cent of China's population, the city had provided one-fifth to one-fourth of central government revenue (Jacobs and Hong 1994: 226). Many Shanghainese resented these expropriations, not least because of the continued deterioration in Shanghai's own infrastructure.

An article in *Duzhe Wenzhai* (*Readers' Digest*) titled 'Great Shanghai, can you still carry China?' commented that when Shanghainese visit Beijing and see its new, tall buildings they will feel '[o]ut of each of these ten buildings, five were built with Shanghai's money!' (*DW* 1992: 43). According to this article 'some people calculate' that if since 1949 the proportion of Shanghai's wealth handed over to the central government had been the same as other places 'at the very least it would now have attained the same economic level as Singapore.' It adds that in the ten years 1979–88, Shanghai provided enough money to the central government to build two cities the size of Shanghai. I often heard the complaint that 'just one district in Shanghai gives as much to the central government as the whole of Guangdong province.' Since in the early 1990s Shanghai contributed at least 12 times as much to central government revenues as Guangdong this seems a reasonable estimate (Jacobs and Hong 1994: 228). Indeed, in 1992, just one Shanghai company, the *Shanghai Cigarette Company*, paid almost as much tax as the whole of Guangzhou Municipality (Jacobs 1997: 190, Note 43).

In the early 1990s, the sense of a Shanghainese identity, fostered through a feeling of shared unfairness, was very evident to me. This resentment may have become more pronounced during the reform era just as the very policies which underscored it were in the process of being ameliorated, that is, as Shanghai retains a higher proportion of its revenues and there is a greater degree of local autonomy. There are also increased possibilities for comparison – Shanghainese can much more readily travel to Beijing – and it is only recently that figures of taxes handed over by Shanghai Municipality to the central government have become more accessible.

OPENING SHANGHAI'S BOUNDARIES: IDENTITIES IN THE REFORM ERA

The reform era has witnessed a flow of both economic and political power from the centre to the regions. Evidence of this is the emergence, since the late 1980s, of regional economic protectionism. Shanghai's reintegration into the world economy is paralleled by an increase in the power and influence of the city authorities and business enterprises. In popular perceptions, the central authorities are losing their grip; as one Shanghai resident succinctly remarked, 'they say that the central authorities are in control, but in reality each place looks after itself.'

An example of increasing local autonomy which may serve as a microcosm of wider changes concerns entrance exams for Shanghai university places. Before the reforms applicants took a unified, national exam. Entrants now take unified Shanghai or Jiangsu province exams. In 1993, Shanghai's Industry University began to set its own entrance exam, in the same way as Shanghai's universities had done before 1949.

Shanghai's boundaries have become far more porous. With the opening up of Shanghai's economy and large-scale construction works under way, the city is once again a powerful magnet for capital, tourists, entrepreneurs, and migrant labourers. Migration patterns are becoming closer to those of the pre-Maoist period. Shanghainese are no longer compelled to leave the city and rural migrants have more opportunities to work and live in Shanghai. Since the late 1980s, large numbers of rural residents have come to Shanghai in search of employment. Shanghai's 'floating population', that is, people without Shanghai household registration, rose from just 4 per cent of the population in 1982 to over one-quarter in the mid-1990s (White 1994: 86). Most migrants are from rural areas of Anhui, Jiangsu, Zhejiang, and Shandong, and they engage in small-scale peddling and trading, construction work, agricultural work on farms in Shanghai's suburbs, or work as household servants. The vast majority of Shanghai's current frenetic construction work is being carried out by migrant labourers. As legal controls have relaxed, Shanghai factories, especially in the Pudong new development zone, increasingly employ non-Shanghainese labour. Companies send out labour recruiters to distant provinces and arrange for workers to come to Shanghai. They are employed on low wage rates and must be housed and fed by the companies.

Apart from maids, who live in residents' households, migrants are generally segregated spatially from the resident population. Construction gangs mostly live in wooden huts or under canvas awnings. Their recruitment and organisation are often dealt with by autonomous labour bosses, an occupation well known in pre-1949 China. These figures were demonised as cruel exploiters in propaganda literature such as Xia Yan's (1959) semi-fictional account *Indentured Labourer* (*Baoshen Gong*). Market traders and the unemployed congregate around suburban parts of Shanghai and especially at the intersection of urban/suburban transport nodes. Less successful migrants occupy marginal spaces within the city – they sleep on the streets, beg, and may scavenge amongst the rubbish in such places as the bank of the pestilent Suzhou Creek.

Since the 1970s, the state's ability to control where people live has gradually diminished. However, although weakened, the *hukou* system is still important. Until 1999 at least, when Shanghai permitted professionals with at least a bachelor level degree who found a job to settle in the city with permanent residential status, there were complaints that only those engaged in low-status jobs could circumvent the *hukou*. A city *danwei* could recruit people without a Shanghai *hukou*, but this was very costly. In one instance, I knew of a *danwei* paid 60,000 *yuan* to obtain a *hukou* and also had to arrange accommodation for the employee. Non-Shanghainese could obtain a Shanghai *hukou* if they came to care for an elderly relative or to replace a relative who had left Shanghai. In one case in my acquaintance, it took three years to circumnavigate the bureaucracy involved. Thus the boundaries are differentially 'porous'.

With the relaxation of migration controls in the reform era, same-native-place relationships are becoming of renewed importance. Non-Shanghainese enterprises are being attracted to the city. For instance, *Chuan Meizi*, a chain of Sichuanese restaurants in Shanghai, employs only staff recruited from Sichuan. At one of these restaurants a waitress explained that her anxiety over coming to Shanghai on her own was reduced since the employers were *lao xiang* (people of one's native-place). Giddens describes 'the local community as a place' as one of the components of trust in pre-modern cultures which will be transformed by modernity (1990: 102). It is, therefore, ironic that this basis of trust is becoming of renewed importance in a society in which the avowed aims of the state are 'economic development' and 'modernisation'.

Since social boundaries are called into being by the exigencies of social interaction, it is of particular importance to pay attention to Shanghai residents' comments on rural migrants. However, before examining the impact of these migrants upon identities in Shanghai I outline representations of contrasts between Shanghainese and Beijingers; a set of oppositions which provides evidence of a redefinition of Shanghainese identities in the reform era.

Shanghainese/Beijingers

The following series of oppositions is a compilation from comments made by Shanghainese. Most informants expressed morally positive views of Beijingers. Even Beijingers' perceived ready resort to violence was taken as evidence of their straightforwardness. The only real note of discord was the occasional suggestion that they were arrogant, a characteristic attributed to Beijing being the city of government.

Shanghai (haipai)	*Beijing*
Financial and commercial centre	Political centre
Open (*kaifang*)	Closed (*bisi*)
Immigrant population, mixed race[17]	Indigenous in population and culture
Future	Past, backward looking
Literature	History
Popular culture (comic plays)	'Serious' culture (Beijing opera)
Mental action, arguing	Physical response, fighting
Concerned with matters that affect them personally	Concerned with national affairs
Sharp, clever	Straightforward, easily taken in, simple-minded

To this list I add the comments of two informants. A Shanghainese professor told me:

> Shanghainese are open-minded (*kaifang*) and 'coastal-style' (*haipai*) – they can accept Western things. But Shanghainese exclude outsiders (*paiwai*).[18] They see Beijingers as *tu* (unrefined – *tu* also means soil, earth; local, native; indigenous) who just drink tea whereas Shanghai people drink beer and beverages. Shanghainese are shrewd.

A young teacher remarked that Shanghainese have a better relationship with foreigners than do other Chinese because of Shanghai people's historical interaction with foreigners. He felt that:

> Northerners have still not lost the Qing dynasty sense of superiority. It is Shanghai that most accepts Western culture. Guangzhou is developed but *tu*, for example, Cantonese don't eat Western food, they are still stuck with the same old way of doing things. Shanghainese, by contrast, visit Western-style restaurants and wear Western-style suits. So Shanghai is the best place to be open to the outside.

The conflation of the terms *kaifang* and *haipai* in these comments is particularly interesting. *Haipai* – 'Shanghai-style' or more loosely 'coastal-style' was a term originally used to describe the distinctive way in which Beijing opera was sung in Shanghai. It was subsequently used to describe the school of literature (*haipai wenxue*) which flourished in Shanghai in the 1920s and 1930s. As a genre it was experimental, Western-influenced, and iconoclastic. The term may also be used of an individual's style, say, of management. As outlined in Chapter 1, the term *kaifang* has various resonances. It denotes the 'Open Door' policy, and in everyday use may mean 'openness' or 'open-mindedness' with a range of evaluations from being broad-minded to morally lax. Many Shanghainese considered Shanghai more *kaifang* than, say, Beijing because it is a city composed mainly of immigrants, and because it had been a cosmopolitan city in the past. Moreover, since Shanghainese were already *haipai*, in a sense they had been *kaifang* before the *kaifang* policy.[19]

The self-conception of Shanghainese as intelligent and sophisticated urbanites was often vocalised. The notion of Shanghainese as shrewd 'maximisers' was evident in comments people made to me about the demonstrations in Shanghai during Spring 1989. For example, informants contrasted the way Shanghai's *laobaixing*, unlike those in Beijing, backed down from a physical confrontation with the army. They considered this both as evidence of Shanghai people's 'smartness' and illustrative of Beijingers' courage and concern with national affairs. In 1989, I met Shanghainese who felt no reason to engage in the demonstrations; they considered them to be part of a struggle for power in Beijing and, therefore, of no concern to themselves.

'Outside people'

Immediately after Spring Festival 1993 large numbers of rural migrants 'flowed' into Shanghai seeking work, spurring complaints by residents, and consternation in the local media. A Shanghainese friend remarked that it was only at such times that one could see Shanghainese identity asserted. The barrier between Shanghainese and *waidiren/nadinin* (non-Shanghainese – see below) was at its most tangible at this time. I had the sense that these 'outsiders' were regarded as a part of a threatening Other, overwhelming in its numbers and poverty.[20] This influx of *waidiren* produced a siege mentality. A newspaper report described these people using terms formerly given to armies from these areas, for example, *Xiang jun* (Hunan army), *Wan jun* (Anhui army), *Su jun* (Subei army), and *Chuan jun* (Sichuan army). If *waidiren* were perceived as a threatening army then the battle sites were the streets, pavements, shop counters, and buses of the city.

The fear of chaos has deep cultural roots in China. Shanghainese often pride themselves that their city is well ordered. Rural migrants were displaced people who brought disorder and aroused the fear of chaos. The media described the arrivals at this time – many thousands of whom slept outside the train station in the freezing cold, wet Shanghai February – as 'blindly flowing' (*mangliu*). Such descriptions deny any rationality on the part of these migrants, contributing to a sense of them as an irrational and potentially dangerous 'Other'. The image portrayed of them is akin to the traditional 'hungry ghosts' who roam the land (Wolf 1974). Sedentary residents may fear migrants as they fear ghosts – both may be 'angry because they are hungry and homeless' (ibid.: 170).

Many of these arrivals in Shanghai hoped to become *mingong* (migrant labourers) and need to be explored within the wider category of *waidiren* of which they form a part. The lack of a proper English term for *waidiren* alerts one to the distinctive nature of this indigenous category. *Waidi* is defined as 'parts of the country other than where one is' (CED 1988: 705). With the suffix *ren* – 'person', a *waidiren* in Shanghai is somebody from another part of China. However, in everyday use *waidiren* often seemed to be restricted to non-urban people. In this sense it is synonymous with the term *xiangxiaren* (*xiang ho nin*) which the dictionary describes as the neutral 'country folk', 'person from the countryside', but which, in Shanghai at least, has distinctly negative connotations. Negative perceptions of rural Chinese portrayed them as dirty, stupid, ignorant, backward, and poor.[21] I often heard Shanghainese complain about 'country bumpkins', for instance, for blocking crowded buses with bulky bags or obstructing traffic when they dragged heavy loads through the city. A survey of 1,000 migrant workers conducted in 2000 indicated that they well aware of this prejudice. Many complained they were paid less than Shanghainese counterparts for doing the same type of work, while 17.7 per cent said they were 'often looked down on by Shanghainese' (*SS* 7 July 2000: 3).

A recent slang term, which not all informants knew, is *bazi*. This term probably derives from *xiangbalao* 'country bumpkin'. One informant described *bazi* as 'those from the countryside who have money but don't know how to use it' or who 'have money but you can see that they are outsiders.' I also heard this expression used of Taiwanese. On one occasion I overheard some workers in a Taiwanese-owned company talk about '*Taibazi*' (i.e. Taiwanese bumpkin). When I asked who this was they became embarrassed and told me that this was how they referred to their Taiwanese boss behind his back. Another instance of when this term was used provides an interesting example of 'front' and 'backstage' impression management. A friend introduced me to a former classmate who worked in a real estate company. Several times the latter mentioned that their customers included 'Taiwanese compatriots' (*Taibao*). As we left my friend was much amused by this, suspecting that the old classmate would undoubtedly use the term '*Taibazi*' on other occasions.

Mingong – migrant labourers – are the most visible (Chinese) 'outsiders' in Shanghai. A state *danwei* employee told me that 'non-Shanghainese want to come to Shanghai in the same way as Shanghainese seek to go abroad.' Most *mingong* in Shanghai are from rural China. A university lecturer described *mingong* in the following way:

> These are the people who do most of the hard manual labour in Shanghai. They are a social problem because they have no houses, live together, and have no *wenhua* or self-cultivation. Many crimes in Shanghai are committed by *mingong*. They have no household registration and the police cannot control them. Without them to build new roads and housing Shanghai's construction would not happen. But they make Shanghai's society unstable.

This is a typical representation of *mingong*. *Mingong* are regarded as a necessary evil – essential for Shanghai's construction but also the source of public order and social problems. *Mingong* and *waidiren* generally are regarded by many Shanghainese as a considerable threat. They are blamed for making the city even more crowded and for committing many crimes.[22] One informant described *mingong* as 'doing the kind of jobs that used to be done by Subei people.' It is my impression that the kind of opprobrium once reserved for Subei people is now increasingly transferred to *mingong*.

BEING SHANGHAINESE

Some tastes/flavours of shanghai

Benedict Anderson suggests that it is important to distinguish the style in which communities are imagined (1983: 15). Anthony Cohen stresses that people often 'experience their distinctiveness not through the performance of elaborate and specialised ceremonial but through the evaluation of everyday practices' (1982: 6). In Shanghai, I also found that 'the sense of belonging' was evoked in rather mundane circumstances such as the use of language and joking, through 'processes which occur close to the *everyday* experience of life' (ibid.). With a Shanghai resident in her early forties I discussed the ways in which one might tell the regional origin of those who live in Shanghai. She said that one could visibly distinguish Cantonese 'because their faces are different'. Subei people were 'too obvious' – from their behaviour, dress, and dialect. Other groups, she felt, were less visible but could be distinguished by the food they ate.

Building upon these indigenous means of ascribing people to different categories, the representations outlined above, and responses to more direct questions about 'Shanghainese' identity, it is possible to provide some senses of what is considered 'Shanghainese'. It should be noted that the physical characteristics required to be 'Chinese' apply equally to 'being Shanghainese'. I concentrate in the following upon dialect, cuisine, notions of style and taste, imputed characteristics and behaviour. Each of these are means by which lines of demarcation were drawn between Shanghainese and non-Shanghainese and evaluative judgements made of different types of people residing within Shanghai. First it is important to distinguish contesting representations of where 'real Shanghainese' are to be found.

Pudong or not Pudong: The 'Real' Shanghainese?

Many Shanghai citizens are only first or second-generation residents of the city and described their family home (*laojia*) as being elsewhere in China. People whose families had deeper roots, whose ancestral line was in Shanghai, were generally very proud of this. As a rule of thumb I was told that those whose families had been in Shanghai over one hundred years were 'people of this place', while others were seen as 'coming from outside'. In practice, however, anyone born in Shanghai could describe themselves as Shanghainese. A university lecturer, himself proud of being Shanghainese, remarked that 'Shanghai people are cross-breeds, only those in Nanshi district are local Shanghainese. The rest are from all over China.'

I had anticipated that Nanshi would be regarded in this way, since it is the site of the old city. Earlier Western visitors considered this 'the real Shanghai' (Gamewell 1916: 140), replete with 'enough... foul-smelling alleys, streets of gay shops, beggars and crowds, to satisfy most lovers of the haunting allurements of the Orient' (ibid.: 142). Until 1911, Nanshi was encircled by the medieval city wall, and its former location is now the circular route followed by the Number 11 bus. This seems straightforward, but another resident told me 'people from Nanshi are no good, they are all immigrants from Subei.' If the residents of Nanshi are not the 'real' Shanghainese, then perhaps one must look elsewhere. One informant told me that his mother was born in Pudong and described her as a 'true Shanghainese'. However, there seemed to be considerable ambivalence as to whether Pudong was Shanghai or not. Often people spoke of going *from* Shanghai *to* Pudong, or vice versa.

Even in a single conversation a person may both describe Pudongers as 'real Shanghainese' and distinguish between 'Pudongers' and 'Shanghainese'. The confusion is evident in the comments of a retired man who told me that 'Pudongers are real Shanghainese... Shanghainese are not prepared to move to Pudong, it is lower one level.' I have no neat solution to this paradox, one, which, it should be said, existed only for myself as an analyst. This instance highlights the extent to which an anthropologist is dealing with flexible and fluid notions which may, or may not, eventually 'congeal' or become systematic. In everyday contexts when people spoke about 'Shanghai' and the characteristics of 'Shanghainese' they seemed usually to refer only to the ten urban districts of Puxi (the west bank of the Huangpu River) and their residents, and not Pudong (the east bank of the Huangpu River) or the suburban counties of Shanghai. However, there was no need for them to specify *where* Shanghai is when discussing 'Shanghainese'. Although evidence that one was born within Shanghai's political boundaries would constitute 'proof' of officially being 'Shanghainese', in other respects 'being Shanghainese' is a de-territorialised notion, involving a composite of certain ways of behaving.

Speaking properly

In China, dialect is a crucial marker in definitions of Self and Others. It is a key way in which distinctions between 'inside' and 'outside', inclusion and exclusion, are created. Since dialects of Chinese differ as much as Romance languages this creates a very real boundary – if Shanghai citizens speak in Shanghai dialect, other Chinese, who do not speak a Wu dialect, will be excluded.[23] An article in the *Shanghai Star* observed that 'Where both Shanghai natives and people from other places are present, Shanghainese sometimes use the dialect as a test to judge whether somebody belongs to their group or not. Here the dialect becomes a natural barrier against any "infiltration" by outside people' (*SS* 2 March 1999: 2). The central importance of language was evident in an informant's response to my question: In Shanghai who are *waidiren* ('outsiders')? – 'People who cannot speak Shanghai dialect.' Similarly, a translator in a joint venture company in her early twenties, who felt that 'the Subei people in Shanghai now are second and third generation and have been assimilated', explained that 'among our generation there is no conception of Subei people contrasted to Shanghainese, we are all Shanghainese, we all speak Shanghai dialect.' Another resident remarked that although Shanghainese can understand *putonghua*, if one speaks to them in Shanghai dialect they 'immediately feel an intimacy (*qinqigan* – literally 'a feeling of being relatives') and a 'tacit understanding' in the relationship. It is important from an emotional point of view.'

Shanghai dialect is clearly an important focus for a Shanghainese identification. However, the confusion over who are 'real' Shanghainese spills over into the dialect. I was often told that Pudongers speak 'true' or 'standard' Shanghai dialect. However, people may also distinguish between 'Shanghai dialect' and 'Pudong dialect'. Some respondents, including a magazine editor, told me that 'the most standard Shanghai dialect is spoken in Nanshi and Huangpu districts.' A little later he added that 'no Shanghai dialect exists.' This assertion was based upon a perception that the various waves of immigrants to Shanghai had distorted and submerged an original 'pure' dialect under the admixture of their own dialects and vocabularies. Many respondents described Shanghai dialect as a 'mix' or 'blend' – and heavily influenced by Ningbo-ese and other dialects. English is another encrustation. One man remarked that his 82-year-old father, who had worked in a foreign bank, still used some pidgin English such as *te le fen* (telephone). A new rising tide was depositing Cantonese terms upon the dialect. Within the city zone itself people could not distinguish differences in dialect based upon spatial location. Instead, indigenous categorisations stressed differences based upon educational level with, for example, contrasts between 'cultured' and 'slang' or 'city well language' (*shijingyu*) Shanghai dialect.

R.D. Grillo notes that languages and their speakers are usually of unequal status, power and authority, and that 'there is commonly a hierarchical ordering of languages, dialects and ways of speaking' (1989: 1). Many campaigners of the 1919 May Fourth Movement considered that a common language was essential to modernising China. In 1956, *putonghua* was officially adopted as the national language to be used in government and public life and promoted in all educational institutions – it is the 'dominant language' in the Shanghai diglossia.[24] Shanghai dialect was gradually excised from official contexts and the media. Local newspapers such as *Xinmin Wanbao* now occasionally use a few words of Shanghai dialect. However, a magazine editor told me that the media 'dare not use more because of pressure from above.'

Shanghainese often assert a sense of pride in the dialect. For instance, some pointed out that it retains much classical Chinese – Tang poetry is said to retain more of its original rhyme when recited in the dialect. Others considered the dialect 'vivid', 'rich', and 'colourful' since it has 'vocabulary from all over China'. Informants would stress that some dialect vocabulary cannot be translated into *putonghua* and that even when similar to *putonghua* it has a 'different flavour' – and this may be a useful metaphor to conceptualise the relationship between 'Shanghainese' and 'Chinese' identities.

Eating properly

Food is a key marker through which Chinese identity is expressed. Any researcher in China soon becomes aware of the seemingly endless discourse on food and eating. It does seem that '[f]or the Chinese... food is a central feature of ethnicity, a basic statement about what one *is*' (Anderson 1988: 211). Eating 'Chinese food' in the correct way is a key component of 'being Chinese'. It is a prime instance of the way 'consumption habits, deemed natural as skin, are criteria for membership and become weapons of exclusion' (Douglas and Isherwood 1978: 85). For instance, chopsticks are considered so 'Chinese' that it is believed foreigners can scarcely learn to use them. During the peak of the Cultural Revolution, when fierce campaigns sought to distinguish 'enemies of the people', even such habits as drinking coffee and eating foreign foods could be used against someone as 'weapons of exclusion'.

Each festive day has its special foods. At the Mid-Autumn Festival, for instance, moon cakes, taro, lotus, water chestnuts, and duck are eaten. Such festive foods invariably have stories and myths associated with them. As a person consumes these foods, ideally alongside other family members, the stories may be recalled or told to youngsters. Thus alongside the food, the eater ingests the social and cultural values of 'being Chinese'. In a sense the participants eat themselves into being 'Chinese'.

Cuisine also plays a part in the construction of regional distinctions. The comments on Beijingers and Cantonese presented above highlight distinctions of this kind – Shanghainese open-mindedness, modernity, Western orientation, and sophistication as manifested in their consumption of Western meals, beer, and other beverages were favourably compared to Beijingers' tea drinking, and the inability of Cantonese to appreciate Western food. Instances where the regional origin of Shanghai residents may not otherwise be 'visible' includes Ningbo-ese. A female informant remarked that one can only tell Ningbo-ese from the food they eat; Ningbo-ese prefer salty, pungent foods such as 'stinking bean curd', thus 'their neighbours can tell where they are from.'

I encountered the symbolism attached to food in my own activities. One morning, with a family, I ate a breakfast of rice porridge (*paofan*), flat bread (*dabing*), and fried dough sticks (*youtiao*). This was described to me as 'the most typical Shanghainese breakfast.' On another occasion – as so often as an outsider I only become aware of boundaries by transgressing them – I was planning a train journey out of Shanghai with some Chinese friends when I suggested that we take some steamed bread to eat on the train. The response was that this would make us like 'country bumpkins' and that we had better take something else instead.

Dressing correctly

Style and sophistication were often regarded as key markers of being Shanghainese. A female respondent noted that one could often distinguish the regional origin of people by their aesthetic taste. She remarked that:

> Shanghainese are really good at dressing up, they like softer colours and have a good sense of colour co-ordination. Subei people like bright green and bright red – it looks very vulgar. They also wear different colours all jumbled up. It is becoming harder to spot *waidiren* as they dress better now. This is especially true with Cantonese, you cannot distinguish them by their clothing, they are integrated with Hong Kong and Taiwanese, their clothing is Hong Kong-style. However, you can tell other *waidiren* by their clothing.

After being compelled to abandon adornment during the Maoist years, fashion had returned to Shanghai with a vengeance. It was increasingly important to be *xiaosa*, meaning 'stylish', a term made popular through a Taiwanese pop song. Shanghainese, the younger generation especially, had abandoned blue and green 'Mao suits' and black canvas shoes. Such apparel marked out the wearer as a 'country person'. It was a source of considerable amusement when foreign women wore such 'peasants' shoes'. It was common to see men with the brand label of their suits prominently displayed on their jacket cuffs. A young teacher gleefully told me that 'these are all *xiangxiaren*, they're afraid that others won't be able to judge the price of the jacket from its appearance.' In explaining the term *xiangxiaren* to me, one informant suggested that somebody who did not recognise a famous brand label may be quizzed 'are you a *xiangxiaren*?' However, it appeared that dressing correctly was still not enough. A wealthy young share dealer from Hunan studying in Shanghai complained to me that Shanghainese are 'urban petty bourgeois' who 'exclude outsiders'. He added that 'even if you wear expensive clothes, Shanghainese will still look down on you if you are not Shanghainese.' Such notions of fashion and style also intersect with emergent consumer and generational identities – significant features in Shanghai today.

Behaving properly

Various characteristics and types of behaviour were routinely ascribed to 'Shanghainese', both by themselves and others. Extremely common was the notion of 'cleverness'. This was described in various ways, ranging from the unambiguously positive *congming* (intelligent or clever), to *jingming* or *men ke jing/menkanjing* (sharp, astute, shrewd), and *xiao congming* (cleverness in petty things). Typically, popular representations locate Shanghainese as mid-way between Beijingers and Cantonese; for instance, Beijingers are too honest, the latter too shifty. Both are frequently depicted as insular, Beijingers because of a concern with national affairs, and Cantonese by virtue of their attachment to things Cantonese – as one informant told me, they 'exclude outsiders and have a strong sense of shared native-place. Shanghainese, by contrast, are outward looking.' A retired Shanghainese university lecturer told me:

> Shanghainese are very clever, they have a high *wenhua* level and have seen a lot. When outsiders come to Shanghai, Shanghainese look down on them and call them 'country bumpkins'. Shanghainese are arrogant, to them 'outside' includes Beijing and Guangzhou, not just the countryside.

This informant considered that 'Shanghainese may be like this because they have engaged in business too much.' This is associated with a common perception that business people are dishonest. By comparison peasants were regarded as *laoshi*, a term which means 'honest', but also has the connotation of being gullible and easily duped.

Attention to bodily hygiene also played a part in being Shanghainese. A young clerical worker commented that Shanghainese, especially women, 'pay more attention to hygiene, they are clean. Northern girls may not wash every day even in the Summer and in Winter they may not wash for weeks on end.' The common notion in Shanghai that non-Shanghainese bring chaos to the city seems to be paralleled in this depiction of non-Shanghainese as disordered in their bodily hygiene – the 'soiled' outsiders are blemishes on the 'face' of Shanghai. The same speaker also believed that *waidiren* were more generous than Shanghainese – 'they will use all their money to show off. Shanghainese use their money in a way which deploys it most efficiently.' I heard various apocryphal stories in which a *waidiren* and a Shanghainese compare their wealth. In one version, they engage in a type of *potlatch* by burning money and throwing away items. Each time the *waidiren* destroys his property only to find that he has been tricked by the Shanghainese who manages to avoid losing his property.

Finally, I note an instance of a man who had 'lost' his Shanghaineseness. At a wedding I attended in the city, the mother's brother was invited. Although born and brought up in Shanghai, he was rusticated during the Cultural Revolution and had not returned to the city. This man insisted that the bride and teetotal groom respond to his toasts by drinking down glasses of beer and became angry when they refused. The bride attributed his unreasonable behaviour to the fact that he was no longer Shanghainese, but 'completely a country person'. This relative could no longer speak Shanghai dialect, and his behaviour, including his style of consumption, was no longer that of a Shanghainese.

The vitality of contemporary 'Shanghainese' identities

Before carrying out research in Shanghai I had speculated on the degree to which a separate and distinctive Shanghainese identity might be asserted. Wallerstein (1979: 184) writes that 'ethnic consciousness is eternally latent everywhere. But it is only realised when groups feel either threatened with a loss of previously acquired privilege or conversely feel that it is an opportune moment politically to overcome longstanding denial of privilege.' With several decades of large-scale expropriations of Shanghai's profits by the central government, increased local autonomy and regional disparities, and an influx of rural migrants during the reform era, there would seem to be fertile ground for the emergence of assertive regional 'voices'. I had expected to find an increased assertion of local identity, and assumed that this would in some ways be oppositional to a Chinese identity. These hypotheses were only partially borne out by the evidence. My findings suggest that whilst residents may assert a Shanghainese identity, and that 'people from Shanghai unabashedly proclaim the superiority of their native-place' (Thurston 1983: 23), nonetheless this was not in any sense oppositional to a concurrent identification as 'Chinese'.

I have highlighted the coalescence of Shanghainese identity when faced with an influx of migrant workers. This influx may be taken as a message about the relative prosperity of city and rural areas – their presence an indication of Shanghai's economic progress and the poverty of rural China, and of an increasing divergence between the coastal and interior regions. This may reinforce the sense of Shanghainese superiority and the fear that rising regional inequalities are a potential source of social instability.

The extent to which migrant workers are held to constitute a threat to the livelihoods of resident workers is a vital issue. In most instances, like Lynn White, I encountered 'grudging acceptance of migrants' (1994: 90–1); they were regarded as fulfilling valuable functions, for instance, as construction workers and maids and supplying fresh food as market traders. Generally these were occupations which were too lowly paid or unpleasant to appeal to residents. Despite this, residents occasionally expressed resentment that migrants earned more than themselves. I also heard murmurings of discontent that lowly paid non-Shanghainese workers were undercutting the wages of Shanghai residents. In Chapter 1, I mentioned a newspaper description of migrant workers as a 'guerilla force... stealthily entering [Shanghai's] factories' (*XMWB* 22 July 1993: 12). This article described them as presenting a 'threat' and a 'challenge' to redundant Shanghai female factory workers getting work again.

The owner of a clothing factory in Pudong, I encountered utilised this 'guerilla force'. He told me that he employed migrant workers from Anhui on a salary of 200 *yuan* per month – a level that Shanghainese would not accept. To circumvent *hukou* regulations he provided these workers' accommodation and meals. This employer had all the advantages of a workforce which was cheap, renewable, dependent, and had limited welfare entitlements. Information on the extent of such practices is difficult to obtain (including for government statisticians), but anecdotal evidence suggested they are increasingly common.

I have drawn attention to the coalescence of local resentment in the face of expropriations by the state. Two (perceived) instances of this occurred during 1993 – over the East Asian Games and Beijing's bid to host the Olympics in 2000. The East Asian Games were held in Shanghai. However, I heard Shanghainese complain that they were having to pay for an event which would bring national prestige, which for many equalled benefits for the Party elite in Beijing. This resentment was also apparent as China sought to hold the 2000 Olympics. Once again, a common complaint was that Shanghai people would have to finance this event, but that all the benefits would go to Beijing. None of these voices appeared in the local press, although some informants gained satisfaction from evading the overlapping collections for this event which were carried out by *danwei*, schools, and residents' committees.

In many countries such a sense of resentment, and the problems caused by migrant labour, are a source for 'racist' movements. Despite apparently fertile soil for assertive regional 'voices', and the persistence of senses of Shanghainese identity, I found little political articulation of these feelings beyond such 'weapons of the weak' (cf. Scott 1990) as grumbling and complaining, and occasional diatribes in the local media against rural migrants. An obvious response is that the Chinese state would prevent any such assertion. However, I also found little commitment to putative 'emblems' of ethnic identity such as the dialect.

Despite the pride, Shanghainese sometimes expressed in their dialect I found no evidence of a political assertion of Shanghainese identity, such as a desire to actively promote or propagate the dialect. For instance, I never heard anybody complain about the lack of media in Shanghai dialect. Young people greatly appreciated popular music in Cantonese dialect and *putonghua*, but when I ventured the possibility of a pop song in Shanghai dialect this was invariably greeted with derision. In the case of *huju* – Shanghai opera – my informants described it as 'Shanghai *wenhua*', but also as inferior to Beijing opera, and as appealing only to 'Shanghai's peasants' and 'those without *wenhua*'. In addition, if people used Shanghai dialect on the radio or television they frequently apologised for this, saying that their inadequacy in *putonghua* (often due to lack of practice) made it easier for them to use the dialect.

Intellectuals tended to speak *putonghua* with their children. They considered facility in *putonghua* as the child's route to success, and seemed to feel at most only a twinge of regret that their children did not, and sometimes could not, speak the dialect. It seemed that their identity as parents overrode that of being Shanghainese. Grillo remarks that in some cases certain ways of speaking have considerable prestige – such as upper-class English – but are not always universally admired or respected (1989: 171). In Shanghai, by contrast, many Shanghainese told me that they liked the Beijing dialect to which *putonghua* is closely related.

Reactions to my own attempts to study the dialect were informative.[25] They highlight the perception, and it seems acceptance, that *putonghua* is the speech of education, knowledge, and ultimately power, whilst the dialect is 'only for conversation'. If I tried to use the dialect people were pleased. But if I suggested that I wanted to study it in an academic context this usually provoked disbelief and bemusement. If my wish to study the dialect was taken seriously I would usually be told that this was a waste of time 'because Shanghainese can all speak *putonghua*.' If 'being Shanghainese' is to include a political dimension one would expect more commitment to 'Shanghai culture'.

In private conversations people occasionally suggested that Shanghai would be more prosperous if it were independent. One academic I spoke with felt that China should split up into its provinces. He considered this necessary because

'China is ossified and bloated. With it being so large, the economic and political problems are too hard to deal with.' However, he added that few acquaintances shared this idea, nor would he dare say this in class since students would inform the authorities and get him into trouble. A scientific research worker also considered it 'a shame that Shanghai is not independent, it could overtake Hong Kong if it was.' However, she considered such a development out of the question, not least because Shanghai gives so much money to the central government.

It seemed that whilst national expropriations aroused resentment, and migrant workers could stimulate a sense of Shanghaineseness, the sense of 'all being Chinese' was powerful enough to preclude the development of an assertive regionalism in Shanghai. I found no evidence of local ethnicity taking on 'the natural appearance of an autonomous force, a "principle" capable of determining the course of social life' (Comaroff 1987: 313). With a local family I watched the special programme broadcast during the Mid-Autumn Festival. The programme included selections of operas from different parts of China. As we watched, one of the family commented that the stories acted out in various dramas were the same all over China, but that the style in which they are acted out differs. I suggest that this is a highly apposite analogy for the relationship between 'Chinese' and Shanghainese identities.

Further consequences of intra-national porousness

If increasing decentralisation and the influx of migrants tended to enhance a sense of Shanghai distinctiveness, there were other consequences of the increasing porousness of Shanghai's boundaries in the reform era which may pull in a different direction. Alongside the inflow of migrants was a broader flow of people both into and out of the city. For instance, with rising prosperity and reduced travel restrictions Shanghainese could now leave the city on business trips, as tourists, or honeymooners. In the late 1980s and early 1990s some Shanghainese headed for 'the south' – the frontier regions of Shenzhen and Guangdong which, because of their early economic liberalisation, had become a preferred destination for economic migrants from Shanghai. In many respects, the differences between Shanghai and other parts of China, especially other coastal regions, were becoming less distinct.

Although many people I interviewed gave their *laojia* (home place) as somewhere out of Shanghai, the degree of interaction people had with their *laojia* varied considerably. Relationships between Shanghai households and provincial relatives occurred along a scale from non-existent to frequent, extensive, and intensive relationships. The latter were most likely among first-generation migrants, especially if they were influential in some respect. In some instances the destruction of tombs in rural areas by Red Guards during the Cultural Revolution had severed vestigial ritual links with the countryside.

The relaxation of travel restrictions has enabled visits to and from the countryside to be much more frequent. Amongst one first-generation migrant family in my acquaintance, interaction with rural relatives in Anhui was intense. Along ties of relatedness flowed information, goods and people, with frequent visits by both maternal and paternal relatives. The father had moved to Shanghai in the 1950s. He maintained links with Anhuinese friends who had come to Shanghai at the same time. He also remained embedded in a complex web of personal relationships with rural relations. This included frequent reciprocal visits on ritual and festive occasions, notably Spring Festival and funerals. Visits, with or without notice, by rural relations – sometimes very distantly related – were common. The motives for such visits included petitioning for assistance in disputes in the home village, seeking help with medical treatment, or to gain access to Shanghai educational establishments. His house was also a place to stay while visiting Shanghai.

The already high degree of permeability in this household across the city/rural boundaries had been enhanced by new technology. This family had had a private telephone for some years and recently an uncle in the countryside had a phone connected. This direct link greatly increased the possibility for contact and involvement in day-to-day family activities and disputes. It is an instance of the way modern technology can allow 'traditional' ties to be resuscitated and/or enhanced. More generally within China, new technologies were overcoming the 'friction of distance'. For instance, the Shanghai share market, already an important forum through which the city has rewritten itself into the Chinese map, has an increasingly sophisticated communications network, including satellites, which link up many parts of China to the Shanghai market.

Between 1966–76 a majority of young people who graduated from high school were sent to the countryside for up to ten years. This policy gave almost an entire generation of Shanghainese direct experience of rural China. Men who did this are referred to as *chaxiong*, an abbreviation of the term *chadui luohu xiongdi* – 'brothers who went to settle in the countryside', and women are termed *chamei* – '*chadui* sisters'. Bonds of friendship formed in these unique and often difficult circumstances, which include shared knowledge of the distinctive language of the period, shared difficulties in returning to Shanghai, and similar age, formed a basis for mutual understanding.

Those socialised during the Cultural Revolution, and especially those sent down to the countryside, often claimed an inability to convey their experiences to younger people. Indeed, amongst many of the present young generation of Shanghainese I found an extreme degree of ignorance about rural China. It seemed that for them rural China was at least as much of a 'foreign country' as was metropolitan Shanghai for myself as an urban 'outsider'. Informal gatherings among former rusticated youth were common. I vividly recall an afternoon spent with a group of former rusticated youth as they sang along to karaoke versions of revolutionary songs from this period (in multiple senses an alien language to younger Shanghainese) and expressed a piquant mixture of bitterness, betrayal, and nostalgia for their younger days.

In the entrepreneurial reform era, *chaxiong* or *chamei* may be an extremely valuable resource since they are now engaged in widely differing occupations, and in other parts of China. A glass factory worker I met in Shanghai had a second job selling bulk orders of leather bags and wallets along the Russian border in Heilongjiang. This trade utilised connections he had made during his 11 years in Heilongjiang from 1967–78. A successful writer who lived in a high-rise flat – where interaction between neighbours was usually minimal – told me that both she and her neighbour were former rusticated youth; she had gone to Yunnan and her neighbour to Heilongjiang. The writer felt a 'special feeling' for her and made up her redundancy money in return for housekeeping work. In addition, the writer intended to set up a company which would employ this woman as a secretary.

There were *chaxiong* and *chamei* at all levels of Shanghai society, including amongst the local Party elite which contained at least two unofficial groups of people – one which had been to Heilongjiang and another to Chongming Island. A local journalist told me that *Heixiong* ('Heilongjiang brothers') who were now high officials regularly met up, had meals together, and helped each other. Such groups of people who had spent time in the same place bear a resemblance to pre-1949 native-place associations, although in the case of these two groups of high cadres it appears that they only provided support for those already in positions of power.

Although Shanghai is very much an urban environment, the daily act of eating reminded people of their link to the countryside. A retired man told me that 'in China it takes eight peasants to support two urban dwellers.' I was struck by his conceptualisation of a direct relationship between the food he consumed and the physical labour of farmers. This sense is in stark contrast to the overwhelming commodification of food buying and consumption in the West. In addition, there was an emphasis upon the freshness of food; many items were bought daily and fish, for instance, was bought whole and alive. People's diet, therefore, was still largely dependent upon the rhythm of the seasons. It is interesting to speculate how far my informant's lack of alienation from food production was the product of years of Maoist propaganda. In the reform era as a whole, consumers are perhaps even more aware of the origins of their food since the re-emergence of private markets involves them in daily interaction with peasant vendors. However, such direct links to the countryside and the seasons have begun to weaken since the late 1990s with the greater availability of prepared, frozen, tinned, and imported foods.

Finally, in this section, I note the Cantonese influence upon Shanghai. In the nineteenth century many Cantonese were attracted to Shanghai – a stereotype persists of the Cantonese comprador. Older informants recalled that before 1949, Cantonese ran businesses such as the *Hualian* and *Wingan* stores. In the second half of the 1990s a Cantonese presence again became evident in Shanghai. Many restaurants now profess to serve 'Cantonese-style food'. Additionally, Cantonese breakfast eating has become popular; culinary recognition of this region's growing economic importance.

I heard contrasting views about Cantonese people. A young teacher stated that until recently Cantonese were looked down on in Shanghai. He felt that money had now become the main criterion for judging people's worth, and that since Cantonese are rich Shanghainese no longer look down on them. However, a more frequently expressed view was, as one university student remarked, 'Cantonese are *baofahu* ('*nouveaux riches*'), they have money but no *wenhua*.' A young Shanghai businesswoman concurred that Cantonese are *baofahu* – a term with a distinctly derogatory meaning – and added that, by contrast, Shanghai is an 'aristocratic society'.

SHANGHAI'S RE-INTERNATIONALISATION

> Mao Zedong had a closed-door policy. Deng Xiaoping opened the window and let the wind (*feng*)[26] come in, people could see what the West was like.
>
> (Joint venture employee's comment)

The increased porousness of Shanghai's boundaries within China has been paralleled by an opening to the outside world. In 1984, Shanghai was one of fourteen coastal cities granted special privileges and license to engage in foreign trade. In the 1990s Shanghai's re-internationalisation gathered apace and brought significant changes to the social, cultural, economic, and physical landscapes of the city. In direct contrast to the policies of the 'closed door' and autarky pursued under Mao, China is now being integrated into the 'world of culturally, socially, and economically interconnected and interdependent spaces' (Gupta and Ferguson 1992: 14). My own unsupervised visits to people's homes were indicative and expressive of this change; China's 'open door' paralleled by households' open doors.

A fashionable term frequently used as a metaphor for China's reintegration into a global space is *jiegui*, *jie* meaning 'to connect' or 'join' and *gui* 'rail, track' or 'course, path'. This expression indicates an acceptance that the Chinese state is willing, to some extent at least, to adapt its 'socialist road' to economic development to one where the agenda is set externally. As part of the process of *jiegui*, China has begun to make significant changes to its economic and legal framework. For instance, in 1993 China *jiegui*ed the Western accounting system and in January 1994 the dual currency system was abolished.[27] Another term used almost daily in news broadcasts was 'reach international levels' – often used of factory production quality. To *jiegui* in such ways was officially described as essential for China's economic growth and, for instance, to enable China to accede to the World Trade Organisation.

Re-internationalising Shanghai

> Vigorously develop Shanghai, open up Pudong, serve the whole country, face the world!
>
> (1 October 1993, National Day slogan on Shanghai's Bund)

A key aim of the 'Open Door' policy and associated legal changes such as the first Joint Venture Law in 1979 has been to 'involve global investors, traders and economic institutions in modernisation' (Zhao and Womack 1994: 147). Since 1978 there have been moves to decentralise the economy, in accordance with the general tenet that some should be allowed to get rich first. Local *danwei* and private businesses have been granted greater autonomy in dealing with foreign countries. For instance, they can negotiate directly with foreign buyers and suppliers. Shanghai enterprises increasingly look towards international markets and do their best to escape the rigid, vertical hierarchy which formerly linked them to ministries in Beijing. It is likely that China's recent accession to the World Trade Organisation will further this process since it will be of most advantage to coastal regions such as Shanghai.

In 1984 provinces were granted the right to retain 25 per cent of their foreign exchange earnings, and in 1985 enterprises allowed to retain 12.5 per cent of their foreign earnings. This was increased to 70 per cent for key export sectors in 1988 (see World Bank 1990). In the 1990s, state policies began to promote Shanghai as an international financial and commercial centre. Controls have been relaxed to allow free access for foreign companies, especially in the Pudong New District. Daily newspaper and television reports herald the arrival (or return) of foreign companies such as *Panasonic*, *LG*, *Sony*, *IBM*, *Unilever*, and *Volkswagen*. Between 1979 and the end of 1998, Shanghai approved 18,984 foreign-funded projects with a total contractual investment of $34.9 billion (Shanghai Today 2000). By mid-1997, foreign-funded enterprises accounted for 32 per cent of the city's industrial output (*SS* 27 June 1997: 2). In 1999, these enterprises accounted for just under 60 per cent of all foreign trade in the municipal area (HKTDC 2000). By early 1999, the *Volkswagen* joint venture, set up in 1984, had produced 1.15 million cars, and accounted for over half of China's domestic automobile market (*SS* 5 January 1999: 6). In March 1997, General Motors signed a joint venture contract with the Shanghai Automotive Industry Corporation to manufacture Buick cars. This $1.52 billion project was the largest Sino–US joint venture so far. The first Buicks rolled off the assembly line in December 1998.

New sectors are opening up to foreign investment. For example, by the end of 1996, 193 overseas financial institutions had opened in Shanghai (SWB FEW/0477 WG/6 12 March 1997). The retail sector is also increasingly open to foreign companies. The 'Open Door' has allowed foreign consumer items to flood into China, and Shanghai's restaurant scene is also being re-internationalised with Korean and Japanese restaurants and fast food chains such as *Kentucky Fried Chicken*, *McDonald's*, and *Starbucks*.

Increasing numbers of foreigners now come to Shanghai. Until the mid-1990s the living space of non-Chinese nationals was strictly controlled and mainly limited to university campuses, expensive hotels, or specially designated housing often located near the airport on the outskirts of the city. Unless they had relatives in the city it was not usually possible for foreigners to live in a local household or to rent private accommodation. Similarly, all smaller hotels had received instructions from the city government prohibiting them to accept foreigners (including 'fellow country persons' such as Taiwanese) as guests. I was told that this was for the 'safety' of foreigners.

Foreign enclaves such as the prestigious *Shanghai Center* on Nanjing Road operate as 'self-contained "mini-cities"' (Gaubatz 1995: 58). Even within university campuses there are walls within walls. Foreign students are generally not permitted to live in the accommodation for Chinese students. Instead, as at my university, foreigners had to live in a building set aside for their use. The only Chinese people permitted to enter this segregated accommodation were teachers and students of the same university, and even these exceptions were allowed access only at certain hours of the day.[28]

In the real estate market, certain property is earmarked for foreign buyers, and other property specifically for local buyers. The two types of currency also served to segregate Chinese and non-Chinese into different spaces (see Note 27, this chapter). In anthropological terms, this segregation could be viewed as a desire to keep polluting matter at a safe distance, an approach with many historical parallels in China. For example, one attempt at containing the 'uncontrollable' outside world was the segregation of foreigners to an island in pre-Opium War Canton. This segregation even included prohibitions on foreigners learning Chinese. During the 1990s segregation diminished significantly. Large hotels and the city's *Friendship Store*, which originally admitted only foreigners, now welcome wealthy Shanghai citizens, and residence restrictions on foreigners are more relaxed. Since the mid-1990s it has become possible for foreigners to rent accommodation in many parts of the city, and in early 2000 there were reports that the bifurcated real estate market would be unified (*SS* 22 February 2000: 1).

Foreign companies are now permitted to lease land in Shanghai. In 1988, for the first time since 1949, a plot of land in Hongqiao district near the airport was leased to foreign investors. This relaxation has begun to re-internationalise parts of Shanghai's 'face'. For instance, Shanghai's main street, Nanjing Road, now has shops such as *Benetton*, and Hong Kong's *Sincere* store has returned to a site only a few doors from its former nationalised store. Further along Nanjing Road the *Shanghai Center*, designed by an American architect, has an international-style hotel, a theatre, various Hong Kong stores including a *Welcome* supermarket, and a Japanese clothes store. In addition, the foreign companies which formerly owned many of the buildings along the Bund are being encouraged to return.

Technological flows

Alongside geopolitical developments and shifting national policies, technological advances have had a significant affect upon Shanghai's 'place' in the world. Until the latter part of the twentieth-century distances within China, and between China and the West, could only be bridged with considerable effort. For centuries waterways were the most rapid form of transportation. Before the construction of railways a journey across China could take many months. This made a coastal port like Shanghai effectively closer to, say, Hong Kong and Singapore, than much of China's hinterland. Even after the development of railways in the 1950s, a train journey from Shanghai to Urumqi in Xinjiang province still takes four days, to Yunnan and the border with Vietnam 5–7 days, to Hong Kong 29 hours, and

17 hours to Beijing.[29] It was only with the development and proliferation of aviation and telecommunication technologies that the spatial and temporal distances between Shanghai and other parts of the world and other parts of China dramatically collapsed. An elderly man reflected on this – he first went from Shanghai to England in 1926, a journey of 31 days by boat. In 1948, he made the same journey by flying boat in five days. In the early 1990s he flew to England in just over half a day.

Developments in transportation have been beneficial to Shanghainese who have taken the opportunity provided by the (half) open door to go abroad to work or study or, increasingly, as tourists. Similarly, since the late 1970s many families have renewed relationships with relatives abroad, especially in Hong Kong and Taiwan. This new mobility provides for knowledge and images of other places to be brought or sent back and for comparisons to be made of the recent history and current state of these locations and Shanghai.

Of perhaps greater significance than the physical movement of people is Shanghai's reintegration into the 'global space of electronic information flows' (Morley and Robins 1989: 22). Listening to radio broadcasts by stations such as the BBC *World Service* and the *Voice of America* is no longer described by the Chinese state as 'secretly listening to the enemy radio station'. Indeed, it was often encouraged by teachers as a means to improve students' English. On 5 November 1993, many Shanghainese tuned into the VOA to hear the results of the United States presidential elections. Increasing awareness of alternative systems of government, which appealed to many citizens, did nothing to foster support for the Communist Party's style of government.

With some informants news items from the *Voice of America* were a common topic of conversation. One man I spoke with was astonished to hear a VOA report on the arrest of two Chinese dissidents in Shanghai only hours after it had happened, a story not reported by the local media at all. This man considered it a big advantage of the 'Open Door' policy that the Chinese government could no longer block news. However, it was noticeable that broadcasts from abroad in Chinese were the target of jamming more often than those in English. It is as though the authorities considered it acceptable for the English-speaking elite to hear messages deemed harmful to 'the masses'.

The intersection of changes in the economic structure and new technologies has begun to enable new types of spatial relationship. An instance from a Sino–German joint venture demonstrates the way Shanghai's re-internationalisation has loosened the old boundaries set by the state and permitted new possibilities for action. A worker in this company, which had offices in most of China's main cities, described how, in 1991, the Chinese staff in all its main offices took industrial action by refusing to go on business trips until their wages were increased. They could organise this action because staff travelled often, knew each other well, and could readily transmit news in person or over the phone.

The 'colonisation of leisure' (Sahin and Robinson 1981) by new technologies has been achieved, above all, by television. There is considerable evidence that 'television has dramatically influenced the cultural and political consciousness of the people who live in urban China' (Lull 1991: 2). I discuss the impact of television and other mediascapes more fully below. However, both television and radio – with the important exception of recently introduced phone-ins – provide only a one-way flow of information. Newer technologies such as international direct telephone dialling, fax machines, and computer link-ups such as e-mail locate Shanghai residents with access to the appropriate facilities within an interactive global network. Electronic media of this type, which were unavailable to participants in previous protests, played a crucial part in the demonstration of Spring 1989. I was made aware of the potential power of the fax machine in Shanghai on the morning after the military crackdown on 4 June. Displayed on lamp posts and the burnt-out buses barricading Shanghai's streets were photographs of the violent suppression of the Beijing student demonstrations which had been sent by fax from abroad.

Since 1989, information flows have continued to expand. For example, in 1993 the *Shanghai United Information Network* began trial operations (*SS* 19 November 1993: 3). Using this network, computer users can access 500,000 Chinese characters of information covering 15 categories including stock market, real estate, trade and international affairs. Shanghai's integration into global electronic networks seems set to continue, not least because the rapidly growing telecommunications sector is now Shanghai's second largest industry and being strongly promoted as a 'pillar' of the city's future economic development.

The full implications of these developing technologies are uncertain, even in the countries where they were first developed. However, they clearly create a dilemma for the Chinese Party-state. It is relatively easy to restrict the flow of people such as foreign journalists and dissidents, and hard copy such as books and newspapers, but the circulation of electronic products is much harder for nation-states to control. The state actively promotes 'modernisation' – this includes importing the latest communication technologies, whilst attempting to control the 'spiritual pollution' it may transmit.

Elisabeth Croll argues that the perceived threat to 'Chineseness' through the import of things Western lies at the root of the now almost permanent 'spiritual pollution' campaign (1994: 220). The Communist Party may well fear that if it loses the battle to define what is 'Chinese' then it will also lose its ability to govern. This is increasingly an elusive ambition. Experiences in the West with, for example, transnational computer viruses, computer hackers, and digitally transmitted pornography provide an indication (and an analogy) for what the Chinese authorities will increasingly face. Moreover, it is often the young who can manipulate these machines whilst their elders may not even realise their potential. An informant's comment (itself borrowed from another cultural heritage) on the impact of *gaige kaifang* seems especially apposite: 'When you remove the cork from the bottle the genie flies out. One cannot put him back into the bottle again.'

Cultural flows/mediascapes

> Nothing in the policies of the Deng years has been more dangerous than the attempt to half-open frontiers and minds.
>
> (William Jenner 1992: 94)

There is abundant evidence of Shanghai's growing cultural re-internationalisation. Most universities have some foreign students and one or more foreign teachers. International schools have been set up and the European Union-funded China Europe International Business School offers MBA courses. An International Cultural Exchange Organisation, the first of several which describe themselves as non-governmental, was set up in 1986. In November 1992, the *Shanghai Star*, the city's first post-1949 English-language newspaper, began publication, at first weekly and since early 1994 twice weekly. In the theatre, too, there is a re-engagement with the outside world. For instance, I saw a stage version of the *Joy Luck Club* by the American Chinese writer Amy Tan – a co-production with an American theatre company.

Perry Link describes a 'post-Mao rush to explore the outside' (1989: 29). Several informants recalled the excitement with which they had queued to buy and devour each newly translated Western book in the early 1980s. Alongside and contributing to a general proliferation of popular media and a commercialisation of culture since the death of Mao, there has been a huge growth in the import of popular cultural items. These items include music, literature, television shows, films, advertisements, and fashions. Diverse foreign books and magazines have been translated, although some controversial works are prohibited and available only to those with 'connections'. Also popular are books and articles by Chinese migrants which describe foreign countries and their life abroad. The latest foreign films are readily available in the form of pirate VCDs; in early 2000 these discs cost just 10–12 *yuan* each. Imported music pervades numerous Shanghai karaoke bars and discotheques such as Babylon, DKD and Judy's. On my university campus the loudspeaker system, which would once have been devoted to political exhortations, broadcast a daily lunchtime diet of music by Western bands such as *U2*, *Pink Floyd*, and the *Beatles*. A favourite radio programme of many young people was a Sunday morning broadcast of popular music hosted by a disc jockey from Scotland.

Although cultural imports from the West have increased it is *gangtai* (Hong Kong and Taiwan) popular culture which is especially pervasive (see Gold 1993). In Shanghai, *gangtai* fashions, cuisine, music and so forth are widely emulated. This influx is affecting the Shanghai dialect; for instance, the Cantonese terms *da paidang* (street food stall), *da di* (call a taxi), *tso hiu hu/chao youyu* (get the sack – literally 'stir-fried octopus'), and *xiaosa* (with style, carefree) were coming into common use. Each of these terms could be construed as having a synecdochal valency; for example, *da paidang* indicates the re-emergence of small-scale private enterprise, *da di* the rise of a new moneyed class, *tso hiu hu* the end of job security, and *xiaosa* the new importance of fashion and the rise of individualism and even hedonism.

Of all the various cultural phenomena, television beamed into the heart of people's homes is perhaps the key channel of the cultural re-internationalisation of Shanghai. Television is a key medium in the 'mediazation of modern culture' (Thompson 1990: 3), which enables individuals 'to participate in a realm of social experience which is no longer restricted by the sharing of a common locale' (17–18).

The rapid growth of televisual media in Shanghai and the re-internationalisation of its images has had a profound effect upon residents' perceptions of their city and the world around them. In significant ways, electronic media and above all television, as the dominant cultural medium, re-sites and re-places individuals in new types of relationship to their own society.

Ulf Hannerz (1992: 223–4) raises the question of whether global cultural flow leads to global homogenisation or to increasing cultural diversity and the building up of national identities. I suggest that the consequences of proliferating media images are highly ambiguous. They can contribute to and construct both national and Shanghainese identities, they can also contribute to the deconstruction or renegotiation of these identities as well as providing 'raw material' for the construction of other forms of identities (see also Yang 1997). It is to these overlapping and, at times, conflicting potentialities that I now turn.

Benedict Anderson (1983: 39–40) describes the act of reading newspapers as creating a certainty of the existence of an imagined community amongst its readers. Drawing upon this approach, Hartley argues that television is 'one of the prime sites upon which a given nation is constructed for its members' (1987: 124). Television penetration in Shanghai is almost complete; most families have at least one television. With the lack of alternative leisure pursuits and limited free time it was evident that Chinese television 'diffuses its messages into the culture in a way that has no parallels' (Lull 1990: 145); the most common evening occupation of most of my informants was watching television at home.

There is ample evidence of Chinese television's role in constructing an imagined Chinese nation. Television presenters, for instance, frequently refer to 'the ancestral land' (*zuguo*), 'our China' (*women Zhongguo*) or 'our nation' (*women guojia*). These may be regarded as a constant reaffirmation that the speaker and listeners belong to a single homogenous community of Chinese people, all are members of the Chinese nation, literally the 'nation-family' (*guojia*). Media representations contribute to collective knowledges, creating 'a cultural resource shared by millions' (Scannell 1988: 22). A programme such as the variety show broadcast from Beijing on *China Central Television Station* on Spring Festival eve attracts an audience of hundreds of millions. It is an important site – a contemporary ritual of sorts – which provides its viewers with 'the temporal authentication of their existence as members of a synchronized national community' (Morley and Silverstone 1990: 42). Both the content of the programme and, arguably of more importance, the shared belief that all over China others are watching this same programme and participating in this Chinese festival, may be regarded as supporting the view of television's role in the construction of the imagined community of the 'nation-family'. The Chinese state actively engages in such a project; festive programmes have a lengthy build-up and each year attempts are made to make them more lavish and spectacular.

For political leaders, broadcast media have the potential for enormous opportunities and unprecedented risks. Skilful politicians who successfully master 'the art of managing visibility' can exploit this by, for instance, fireside chats and local walkabouts whilst danger lies in emotional outbursts and impromptu remarks.

Chinese political leaders have rarely attempted to utilise 'the artificial intimacy of the television or radio' (Jenner 1992: 184) to promote themselves. However, television's potential to mobilise popular opinion was dramatically demonstrated by Deng Xiaoping's brief public appearance at Spring Festival 1992, an 'act which electrified the whole country' (Pye 1993: 414). In subsequent years Deng's television appearance at Spring Festival became an annual ritual – in part, to assure citizens that he was still alive.[30] An important part of this contemporary iconographic ritual was the physical location of these 'appearances'. In the early 1990s, Deng chose Shanghai and Shenzhen, thereby endorsing the reform policies and focusing the national gaze upon events in these places.

Political leaders stick to carefully stage-managed media appearances and rarely appear in live broadcasts. Many are distinctly 'media unfriendly' and their media appearances can leave them open to ridicule. For instance, many Shanghai government officials speak extremely poor *putonghua*. Some Shanghainese took this as evidence of their lack of education (and hence unsuitability for their government roles). An instance of this occurred during the live broadcast of the 1993 East Asian Games opening ceremony. A leading Shanghai official made a speech in which he inadvertently, and apparently without noticing, welcomed the '*guaibin*' (strange guests) instead of '*guibin*' (distinguished guests)! I watched this programme with a large family group – many people had been given the day off and told to stay indoors so as to keep the streets clear – who all burst into laughter at this error.

Television images may re-orientate viewers' perceptions of their community in unexpected ways. In Britain I watched a documentary on Mao Zedong with a Chinese citizen. My friend had grown up in Shanghai surrounded by images of Mao, but found it remarkable to see him moving. In China, portrayals of 'the Great Helmsman' had always been static, an all-seeing, omnipresent icon. A moving Mao was not only unfamiliar but reduced in stature, a human figure with human frailties.

During the 1989 student demonstrations, television's role in constructing a national imagined community and the potential dangers in this for the Party were abundantly clear. Television images such as the film of hunger strikers on Tiananmen Square and the meeting between Li Peng and student representatives fuelled Shanghainese viewers sense of involvement in a national event. Further more, mass communications allowed demonstrators across China to pattern their protests closely on those in Beijing. One may find evidence here for the media's role in constructing a national community. However, the plurality of communities which are 'imagined' may be quite different from the one the state intends. In the months after 4 June there was a daily diet of programmes designed to convey the message that the demonstrations had been 'counter-revolutionary turmoil'. Some people I spoke with accepted this message, however, many did not.

It has become increasingly difficult for the Chinese state to inculcate its message when many of the 'audience' are sceptical or indifferent. Recent developments such as the proliferation of channels, satellite television, and devices such as video cassette recorders and video compact disc players, all tend to foster a more fragmented social world than that of traditional national broadcast television. In an increasingly competitive cultural market place, with many alternative and divergent images, state propaganda officials face an uphill task to 'sell' their message.

An especially ambiguous aspect of electronic media is its ability to 'transgress national boundaries' (Hartley 1987: 124). In Europe, Hartley argues that this occurs in three main ways: the broadcast of programmes such as the Olympics and 'aid shows'; transnational ownership and control of production and distribution; and international sales of programmes. In Shanghai, the broadcasting of 'global events' has begun to transgress China's national boundaries. However, as consideration of Hartley's example of the Olympics suggests, the impact of this is ambiguous. Such events may bolster the national imagined community; the Chinese government places great stress upon sports events and the achievement of national success in them. China's success in the Sydney 2000 Olympics was widely trumpeted as evidence of China's international status and prestige, and it afforded an opportunity to re-energise the campaign to bring the 2008 Olympics to China. Conversely, events such as the July 1985 Live Aid concert, which was screened to one billion viewers in 150 countries including China, may appeal to 'the ability to feel affinities across national, ethnic and cultural divisions, to imagine a community beyond the boundaries of the known' (Hebdige 1988: 219).[31]

Political controls still prevent transnational ownership within China. However, there is considerable screening of foreign-made programmes. Where Cultural Revolution China had a strictly controlled and limited range of images the reform era has ushered in a vast increase in the range, availability, and divergence of images. Recently imported television programmes include an American comedy serial *Growing Pains*, a British comedy serial *Some Mothers Do 'Ave 'Em*, and regular screening of British football matches. As I noted in Chapter 1, the influx of images from other countries had a profound effect upon many Shanghainese. Not only were viewers dismayed by the glaring disparities in living standards, but they also noted discrepancies between the style, genre, and content of foreign and the Chinese media. Images of the West and wealthier Asian 'tiger' economies, which were clearly at odds with official pronouncements, contributed to an undermining of the Party's credibility at the same time as providing alternative images of how things were or could be.

The extent to which foreign ideas and genres now influence Chinese programmes is also extremely significant. The influential and controversial *River Elegy* series was an obvious instance of this. The series format drew heavily upon Western television documentary styles. In addition, the script referred to an extensive range of Western ideas which formerly could not have been voiced – Marxism, of course, had been an exception – and used them to analyse China's current situation. A middle school teacher told me that students had demonstrated in 1989 because of changes brought about by *gaige kaifang*. Above all, she believed, 'before the reforms people heard and saw nothing about the outside world. Now they could compare with the rest of the world and see China's true state.'

More generally, global communication systems 'lay an abstract space over and across territorial configurations' which renders the very idea of boundary, such as the frontier of the nation-state problematical (Morley and Robins 1989: 23). In Shanghai, for instance, the number of television satellite dishes is increasing. These enable viewers to watch, for example, broadcasts of *Star Television* from Hong Kong. Satellite television is common in expensive hotels, companies, and newspaper offices. Private homes may also have satellite television, even though it was supposedly illegal to install personal satellite dishes. Satellite television is subject to other indirect restrictions. For instance, *Star Television* has sought to safeguard its access to the mainland China market by reducing the sex and violence content of its broadcasts and reducing news coverage. These moves included *Star* dropping *BBC World Television* from its broadcasts following the Chinese government's criticism of BBC programmes deemed critical of the regime. As an executive of *Star* commented wryly, in China 'no news is good news' (BBC2, 20 February 1995).

The demonstrations of May–June 1989 provided ample evidence of the way in which television 'enables individuals to experience events which take place in locales that are spatially and temporally remote, and this experience may in turn inform or stimulate forms of action or response on the part of recipients' (Thompson 1990: 17). The demonstrators were aware that their political drama had a global audience and at times played their role accordingly.[32] The style of the demonstrations was clearly affected by foreign symbols (see Pieke 1996: 200; Wark 1993; Watson 1992: 79–80). Chinese student demonstrators adopted headbands with slogans written on them, a practice they had seen on television film of demonstrations in Korea and Japan. Shanghai students had their own 'Goddess of Liberty', a copy of the statue which had been placed in Tiananmen Square by Beijing students, and which in turn was modelled on the American Statue of Liberty. Many banners had slogans in English, clearly an attempt to appeal to an international television audience. Theorists such as Joshua Meyrowitz would take this as evidence that electronic media have 'homogenised places and experiences' (1985: viii). The replication of the same images and products in different places may give this appearance, but I would argue that the way they are appropriated, understood, and the effects they have may vary enormously. For instance, I suspect that few of the students calling for 'democracy' during demonstrations in 1989 wished to enfranchise China's rural population. Moreover, the eclectic array of borrowed cultural forms from diverse locations were reassembled to produce a unique collage.

If television images are ambiguous for Chinese identities, then what of Shanghainese identities? Is there any evidence of a strengthening of local identities, the 'recreation, the reconstruction of imaginary, knowable places in the face of the global post-modern' (Hall 1991: 35)? Presenters on the two main local television stations – *STV* and *Oriental Television Station* – frequently spoke of '*women Shanghai*' – 'our Shanghai'. This constant reference can be regarded as a means of both creating and/or reinforcing a sense, or senses, of being Shanghainese. During the reform era Shanghai has become a more productive cultural centre with far more radio and television programmes made in the city and about events which occur there. One consequence of this is that the local dialect had begun to achieve more prominence. This was especially apparent with the post-1991 proliferation of radio phone-ins and live television programmes. In these, local (non-professional) participants frequently used the dialect. In 1995, *Debt of Conscience*, a drama about the Cultural Revolution generation, became the first television drama in the Shanghai dialect to be broadcast nation-wide. Such developments, which are likely to increase as Shanghai's increasing prosperity helps to foster a cultural renaissance, may presage the strengthening of local identities and loyalties.

As with other cultural products *gangtai* influence was especially pervasive, with many imported serials and advertisements. Locally made television programmes increasingly copied *gangtai* formula. In the media, overseas Chinese were generally represented as 'insiders' but to an extent they straddle the 'inside/outside' divide. Cultural Revolution rhetoric which depicted overseas Chinese as potential spies would, presumably, have fostered a perception of them as outsiders. However, during the reform period the Chinese state has made a particular effort to reconstruct relationships between mainland and overseas Chinese in an attempt to attract investment. Investment by overseas Chinese has been crucial to construction throughout the coastal region of China. Some Chinese economists use the term 'greater China economic circle', including the People's Republic, Taiwan, Macao, and Hong Kong. From an ideological standpoint the involvement of overseas Chinese is less problematic than that of 'foreigners'; the state has a vested interest in stressing their 'Chineseness'.

The Chinese media often applauds the positive role of overseas Chinese in China's current reconstruction. During the 1993 Mid-Autumn Festival evening variety programme broadcast by *China Central Television Station*, for instance, the presenters made frequent reference to Taiwan, Singapore, and Hong Kong 'friends'. Acts were included from these places and the presenters stressed that 'we are all children of the dragon'; a description which emphasises common ancestry and hints at China's desire to emulate the economic success of the 'Four Little Dragons' – South Korea, Singapore, Hong Kong, and Taiwan. It was notable that Shanghai's *Oriental Television Station* has a separate section on its news devoted to events in Hong Kong.

Thomas Gold argues that the largely one-way flows of cultural imports from 'peripheral China' are 'redefining the essence of what it means to be a "modern" Chinese' (1993: 907). In the case of Shanghai, I agree with this to an extent but with certain reservations. First, I would add that it also contributes to notions of being a 'modern' Shanghainese. I gained the strong impression that Shanghai citizens often felt a closer cultural affinity to Chinese compatriots in Hong Kong or New York than rural mainlanders. When talking about Shanghai, for instance, they often compared it to these two cities, and never to cities such as Bombay or Bangkok which an outside observer may consider more apposite. An article in a local newspaper approvingly described Shanghainese as 'China's Americans' (*SWYB* 5 March 1993: 2). Second, there is a sense in which this is a recreation of a global Chinese culture which was disrupted in 1949. Watson (1992) argues that this is a new sense of cultural identity which has been created by such phenomena as global media. However, before 1949, treaty port cities such as Shanghai, Canton, and Hong Kong 'shared analogous and specific cultures and economies' and had more in common with other overseas Chinese communities than rural inland provinces (Bergère 1989: 28, 43). The re-internationalisation of Shanghai has reactivated these ties and electronic media actively facilitate this process. Increasingly there are 'overlaps and commonalties' (Yang 1997: 309) in the programming watched by overseas Chinese communities and those on the mainland. Moreover, as Gold points out, since it was Shanghai refugees who pioneered the Taiwan and Hong Kong entertainment industries, '[o]ne could argue that the spread of *Gangtai* popular culture on the mainland now represents a return of Shanghai culture' (1993: 909, Note 6).

A third reservation is that the influence of *gangtai* culture can be exaggerated. I found that Shanghai residents would 'pick and mix' the desirable aspects of many different places. Shanghainese often expressed rather condescending views towards such 'upstarts' as Hong Kong, Taiwan, and Singapore. Moreover, the notion that overseas Chinese are 'insiders' was far from universal. I often heard people complain that land in Shanghai was being 'sold/rented to foreigners'. Yet in many instances this land was being rented to overseas Chinese from Taiwan or Hong Kong. I noted above the appeal of New York; this was not solely for the Chinese diaspora there, but a more general attraction to New York as an appropriate metropolitan model. During 1993, an extremely popular television series was 'Beijinger in New York',[33] the first full-length Chinese-made television drama filmed on location in the West. Although featuring Beijingers, the New York setting may have had a special resonance in Shanghai, where residents sometimes described their city as similar to New York, considering both as cities of immigrants and entrepreneurial flair. The development of such programmes also indicates the way in which cultural boundaries in coastal cities such as Shanghai increasingly crisscross each other to form interlocking networks in which there is no single centre (see also Yang 1997: 313–14, Note 15).

I have shown some of the ways in which global cultural flows and the 'mediascapes' (Appadurai 1990) they create contribute to the sustenance, creation, redefinition, and/or deconstruction of an 'imagined community' of Chinese and/or of Shanghainese. These mediascapes also enable many other potentialities. It is necessary to inject a greater degree of complexity into the notion of a single monolithic entity which Anderson's notion of an imagined community seems to posit. Self-identification with various, potentially mutually antagonistic, imagined communities is possible. These identities can be conceptualised as akin to transparencies of varying density, hue, and content, layered one upon the other.

The proliferation of media addressed to different audiences at different times and places provides the potential for diverse imagined communities. I am drawn to Appadurai's (1991) focus upon the importance of the imaginary in 'imagined communities' and especially his emphasis upon the extent to which mass media images 'present a rich, ever-changing store of possible lives' (197). Alongside membership of an imagined community of mainland Chinese people and/or Shanghainese, the same participant could also be part of an imagined community, for example, of film fans (the live Oscars), international football fans (watching British football matches is very popular), old people (reading *Shanghai Old People's Newspaper – Shanghai Lao Nian Bao*), or a transnational Chinese community (watching *Star* satellite television, for example). Shanghai radio had hourly updates of share prices on the Shanghai exchange and the major world stock markets. This could contribute to the imaginary construction of a community of Shanghainese share dealers and/or members of a global financial market.

In Shanghai today, the 'images, ideas, and opportunities that have come from elsewhere' (Appadurai 1991: 199) include those provided by the reintroduction and rapid growth of increasingly sophisticated advertising. This plays an important role in fostering aspirational identities. Television programmes, especially at peak times, are framed and interspersed by advertisements, often for products made by foreign companies. Viewers are enticed by *Marlborough* cigarettes, *Hitachi* video recorders, *Colgate* toothpaste, and *Omo* washing-powder – one of the latter's advertisements being a direct translation of a British advert from the 1960s. Often the rights to screen popular (usually American) films and series are sold cheaply to Shanghai television stations on the condition that adjacent advertising slots are filled by advertisements of the distributors' choosing. As advertisers begin to target specific audiences this provides material for the construction of imagined communities of consumer identities – for instance, of *Nike* wearers or *Marlborough* smokers – and reinforces differences between groups.

To posit the potentiality for diverse imagined communities does not, of course, tell us the extent to which an individual 'buys into' any particular community or communities – we cannot simply *read* this from the content. For instance, although the front-page of *Xinmin Wanbao* generally replicated that of the main national papers, many people told me that they 'never read the front-page'. Additionally, like Andrew Nathan, I found many 'decipherers and skeptics' who when viewing Chinese media 'often reached conclusions opposite from those intended for them' (1986: 180).[34] Belonging is multifaceted and subject to flux. Electronic media's role in forming, sustaining and recreating identities is complex. As Peter Dahlgren found with television news, even this single mode of broadcasting 'facilitates a plurality of subjectivities which can become mobilised in different settings' (1988: 297–8). Taking television viewing as an analogy for identity, sometimes one is thoroughly captivated by a single programme, at other times one is torn between different channels, a remote control can be used to zap from channel to channel, one's attention may drift on and off a programme, people may talk over or engage in some other activity whilst it is on.

Often the appeal of *gangtai* culture was its stress upon individual emotion, fun, and relaxation (Gold 1993: 913–14). In this way 'it helps to carve out a private sphere' and 'institutionalizes the zone of indifference' (924). For instance, when I asked informants about the appeal of karaoke I was invariably told that it gave people an opportunity to *fahui* – to give full rein to their feelings.

China's largest disco, JJ's, opened on Shanghai's Yanan Road in 1992. JJ's has room for 1,000 people – in Asia only a disco in Tokyo was larger – and was set up by an American overseas Chinese. The lasers, stroboscopes, video displays, music, and disc jockeys were all imported. One fan commented that JJ's was an example of something good that had come out of the *kaifang* policy, adding that previously in Shanghai the only modern discos were in tourist hotels which required FEC for the entrance fee. By contrast, JJ's was open to 'ordinary Shanghai people' because one could also pay in *renminbi*. However, the entrance fee (27 FEC or 32 RMB) made it the domain of the relatively affluent such as joint venture employees or business people. Moreover, like many other cultural imports, its appeal was almost exclusively to the young. These new cultural phenomena (fashion was another) served to create and contribute to a growing cultural divide between young and old – the authorities being firmly in the latter camp. Visits by popular singers from Taiwan and Hong Kong also attracted the relatively affluent young. A new word – *fashaoyou* (literally 'fevered-friends') – had been introduced from Hong Kong to describe the behaviour of fervent fans. Fans paid touts up to 400 *yuan* for tickets originally priced at 100 *yuan*, behaviour which provoked incomprehension among older generations. By contrast, at performances of Shanghai opera (*huju*) – where audiences tended to be elderly – tickets priced at 10 *yuan* could often be bought for just 2 *yuan*.

Dick Hebdige (1988) argues that for British working class youth in the 1950s and 1960s American and Italian products provided a space in which oppositional meanings to the dominant traditions of British culture could be negotiated and expressed. For these young people American popular culture 'offer[ed] a rich iconography, a set of symbols, objects and artefacts which [could] be assembled and re-assembled by different groups in a literally limitless number of combinations' (ibid.: 74). Similarly, in the emergent youth culture of contemporary Shanghai, youngsters appropriated commodities, especially from America and Hong Kong, 'to mark out aspirational differences in the social domain through the invocation of an exotic elsewhere' (ibid.: 9). Some of Shanghai's more luxuriant bars and discos, for instance, replicate exotic locations – ancient Egypt at one, an Irish pub at another, and are fine examples of 'the unyoking of imagination from place' (Appadurai 1991: 202).

It would, however, be overly simplistic to consider venues such as JJ's and karaoke bars as indicating solely a generational cultural divide. High Party officials were widely believed to make money from such entertainment centres. An article in Shanghai's mass circulation *Xinmin Wanbao* hinted at the existence of high-level backing for karaoke bars where sexual services and extortion took place (*XMWB* 9 July 1993: 13). The absence of follow-up articles suggests that it touched a raw nerve.

Spatial mobility/sociological differentiation

Shanghai's re-internationalisation and increasing spatial mobility is affecting sociological differentiation within the city. Foreign-invested companies, for instance, offer new employment opportunities to (mainly) young, well-educated Shanghainese residents. The economic and social position of employees in these companies is generally quite different to those for employees within state *danwei*. For example, foreign-funded ventures do not usually provide housing for employees, nor do they have official Communist Party structures within them. The need to mediate between foreigners and Chinese has allowed for a revival of the old role of comprador. A businesswoman in a trading joint venture company described her role to me as a *maiban* – a comprador. Although this term was not generally used, this occupation is returning to Shanghai in practice if not in name.

Often considerable status was attached to those who have studied abroad. To have been a 'student abroad' (*liuxuesheng*) is an identification one keeps for life. An academic told me that students considered it 'glorious' to obtain the gilding of having studied abroad (*chuguo dujin* – literally 'the gold plating which comes from having been abroad.' A dictionary definition says of *dujin* 'get gilded – formerly said of students who went abroad to study in order to enhance their social status' (CED 1988: 167)). He added that a PhD gained abroad – a *yang boshi* – is considered more valuable than a Chinese PhD – *tu boshi*. This is the re-emergence of a social stratum familiar in pre-1949 China and which was immortalised in Qian Zhongshu's (1947) satirical novel *Fortress Besieged*, which depicts the life of Chinese students who studied abroad in the 1930s.[35]

So many people have gone abroad that a term has been coined to describe 'left behind women' (*liushou nushi*). In 1991, a play performed in Shanghai used this expression as its title '*Liushou Nushi*'. Those who have worked abroad and returned to Shanghai form a part of the *nouveaux riches* in Shanghai. A local stereotype was that they can place the savings of two or three years work in Japan in the bank and live off the interest (*chi lixi* – literally 'eat the interest'). A fictional account, *Shanghai's New Aristocrats* (Fan 1992), focuses upon characters of this type.

Some Shanghainese seek to acquire a foreign passport. A young businesswoman hoped to become an overseas Chinese in this way. She stressed that it was not her intention to live abroad, rather, a foreign passport would enhance her status within China. It would, for example, entitle her to buy soft sleeper train tickets which were officially reserved for those with the rank of section chief or above and foreigners. It would also allow her greater freedom to come and go from China and within China – tax evasion was also a part of this freedom. Instances such as these highlight some of the new realms and layers of complexity which Shanghai's reintegration into the global economy has already begun to produce in the daily lives of its citizens.

CONCLUDING REMARKS

In this chapter, I hope to have given an ethnographic portrayal of the increasing porousness of Shanghai's boundaries both to global and intra-national flows. The consequences for identities in Shanghai of the shifts away from the pre-1980s model of autarchy with cellular honeycomb, and limited horizontal linkages are extremely ambiguous. There is evidence to support those who anticipate 'forces within modernisation that sustain and even encourage ethnicity's growth' (Burgess 1978: 278–9). However, there are also countervailing tendencies which fracture and deterritorialise identities. Identities in contemporary Shanghai are, perhaps increasingly, multiple and context-influenced.

In the case of senses of 'being Shanghainese' I have shown that there is considerable vitality to such identifications. The decentralisation of economic and political powers, central government expropriations and, above all, the influx of rural migrants, all provide the potential for distinctive and assertive Shanghainese identities to develop. Although this could provide the basis for a more overtly political assertion of regional 'voices' I found little evidence of this.

I have demonstrated the extent to which Shanghai citizens engage in 'orientalising'. The delineation of various regional stereotypes expressed by Shanghai residents provided a 'mirror' for self-definitions of 'being Shanghainese'. My findings highlight the extent to which regional identities contribute to 'different meanings of being Chinese' (Siu 1993: 19). Despite this, I also gained an overwhelming sense that Shanghainese identities were not oppositional to concurrent identification as 'Chinese'. Indeed, an indispensable component of 'being Shanghainese' was to 'be Chinese'. In Shanghai as in Guangdong, often regarded as one of China's most independent provinces, there is 'a definite commitment towards the larger polity' (Siu 1993: 21). Shanghainese may demand better treatment from the central government but as residents *of* Shanghai and not *as* Shanghainese. On this part of the China coast, and I suspect elsewhere in China, 'multiple identities exist which are mutually reinforcing' (White and Cheng 1993: 190). To adapt a vogue phrase, 'being Shanghainese' is being Chinese with Shanghai characteristics. In the following chapter, I disaggregate identities further by investigating the different types of representations which were made of those who live in different parts of Shanghai.

Horizontal integrations have, variously, helped to sustain, redefine, and/or deconstruct imagined Chinese and Shanghainese identities. Various 'horizontalising' trends are reducing Shanghai's distinctiveness within China. In the reform era, Shanghai is less obviously at the vanguard in comparisons of wealth and 'modernity'; until 1991–2, at least, many saw it as having been overtaken by Shenzhen and Canton. Additionally, greater freedom of movement within China has reintegrated Shanghai into flows of tourists, relatives, business people, and other transients.

During the Maoist era China's international frontiers were relatively tightly sealed; flows of information, people, and products both into and out of the country were limited and strictly regulated. There was little to challenge views of what 'China' and 'being Chinese' was or should be. Shanghai's increasing re-integration into global cultural flows has had far reaching consequences. In some respects, this is simply a return to the pre-1949 situation in which Shanghai was closely linked with other commercial entrepôts and the Chinese diaspora. There are, however, at least two distinct differences. First, contemporary Shanghai is no longer a highly productive cultural centre but, rather, is dominated by cultural imports, many from the Chinese diaspora in Hong Kong and Taiwan. There is an increasing 'compradorisation' of the Chinese avant-garde, for instance, in the form of contracts between Hong Kong and Taiwan music producers and mainland Chinese film makers and musicians (Barmé 1992: 13.29). It remains to be seen whether Shanghai can re-emerge as a cultural centre for the Chinese-speaking world; there is a great deal of lost ground to make up. There is much to support Tu Wei-ming's view that 'the periphery will come to set the economic and cultural agenda for the centre, thereby undermining its political effectiveness' (1991: 12). Second, new technologies enable a far more rapid and extensive influx of communications and images, although the degree of access to them produces new forms of differentiation.

Undoubtedly 'media-derived meanings can contribute to a sense of belonging and community' (Dahlgren 1988: 288). Skilful politicians may, for instance, seek to bolster the sense of shared national feeling through television programming. However, in place of a 'captive audience' government propagandists must now vie in the cultural market place (see Barmé 1999). The Open Door has undermined the Communist Party's attempts to control hearts and minds; both social life and public opinion have grown more disparate and autonomous. In fracturing the monologic state discourse, transnational cultural flows provide the material for diverse non-territorial identities. Ulf Hannerz comments that the 'media gives us more contemporaries' (1992: 30). For urban Shanghainese their contemporaries tend not to be the rural migrants on their doorstep (at times literally so), but images of successful migrants (or their descendants) in the Chinese diaspora and other 'modern' metropolitans. These models provide positive images of what Shanghai can (and many say ought to) be, whilst the influx of indigenous non-Shanghainese migrants heightens senses of what Shanghai should not be. The irony is that it is largely these stigmatised migrants who are building the 'new' Shanghai; a city whose 'modernity' and 'internationality' bolsters senses of Shanghaineseness which excludes those who have made it possible.

Global mediascapes facilitated by new technologies and allied with China's burgeoning media provided residents with diverse 'landscapes of images' (Appadurai 1990: 9) and a far greater range of imaginary others. Tu Wei-ming (1991) stresses especially the 'transformative potential' of the *gangtai* periphery. Whilst acknowledging the 'destructive power of the center' (15), Tu sees the potential for the periphery to participate in 'creatively constructing a new vision of Chineseness' (28). Amongst Shanghainese residents, who stressed the openness and outward-looking characteristics of 'being Shanghainese', I found a willingness to embrace cultural products from elsewhere. However, I conceive of these flows as also having more diffuse, diversifying effects. Global cultural flows and rising prosperity provides an increasing repertoire of, and greater scope for conscious choice in, possible identities and communities to belong to. These include a range of 'aspirational identities', such as consumer and youth sub-cultures.

Finally, it should be stressed that 'Chinese culture' and 'Chinese identity' are not monolithic, unchanging entities but dynamic and shifting landscapes. Those who predict the deconstruction of China, or the demise of the Communist Party for that matter, underestimate the ability of people to adopt and adapt. What are conflicting identities from an outside analyst's viewpoint are often non-discursive, not reflected upon in people's daily lives.

3 The walls within: Shanghai inside out

The previous chapter dealt primarily with the impact of flows from outside the city (*chengwai*). In this chapter, the focus moves to differential representations of places and people within the city (*chengli*), the experiences of inhabiting different kinds of space within Shanghai, and the ways in which different people negotiate these spaces.

Each visitor and resident will have their own mental map of Shanghai, a map based upon memories, gossip, and experiences, which is both contingent and subject to redrawing. My intention here is to pore over some indigenous 'charts' of Shanghai as they were represented to me by citizens of the city. Of particular interest are ways in which linkages were made between place and identity, between physical and social boundaries. Special attention is also paid to changing features of the work unit and home 'styles', and changing modes of transcending space.

During a long, free-wheeling conversation with a young working couple, the wife described her life and that of her husband to me as consisting of 'two points and a line' (*liang dian yi xian*). They explained that this description, which is also used in local newspaper articles, conveys the simplicity, regularity, and monotony of the lives of the vast majority of Shanghai's working population. Their lives, their time, and energy, were spent predominantly at home, the work place, or commuting between these two places. The adoption of a five-day working week in 1994 gives residents more time at home, but on work days many people commute for up to three or four hours per day, and this leaves little time or energy for alternative activities. My investigation builds upon this indigenous model and examines ways in which its content was changing and new alternatives, including new types of 'line', emerging.

Each of the two points, the home and the work place, are taken as 'enclosures'. Within Shanghai there is considerable evidence that both physical and social walls are being breached. One informant commented that 'before *gaige kaifang* Shanghai was stuck in a frame, now it has been loosened up.' Below I highlight trends for work places to become less enclosed and encompassing, and for homes to become more enclosed and bounded. I commence, however, by outlining ways in which the cityscape has begun to alter since the mid-1980s. I then examine a significant way in which places within Shanghai and their residents were differentially marked and assigned to an 'upper' or 'lower' status.

THE CHANGING CITY ENVIRONMENT

Shanghai citizens often complained about the over-crowding and lack of improvement in the city's infrastructure and physical appearance during the Maoist era and until at least the mid-1980s. In the late 1970s, in a city without high-rise housing, the population density of Shanghai was five times that of London. A typical comment was that after more than 30 years of Communist Party rule, the best architecture in the city was still that built by foreigners and the tallest building still the 78-metre tall Park Hotel built in 1934. Many informants cited this stagnation as symptomatic of a more general lack of change.

In the late 1980s, new construction began to radically alter the cityscape. By the mid-1990s, fuelled by real estate speculation, Shanghai was in the midst of a building boom. After years of neglect, there are many projects to improve the city's housing and infrastructure. In central Shanghai, residential housing is being demolished to make way for roads and redevelopment, including land leased to foreign companies. There are many new high-rise luxury hotels – a 93-metre tall hotel completed in 1983 finally exceeding the Park Hotel after half a century. There is also the widespread construction of elevated roads, underground railways, numerous shopping malls and plazas, and the large-scale development project in Pudong.

Informants generally anticipated that these construction projects would bring improvements and, as a factory worker in her early forties commented, this redevelopment gave her 'a feeling of newness.' However, in the short-term these projects often created even greater congestion, and Shanghainese described this inconvenience as the price they must bear to 'repay the debt' of no construction in the past. People expressed resentment that this debt had built up because Shanghai had contributed so much money to the central government.

Advertisements proliferate and a profusion of neon signs light the main commercial areas. Walking along Nanjing Road opposite the Peace Hotel with a local businessman in his late thirties I commented to him on the profusion of bright lights. Concurring, he added, with great approval, 'Shanghai is returning to how it was in the 1930s.' He paused before continuing, 'now China is the Communist Party's, and they have to make Nanjing Road brighter and the life of the *laobaixing* better than it was then, or it will be seen as a failure.' He was clearly full of optimism. It is ironic that returning to how things were six decades ago should be construed as the measure of success.

UPTOWN, DOWNTOWN SHANGHAI

Within Shanghai, local residents drew a distinction between the *zang tsa ko* (*shangzhijiao*) – 'upper corner' – and the *o tsa ko* (*xiazhijiao*) – 'lower corner'. The Chinese terms *shang* (upper, higher) and *xia* (low, under) are used in much the same ways as these socio-spatial metaphors are in English (see Lakoff and Johnson 1980: 14–21). Thus *shang* indicates political superiority as in *shangji* – higher authorities – and being morally or qualitatively superior as in *shangdeng* – high, superior quality. By contrast, *xia* includes things both physically and morally base as in *xialiu* – lower reaches of a river; low-down, obscene.

Although, as one informant remarked, it is not possible to draw a precise line on the map of Shanghai (see Maps 1 and 5) to demarcate *shang* and *xiazhijiao*, amongst people I encountered I found a broad consensus on how different parts of the city should be assigned. The *shangzhijiao* included Jing'an district and the northern parts of Xuhui, Luwan, Huangpu districts, particular roads included – Nanjing West, Beijing West, Huaihai, and Yanan West. The *xiazhijiao* included especially Zhabei, also Putuo, Yangpu (especially in the south west), the southernmost part of Xujiahui, Chongning, parts of Hongkou, and Luwan south of Jianguo Road (especially Dapujiao Road).

Shang areas may have *xia* parts within them and vice versa. For instance, whilst overall Yangpu is *xia* it also has places, such as Fudan and Tongji Universities, which are *shang*. Hongkou was generally regarded as neutral – as possessing both *shang* and *xia*. Most divergence from this 'map' of Shanghai involved the 'border' areas between *shang* and *xia*. One of the few sites over which there were contesting views was Nanshi – the district containing the old city. Some placed it firmly in the *xiazhijiao*, others considered it neither *shang* nor *xia*. One suggestion was that 'Nanshi used to be *xia* but is now middling.' To describe it as *xia* accords with a Western imperial discourse which found numerous contrasts between the 'model settlement' and the 'Chinese native city' – the former invariably positive and the latter negative (see Gamble 1991).[1] I speculate below on why the status of Nanshi may be rising.

I also asked how Pudong should be considered. A doctor responded that 'Pudong is really poor (*cha* – this can be 'poor' in the sense of poverty or quality), even lower than the *xiazhijiao*.' Equally typical was the response of a young man who replied that 'Pudong is completely different – this is a difference between Shanghainese and country bumpkins.' He laughed and continued 'once you cross the Huangpu River it is considered the countryside.' Similarly, an editor described the *xiazhijiao* as 'like the second world' and Pudong as 'like the Third World'.

On 18 April 1990, China's Premier Li Peng announced that a 350 square kilometre site, Pudong New District, was to be made a national development zone. There has been substantial development in Pudong, including the city's new International Airport. Additionally, Pudong has been physically integrated into the rest of the city by the construction of the Nanpu and Yangpu bridges, a Metro line, and two under-river tunnels. It will be interesting to examine how representations of Pudong change in coming years. Intimations of Pudong's changing status were already apparent. Until recently a popular saying commented: 'It's better to have a bed in Puxi, than a whole house in Pudong.' This assessment had begun to change – a young architectural worker told me that she had recently chosen to work in a company in Pudong. She added that her mother, who was born in Pudong, had been very keen to leave Pudong to study and work in 'Shanghai'. She commented that 'it's very different now, Pudong was seen as the countryside.

In the past Pudongers had to cross to Puxi to buy many things they needed, now Puxi shops are opening branches in Pudong.'

The basis of the distinction

When I asked people what they considered the origin and content of the distinction between the *shang* and *xiazhijiao*, five main types of factor were mentioned – historical, housing and environmental, socio-cultural differences, occupational and economic status, and the regional origin of inhabitants. Although different informants might stress one factor more than another there was a broad degree of consensus. In addition, the factors were invariably regarded as linked and mutually reinforcing.

It was often remarked that the *shangzhijiao* accorded with the former French and International Settlements. These were described as having been the most prosperous with the best housing. It was 'where foreigners lived' or, as a young teacher remarked, 'where people with status lived.' The editor mentioned above observed that 'Huangpu district is in-between *shang* and *xia*, inclining towards *shang*. It was where businessmen, compradors and those who worked for foreign banks lived. Therefore, they could not be without *wenhua*.' Informants considered the current positive evaluation of the *shangzhijiao* area as a continuation of its historical pre-eminence. The former French zone was the most highly rated *shang* area, the Japanese zone the lowest, and the International Settlement area in-between these two. By contrast, a Communist Party member in his sixties described the *xiazhijiao* as being the pre-1949 Chinese-run part of Shanghai. A resident of Yangpu observed that 'the level is lower in Yangpu. No foreigners lived in Yangpu.'

Some informants believed that the terms *shang* and *xiazhijiao* had only emerged during the reform era. However, a Huaihai Road resident in her fifties had first heard the terms used during the early 1970s. She believed that they would not have been used any earlier in the Cultural Revolution as 'then everyone was supposed to be equal.' A teacher felt that 'before the Cultural Revolution the *shang/xia* difference did not matter so much. Then people from these areas did not meet, so there was no conflict. But when Mao Zedong carried out the Cultural Revolution and, for example, people from Zhabei were moved to the *shangzhijiao*, contradictions arose.'

Housing, architecture, and general appearance were described as key components of being *shang*. It was noted, for example, that many houses in the *shangzhijiao* are Western-style and have gardens. One woman, a resident of Yangpu, observed that before 1949 places such as Jing'an were where the rich lived and that it still has many villas. She asked rhetorically 'how many villas are there in Yangpu district?' These architectural differences were still considered important, even though many of the foreign-designed dwellings intended for single households were now divided among several families.

Shang areas were said to have a lower population density and be cleaner and quieter. One man compared Fudan University – considered a *shang* area within the *xia* Yangpu district – to the *xia* Zhabei district: 'In Fudan's space people do not disturb or influence each other. But in Zhabei people are mixed-up together, for example, three generations live together. There is no quiet environment in which to study and improve one's *wenhua* level.' Traditionally several generations living together was regarded as the ideal family and accorded high prestige. By contrast, in contemporary Shanghai, the concept of 'five generations under one roof' is generally associated with over-crowding and families condemned by inadequate housing space and poverty to reside together. Space is of particular concern to Shanghainese because of its scarcity. In 1987, before Shanghai's building boom began, the downtown population density averaged about 40,000 people per square kilometre and reached 160,000 in the most densely populated downtown areas (*SS* 12 January 1999: 4).

Inferior housing with poor, often communal, washing and cooking facilities was said to characterise the *xiazhijiao*. A former resident of Huaihai Road commented that *xiazhijiao* areas are 'rubbishy places'. This informant recalled that before 1949 Zhabei, Nanshi, and Putuo had dwellings called *gundilong* ('rolling along the ground dragons') which were simply bamboo frames covered with matting. He added that 'this is where what we now call *mingong* (migrant workers) lived. Like contemporary *mingong* they did all the hardest manual work and Shanghainese, as now, had nothing to do with them.' A doctor reckoned that even though the old slums had gone, the population density was still much higher and incomes lower in these districts.

Architectural differences were closely associated with notions that there were differences of 'cultural/educational level' or 'quality' (*suzhi*) between residents of the *shang* and *xiazhijiao*. It appears that educational level and indicators of material well-being were correlated, as though the former legitimated, implicitly, the latter. Huaihai Road and areas adjacent to it were considered especially *shang*. A university lecturer in her early forties who was born and brought up on Huaihai Road felt that 'there were more codes of conduct there. There was a distinct demarcation line between us and those brought up elsewhere. We dressed more smartly than those in other areas, had better manners, were more civilised and had more etiquette.' It is interesting to bear in mind that this woman is describing a childhood in the 1960s, including the early Cultural Revolution, when the rhetoric of egalitarianism and equality was at its height.

A local education bureau cadre told me that in the *shangzhijiao* far more students pass university entrance exams than in the *xiazhijiao*. He added that those who go abroad from Shanghai are mostly from the *shangzhijiao*. This view was shared by a university student from Yangpu district who told me 'in my imagination I have the idea that the *shangzhijiao* has a connection to overseas. For example, people there have relatives abroad or have studied abroad.' People in the *shangzhijiao* were also said to pay attention to 'outward appearance' – to dress and make-up. As one resident of a *shang* district remarked, 'as soon as you look at somebody, you can tell if they're from *shang* or *xiazhijiao*. The latter are uncouth (*tuli tuqi* – literally they have 'the air or manner of soil') and vulgar.' More generally, the 'atmosphere' (*fengqi*) of the *xiazhijiao* may be described as bad and these areas as dirty and chaotic. A doctor told me that in the *shang* areas, to say of a neighbour '*dige nin si ho tsa ko leige*' (*zhige ren shi xiazhijiao laide*) – this person has come from the lower quarter – is to impugn their character and behaviour.'[2]

The pre-1949 occupational and economic differences between the *shang* and *xiazhijiao* appear to have persisted in contemporary Shanghai. The doctor remarked that before 1949 in the *shangzhijiao* 'people's quality and education were high and they had good white-collar jobs. Refugees went to the *xiazhijiao*, they were lower-strata people. Since 1949 there has been a continuation of this distinction.' The *shangzhijiao* were considered to have more professional workers and places such as Xuhui district were where 'old cadres' and officials lived.

A high proportion of industrial workers and other 'low-status' occupations was described as characterising *xia* areas. A young architectural worker told me '*xiazhijiao* are where industrial workers live, they are rough, comparatively poor, and people have more children.'[3] An academic's view was that:

> In Yangpu district there are many industrial workers and this is *xiazhijiao*. People who want face do all they can to move to the *shangzhijiao*, even though the housing there may be worse than where they moved out from. Some girls want to marry somebody who lives in the *shangzhijiao*, (laughs) so if you live there it's easier to get a wife.

A resident of Yangpu described this district as *xiazhijiao* 'because many poor people live here.' A scientific research worker remarked that in the *xiazhijiao*, people's incomes and social status were lower. He contrasted this to a *shang* area such as Xuhui and especially Kanping Road: 'If you say you live there others will know that your status is high. Government people with special power can live there.' He continued 'in my *danwei* the leaders live in comparatively bustling places, but the workers mostly live in the countryside. If somebody from Zhabei gets rich they will want to move to the *shangzhijiao*.'[4]

Regional origin was often mentioned in descriptions of the *xiazhijiao*. Specifically, a high proportion of Subei people was closely associated with an area being *xia*. A scientific researcher told me 'there are many Subei people in Zhabei and they form a small society – it is dirty, chaotic, and poor.' In popular stereotypes there is often a coalescence between regional origin and occupation. The comments of a young teacher were typical, 'areas were *xia* because they were industrial districts with many industrial workers and especially non-Shanghainese workers. Putuo district is still a complete mess, they're all Subei people.' Similarly, a long-term resident of Huaihai Road remarked that residents of the *shangzhijiao* area of Xujiahui described another part of Xujiahui as being *xiazhijiao* 'because many Subei people lived there.' It was notable that in describing the *shangzhijiao* regional origin was not mentioned. One young man considered that Nanshi was not usually called *xiazhijiao*, even though its housing was very dilapidated, because 'it is where "old Shanghainese" (*lao Shanghai*) live.' It appears that the dominant social group acquires a degree of 'invisibility'; the situation is comparable to that of the WASPS – white Anglo-Saxon Protestants – in America.

Changing views of the *shang/xiazhijiao*

A man in his sixties felt that the difference between the *shang* and *xiazhijiao* was at its greatest during the Maoist period 'because no new houses were built at that time, it was like two different worlds.' Most of my informants felt that the *shang/xiazhijiao* distinction had weakened during the reform era. In part this was attributed to the demolition of poor quality housing and the construction of much new public housing since the late 1980s. In the mid-1990s, for instance, the downtown Huangpu district was being depopulated at the rate of 10,000–30,000 people per year, with residents usually being rehoused in suburban areas. The new opportunities for wealth-making which the reforms had provided also played a part in reducing the distinction. A young architect felt that until recent years there had been a clear difference in wealth between the *shang* and *xiazhijiao*. Now, however, one could not say clearly where the rich lived since people, for example, in Yangpu might become wealthy through business. In addition, if they became rich and wished to buy property, most commercially available housing was not in the *shangzhijiao* but in suburban areas such as Hongqiao.

A young businessman felt that the concept of *shang* and *xiazhijiao* had also weakened because of a 'change in people's way of thinking'. He observed that:

> Money is now used to judge a person's worth. Previously *wenhua* was the most important thing. It didn't matter if you were poor. Manual work and service jobs were regarded as low-status, *xiazhijiao* occupations. But now this is not the case. For example, before hairdressing and bar work were considered low-status occupations, but now they may be regarded as high-status. If they have money this gives them status.

An interesting aspect of these comments is that the 'before' time period referred to is the pre-reform era when state rhetoric stressed minimising differences between mental and manual labour. Although I found that many service occupations were still regarded as inferior, this does not, of course, affect this informant's perception of a shift.

This businessman felt that Nanshi district was no longer considered *xiazhijiao* because many residents engaged in business and might be quite well off.[5] However, a former resident of Huaihai Road considered that Nanshi was still *xiazhijiao*. She agreed that 'many people in Nanshi are richer now' but added:

> This doesn't matter, these people are *getihu* whose *wenhua* is insufficient. People may praise them to their face, but in their hearts they still despise them and don't want their children to marry them. They feel that in the past they were really poor, their home didn't even have a single decent chair, now they're rich, but they're still really rubbish. In Huaihai Road many people have mahogany furniture.

This woman is using the 'traditional' criterion which seeks to associate *wenhua* with wealth, in contrast to the previous informant's stress solely upon wealth as a key signifier of status. Significantly, my female informant retained a strong sense of moral superiority on the basis of her upbringing in Huaihai Road, a commitment not shared by the young businessman. A mutual friend described the latter as having been brought up in the *xiazhijiao*, in a home with 'three generations living together.' As noted above, the traditional prestige accorded several generations living together is reversed, for in Shanghai it now serves as a synonym for poverty.

The persistence of the notions of *shang* and *xiazhijiao* demonstrates the failure of the Maoist rhetoric which sought to reduce differences between mental and manual labour and produce an egalitarian society. In practice, the relative status of different types of labour appears to have been unchanged even entrenched – white-collar occupations were still highly regarded and manual work and service jobs looked down upon.[6] It was striking that none of my informants used the term *jieji* (class) in the discourse on *shang/xia*. My older informants especially would have been well-versed in the vocabulary of class. It may be that the ideological overtones of *jieji* are just too overwhelming. The nearest informants came to this terminology was to use the terms (translated from English) of 'white' and 'blue'-collar. Instead, in the *shang/xia* discourse people used a geographical idiom to describe what an outside observer may consider as largely class distinctions.

In the previous chapter, attention was drawn to the way in which Maoist rhetoric sought to overcome urban–rural distinctions. Evidence suggests a sharp disjuncture between this rhetoric and the actual consequences of socio-economic policies which appear to have reinforced this divide. Emily Honig (1989a, 1990) argues that prejudice against Subei people persisted after 1949 as a consequence of state policies. Similarly, I would argue that post-1949 socio-economic policies also contributed to entrenching the *shang/xia* distinction. Lack of capital investment in the city enabled pre-existing inequalities to persist: for instance, most of the better housing and schools, and the main entertainment centres, were still in the *shangzhijiao*. The limited degree of social mobility, including inability to change jobs or move residence, of the pre-reform era, also helped entrench these inequalities.

The case of the lecturer in her early forties who had been brought up on Huaihai Road illustrates the persistence of distinctions. She described schooling in the Cultural Revolution as haphazard and limited. Her (well-educated) parents often kept her at home and educated her themselves. It seemed that whilst educational provision generally had deteriorated, families such as hers could ameliorate the consequences of this. In other words, policies designed to bring about equality tended to have the opposite effect.

A further irony is that the *shang/xia* distinctions only appear to have been declining in importance during the reform era, when little attention is paid to egalitarian ideological imperatives. For instance, the status of some service workers has risen and the previous correlation of *shangzhijiao* with wealth and *xiazhijiao* with poverty are beginning to alter. Architectural changes are also reducing the *shang/xia* distinction. Until recently new, better quality public housing was mainly allocated to those with (politically) higher status jobs or good connections. Since the early 1990s there has been extensive housing demolition in the inner city area with residents being relocated to suburban areas. Some one in four Shanghai residents now lives in a new home, with 1.5 million living in homes built during 1993–5 (SWB 1996, 17 January). These developments were such that by the end of the 1990s many informants considered the *shang/xia* distinction had ceased to exist.

There are, however, also ways in which new boundaries are being (re)created. For instance, in 1993 Huaihai Road was extensively refurbished and many of its stores now sell expensive, imported goods. A retired resident of Luwan district recalled that when he was young, Huaihai Road was 'very refined', with relatively few people, many jewellery shops and Western-style restaurants. It was of 'superior quality' (*gaodeng*). He noted that the city government intends to make Huaihai Road more *gaodeng*; 'we can already feel that this has happened, the *laobaixing* are afraid to enter the shops on Huaihai Road, they cannot afford the prices.' The role of boundaries created by consumption styles is taken up in the following chapter.

TWO POINTS: WORK PLACE/HOME

Although Shanghai's sixteenth-century city wall was demolished in 1911, regarded as a 'relic of medievalism, out of keeping with modern China' (Pott 1928: 192), many walls remain in contemporary Shanghai. Both *danwei* and residential areas are often clustered in walled compounds. It seems reasonable to depict them as 'enclosed' spaces. The spatial metaphors people used when talking about *danwei* appear to support the notion of them as bounded, discrete entities. For instance, a person who left a state *danwei* and moved to a joint venture was said to have *chulai* – 'come out' or 'emerged'. In a similar way, the unemployed may be described as 'remaining in society' as opposed to being 'in' a *danwei*, and laid-off workers were said to 'come down' (*xialai*) and to 'go to society' (*dao shehui*).

Shanghai has many 'new villages' (*xincun*) which were built in the early 1950s. The intention was that these villages, which were located in close proximity to residents' workplaces, would provide accommodation and integrated community facilities for workers and their dependants (see Fung 1981: 281–2). One 'new village' I visited was bounded by a wall; it had a nursery and a primary school, various shops, and repair centres. Until their teens a young person could easily live enclosed within this small circle. As in many residential areas, the people to whom the flats had originally been assigned were all employed in the same *danwei*. Socio-spatial organisation of this type produced a form of urban life that was 'unusually sheltered' (Naughton 1995a: 25).

The incorporation of a new, adult female family member through marriage involves a number of rituals which highlight the sense of a journey from one bounded unit to another. I watched a wedding video of one couple's spatial and ritual journey. As the bride left her home in Shanghai's Songjiang county, just before she stepped into the car, she removed her shoes and put on a new pair. The bride later explained to me that this was because she should not take any of her natal home's soil with her – it is said to represent either its wealth or bad luck (the bride was not sure which was intended). The bride also had to cross flames upon arrival at her new home with the family of the groom.

Although the bride's marital journey involved elements symbolising separation and the transfer of rights and obligations, it also incorporated elements which stressed the creation of an ongoing relationship between the two families. This was symbolised in a ritual carried out when the groom arrived at the bride's home to collect her. A 'custom of the place' was for the groom to present six gifts including a fish. When the groom left with the bride, the bride gave him eight gifts including the fish. The fish was especially important because it 'swims back and forth' a homonym of which means 'to come and go'. A participant explained that this signifies the hope that there would be a good relationship between the two families, with many reciprocal visits.'

Boundaries and enclosures

Both at my university accommodation and when visiting people in the city I often felt that the various entrances and boundaries were like Russian dolls – each one opened revealed another doll in a seemingly endless succession. At my accommodation the main gate of the university had gatekeepers. The entrance to the foreign students building had permanent doormen to keep out all Chinese except teachers and students of the university. Each floor had a worker employed to clean the corridors and communal areas. It seemed like a series of ever finer filters designed to exclude outsiders and prevent contacts deemed 'undesirable'.

On a visit to an ordinary flat I noted the following: the compound is enclosed by a wall, there is a gate through which a car could pass, but often only a small gate just large enough for a bicycle and rider to pass through is kept open; usually there are people observing who enters or leaves. Beside the entrance to the building (one of several in the compound) is an office manned by several elderly people. In addition, a group of people invariably sit in this area talking or knitting; the lift has an operator; each of the four quarters of each floor has a door which can be locked; the flat itself has a barred metal outer door and an inner wooden door.

William Jenner in *The Tyranny of History* (1992: 83–102) has written convincingly about the persistence of walls, boundaries, enclosures, and compounds of various types throughout Chinese history. He describes, for instance, the way walls – both literal and symbolic – have been erected to keep foreigners out. As I have shown in the previous chapter, many Shanghainese conceived of national 'walls' in a similar way to those described by Jenner. At another level Jenner describes the way '[o]ffices, factories, schools, and housing projects are walled or fenced off and gatekeepers put in place to monitor the movements of all who come or go' (86). However, my informants generally did not share Jenner's view that these walls were detrimental and oppressive. I suggest that the cultural significance of walls may vary. The potential for surveillance in the residences described above was clearly very great, but informants did not usually consider this a problem. Indeed people were more inclined to complain when these gatekeepers were absent, feeling that they enhanced security. In China, the degree of enclosedness appears to bear a relationship to status. In imperial times Emperors' bodies were enclosed within myriad enclosures inside the Forbidden City. This practice continues with the current political leaders who live within a modern equivalent of the Imperial Palace at Zhongnanhai. The homes of poor people, by contrast, are far less enclosed, and daily activities such as food preparation and hair-washing become public events.

Jenner notes the fear of *luan* ('chaos') in China. However, he overlooks the extent to which many Chinese people consider walls, boundaries, and surveillance as valuable and essential means to prevent chaos. Attitudes towards control may have varied over time in Britain. For instance, Forbes describes, with admiration, the degree of orderliness he found in Shanghai in the 1840s. He describes how most by-streets had a small gate at each end which was locked at nine o'clock and that '[s]ometimes each house, but invariably each street, has its watchman, who patrols all night beating a small drum' (1848: 21).

Many informants complained to me that crime in the city was increasing, although they considered Shanghai relatively secure and well-ordered in comparison to other parts of China. A young Shanghainese woman told me that she felt safe in Shanghai at night. She felt that Shanghai people 'keep within bounds'. In this sense it seems that 'walls' provide a haven, a retreat, a non-porous private sphere.

The work place (*danwei*)

Chinese state *danwei* represent the epitome of a socialist planned economy. Mayfair Yang's (1989a: 31–2) description of *danwei* as 'total institutions' since they 'oversee functions of production and reproduction, social welfare, indoctrination and surveillance' captures effectively and succinctly the nature of the *danwei*'s impact.[7] Under this (Maoist) model the *danwei* is responsible for the supply of housing, social security, medical care, income, and social status. Party cells in each *danwei* and the maintenance of personal dossiers on each worker ensured that the state 'penetrated into every corner of the shopfloor' (You 1998: 4). Associated with the *danwei* system is a high-level of both job security and worker dependency upon the enterprise.

A particularly high degree of inclusivity (and exclusivity) is found in large state enterprises such as the *Jinshan Oil and Chemical Plant*.[8] The Jinshan plant is like a small-scale city; it provides everything from nursery and primary schools to shops, recreational and leisure facilities and even a university, old people's home, television station, hospital, and crematorium. Workers may be encapsulated in the *danwei* at all stages and in all points of their lives. A Jinshan executive described this *danwei* to me as the 'mother and father' – it considers itself responsible, for example, for helping introduce potential marriage partners.

Danwei tend to be not only physically walled off but also to induce a degree of mental isolation.[9] For instance, a teacher told me that 'anything beyond our *danwei* is distant and we take little interest in it.' I had the sense of her *danwei* as not only literally, but also a socially enclosed space. A younger state *danwei* employee told me that 'when you enter a *danwei* yourself becomes the *danwei*'s, all aspects of your life are contained by it. It has no connection to society.' In many instances, the only way to negotiate the vertical hierarchies of such cellularised units was to utilise *guanxi* – particularistic relationships. Within *danwei*, the existence of a zero-sum relationship between co-workers could engender tensions and rivalries, in particular in matters concerning the allocation of housing and promotion.

During the Maoist era spatial controls over people were generally very strict.[10] Work units were 'multi-functional compounds' and the 'work-unit compound became a miniature city within its walls... entered through a guarded gate' (Gaubatz 1995: 30). A former 'counter-revolutionary' recalled how during the Cultural Revolution he had not been allowed to use the main gate of his *danwei*. Instead he and other 'cow demon and snake spirits' (*niugui sheshen* – 'forces of evil; class enemies of all descriptions' CED 1988: 499) were compelled to enter and exit via a hole in the wall designed for rubbish collection. He described the Cultural Revolution as a time when he had been 'denied the right to be human.' This denial was here symbolised by the prohibition on using the entrances and exits of humans. This man had no choice but to be associated with a state *danwei*, access to which was controlled by political 'gatekeepers'. Ultimately a suicide attempt was the only 'route' he felt remained open to him.

During the reform era the 'total institution' model of Chinese *danwei* has been undermined by changes in the overall economic structure and within *danwei* themselves (see You 1998). In the 1990s *danwei* became increasingly permeable and porous entities, with vertical linkages eroding and wide-ranging horizontal networks becoming more important. Both the proportion of workers in such *danwei* and the degree of inclusivity of *danwei* has decreased. Functions formerly dominated by *danwei* are being disentangled. Important changes include the extensive sale of housing since the second half of the 1990s, the erosion of welfare benefits and moves towards the introduction of insurance schemes to replace *danwei*-based benefits, and the cessation of political study sessions in most *danwei*. The adoption of 1–5 year labour contracts, first introduced for new employees in 1986, has also reduced job security. In the most extreme cases, *danwei* become 'empty shells' in which city employees are made redundant and production transferred to the countryside.

The new 'socialist market economy' offers workers alternative sources of income and status beyond the *danwei*. As labour increasingly becomes regarded as a commodity it is 'tradeable' and transferable. Workers are freer to move from one state *danwei* to another and between state and collective enterprises. There are also opportunities for workers to engage in sideline occupations, move to private companies, joint or wholly foreign-funded ventures, or to establish themselves as private entrepreneurs (see page 33). A worker in a large state *danwei* contrasted the lack of freedom in his parents' youth to his own situation. In the

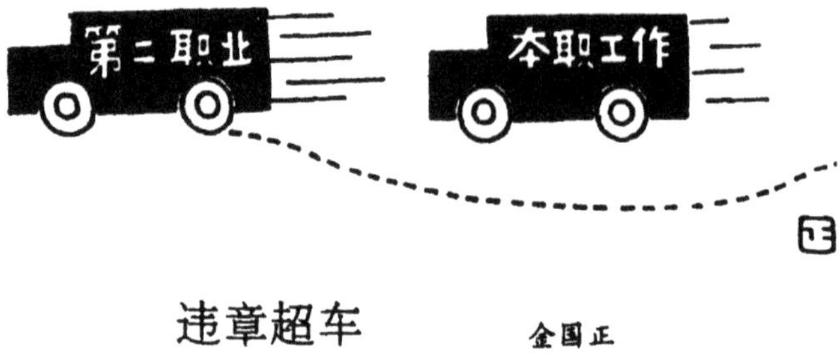

Cartoon 3.1 'Illegally Overtaking'. The first truck is labelled 'second job', the second truck 'one's job' [i.e. one's state allocated job].

Source: *XMWB* 30 March 1993.

past workers dared not question the authority of *danwei* leaders, now workers 'say what they like about them, so long as they are out of earshot.' This worker added that when leaders gave instructions 'people such as myself now consider, "is this advantageous to me?" Only if the answer is yes do I carry out the task.'

Danwei retention of individual dossiers still gives them an important degree of control over employees. For instance, permission to get married or for a passport is given through this dossier. However, it is increasingly possible for those with sufficient money to buy their way around *danwei* attempts at control; for example, employees who had signed contracts could break them by paying 'compensation'. Some of my informants had an extremely complex bureaucratic existence. In several cases, their dossier was not at their current place of work but at a *danwei* they had previously worked at. Sometimes retaining the dossier at the former work place was a strategy – good personal connections there would make it easier to obtain bureaucratic permissions. In other cases, workers had left *danwei* without permission and would deal later with the consequences of this invisible 'cord'.

Tearing down the walls

Many official institutions, including schools and local government offices, have *poqiang kaidian* (broken down the walls and opened a shop) in an effort to increase revenues. Units have been aided in this practice by the way in which, during the Maoist period, each *danwei* aimed at self-sufficiency, a feature derived from the Communist Party's origins as a guerilla organisation. A university, for instance, may have a bakery, printing factory, hospital, laundry, and a lorry division. With the reduction of state funding each section now independently attempts to engage in commercial activities to try and make a profit. The breaking down of school walls to set up shops is both a literal instance of changing boundaries and a microcosm of wider architectural and social trends in the city. In particular, it demonstrates the blurring of what used to be quite segregated spaces or spheres.

Since 1988 schools have been allowed to start shops, factories, and educational courses to make money. One of the first schools to *poqiang kaidian* is located in a busy part of Hongkou district. After unsuccessful attempts at producing and selling radios the school *poqiang kaidian*.[11] This development may be taken as indicative of a wider shift from a stress upon production to one upon consumption. One wall of the school was converted into 60 shop fronts – closed off at the rear where they backed onto the school – and these were rented out. This school was successful in its commercial ventures because of its location on a bustling 'city mouth'. In the first year, 1988–9, the school made 1 million *yuan*. In 1992–3, it made 4.7 million *yuan*, vastly more than the 800,000 *yuan* provided by the city Education Bureau to this key school.

The school's successful *poqiang kaidian* soon encouraged many other businesses to move to this area. This commercial success brought a danger to the school. The covetous local authorities wanted to relocate the school, knock down the current single-storey shops and replace them with high-rise buildings which it could rent out at high rents.[12] However, one teacher felt that this danger had receded because 'now everyone is going into business, there is more independence, and the state can no longer simply confiscate property in this way.' These comments are indicative of wider changes, most particularly the greater degree of individual 'space' and the increasing autonomy of social and economic life at the expense of state power. In the summer of 1994, the school set up a joint venture with a Hong Kong company to develop this zone. This venture was with a former pupil who was now a businessman in Hong Kong. A teacher noted that the school would fear losing out if it dealt with a stranger.

Commercial success has brought big changes to the school. The premises have been refurbished, teachers receive higher salaries and many fringe benefits – newly appointed teachers receive a higher salary than head teachers of many Shanghai schools, the library has been computerised and 'can buy as many books as it likes'. The school has bought large colour televisions, video machines, and a satellite television. In addition, 600,000 *yuan* has been spent on setting up a school television station.

In 1992, the school embarked upon another money-making venture. It bought a 5,000 square metre plot of land in the Zhoushan Islands and formed a joint venture with a Hong Kong company to develop the land as a tourist resort and conference centre. I was told that an important reason the school had entered into this project was because it had 'too much money and people were jealous'. By using the money in this way it would be safer because then 'people could not see it.'

This school is a remarkable instance of persistent privilege. It was built in 1913 as a private boys' school for foreign children. After 1949, as one of Shanghai's 26 key middle schools (out of a city total of 800) it was still marked out as a privileged place. Parents try hard to get their children into a key middle school. An education bureau cadre admitted that 'if children attend a key school they have a good chance of going to university. Otherwise they have almost no chance.' In 1992, at this school, all its final-year students won university places. It provides excellent facilities and can attract high-quality teachers. Whereas many university graduates did their best to avoid becoming school teachers, graduates of Shanghai's top universities were competing to be appointed as teachers at this school.

This case study provides a microcosm of many trends in contemporary Shanghai. In a literal sense, by 'breaking down its wall', the school had affected the appearance of the city. The school's vertical links to the Shanghai Education Bureau, and through it to the State Education Commission in Beijing, had diminished in importance now that they provided only around one-sixth of the school's funding. In their place, the school was embroiled in a much more complex network of relationships – both personal and contractual – with former pupils, commercial organisations, and local government departments. Although all the staff and pupils were affected in some way by the *poqiang kaidian*, the school tried to contain and control these activities by appointing two teachers as 'gatekeepers' to act on behalf of the school in its commercial transactions.

This example also highlights the growing inequalities within the city. As a key school, this school already received state funding in excess of ordinary middle schools. Its commercial success, largely based upon its prime down-town location, now placed it in a 'super-league' with few peers. Entrance to this school was still open to children in its catchment area. However, as with other key schools, parents may attempt to use the 'backdoor' – including the use of 'connections' and bribery – to enrol their children. Others may use 'household registration strategies'; for instance, one mother I knew moved her daughter's household registration to her grandmother's house so as to be in this school's catchment area. Shanghai already has several private schools and there is an incentive to make this a fee-paying school.

I noted above the reduced degree of enclosure of *danwei* in the 1990s. However, in the case of this school a rather different scenario had developed. This school was now able to offer a much more comprehensive array of socialist-type benefits to its employees. Thus, whilst its employees are now free to leave this *danwei*, they may be reluctant to leave since they would lose these benefits – they remained tightly 'bound' to the *danwei*, although the nature of the link had altered.

Beyond the *danwei*

Workers who leave state *danwei* separate themselves to varying degrees from the surveillance and control of the state. Joint ventures and foreign-funded enterprises are less intertwined with the state. However, it would be mistaken to conceptualise them as necessarily 'freer' environments. Amongst informants considering working in joint ventures, higher salaries, better promotion prospects, and more interesting work were often weighed against the *loss* of personal freedom. It was widely believed that foreign-funded ventures applied much stricter attendance regulations and expected more intensive work than state *danwei*. In addition, since many of these ventures did not provide accommodation, employment in them often meant that employees must continue to live in the parental home. Thus increased freedom in the sphere of employment may well be offset by less choice in where one lives.

Other possibilities for workers may offer a less constrained existence. An archetype of mobility were the private motorcycle 'taxis' which proliferated in Shanghai during the early 1990s. More generally, *getihu* often inhabit lateral or liminal niches between units. Small-scale enterprises within the city are spatially dispersed and differentiated and provide new locales to earn a livelihood. Zhapu Road, for example, a narrow street in central Shanghai, with a high concentration of private restaurants and neon lights, is described by some as 'little Hong Kong'. The re-legalisation of private enterprise has also allowed a recolonisation of public spaces by private traders and hawkers.

Wujiaochang, on the north east outskirts of the city, has many *getihu*. It constitutes a liminal zone, a place of rural–urban interaction. It is in such spatial margins, as with social margins, that change is particularly rapid. Informants told me that until recently this area had been 'rural'. Wujiaochang now has many street stalls – often run by moonlighters. Informants sometimes described this area as chaotic and disorganised. As such it can be contrasted with, say, the Hongqiao district around Shanghai airport. This is another marginal zone – it is where most early foreign investment and residence was allowed (and contained). A young lecturer described, with great approval, Hongqiao development zone as 'completely foreign-style'. From this and other conversations, it was evident that his view of 'foreign' included notions of modernity, progress, order, and organisation.

Those who had succeeded in the share market (see Chapter 5) also inhabited very different socio-spatial environments. Wealthy share dealers sometimes resigned from their *danwei*. They could choose to be based at any of the city's three hundred plus dealing centres. These centres, which attract clusters of shops and restaurants around their vicinity, are a striking instance of a new type of place. Share centres have rooms divided into various categories, with separate dealing rooms for large-, medium-, and small-scale dealers. This spatial hierarchy matches a wider process whereby wealth, rather than primarily political status, provides access to more space, comfort, and access to information. Access to the *dahushi*, dealing rooms for the use of wealthier dealers, is generally restricted to those with capital in excess of 500,000 *yuan*. It is also becoming possible for wealthy dealers to operate from home by telephone.

The different type of work place which the *dahushi* constitutes was evident in conversations with wealthy dealers. I asked two such dealers – one a retired engineer, the other a former factory worker – relaxing in the black vinyl chairs of their special dealing room, how they would characterise relationships between fellow dealers. They both felt they were quite good and believed that this was because, unlike in a *danwei*, there was no relationship of profit and loss between them. Thus, for example, if one person made money it was not at the expense of somebody else in the same room. In a *danwei*, by contrast, there was such a zero-sum relationship, with competition over housing and other entitlements. In addition, the lack of mobility in Chinese *danwei* meant that workers were often colleagues for many decades. This might foster strong bonds of friendship, but it could also mean that resentments and rivalries smoulder for years. In some instances workers must work alongside those who had denounced them or were on opposing sides in previous factional disputes.

I gained useful insights into small-scale share buyers in an interview in November 1993 with Zhao Huanan, author of the play '*OK Stock*'. Before writing this play, Zhao conducted research among such buyers. He described the crowded dealing room and the space around its doorway as a 'small society since it is composed of people of every *wenhua* and occupational level. These people have only one objective, to buy and sell shares.' As a place to interview people he felt that this small society possessed a great advantage; 'the interviewee is in a place distant from their home and *danwei*. He is a complete individual in this market place.' Zhao considered that under these circumstances people expressed themselves very honestly. There was a 'high degree of transparency because there is no relationship of profit and loss between share dealers. At home or in the *danwei* they would all have something they wished to conceal and would not fully reveal themselves.'

Social and spatial boundaries were also transgressed during the demonstrations of Spring 1989. For several weeks demonstrators colonised the city's main streets including the road area along the Bund. Whilst this carnival-like atmosphere prevailed some of the boundaries between Shanghai's vertically discrete units were weakened. Even though students demonstrated under their particular units' banners, there were many instances when barriers between them and Shanghai's 'common people' were visibly transcended – this was apparent in the way bystanders supplied demonstrators with food and drink. In subsequent conversations, local people portrayed the demonstrations as a product of the reforms and the changes brought about by the 'Open Door' policy.

THE INNER CIRCLE: HOME SPACES

> They don't put in much effort at work, (laughs) but once they get home they're really busy.
>
> (Middle-aged female clerical worker talking about Shanghainese men)

For many foreign visitors Shanghai induces a sense of claustrophobia. The slow-moving crowds on the streets, and the density of humanity jammed into buses and shops, confront even the most transitory visitor. Local residents also frequently lament 'there are too many people!' With space at such a premium it was, perhaps, hardly surprising that my informants could invariably tell me the precise dimensions of their accommodation. It was evident, too, that the family and home – which are conflated in the Chinese *jia* – were of central importance to most of my informants. Family structures in Shanghai exhibit a high degree of conformity when compared to a West European city. The vast majority of people marry and have a single child. Most alternatives to this pattern are either illegal or socially unacceptable – such as having more than one child or living together without marriage – or an indication of social failure. An instance of the latter would be

Cartoon 3.2 'The Last Big Dish'. The television screen shows that it is the start of the New Year's Eve variety programme.

Source: *XMWB* 22 January 1993.

a childless marriage, although some recent press coverage of a new phenomenon DINKS – 'double income no kids' – suggests a modification of this traditional view. Divorce rates are rising but still low, and often considerable stigma is still attached especially to female divorcees.

Material considerations conjoin with cultural imperatives to stress the importance of marriage. In particular, *danwei* generally only allocate housing to married couples. In Shanghai, as in rural China, the core kin group are, above all, those who eat together on key ritual and festive occasions. At Lunar New Year in particular, scattered family members should return home. The family eat and remain cloistered together until after the mid-day meal on New Year's Day.[13]

Inadequate housing was regularly cited by Shanghainese as *the* main problem in the city. During the early years of Communist Party rule considerable attention was paid to rehousing slum dwellers. However, after the early 1950s, there was little new housing built or renovation of the existing housing stock. In addition, an inflow of people contributed to a per capita decline in living space. Between 1949 and 1965 per capita living space in Shanghai declined from 3.7 square metres to 2.15 square metres (Howe 1968: 79). The rent burden, however, was quite low at about 8 per cent of average income.

Scarcity of housing constrained most residents' lives. In university dormitories, for example, seven or eight students shared a single room. The amount of personal space for each student consisted of a bunk bed and a small cupboard; they had to use great ingenuity to minimise conflicts and retain any degree of privacy. Access to housing plays a part in decisions to marry. Most young adults remain bound to the parental home by lack of affordable alternative accommodation. Frequently adult offspring have no separate room of their own. Since *danwei* do not allocate accommodation to unmarried employees non-marriage is rarely an option. Even after marriage a substantial proportion of couples still have to live with the bride or groom's parents while they wait for a *danwei* allocation of housing. It was my impression that many couples would prefer to have a flat of their own. Housing could, therefore, be an important criterion in mate selection. I visited a young couple who lived in a large flat (over 70 square metres) inside a compound of buildings belonging to the military. The flat was given to the husband by his father, a retired senior army officer. The wife told me that her husband's ability to provide this flat was an important factor in deciding to marry him.

The retired often take responsibility for '*madasaodaiban*', that is, to buy food, do the washing and cleaning, look after grandchildren and carry out tasks for the children. Elderly parents who still support their children are called *lao huangniu* – old oxen. Parents may speak of being fleeced (*gua*) by their married offspring – this may be said with affection or real bitterness. This *gua* covers financial aid and labour, including contributions to the costs of raising grandchildren. A grandfather described three generations living together as 'troublesome' and 'complicated', and complained that inter-generational conflicts over expenses and different lifestyles could only be tackled by the older generation 'keeping their mouths shut tight and their pockets loose' (*zuiba yao jin, koudai yao song*). In his estimation, both generations now wished to live separately, and he expressed his strong approval for this 'foreign method'. Developments during the reform era which may promote this trend include the rising level of young people's salaries – especially those of the well-educated – the increase in housing construction, and the emergence of a housing market. The ideal now is for the two generations to live separately but close at hand.

In a city the size of Shanghai there is inevitably a diverse array of living environments. Moreover, the experience and perception of these environments will differ in accordance with a range of sociological factors such as age, gender, and occupation. For instance, the spatial world of the elderly is often especially restricted. Shanghai's densely packed main streets and pavements are a hazardous environment for the elderly. Often the elderly are spatially marginalised within households. After their children marry, parents generally move into a smaller room and the new couple take over the largest room. The best accommodation is accorded to those who are the most (re)productive. A local documentary programme showed how an elderly woman slept on the balcony of her flat while her married children occupied the main room. Parents may have to spend part of the day outside in order to give the young couple some privacy.

Despite such experiential differences it is possible to outline larger trends which are under way in the reform era. In particular, as work places are becoming less inclusive and less bounded, I observed a tendency for homes to become increasingly bounded, discrete, and privatised. A combination of political, economic, and socio-cultural factors are involved in this trend and it is to the inner circle of the home, and an examination of these factors, that I now turn.

Privatising the home

The increased discreteness of the home was particularly important for those who had been persecuted in the past and whose homes had been subject to outside encroachment. When asked about the impact of the Cultural Revolution on interpersonal relations the starkest portrayal was that even husbands and wives and parents and children could be pitted against each other. However, the fact remained that if one could trust anybody it was most likely to be close family members. In these circumstances, the core family group could be strengthened as people retreated to the household as the only safe haven in a society full of risk and uncertainty.

Several informants described the 'reach of the state' as having been much closer to their everyday lives in the past. A number described how their homes had been searched by Red Guards. The fear of such searches must have spread well beyond those who were actual victims. Outsiders' control over private space could extend to the absurd. One family I visited had been searched three times by Red Guards. Three people lived in their two-room flat. This was considered too much space for a family with their 'bad' class background, but the extra room was too small to be given to anybody else. The solution was to seal up the room with a strip of red paper – with the name of the revolutionary group giving the order and the date – glued across the door forbidding entrance. In the same household, I admired a large mahogany dresser (an obvious sign of pre-1949 wealth). Unable to move this large, heavy piece of furniture, the Red Guards again resorted to the red tape, prohibiting the cupboard being opened!

Even when not physically entered, the home space could be subject to incursion. Neighbourhood Residents' Committees operated as low-level surveillance organisations which enabled the reach of the state to transcend the physical boundaries of the home. A member of a family which had been 'under the supervision of the masses' during the Cultural Revolution recalled how the head of the local Residents' Committee would deliberately do his exercises outside their window. He would rest his leg on the fence outside their ground-floor flat, ostensibly carrying out his exercises, but in practice watching their activities. As I comment in Chapter 1, Residents' Committees have now lost much of their overtly political role and instead concentrate upon running small-scale enterprises. This shift is part of the wider post-Mao depoliticisation of everyday life which has involved a general reduction in the number of communal activities. Elderly residents had been the main beneficiaries of Residents' Committees welfare activities, and they tended to be critical of the Committees' focus upon commercial ventures since this often brought a downgrading of community-based welfare services.

Furnishing desire – the urge to decorate

Many Shanghainese invested much of their energy and financial resources on their homes. A Shanghai resident explained that 'people place great importance upon their homes because the wider society has many things which oppress them. The home is a small heaven. Everything outside their home is not their world.' This informant considered the historical context important in this retreat to the home, remarking that 'previously outside the home people could not speak the truth and had no real friends. Outside one was fearful and without a sense of security.'

In these circumstances, the home offered at least a relatively greater degree of safety and security.

The stress upon the home as a 'symbolic investment' is apparent in the craze for decorating and home furnishing. The resident noted above described an historical progression in this. He recalled that in the late Cultural Revolution many people began to engage in hobbies such as making small gasoline stoves. This was followed by a craze for making radios and sofas, and then by home decoration. At first people made their own furniture. With higher incomes and a greater variety of consumer goods – fabrics, furniture, and fittings – such items can now be bought. He considered the emphasis upon the home as 'a kind of passive opposition to society.' However, he stressed that the individuals concerned would not explain it in this way. He associated this with Shanghai people's general lack of concern about things that do not directly concern them; some feel they cannot control things beyond the home, others are afraid of trouble if they do. He concluded that 'apart from their homes, people take no interest in anything else. The circle in which Chinese people live is getting smaller and smaller.'

Most Shanghainese have few avenues for fulfilment outside the home. The high population density and the paucity of cultural facilities – from sports facilities to clubs and more engaged forms of civil society – ensure that for most people home is the main site of leisure and recreation. Like Deborah Davis I found that this 'inward gaze' was apparent in the way household interiors were generally 'devoid of all connection to the state, the party, or the workplace' (1989: 95). Davis describes this as an explicit rejection of state intervention in private space and a popular resistance to state power. Although I accept that resistance to state intervention may be an *outcome* of these individual choices, I suggest – as the remarks of the informant above indicate – that this formulation exaggerates the degree of conscious agency involved.

Both outside observers, who often engage in a search for resistance to the state, and my own informant, may overlook other features of the urge to decorate. Many home decorators expressed great pride in their achievements. Only a fully fledged ethnography of home furnishing could do this topic justice but I will make a few comments.[14] Geremie Barmé contrasts the home to the outside world and the *danwei* which are largely 'unmalleable'; he observes that 'people with economic means are increasingly anxious to change their immediate environment, translating their visions of individual comfort and bourgeois life into their own apartments' (1992: 13.22). Even those with slender means sought to creatively inscribe their personality on their living space. One man, a true *bricoleur*, showed me the dining room, just large enough for a small table and chairs, he had constructed at the back of his flat. He proudly explained that all the items employed in its construction had been salvaged or obtained by 'connections', and could discourse at length on the origin of each.

New technology is also facilitating the privatisation of the home and promoting the atomisation of Shanghai into nuclear households. Television watching alongside the core family group is the dominant leisure activity. In addition, since 1993 air-conditioning has been installed in many households – in 1993, there were just five air conditioners per hundred households, by 1996 there were 50 (*FT Survey* 1998: 19). In the old-style housing high temperatures had a centrifugal effect, forcing people out of their crowded stifling homes and onto the streets where they mingled with neighbours. Air-conditioning has precisely the reverse effect; it only functions when doors and windows are kept shut.

A significant policy shift which was promoting the privatisation of the home and underpins the desire to furnish is the marketisation of housing. Until the early 1990s most residents had no alternative to renting housing from their *danwei*.[15] *Danwei* generally allocated housing on the basis of a points system based upon various criteria such as number of people in the household, age, length of employment, and rank. In 1993 rents were still very low; the rent for a standard flat would be about 20 *yuan* per month. However, at this time, a city wide policy began to marketise housing by raising rents and encouraging occupants to buy their homes.[16] In one 'new village' in Yangpu district, encouraged by being told that their rents were about to rise dramatically, some 70 per cent of residents bought their properties for just 250 *yuan* per square metre.[17] Even when new housing is allocated, occupants now usually have to contribute a percentage of the cost.

A commercial housing market is also developing. Real estate agencies re-emerged in the 1980s, but only flourished after 1991. By 1993, there were as many as 1,000 real estate agencies. A worker in one agency remarked to me that 'those who rely on salaries cannot buy the housing we sell.' Their properties were sold mainly to those with overseas connections or who had earned money abroad, overseas Chinese, or wealthy businessmen such as the bosses of private enterprises. Initially housing had to be paid for in advance. However, with the sale of public and *danwei* housing, a more vigorous local housing market has begun to develop. In 1998, China's newly appointed premier, Zhu Rongji, announced the commercialisation of China's property market (*FT* 20 March 1998: 1). This top-level endorsement provided a qualitative boost to home-ownership in China, it also signalled the widespread availability of mortgages (*FT* 26 May 1998: 4). Individual home mortgages can be secured for a maximum of 70 per cent of the purchase price and can have terms of up to 20 years. There are also tax incentives and compulsory salary based housing funds to encourage home ownership. In 1998, sales of housing in Shanghai totalled more than 7 million square metres, an increase of 80 per cent over 1997 (*SS* 29 January 1999: 6). In 1999, local buyers purchased a total area of 11.29 million square metres of property in Shanghai, an increase of 68.3 per cent over 1998 (*SS* 11 April 2000: 11).

Changing home styles

During the reform era there has been a substantial increase in state investment in housing. More new housing was built in Shanghai between 1979–89 (40 million square metres) than between 1950–80 (23.13 million square metres) (see Davis 1989: 99; Pellow 1993: 399). The city government has set targets to rehouse all those in cramped living conditions; one target was to rehouse 31,808 families with less than 2.5 square metres of living space per person by the end of 1992

(*SS* 18 December 1992: 2). A goal for the end of 1994 was to rehouse all those with less than 4 square metres per person – although at the end of 1998 over 10,000 families in this situation had yet to be rehoused (*SS* 12 January 1999: 4). Average living space per person rose from 7.21 square metres per person in 1985 to 8.1 square metres in 1997, with a target average of 10 square metres for the year 2000.

The redevelopment of large tracts of the city in the 1990s has been rapidly changing the type of accommodation of many residents, and high-rise living is becoming much more prevalent. In 1980, Shanghai had just 11 buildings with between 16 and 29 storeys, and none above 30-storeys. In 1995, there were 811 buildings with 16–29 storeys, and a further 53 with more than 30 storeys (Statistical Yearbook 1996: 108). To bring out the significance of this shift it is necessary to compare the two types of living 'style' involved.

Parts of Shanghai with low-level high-density housing, such as Nanshi, with its tiny houses and crowded alleyways, are visibly very different to the new high-rise housing compounds. In *shi kumen* – alleyway houses built on a grid of lanes – up to eight families may share one building, in which, generally, washing, toilet facilities, and kitchen areas are communal. The cramped living conditions, along with strict controls over migration, facilitated a residential stability which Parish and Whyte argue allowed 'rather traditional relations – *gemeinschaft*' to reappear in Chinese cities (1984: 355). Informants commented that although living conditions in Nanshi were poor, relationships between neighbours were good – they all knew each other and would help each other, for example, to look after children. On one occasion, I visited Nanshi accompanied by a former resident who now lived in a high-rise flat. He felt nostalgic for life in Nanshi and missed the closeness of relationships between neighbours and the frequent visits they made with each other. He contrasted this situation with his new accommodation where there was little or no contact with neighbours.

In Hongkou district, I visited the home of a factory worker, his wife and eight-year-old son. The couple both worked in a large state glass factory. They lived in a high-density residential area, just ten minutes walk from the factory, in pre-1949 housing built by the factory for its workers. Their house was in a small compound comprising four households which shared toilet facilities and a common entrance onto the street. Most neighbours worked in the same factory and, like my host, had spent 10–11 years in Heilongjiang from 1967–78. The extent and depth of the shared experiences of the residents, with neighbours' lives interwoven in diverse ways, imbued this corner of the city with a distinctive character.

I was invited to join the family for a meal. This was cooked at their home and on the cooker of the family next door. The large round dining table was borrowed from another neighbour. Their home consisted of two floors, a bedroom upstairs and a downstairs living room. The kitchen was outside the front door, jutting out from the front of the building. It had two gas rings and a sink and was only big enough for one person. There was no space to prepare food, this was done on the plain cement floor of the downstairs room. In this compound, interaction with neighbours was frequent and unavoidable. Privacy was limited, the exits and entrances of residents and visitors were all visible. The shared toilet facilities, front doors side-by-side, and outside cooking areas provided many opportunities to observe neighbours and to engage in conversation.

Some six-storey buildings, often with shared washing and cooking areas, were built in the early 1950s. During the reform period true high-rise dwellings have been constructed. Previously, China's indigenous elevator technology was too poorly developed to allow the building of high-rise blocks. The appropriate technology could not be imported until the reform era – an interesting spatial outcome of the 'Open Door' policy. High-rise living, which is becoming the experience for an increasing number of Shanghai residents, brings a marked privatisation of experience.

Many informants told me that people preferred the new high-rise housing because it was 'one flat, one household', that is, each household has its own kitchen and toilet. This separation reduced the number of arguments between neighbours; contact between them was now so infrequent that they might not even recognise each other. Families which were rehoused often moved to suburban areas of the city, away from old friends, relatives, and neighbours. One informant suggested that living in such accommodation decreased the prejudice against Subei people 'since people will not even know if their neighbours are from Subei.' However, informants also noted a negative side to high-rise dwelling. A retired man told me that house-breaking had become more common. He considered a combination of high-rise accommodation and women going out to work – thereby leaving homes unoccupied during the day – as the key factors behind this increase. In the old, low-level housing, neighbours all knew each other and would notice any strangers.

Differences between the two types of housing were very apparent. Residents of high-rise blocks lived in far more discrete spaces. The fear of crime, allied with a decline of mutual neighbourhood surveillance, increased the privatisation of experience. A *Jiefang Ribao* article described how 'more and more households are becoming "closed-style"' with families locked in by doors and steel gates and 'distanced from the outside world' (*JFRB* 13 June 1993: 10). As China's national 'door' opened many families installed outer metal doors to their flats. Fear of burglary was invariably the rationale for fixing such doors. The physical openness of many low-level homes contrasted with the multiple doors in high-rise dwellings. Although homes were increasingly encloistered, various 'outside' objects were incorporated into them. Almost every home I visited had a glass-fronted cabinet which displayed items considered 'attractive' by the residents. These often included wedding gifts, sometimes in unopened boxes, and mementoes from places visited by the household or the gifts of friends. Most cabinets contained at least one foreign item. Popular items were *Nescafé* coffee, a bottle of 'foreign alcohol' such as French *XO Brandy*, even dried milk and, in one case, an unopened packet of *PG Tips* tea. The presence of these foreign objects indicates both the 'breach' in the Chinese wall, and the extent to which such objects were considered prestigious.

In the evidence presented above, there are aspects which both support and undermine David Harvey's thesis of the 'urbanisation of consciousness'

(1989: 229–55). In Harvey's view, with capitalism and urbanisation, the family 'provides a haven to which individuals can withdraw from the complexities and dangers of urban life or from which they can selectively sample its pleasures and opportunities.' My findings suggest that individuals were often forced to withdraw from the wider society when the Chinese state was at its most virulently anti-capitalist. Of the factors promoting this withdrawal in the (capitalist-orientated) reform era, only new technologies such as television and air-conditioning, taken as products of a consumer economy, play the type of role Harvey suggests. However, set against this, communication technologies pull in the opposite direction, and the commercialising economy presents new motives to extend contacts beyond the family. In this final section I will indicate the role of electronic media in both linking and severing the home from the 'outside'.

Alternative places

During the reform era there has been a proliferation of locations that are neither work nor home places (see Wang 1995: 149–72). Particularly notable are various sites for conspicuous consumption which have emerged, or re-emerged, including karaoke bars, discotheques, night-clubs, bowling alleys, saunas, and restaurants. Since the mid-1980s over 1,000 karaoke bars have opened in Shanghai, and during 1992 alone an average of ten new restaurants opened each day. The polarisation of incomes has been matched by a polarisation of leisure sites, as many of these sites are far beyond the price range of ordinary Shanghainese. From around 1993, numerous expensive health and social clubs opened. Private karaoke rooms, with rental prices often in excess of 500 *yuan* for an evening, are also particularly exclusive locations. These places are indicative of rising inequalities and of the way money can now buy exclusivity. Many informants also considered such places as indicative of the trend for money to exert a stronger influence than morality – they associated these places with waste, corruption, and prostitution.

Privacy is a luxury in short supply for most Shanghainese. Before the late 1980s, for example, courting couples had few places to go. They would congregate on the Bund after dark or head for the parks where they faced competition from elderly men playing chess or taking their pet birds for a stroll. Unsurveyed spaces, dark corners, were at a premium. With the commercialisation of leisure there are now more possibilities for young people to find relatively secluded places. For instance, many Shanghai cinemas now provide double seats. In 1990, a cinema ticket had usually cost under 1 *yuan*; the new double seats are 10–20 *yuan*. This seating facilitates a privatisation of experience in a semi-public space, but only for those who can afford the cost. The proliferation of dimly lit coffee houses, with highly priced snacks and hefty cover charges, are another example of this trend.

Reopened Christian churches offer a quite different type of place. An elderly churchgoer described his local church to me as 'very different to the rest of society.' He contrasted the quiet and orderly fashion in which people left the church with the way people tried to grab seats on the buses, 'not caring if there is an elderly person or a woman with a baby.'

These few examples of new alternative places highlight the increasing diversity and fragmentation of social life in contemporary Shanghai. In the case of the church, my informant stressed that it was an 'orderly' place in contrast to the disorder 'outside'. Karaoke bars and nightclubs, by contrast, are more morally ambiguous places, which some described as 'chaotic'. Other important sites include restaurants and shops; the types of consumption these are believed to involve are examined in Chapter 4.

CONNECTING LINES

Commuting lines

Residents who commute to work often told me that this journey – it could take three and a half hours to cross the city – used up far more energy than they ever expended at work. Most citizens travel by bus or bicycle – there were some 6 million bicycles in the city by 1997 (*SS* 10 June 1997: 3). Since the mid-1990s city bus services have improved, but they can still sometimes be so tightly packed with passengers that the doors cannot be closed. This degree of crowdedness is, itself, constitutive of some informants' notions of Shanghaineseness. For instance, a young library worker told me that she felt a *moqi* ('tacit agreement') when travelling by bus, a shared feeling with her fellow passengers. Notions of Shanghainese identity extended to 'correct' ways of standing on cramped buses. I was assured that Shanghainese ingenuity had designed the most efficient way to stand on these – those who did not know these unwritten rules were rural outsiders.

The number of motor vehicles is rising rapidly. Between 1992–7, the number of cars in Shanghai – many of them *Santana* brand vehicles produced in the city's *Volkswagen* joint venture plant – almost doubled to 520,000, plus a further half a million mopeds. There are still relatively few private cars, just 8,000 were registered at the end of 1999 (*SS* 28 January 2000: 4). Congested roads and minimal parking spaces undoubtedly deter the minority who are wealthy enough from buying cars. Despite this there has been a marked increase in the number of expensive foreign cars on Shanghai's streets. These belong mainly to foreign businessmen and companies, Party and government organisations, state-owned enterprises and institutes, and private businessmen. Private car ownership is still considered a mark of elite social status.

Electronic 'lines'

> At an exhibition of pictures by children in the Shanghai Art Exhibition Centre for Children's Day on 1 June 1993 a picture by a nine-year old caught my attention. It showed a child with a mobile phone and above him a representation of a goddess in the heavens also with a mobile phone. A caption

> showed the message the boy is giving the goddess: 'Goddess of Rain, on 9 May [Author's note – the day of the opening ceremony for the East Asian Games], please don't let it rain.'

No matter which means of transport one uses, physically moving from one place to another consumes both time and energy. Electronic media, as the young artist realised, 'make possible new forms of social interaction, modify or undermine old forms of interaction, create new foci and new venues for action and interaction' (Thompson 1990: 225). Various theorists have written on the way electronic media separates social interaction from physical locale (e.g. Meyrowitz 1985; Thompson 1990; Fitzgerald 1991). In this section I outline the role and impact of three types of machine – the telephone, pager, and mobile phone before concluding with the impact of television on boundaries in Shanghai.

In Shanghai, the type of communications device a person had access to was often a reasonable indication of their social status. At the lowest level are those who rely upon public phones. These phones usually serve several dozen households. Calls are taken and made from small booths staffed by elderly local residents. Incoming callers leave their name and number and one of the booth's staff emerges from the hut and summons the person sought with the aid of a megaphone.

Installation of a home phone ensured a much greater degree of privacy, although the size of many dwellings meant that family members might be able to overhear calls. The use of a private phone and the privatisation of experience it brings has only become possible during the reform era. At first, only those with 'connections' (sociological 'lines') and/or status could have phones installed. By the early 1990s phone installation was available to those who could afford the expense. In 1992, it cost about 3,500 *yuan* ($608) to install a phone – a local newspaper pointed out that this was the equivalent of a year's salary for many people (*CD* 13 March 1993: 3). By the end of 1998 Shanghai was expected to have 4.3 million private telephone users, making 12.6 billion phone calls per annum (*FT Survey* 1998: 18).

Telephones make the use of connections (*guanxi*) much more convenient. In using *guanxi* the actual connection one requires is often reached indirectly via another or several other people. Negotiating such a chain by physically going from place to place would be extremely time and energy-consuming. The telephone enables one to pass rapidly along the links of sometimes very elaborate chains.

In the previous chapter, I described an instance where the installation of private phones had reinvigorated what may be construed as 'traditional links' between urban and rural relatives. The telephone can also 'reinvent' traditional rituals. For example, at Spring Festival people should visit relatives and the streets are thronged with people carrying large round cakes and bottles of alcohol. However, one can only visit so many people, and the telephone enables some of these ritual 'calls' to be made from home. An element of competition appears to creep into this – it is considered best to phone others before they phone you. This competitive reciprocity may follow over to the following year.

Since the early 1990s pagers have become common – by May 1997 there were some 1.9 million in use in Shanghai (*SS* 16 May 1997: 3). A young woman who described herself as a 'broker' told me that for her the pager is 'an opportunity', 'a line' (*xian*), and 'a route' (*lu*) (see page 21–2). A saleswoman, who had been issued with a pager by her boss, felt differently about her pager. The description of her new pager's effect upon her life seemed to liken it to a kind of electronic tagging device. Soon after she had been issued with it I asked her what difference it had made. She replied that she felt 'caught' and 'lacking freedom'. She added that in contemporary Shanghai, communication links of this type had become very important, while before it had not mattered. She explained that this change was due to increasing commercialisation and a new sense that 'time is money'. These two contrasting views on pagers show the ambiguity of this device. For one informant it was a source of opportunities, for the other an infringement upon her personal space, an invisible line which bound her. These examples illustrate the way in which the global phenomenon of 'time-space compression has not been experienced by all in the same way, whilst some initiate its operation others are constrained by it' (Carter *et al.* 1993: viii).

Information has become much more important in the reform era. In Maoist China information was limited and access to it strictly controlled – there was primarily a vertical flow of information within units controlled by the state. As I showed in Chapters 1 and 2, during the reform era the state's near monopoly over the control of information has been fundamentally undermined. The new importance of communication devices both facilitates and attests to the proliferation and dissemination of information.

More sophisticated pagers can store simple messages and provide information such as the latest share prices. However, the most prestigious means of communication is the mobile phone (see page 157–8). Mobile phones and pagers make possible a quite different lifestyle from the 'two points and a line' of ordinary workers. Following this indigenous description it could be said that these new devices merge the two points into one, with multiple lines radiating to and from it. The user is at the centre of his or her own network and incorporated into the networks of others, rather than being daily conveyor-belted from home to work and back.

Home boundaries in the electronic age

The electronic media of radio and television have entered the homes of most Shanghainese. As I showed in Chapter 2, the material conveyed by these media has the capacity to facilitate both the construction and disassembling of identities at diverse levels. For instance, they sever traditional links between physical and social place; instead of, or alongside, place-related identities, new types of identities can develop.

The effects of electronic media on the boundaries of the home are ambiguous. At one level, television, radio, and home telephones reduce activity in the public sphere and fragment society into discrete households. In China, the development of the home as a cloistered environment may be even more attenuated as result of the impact of past political campaigns, the spread of high-rise dwelling, and the growing fear of crime which I have outlined. However, at another level these media collapse time and space and purvey global images and locate Shanghainese within a global and national media world. In this way broadcasting spans the private and public spheres through, for example, the domestication of standard national time (see Scannell 1988). Additionally, the sitting room becomes the place where 'the global meets the local' (Morley 1991); once public events now 'occur' in the living room. Paradoxically, as these media promote a separation from neighbours, they join viewers with (or, at least, enabled them to gaze upon) people, places, and events they would otherwise never encounter – distance and intimacy becoming increasingly disjoined.

CONCLUDING REMARKS

In this chapter, I first outlined significant changes which are taking place in the cityscape of Shanghai. Through the 1990s, after more than two decades of stagnation, profound physical ruptures and dislocations began to alter the 'face' of the city. A theme of this study is to show ways in which identities are contingent and contextual with a wide range of cross-cutting, possible identifications. I pursued this theme by examining ways in which places and people in Shanghai are assigned to an 'upper' or a 'lower' status. The attribution of qualities and identities to people in (or from) different parts of the city provides further strands of complexity. The persistence and apparent reinforcing of these identifications during the Maoist era demonstrates the way in which socio-economic policies of that time often operated to produce consequences in direct opposition to the ideals rhetorically espoused.

I also outlined ways in which work and home places are changing in the reform era. I argue that there appears to be a trend for *danwei* to become less enclosed and bounded and for the home to become an increasingly privatised, cloissonéed sphere. A combination of factors reinforced perceptions of the home as a place of refuge, including the impact of past political campaigns, technological and architectural changes, and the belief that rising crime is making Shanghai a more insecure place.

In the final section of this chapter, I highlighted ways in which differential means of transcending space not only located people within different spatial habitats but was also often indicative of social status. When analysing social differentiation in contemporary Shanghai, rather than use the terminology of 'class', it may be more appropriate to refer, as local people do, for example, to a car-using 'stratum' or a mobile phone-using 'stratum'. These are clear instances of the way in which, in contemporary society, consumption of products can be used to ascribe identities, a theme pursued in the next chapter. I have also shown some of the ambiguous effects of electronic media. They make 'connections' easier and new types of links possible, but at the same time they create new boundaries and new types of exclusion.

4 Consuming Shanghai: hairy crabs, ghosts, and Christmas trees

Shanghai is in the midst of a consumer revolution. Evidence of this is readily apparent in the well-stocked stores and Hong Kong-style shopping plazas packed with shoppers, the proliferation of advertising billboards, neon signs, numerous lavishly furnished new restaurants filled with diners, expensive nightclubs, karaoke bars, jewellery shops, and fancy bakeries. The once drab clothing of its inhabitants, especially that of the young, has been replaced by the latest fashions and accessories. On the television, glamorous and alluring images designed to entice the 'audience' seep into almost every living room, deliberately, or unwittingly, creating new desires and new 'needs'. The consumer 'tide', the 'flood' of consuming, as local newspapers describe it, is there for all to see.

Notions and patterns of consumption include diverse aspects of consuming, whether it be food, clothes, or leisure activities. Through differential modes of consumption a range of social values and senses of identity may be ascribed, expressed, maintained, created, and disputed. Chao and Myers (1998: 351) argue that consumerism is 'strengthening… social, economic, and political ties' between the Chinese people. This chapter takes a contrary perspective, highlighting the fracturing and divisive nature of consumerism and the new stresses and strains which it brings.

The Party-state has looked benignly upon the consumer boom in Shanghai, seeking to take the credit and bask in the afterglow of consumer satisfaction. Satiating pent-up demands may have helped to ensure that there has been no repeat of the events of Spring 1989 – but the processes, forms, and consequences of consumption are multiple and multivariate. Marketing strategists stress the importance of product differentiation and differentiate consumers into ever finer market segments. Differential styles of consumption increasingly divide and fragment Chinese society into discrete status groups, setting off Shanghainese from the rural poor, 'the people' from the Party-state, parents from children, rich from poor, and present from past.

The two initial sections of this chapter locate consumption in contemporary Shanghai within an historical context: the first examines the factors which restricted the development of popular consumerism during the Maoist period; the second outlines the structural and ideological changes which have made possible the emergence of popular consumerism in contemporary Shanghai. The third section notes the indigenous notion of rising consumption levels as an indicator of 'progress', and also the stresses and tensions created by this phenomenon. I then outline the new importance of money and the rise of consumption in courtship and marriage rituals. The fourth section focuses upon the semantic field of 'eating'. In particular, I examine ways in which food-based analogies and metaphors permeate the language Shanghainese use to depict many aspects of life, from individual behaviour, to conceiving of the relation between Shanghai and the central government. In the fifth section, I investigate instances of newly emergent forms of lifestyle consumption. In particular, I outline the way small-scale entrepreneurs and young people are portrayed as having distinctive consumption patterns. I then explore the recent craze for famous brand name consumer goods and the re-emergence of Christmas, in part at least, as a new festival of consumerism.

HISTORICAL BACKGROUND TO THE NEW CONSUMERISM

In the 1920s and 1930s Shanghai achieved world renown, and sometimes notoriety, as a 'modern', cosmopolitan, semi-colonial city administered on a basis of *laissez-faire* mercantilism. Fashion, advertising, dance halls, nightclubs, and other forms of conspicuous consumption were ubiquitous features of Shanghai life. The Communist Party regarded Shanghai as a parasitic, consumer city (see Gaulton 1981: 46), which sucked in the wealth of the surrounding countryside – a black stain on the purity of rural redness. When the troops of the People's Liberation Army walked into Shanghai in May 1949 many citizens were struck by their simple, frugal, and unadorned appearance. This was the ethos which was to dominate China, in rhetorical terms if not always in practice, with varying degrees of intensity until the late 1970s. From the mid-1950s onwards 'conspicuous consumption and individual wealth creation were largely regarded as hostile acts by the CCP' (Goodman 1996: 227). In Shanghai, of all places in China, this new order constituted a significant break from the past.

Maoist ideology and socio-economic policies precluded the emergence of popular consumerism. Heavy industry and capital investment were promoted, while consumption, including the production of consumer goods and investment in housing, and services, was sacrificed.[1] Shanghainese recall that 'during the Cultural Revolution shops remained open, but there was nothing to buy.' Apart from a severely limited range of poor-quality consumer goods, wage levels were low and relatively egalitarian – a situation summed up in a satirical expression of that time 'long live 36 *yuan*!' (*san shi liu kuai, wansui*). The combination of low wages, a reliance upon payment in kind (such as housing and medical services), a limited choice of consumer products, and rationing, meant that Maoist China possessed many features of a non-monetised economy.

Advertising was severely curtailed from the 1950s until the late 1970s and 'castigated . . . as the apotheosis of the capitalist religion of consumption' (Stross 1990: 485). Moreover, the ethos of the period discouraged conspicuous consumption and 'bourgeois' habits and lifestyles – drinking coffee and raising goldfish were two examples I was told about. At least some informants believed that Mao Zedong had deliberately kept the masses in poverty, in the same way as he had maintained the 'closed door policy', as part of a deliberate strategy to maintain his own position of power.

At its most intense the prevailing ideology had much in common with that of the Puritans in seventeenth-century England. Rather than hold lavish wedding feasts, for instance, the Communist Party encouraged families to have simple and frugal gatherings with tea and candies (Parish and Whyte 1984: 139). Clothing was functional and personal adornment discouraged. In her autobiography, *Life and Death in Shanghai*, Nien Cheng writes that during the Cultural Revolution '[o]ne could no longer assess a man's station in life by his clothes in China because everybody tried to dress like a proletarian' (1986: 11).[2] At times coercion was used to ensure conformity. Informants told me, for instance, that young women were publicly humiliated in the late 1960s by having the legs of trousers considered too fashionable cut open.[3]

Highly developed organisational and surveillance structures reaching into every work place and residential area, facilitated by the high-population density, ensured conformity (see Parish and Whyte 1984: 236–73). Since wage levels were relatively similar and alternative sources of income extremely limited, people could readily assess the income level of neighbours and would be suspicious if they bought expensive items.

David Parkin has written of 'peoples' propensity continually to make themselves different through objects' (1993: 79). During the Cultural Revolution, in particular, the reverse situation applied – Chinese people had to make themselves appear the *same* – and, of course, markedly different from foreigners and 'capitalist' consumers – through objects. Since the death of Mao Zedong in 1976, people are once again able to assert distinctive identities through consumption.

FROM REVOLUTIONARY SLOGANS TO ADVERTISING JINGLES: THE RE-EMERGENCE OF CONSUMERISM

During the reform era most of the factors which prevented the emergence of a popular consumer society have been either radically changed or, at least, undermined. By the early 1980s, after three decades of shifting ideological campaigns, the Party had lost the ability to use revolutionary rhetoric and political campaigns to spur the masses. The Communist Party was, as Richard Madsen succinctly puts it, 'ideologically dead' (1993: 183). Instead the Party elite perceived the best hope for its own survival in increasing the economic prosperity of the populace – to adapt Marx, the hope was that material prosperity would act as the opium of the masses. The urgency of this task, and the price of failure, was underlined by the demonstrations across China of Spring 1989, the collapse of Communist regimes in Eastern Europe, and the break-up of the Soviet Union.

There has been an unmistakable shift from deferred gratification to a stress upon consumption and material rewards in the present. Income levels generally have risen; between 1991–6, the monthly income of Shanghai residents increased by almost 56 per cent (*SS* 9 September 1997: 3). The city also has a 'new wealthy stratum' (*xinfu jieceng*). A far greater range of consumer products is available, ration coupons are a thing of the past, and there is fierce competition amongst both producers and retailers. In 1988, just ten years after the first reforms, the individual sector already accounted for 17.8 per cent of retail sales compared to just 0.1 per cent in 1978 (Young 1991: 120). In 1998, 37.1 per cent of retail sales of consumer goods were generated by the private sector (HKTDC 1999).

In 1993, a year after Shanghai at last began to take major steps in reform, Chinese newspapers began to describe a 'consuming passion' (*CDBW* 14–20 February 1993: 8) and a 'shopping craze' (*CD* 22 February 1993: 6) in Shanghai. In 1990, retail sales in the city rose by just 0.1 per cent over the previous year; in 1993, sales rose by 33.5 per cent over the previous year (Jacobs 1997: 176). Sales of consumer goods rose in value from 46 billion *yuan* in 1992, to over 132 billion *yuan* in 1997 (*FT Survey* 1998: 19). Numerous jewellery shops opened in Shanghai as China became the world's largest gold consumer (*CDBW* 16–22 May 1993: 8). From the mid-1990s shops offering 24-hour service began to open. With the incentive of material rewards, and increasingly the threat of redundancy, the self-presentation of Shanghai's notoriously surly service workers has undergone a marked transformation. Despite this, for most households buying items such as a colour television involve a lengthy period of saving, with money saved by 'the mouth not eating it'.

Foreign companies have been allowed to participate in the retail sector since June 1992 (see Ho and Leigh 1994). In 1992, the State Council approved the first foreign joint venture retail project, a $100 million scheme by the Japanese company *Yaohan* to build a 120,000 square metre shopping centre in Pudong. By late 1999, over 40 foreign chain stores had been set up in Shanghai, by companies such as the Hong Kong retailer *Sincere, Carrefour* of France, *Chia Tai* of Thailand and *Ikea* of Sweden. These foreign stores now accounted for 6–7 per cent of the city's total retail sales (*SS* 23 November 1999: 7). In 1999, the British do-it-yourself retailer B&Q opened a warehouse store in the city, it added a second store in June 2000. Chinese shoppers regularly flock to such 'new cathedrals of consumerism' (Tomlinson 1990b: 70). During the Maoist era, consumer goods purchased in China were invariably home-produced and the highest cachet accorded those marked 'Made in Shanghai'. Shanghai's re-internationalisation has allowed an increasing influx of foreign consumer items. Whether it be everyday commodities such as shampoo and washing-powder or designer-label suits, foreign consumer goods have replaced Shanghai brands at the top of the status list.

Alongside rising incomes and the increased availability of consumer products is a recognition that one of the new demands of the 'socialist market economy' is to learn how to become a consumer. The resurgent advertising industry is eager to take up this 'educative' role.[4] In late twentieth-century consumerism, media-derived images play a vital role in valuations and notions surrounding products. Mike Featherstone's description of developments in advertising in 1920s

Cartoon 4.1 'Untitled'. Captions are: 'Preferential price', 'cut price', 'discount price', 'sale price', 'best price', 'normal price', 'friends' price'.

Source: *XMWB* 18 April 1999.

America is remarkably appropriate to post-Mao China. He writes that through the new mass media '[w]orkers who had become used to the rhetoric of thrift, hard work and sobriety, had to become "educated" to appreciate a new discourse centred around the hedonistic lifestyle entailing new needs and desires' (1991: 172). Clearly, astute marketing by Western and other advertisers explicitly seeks to fuel the dreams, aspirations, and fantasies of consumers. Foreign-invested retail outlets also play a part in educating consumers. James Watson details, for instance, the way in which the first *McDonald's* restaurant in China provided (literal) consumer education on how to eat its hamburgers (1997b: 28).

The rise of popular consumerism is inescapable on *Shanghai Oriental Radio Station* which devotes abundant airtime to consumer information programmes, including live phone-ins. These programmes constitute not only cheap programming and publicity for stores but also education on being 'consumers'. Experiences in the 'West' are often invoked. For instance, local media have introduced consumers to the 'Western' notion that 'the customer is God'. This was contrasted to the experience of Shanghai shoppers who had become inured to sullen and off-hand treatment by sales staff. Such live programming has also allowed the distinctive Shanghai dialect a prominence denied in the pre-reform era when state-sponsored *putonghua* (Mandarin) dominated. This departure from the script adds to the growing heterogeneity in Shanghai and may help to invigorate senses of Shanghainese identity.

Consumption as the measure of progress

For most people I spoke with the meaning of 'reform and the Open Door' (*gaige kaifang*) was higher incomes, the emergence of numerous free markets with abundant and good quality produce, and the possibility of acquiring consumer durables. The comments of a retired teacher were replicated in countless conversations. When asked about the impact of *gaige kaifang* he commented that:

> *Gaige kaifang* is better than previous policies. In the 1970s and early 1980s the *laobaixing* never imagined that their homes could have a fridge, a television, and a video player. After a few years of *gaige kaifang* every family bought electrical goods.[5] The ordinary *laobaixing* are relatively satisfied. We eat more dishes and less rice. Now sea food is common, before there was only pork.

Official rhetoric that the aim of the reform policies is to increase the standard of living of the common people is clearly an extremely potent and powerful force. However, rising consumer demands bring new pressures…

All-consuming pressures

The commercialisation of everyday life, increased levels of consumption and availability of consumer products has brought an 'economic pressure'. Media and advertising images spur new wants and there is increased social pressure to keep up with one's peers. In the 1950s and 1960s the consumer items people sought cost in the region of 100 *yuan* – a watch, a bicycle, and a sewing machine. In the 1970s and 1980s they wanted a colour television, a fridge, and a washing machine, which, together, would cost around 1,000 *yuan*. An article in *Wenhui Film Times* considered that there were no comparable 'big three items' in the 1990s (*WHDYSB* 5 June 1993: 7). By the late 1990s, even those on average incomes aspired to take foreign holidays, purchase computers and cars and to buy their own homes, the latter an ambition now actively promoted by the state.

Inevitably products are graded in terms of their perceived quality and status. In the case of colour televisions, for instance, this grading extends beyond obvious differences in screen size and brand, to gradations based upon the place of manufacture of the *same* brand. Thus, in Shanghai electronic goods stores *Panasonic* television sets, for example, are clearly marked as 'Made in Japan', 'Made in Malaysia', or 'Made in China' – the price labels descend accordingly.[6] Sets made by state-owned enterprises such as *Changhong* are cheaper still. Subtle and, at times, blatant judgements are made of the value and worth of the person themselves on the basis of the type of products they own, wear and display, and there are strong peer pressures to upgrade products.

Young people who have grown up in the relatively affluent 1980s and 1990s often have especially high consumer demands. Unlike their parents, they take the benefits brought by the reforms and the Open Door for granted and expect much more in the future. Some actively seek success, to be able to enjoy high-class consumption. Their desires are fuelled by media images and advertising which deliberately aims to create a 'cycle of continual dissatisfaction' by playing upon intimate fears and desires (Ewen and Ewen 1982: 73). Young people are increasingly both forced and encouraged to 'look towards money' as the pull of money grows greater and the security of state work unit jobs erodes.

The older generation tend to express relative satisfaction, and feel less pressure to consume on their own behalf. This contentment was exemplified in the comment of a retired man that 'the ordinary people are satisfied now, their demands are low because they are accustomed to poverty.' Many have experienced great deprivations and disruptions in their lives and emphasise the importance of stability. A magazine editor in his mid-fifties epitomised this approach. His aspirations in the public sphere were to 'just muddle along until retirement', adding that 'one of the good things about socialism is that one can eat from the big national pot and muddle along with little effort.' His main hopes were in the private domain – for good health, the successful marriage, and careers of his children, to have his family nearby and to have a grandson. Beyond this, a larger living space and consumer items such as air-conditioning were considered highly desirable.

The older generations are, however, under great pressure to spend on their families' children or grandchildren (see Bin 1997: 49–50; Yan 1997: 62–6). Parents brought up during the Cultural Revolution (1966–76) often feel that the disruptions of this period blighted their own lives and have extremely high expectations for their own offspring. This tendency is heightened by the one-child policy and the typical close proximity of grandparents, such that the financial and other resources of two parents and four grandparents are all focused on a single child – the so-called '4-2-1 syndrome'. The concentration upon the well-being and upbringing of a single child translates into substantial expenditure on children's clothing, foods, education, computers and so forth. *McDonald's* provides an instance of this. Since 1992, *McDonald's* has set up dozens of restaurants all over China. Yan found that many adult customers are brought to these restaurants by their children or grandchildren, and that they 'continue to go there even though in many cases they dislike or cannot afford the foreign food' (1997: 65). No parent wishes to be left out in the competition to meet the ever spiralling 'needs' of their offspring.

There is increased pressure on families when young couples marry. The level of consumption considered appropriate has inflated considerably in recent years. Cynics suggest that courtship itself has become commercialised and is no longer *tan lianai* – 'talking love' – but, rather, 'talking business' (*tan shengyi*).[7] The boyfriend who spends lavishly trying to impress his girlfriend is a popular stereotype. Shanghainese joke that he is under the 'order of the soup' (*tang si ling*), a pun on the name of a character – General Tang (i.e. *Tang siling*) – who featured in a film shown early in the reform era. The homonym caricatures a young man who eats only soup so as to save money to lavish on his girlfriend. A prospective son-in-law, called a *maojiao nüxu* – 'hairy-legged son-in-law' – in Shanghai, is expected to *gue padü/guai paitou* – display style/show off his wealth – by providing gifts for his prospective parents-in-law. Some parents were considered especially greedy (*tanxin*), and to decide if their daughter could marry the young man depending upon the quantity and quality of gifts he brings on his visits.

From the late 1950s and especially during the Cultural Revolution, families were discouraged from holding lavish wedding feasts. Instead, the Communist

Party tried to popularise simple and frugal 'wedding tea parties'. Wedding feasts continued but on a reduced scale, and by the 1970s they had 'retreated back into the home' (Parish and Whyte 1984: 139). The government still warns against extravagance in wedding ceremonies, but most of the former socio-political restraints have been removed and there is considerable social pressure to hold a lavish wedding feast and acquire the requisite array of consumer durables for the new marital home. For instance, both the couple and their families would 'lose face' if the newly weds did not have a new colour television set with at least a 24 inch screen. On wedding days a new home is packed with goods from the traditional eight quilts piled up on the new marital bed to video players and television sets, the larger the better.

A typical wedding meal I attended in 1994 cost 9,000 *yuan* and a further 30,000 *yuan* was spent on consumer items. The cost of the wedding feast itself may be offset by the gifts of money brought by the diners. Guests generally give a sum of money enclosed in a red envelope. In 1994, an average gift was 100 *yuan* per person.[8] It was often remarked that the hosts 'made a profit' on the wedding meal and that extra guests may be invited just to maximise this revenue.

The rise of popular consumerism can be charted in the requirements of young couples who set up home. In the early 1970s, the items they bought comprised the 'thirty six legs' – a table, four chairs, bed, sofa, chest of draws, and a wardrobe. Subsequently it was the 'four machines' – a television, a tape recorder, a camera, and a sewing machine. Currently air conditioners, a video cassette disc player and a large wide-screen colour television are just some of the items considered essential. Terminology drawn from computing is popularly used to describe the division of costs – the groom's side is expected to provide this 'hardware', while the bride's side contribute the 'traditional' items of 'software', such as bedding items. Although there is a tendency for a more equal level of contributions from the bride and groom's families than in the past, the male's side still generally contribute more.

The inflated requirements of weddings mean that children may now rely more upon their parents in order to get married. Parents are under a moral imperative to contribute to these costs, even if they lack these items themselves. Popular stereotypes depict parents as having to eat frugally, wear old clothes, and make do with a black and white television so as to raise sufficient funds. The burden is especially great if a family have more than one son. In one instance in my acquaintance a man with two sons paid out 10,000 *yuan* for the marriage of his first son in 1982 and 20,000 *yuan* for the marriage of the second in 1992.[9] Using a dialect term he commented that his 'wealth (literally his "fat") has all gone' (*hiusi ma la/youshui meiyou le*). He did not envisage paying off the debts incurred until the child of the second son's marriage was seven or eight years old. The inflated requirements of weddings may also increase the dependency of young people on their parents.

Those in state *danwei*, as we have seen, often have to find a second job or source of income in order to acquire the consumer durables now considered essential for happiness and well-being. This pressure to make money is associated

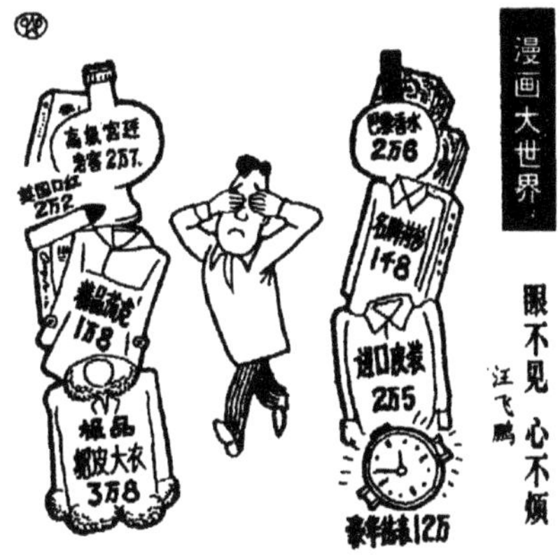

Cartoon 4.2 'What the eyes don't see, does not perturb one'. The articles have labels such as 'Parisian perfume 26,000 *yuan*', 'famous brand name shirt 1,800 *yuan*', 'imported leather jacket 25,000 *yuan*', 'luxurious diamond watch 120,000 *yuan*', and 'English lipstick 22,000 *yuan*'.

Source: *XMWB* 5 December 1993.

with what a deputy restaurant manager described as an 'increasing pressure of material goods.' Formerly a teacher, this woman had changed careers because of this pressure. As a teacher her salary had been just 300 *yuan* ($35) a month, but she wanted to enjoy expensive entertainments such as karaoke and buy expensive consumer goods. She also felt a 'clothing pressure' (*fuzhuang yali*), experienced as a desire to wear expensive famous brand name clothing. These comments provide evidence of the double-edged quality of a monetised economy (cf. Miller 1987; Simmel 1990); money brings both the social advantages of freedom, but also new stresses and constraints. It is to the re-monetising of Shanghai that I now turn.

The God of wealth returns to Shanghai

The rise of popular consumerism during the reform era is part of a general increase in commercialism and commodification. These trends have affected many aspects of life in Shanghai from education, leisure, housing, journalism, and medical services to weddings and funerals. In education, for instance, parents believe that it is necessary to present teachers with gifts to ensure their children are given adequate attention. The same applies to journalists, if one wishes to have an article placed in the media. On the inflating costs of funerals, an elderly man remarked bitterly that he could 'no longer afford to die (*sibuqi*)'. Commercialism is apparent in the explosion of private enterprises and trading activities by units as diverse as schools, residents' committees, local government departments, research academies, and the military.

As we have seen, the Maoist economy possessed many of the features of a non-monetised economy. In the reform era Shanghai's economy has rapidly re-monetised. The cellular, vertical socio-economic structures which formerly encapsulated much of people's lives have been considerably weakened, both by an internal inability to meet workers' demands, and the emergence of alternative sources to meet workers demands. Changing jobs, described in local slang as *huan yi wan fan chi chi* ('change to a different rice bowl to eat') and *tiaocao* ('jumping to another trough'), is increasingly common. A lucky few *chi waihui* – 'eat outside money' – that is, live off money sent to them by relatives abroad, while those with a large bank balance can live off, literally 'eat' the interest (*chi lixi*). The need and desire to make money in Shanghai's newly commercialising economy induces some to take risks. This may involve setting forth into the business world (*xiahai*), or speculation on Shanghai's volatile stock market (see Chapter 5). In the scramble for money, desperate measures such as fraud, theft, and counterfeiting are also increasingly common.

There has been considerable criticism of the new prominence of money. An article in *China Daily* commented that the socio-economic changes had 'revolutionised attitudes toward wealth' and that Chinese people had no choice but to become 'money conscious' (*CD* 15 July 1993: 4). However, it added that in certain cases this had given rise to 'worshipping money', 'idolatry of money', and 'moral degeneration'. My informants could all cite instances of this and felt that China had become a far more materialistic society, one in which 'everybody grabs' (*dajia na*).[10] Official pronouncements condemning such worship of money and stressing the need for 'spiritual civilisation' were either ignored entirely, regarded as empty words, or as hypocritical. The television series *River Elegy* remarked upon Chinese rulers who 'exert their full strength to criticise western life-styles and values, yet they themselves would never refuse to enjoy those super-deluxe limousines and high-class consumer goods' (Su and Wang

Cartoon 4.3 'The mouse has money'.

Source: *XMWB* 29 July 1993.

1991: 151). These criticisms were frequently echoed in the comments of my informants.

Some intellectuals retained at least a rhetorical disdain for money. For instance, a university graduate who is now a successful businesswoman told me that she disliked business people. She described them as having *tongchouwei* – the 'stink of money'. This would seem to be an example of the way notions of cultural distinction (cf. Bourdieu 1984) are invoked – this woman stressed her affinity to 'cultured people' (*wenren*). In this instance, cultural taste was contrasted with the actual taste of money – one may have money but should not 'smell' of it.

Money in Shanghai has various 'Chinese characteristics'. There are few credit facilities and banks generally do not lend money to individuals although, as noted in Chapter 3, mortgages became more common in the late 1990s. Instead funds are borrowed from family and friends. This situation was described to me by a Shanghai economics professor as an instance of the way that China, in contrast to the West, is a 'human feeling country' (*renqing guojia*).

The power of money was frequently mentioned. A state *danwei* salesman noted a traditional saying: 'If you have money you can make ghosts turn the millstone', whilst in a 1990s version people may even say, 'If you have money you can make the millstone turn the ghost.' The increasingly vital role of money was evident in the revival of expressions such as *pulu* (see page 21–2), and *shaoxiang*, 'incense burning'. *Shaoxiang* is a pre-1949 term which has regained popularity. In the same way as incense is burned before heavenly gatekeepers, the bodhisattva, to secure their aid and support, so gifts are laid before more earthly 'bodhisattva' to achieve this end.

Spring Festival appeared to be a time for much 'incense burning'. At this time in 1994, an informant assured me, restaurant owners in Zhapu Road each had to buy 1,000 *yuan* worth of firecrackers from the local police – alongside providing regular free meals – in order to secure their protection. The tradition of giving money to children wrapped inside a red packet (*hongbao*) at Spring Festival also serves as a cover for *shaoxiang*. A sum between 10 and 100 *yuan* is usual, but much larger amounts, destined for the parents, can be handed over in this way.

The new striving for wealth is symbolised in the return of a pre-1949 custom on the fourth day of the lunar New Year to welcome the God of Wealth. Traders set off firecrackers and bought large carp. The carp is considered lucky since its name '*li*' is a close homonym of the *li* in *lixi* (interest). This tradition was dormant until recent years, both because it was frowned upon and since there were few private stores. The main display of firecrackers on this occasion was on Zhapu Road, a street now almost entirely occupied by private restaurants.

Shanghainese transnational Chinese identity

Sophisticated adverts produced in the West, Japan, and the Asian 'little dragons' undoubtedly contribute to the popularity of goods from these places as communicators of both material success and of style. Indigenous mass media, too, often purvey images which implicitly promote the lifestyles of wealthy Westerners and overseas Chinese and the consumerism associated with them. In these programmes the 'furniture, house decoration, cars, clothing, eating and drinking habits, the "look" of the characters... creates images of life-styles which are perceived as being desirable in the eyes of the viewers' (Bocock 1993: 93). The subtlety of these influences makes them at least as powerful as Western advertisements in promoting consumerist lifestyles. In a complex interplay media images stimulate, form, and articulate consumer desires. At the same time they create, fuel, and define standards of success and provide patterns of ways of life (ways of consuming) that many Shanghainese aspire to and seek to emulate.

It would be tempting to consider the predominance of Western and Japanese products as symbols of success as an example of 'cultural imperialism'. Television programmes and advertisements often include a foreigner. The presence of foreigners seems to be metonymical for modernity.[11] In everyday discourse in China there seems to be a conflation and congruence in the use of the terms *waiguo* ('foreign'), *xifang* ('the West'), *xiandai* ('modern'), and *xiandaihua* ('modernity').[12] I would argue that the Chinese state actively sustains this conception by utilising the success of Western products in China as a propaganda tool to advertise its own success. State rhetoric now emphasises, above all, economic development; and popular perceptions are that 'the West' has already achieved this goal. It is, therefore, hardly surprising that Chinese people adopt as their own the symbols of success in the West. A *China Daily* article on fashion in China demonstrates this point. In 1978, Pierre Cardin was the first overseas designer to visit China and '[h]is name is now known to many ordinary Chinese' (*CD* 20 May 1993: 5). Cardin's success is taken as evidence that 'China enjoys rapid economic growth', and events such as Cardin's first fashion show in China 'proved that China had gained international recognition in fashion.' In this article, as in many others, the Western gaze is invoked. Foreign visitors are described as 'amazed' that the 'the daily attire worn by people is so colourful and diversified.' The significance of 'the West' may be particularly important in Shanghai where citizens often proclaim a proclivity towards the 'West' (note the description mentioned in page 102 that Shanghainese are 'China's Americans').

Yan describes the way in which for younger Beijing residents, eating at foreign fast food restaurants such as *Pizza Hut* 'has become an integral part of their new lifestyle, a way for them to participate in the transnational cultural system' (1997: 49). A similar situation applies in Shanghai. However, it is also possible to discern a parallel transformation to that which occurred in Hong Kong. James Watson describes how from the mid-1970s to the mid-1980s *McDonald's* in Hong Kong was frequented by those 'seeking an American cultural experience', but that it has now become a local institution (1997b).

During the 1990s, most Shanghainese acquired the electronic media of radio, television, and home telephones. Shanghainese have long considered themselves as separated by their style and sophistication from China's rural masses. Media images have helped to foster this self-image. As shown in Chapter 2, Shanghainese identify themselves far more closely with affluent overseas Chinese in

New York or Taipei than with the two or three million rural migrant workers so visibly and industriously engaged in reconstructing Shanghai as a modern city. For their part, rural migrants to Shanghai who ostentatiously display their ability to enjoy prestigious consumption patterns may face ridicule. A common belief is that those in Shanghai who display the brand label of their suits on the cuffs of their jacket sleeves are 'country bumpkins'. This provides an instance of the way that '[g]oods can be used as fences or bridges' (Douglas and Isherwood 1978: 85).

THE STATE AS CONSPICUOUS CONSUMER/CONSUMING THE STATE

> The tables were now covered with a profusion of small dishes, which contained all the finest fruits and vegetables of the season, besides many of the most expensive kinds of soups, such as the celebrated bird's nest and others, many of which were excellent even to the palate of an Englishman.
>
> (Robert Fortune 1853: Volume I, 113)

Chinese people frequently assert that food plays a central part in their country's cultural life and speak, for instance, of an 'eating culture' (*chi wenhua*). Food plays a vital role in life-cycle and religious rituals, and festive occasions.[13] Ties of affect within families and between friends are fostered and maintained by commensal meals and the reciprocal exchange of gifts such as mooncakes at the Mid-Autumn festival. In business circles, too, dining is often considered vital in creating and maintaining connections, with foods such as turtle, shark's fin soup, and crab considered especially prestigious for banquets. Generally one person pays for the meal, the diners may be indebted to the meal provider, or each meal may form part of an on-going and 'continuing reciprocation' (Fei 1992: 124–5) between those present. It may well be that 'few other cultures are as food-orientated as the Chinese' (Chang 1977: 11). As one informant remarked to me 'it seems that in China, whatever you do, you cannot do it without a meal.'

Food-based analogies and metaphors constitute a leitmotif through which people talk about, conceive, and evaluate many aspects of the world around them. Chinese people, for instance, routinely describe knowledge as being in the 'stomach' (*duzi*). For intellectuals the *laobaixing* are those who have not 'consumed' sufficient *wenhua*. The topic of eating also provides an innovative avenue through which to examine perceptions of the relationship between Shanghai and the state, and between individuals and the state. In the years after 'Liberation' the state created a new ritual using food. Diners were solemnly fed *yikufan*, a poor meal made up of twigs, grass, and soil. *Yiku* means to 'recall one's suffering in the old society' and this meal, low in nutrients but rich in propaganda, was intended to remind its consumers how people had suffered (*chiku* – 'eat bitterness') before 1949, and to promote a sense of common purpose and belonging to the 'nation-family' of New China.[14]

In recent years, the perception of the state as a provider has diminished, and sometimes even turned upside down. In Chapter 2, I noted the conviction of many Shanghainese that the Chinese state was a voracious consumer of Shanghai's wealth. This was clear in the comment of a university lecturer in her early forties who said that in the three decades after 1949 Shanghai had not changed. It had just 'lived off its past capital' – *chi laoben* ('eaten its old capital') whilst the whole country had 'lived off Shanghai' – *quan guo chi Shanghai* ('the whole country ate Shanghai'). In a similar vein, a young joint venture employee adapted a current slang term for a rich man (*dahu*) in describing Shanghai's relationship to the state, calling the city the 'biggest tax-paying *dahu* of all'. This perception of many Shanghainese was the inverse of the Communist Party's rhetoric which described pre-1949 Shanghai as a parasitic 'consumer city'. This feeling of shared unfairness fostered distinctive senses of Shanghainese identity. However, this was only one aspect of a relationship of symbiotic commensality. If the rest of China was considered to be living off Shanghai, so many people were described as being fed by the state. This applied in particular to those in larger state enterprises; these people have an 'iron rice bowl' and are said to *chi guojia de* ('eat the food of the state') or *chi daguofan* ('eat from the big national pot'). An elderly man graphically summed up the situation in China in the following way: 'China only has one Party, if you don't eat this Party's food, you'll starve.' This comment can be compared to that of a rich share dealer in his mid-thirties who complained that at his work unit 'people just sit around, drink tea and read newspapers all day.' He said that he rarely went to his work unit, and added, 'I don't drink the Communist Party's tea, I can drink my own tea at home.' These two comments illustrate the changes in Shanghai society.

The elderly man describes especially the Maoist era when the 'iron rice bowl' dominated. The Maoist ideal had been to offer workers 'iron rice bowls' in return for their loyalty and commitment to building the revolution. In contemporary Shanghai the term *chi daguofan* ('eat from the big national pot') often serves as a synonym for socialism and has a rather derogatory meaning. It was, as Rofel found in Hangzhou, a synonym for a 'lazy work ethic' (1989: 238). The share dealer depicts the contemporary situation in which the 'unbreakable' rice bowl has been either broken or, at least, begun to leak as workers are hired on fixed term contracts and increasingly face the threat of redundancy. That the younger man did not have to drink the Communist Party's tea may serve as a metaphor for and is emblematic of the newly emergent possibilities for alternative lifestyles and means of livelihood far more independent of the control of the Party-state.

During the reform era it is widely believed that many people have refined the ability to consume and parasitically live off the state, in ways which go well beyond the sense of dependency and idleness imputed to those who *chi daguofan*. Shanghai's countless expensive new and refurbished restaurants are often filled with diners. This proliferation can be ascribed to the commercialisation of the economy and the association between commercial transactions and banqueting. More negatively, Shanghainese often suggest that much of this conspicuous

Cartoon 4.4 'Before retiring'. A cadre busy making the most of his power as a bureaucratic gatekeeper before he retires.

Source: *XMWB* 12 November 1993.

consumption involves *chi gongkuan* ('eating public funds') or *chi laogong* ('eating the Communist Party'). A retired accountant fulminated that this was very corrupt and that it made people very angry. He considered that 'this *chi laogong* is actually eating the blood of the ordinary people. This was why in the 1989 demonstrations the main protest was against official corruption, the *laobaixing* (ordinary people) supported this.'

In May 1989, several dozen Shanghai students emulated those in Beijing and embarked upon a hunger strike outside the city government headquarters on the Bund. The television pictures and descriptions of the hunger strikers – often referred to as the 'nation-family's children' – provoked a strong emotional response among many people. The moral power of this refusal to consume – conspicuous non-consumption – contrasted sharply with the perceived avaricious consumption by high officials.[15]

The manager of a Zhapu Road restaurant confirmed the impression of many Shanghainese that customers were often 'eating public funds'. Customers often asked for receipts, and they would be reimbursed later by their *danwei*. On one occasion I was shown around a newly opened restaurant by the manager. I subsequently described this visit to some Chinese friends employed in a state work unit. I told them that several hundred thousand *yuan* had been spent on furnishings including mahogany tables and chairs and, for example, flying in Taiwanese chefs and ingredients for its opening night. The immediate reaction of my friends was that it must be owned by the state. One of them explained that 'if money is being spent in this way it must be a state restaurant because the state's money can never be used up. If it runs out they just dig out more from the pockets of the *laobaixing*.'

A local slang expression which was indicative of individuals' changed relationship to society and changing social values was *hun ve tci/hun fan chi* (to get a meal just by muddling through) which could be translated as 'putting the minimum effort required into one's job.' A former teacher in his sixties remarked that *hun ve tci* could be contrasted to the term *gongxian* (contribute). He recalled that:

> In the early 1950s people worked very hard, this was to 'serve the people', it was *gongxian*. Then people would have despised somebody who said they *hun ve tci*. Now it's the other way round, even doctors may say they *hun ve tci*. People would consider somebody who said he was 'serving the people' as a fool.

Wealth inequalities

Some Shanghainese have become extremely wealthy during the reform era, but a substantial proportion of citizens has been left behind (see page 38–40). The unemployed and temporarily laid-off, for instance, form a largely hidden underclass unable to participate in popular consumption. For these people, with incomes of 270–400 *yuan* ($33–48) pcm; a meal at *McDonald's* is beyond their means, let alone, for instance, the designer-label ties on sale in Shanghai's fashionable *Maison Mode* store at prices of 900–1,150 *yuan* each.

Metaphors of eating could be used to express the new inequalities which are emerging. A factory worker told me, for instance, that rich share dealers 'eat big meat' whilst small-scale share buyers, such as herself, 'eat small meat'. Notions of expropriation and corruption could also be expressed through gastronomical metaphors. In business negotiations, people speak of the need for '*yanjiu*' to conclude a deal or solve a problem; *yanjiu* means 'to research', but a homonym is 'cigarettes and alcohol', popular lubricants to 'open doors'. Costly foods such as crabs and *Maotai* alcohol act as 'social lubricants' (Anderson 1988: 200) in gift-giving and the use of connections. A piece of doggerel acknowledged this widespread practice: *ma ge va tci, tci ge va ma/maide bu chi, chide bu mai* – the people who buy them don't eat them, the people who eat them don't buy them. The 'appetite' (*weikou*) of officials who accept bribes is said to depend upon how 'greedy' (*tanxin*) they are; the higher the official, the greater his 'appetite'.

It is considered axiomatic that top officials eat foods unavailable to the common people. Informants would assure me, for example, that Deng Xiaoping ate croissants flown in specially from France and that top Shanghai officials drank tea which cost 10,000 *yuan* per *jin*. More visible differences in consumption are also taken as evidence of inequalities. For instance, one informant commented on Zhapu Road restaurants that 'ordinary people cannot afford to eat there, you can tell the kind of people who eat there from the fact they arrive by car.'

In Chapter 2, I noted the importance of the hairy crabs eaten each Autumn. Since this prized food has increased dramatically in price in recent years, this could make comparisons with the past very unfavourable. For instance, one informant remarked that while in the Cultural Revolution crabs had cost just 2 *yuan* per *jin*, they now cost 80–100 *yuan* per *jin*. He remarked that 'my family used to eat them five or six times a year, now not at all.' The ability to consume or exclusion from consumption of these crabs could mark out different status groups. When I asked one informant who could afford to eat crabs, he suggested that they were 'mostly the class with special power and *getihu.*' A front-page article in *Xinmin Wanbao* (17 January 1993: 1) which caught many readers' attention described a couple who paid over 1,000 *yuan* for two large crabs. They refused to tell the journalist their names or occupation but would only comment that 'we are also ordinary salaried stratum.' The journalist and those I spoke with clearly did not believe this.

Instances of conspicuous consumption often provoke the anger of those who 'rely on their salaries to eat' (*kao gongzi chifan*), who complain that they cannot afford many of the products and entertainments now available. Many feel excluded from participating in the 'flood of consuming famous brand names' which are 'gushing' into Shanghai (*WHB* 13 May 1993: 7). Moreover, conspicuous consumption is frequently associated with corruption, the misuse of public funds, or those who have made money in some morally suspect way. This resentment may go much deeper amongst workers who have been laid-off and lack an alternative source of income. A redundant factory worker in her late forties, for instance, contrasted the plight of the several hundred workers at her *danwei* who had been laid-off with the 'hooligan factory manager' who 'eats and drinks at restaurants all day long.'

EMERGENT CONTOURS OF LIFESTYLE CONSUMPTION

Consumption can express and establish differences between social groups. Leiss *et al.* observe that '[p]eople in contemporary society come together in "taste cultures", "life-style groupings", or "market segments", which represent distinctive consumption patterns' (1986: 3). The term 'lifestyle consumers' can be used to indicate people's use of products to assert particular identities. These achieved identities overlap and may cross-cut more territorially based identifications such as 'Chinese' and 'Shanghainese'. On Shanghai television many advertisements promote 'looks' and 'lifestyles'. *Gillette* razor blades, for example, promise to make the user 'even more carefree and fashionable', and *Lux Shower Cream* to 'make (you) female that loves beauty even more attractive.' Traditional gender stereotypes dominate – men are doctors, businessmen, 'experts'; women are pretty, mothers, dancers, air-hostesses. Locations are often of modern kitchens, shopping malls, and 'exotic' places.

In Shanghai, one can find ample evidence of the way 'the person in the big city consumes in order to articulate a sense of identity, of who they wish to be taken to be' (Bocock 1993: 17). In everyday contexts there are many instances of the way the 'consumer is engaged in a continual task of grading goods and occasions and matching them appropriately' (Douglas 1992: 153). In a striking instance of this, I learnt of a work unit employee who regularly carried three brands of cigarettes – imported, good quality Chinese cigarettes, and poor quality local cigarettes. The type of cigarette offered depended upon the man's assessment of

Cartoon 4.5 'Untitled'. Child is saying 'Teacher, this is my name-card.'

Source: *XMWB* 16 November 1993.

the interactee's social status and/or potential instrumental value to himself. A distinct case of wanting to be taken as what one *presents* to others, which may be termed a literal presentation of self.

During the reform years name-cards have become a vital accessory to many professionals and business people in Shanghai. Often one person has multiple name-cards. At the start of an interview an interviewee would usually first hand me a name-card relating to their main profession. As the conversation touched upon differing aspects of their life so other cards may appear relating to sideline activities. In addition, a name-card with the home address might be proffered – the hand-written addition (or omission) of home phone, pager, mobile phone numbers, and Internet addresses adds further degrees of finesse. The presentation of different name-cards could be construed as proffering differing versions of the self, the decision of which cards to give dependent upon considerations including the degree of trust developed.

Lifestyle consumers

Bocock defines status groups as having 'a distinctive pattern of living, of eating, drinking, dressing, entertaining, in short of consuming' (1993: 6). The first distinctive 'status group' to emerge in the reform era were small-scale private entrepreneurs, *getihu*. Typically, *getihu* were portrayed as exemplars of conspicuous consumption, spending lavishly on karaoke bars, clothing, women, and food. They were said to do this to *gue padü/guai paitou* – display their wealth – or to *tse fongdü/chu fengtou* – seek to be in the limelight. *Getihu* are often termed *baofahu* – upstarts, people who have got rich quick. The root of the term *bao* in *baofahu* is 'sudden and violent' (also 'savage, cruel; hot-tempered; stand out' CED 1988: 24) – it may be used to describe the violence of a thunderstorm.

The consumption pattern of *getihu* is popularly perceived in just this way, with their money portrayed as spent wildly, freely, aggressively, with no concern for taste or finesse.

The socialising of *getihu* can be linked to their need to establish contacts. They extend their networks by shared eating and drinking, and thereby developing numerous *jiurou pengyou* – wine-and-meat friends. Those keen to cultivate *guanxi* must expend considerable effort, energy, and cost. Without some degree of 'emotional investment' (*ganqing touzi*) in the form of visits, shared eating and drinking, and so forth, *guanxi* weakens – an outcome conveyed in the saying: when a person has gone, the tea grows cold (*ren zuo le, cha liang le*). The term 'emotional investment' is clearly a highly instrumental conception of human relations and accords well with Smart's (1993) description of *guanxi* as a 'social capital of trust'. Shanghai's new entrepreneurs readily seize every opportunity to widen their *guanxi* network by developing numerous *jiurou pengyou*. This behaviour matches that observed by De Glopper amongst businessmen in Lukang, Taiwan where '[t]he aim seems to be a lot of amiable, matey, but not too intimate ties with as many people as possible' (1972: 320).

Women generally engage less in such socialising. Women with many social contacts may be regarded with ambivalence. At best they may be considered 'strong women' (*nuqiangren*) – in a society where the dominant view is that women should be 'soft and gentle' – and at worst 'loose women'. People with many social contacts are likely to have numerous *jiurou pengyou*, and it is salient that in Chinese conceptions of the properties of foods, wine, and meat are 'strong' foods with masculine connotations.

When analysing social differentiation in contemporary Shanghai, rather than using the terminology of 'class', it may be more appropriate to refer, as local people and newspaper reports do, to a 'car-using stratum' or a 'mobile phone-using stratum' (*dageda jieceng*). In Shanghai, the type of communication device a person has access to provides a reasonable indication of their social status. At the lowest level are those who rely upon public phones and the most prestigious means of communication is the mobile phone. A young office worker described the increasing disparity between rich and poor as Shanghai's most serious problem. He portrayed this as the difference 'between those who lead very hard lives in poor accommodation, and the few who have mobile phones'; a clear instance of the way in which, in contemporary society, consumption of products can be used to ascribe identities.

In 1988, there were just over 200 mobile phones in Shanghai. In the early 1990s, a local stereotype emerged of the businessman wearing a stylish suit, the mobile phone clutched in his hand a symbol of his power and ability to make things happen. The status of the mobile phone is implicit in its slang Chinese name, *dageda* – 'big brother big'. Shanghainese claimed that this term originated in Hong Kong to denote the head of a triad organisation. This genealogy, whether real or imagined, indicates the power and prestige associated with possession of a mobile phone. In 1993, a pager cost around 2,000 *yuan* ($347), but a mobile phone cost 20,000–30,000 *yuan* ($3,472–$5,208). As one informant commented, 'if somebody has a *dageda* you know he's rich, because the most a boss would give somebody is a pager.' Such electronic media make 'connections' easier and new types of links possible, but at the same time they create new boundaries and new types of exclusion both in the sense of the wealth they embody and the access to opportunities they provide which are denied to those who lack them.

Identifications between social prestige and products tend to be transient and ephemeral. Mobile phone ownership is a good instance of this. The exclusivity of mobile phones, and the elite status it accorded in the early 1990s, has already been eroded. In 1982 a Motorola 8500 mobile phone cost 27,000 *yuan* ($3,253), by 1997 it cost 5,000 *yuan* ($602) (*SS* 1 August 1997: 4). The 10,000th mobile phone was issued in December 1992 (*XMWB* 16 January 1993: 2). Six years later, over 1.5 million Shanghai residents had mobile phones (*SS* 21 September 1999: 3). Currently, private car ownership is considered as a mark of elite social status, although this is likely to change as the number of private vehicles increases.

In 1992, Shanghai's popular *New People's Evening Daily* reported that 'yuppies (*yapishi*) have now emerged in Shanghai' (*XMWB* 26 October 1992: 2). The term *yapishi* for this new 'status group' was newly coined, a transliteration from English. This article described them as being 'foreign-style' and mostly graduates from Shanghai's top universities who worked for foreign companies. Distinctive aspects of these young professionals included the way they speak foreign languages fluently, go to big hotels, travel by taxi, and are 'immaculately dressed'. The following section focuses upon the importance of famous brand name clothing.

Famous brand name clothing – the 'uncooked' consumer

Whilst in prison during the Cultural Revolution, Nien Cheng was faced by one interrogator who had hair greased down, good quality clothing, and a gold watch, 'the habitual attire of the capitalist class' (1986: 257–8). She was surprised to see somebody dressed in this way and writes that only later did she discover that this attire marked him out as 'a typical son of a senior army commander.' This instance indicates how styles of consumption may divide and can be expressive of power relationships. In contemporary China, power grows less obviously from the barrel of a gun than from the wallet. Clothing styles are now more diverse and their 'meanings' more ambiguous – they may indicate relations of power (dressed in a new guise) but may also be indicative or expressive of aspirations, commodification, and commercialism, as well as involving indigenous notions of face.[16]

In 1990s Shanghai, commercial products became an important sign of displaying a person's social status. The desire to acquire famous brand name (*mingpai*) products is an obvious instance of this. It provides an example of the way 'consumption involves the incorporation of the consumed item into the personal and social identity of the consumer' (Gell 1986: 112). An article in Shanghai's *Wenhui Bao* (13 May 1993: 7) suggested that in cities such as Shanghai people are 'compelled' to join the trend to buy *mingpai*, and explains that:

> Every commercial product has the symbolic function of displaying the owner's social and economic status, personality, accomplishment, character, and so forth. Particular products ... are always associated with a particular type of person, for example, high class cars are invariably associated with high ranking cadres, wealthy people and film stars, pianos are associated with dignified families, mobile phones with managers, bosses, and high-level company employees.

The article sees the craze for high levels of consumption as led by the propaganda of Western high consumption and the 'gushing in' of foreign famous brand products. Chinese consumers are depicted as too 'immature' (*bu chengshu*, literally 'unripe') to resist such pressures.

The *mingpai* clothing and accessories which people buy or aspire to buy are predominantly American and European products such as imported training shoes and, for the most wealthy, Swiss gold watches and designer-label suits. These products are far more expensive than locally made goods; for instance, at around 600 *yuan* a pair *Nike* trainers cost about ten times more than local brands of sports shoes. Purchase of such goods exemplifies Alan Tomlinson's definition of consumerism as 'the difference between buying an object mainly for its function, and acquiring an item for its style' (1990a: 9). Increasingly, these items become necessities, rather than luxuries, in the serious game of maintaining status at an appropriate level.

The common conflation of notions of 'the West' and 'modernity' was mentioned above. Now that wealth has become a key component in the judgement of a person's worth, imported goods can serve as symbols of success. The acquisition of expensive foreign clothing could also instil a sense of national or local pride. This 'purchasing pride' was evident in the comments of a businesswomen who had bought such clothing. She exclaimed, 'it gives me a sense of pride that as a Chinese and a Shanghainese I can afford to buy such items.' Her comments accord with Simmel's insight that 'the very act of buying is experienced as such a satisfaction, because the objects are absolutely obedient to money ... money provides a unique extension of personality' (1990: 326).

The desire and pressure to buy these products was especially apparent among the young and those engaged in commerce. In many ways these are the two sections of society, most affected by the increasingly marketised economy and for whom style has become 'a powerful medium of encounter' (Ewen 1990: 46). In 1999, a survey carried out among Shanghai teenagers found that as many as 49 per cent preferred brand name products (*SS* 25 May 1999: 9). The emergence in the 1990s of the popular use of the term *baozhuang* is indicative of this 'aestheticisation of social relations' (Ewen 1990: 46). In the early 1990s, *baozhuang* – pack or package – began to acquire the more abstract (English) meaning of the term 'packaging' as used in advertising.

Mike Featherstone stresses 'the importance of appearance and the "look"' in consumer culture (1991: 170). He suggests that with consumer culture a 'new conception of self has emerged' (187). He calls this a 'performing self' which 'places greater emphasis upon appearance, display and the management of impressions' (ibid.). Featherstone writes that in consumerist society 'individuals are required to be "on stage" all the time.' This approach is useful, but has a rather ethnocentric bias. From my interviews and conversations with Shanghainese it appears that the need for individuals to be 'on stage' was particularly strong in China's most virulently anti-consumerist phase, during the Cultural Revolution.

Informants likened the Cultural Revolution period to a dramatic stage in which individuals had to act out certain roles. Indigenous notions of 'face' in Shanghai indicate a conception of public behaviour as involving role-playing; for instance, the dialect term for 'lose face' (*te de/ta tai*) means, literally, a 'collapsing stage'. The key change in contemporary China is the much greater range, diversity, and origin of acceptable 'looks'. In the reform era, the presentation of self and the management of impressions are no longer dominated by relatively monolithic politically inspired notions of style. Instead, it is images purveyed by advertisers and the mass media which increasingly contribute to and are imbricated with the construction of socially acceptable 'looks' and perceptions of the body. Moreover, whereas people in the Cultural Revolution appear to have dressed largely *not* to be noticed, *not* to attract the surveillant gaze, they may now dress to attract an appreciative gaze.

The new stress upon 'packaging' and the associated desire for *mingpai* intersects with 'traditional' notions of face (*mianzi*). Face involves notions of prestige and may be described as a type of 'social capital' (Smart 1993: 402). A person with many connections is said to have a 'large face' (*mianzi hen da*). People wear *mingpai* to display or increase their social status, and many Shanghainese linked this to the way Shanghainese 'want face'. A library worker explained that 'Shanghainese judge people by their clothing, they pay great attention to this packaging.' Now that economic success is often perceived to be the main determinant of a person's worth it is increasingly important for the packaging of the individual – clothing, make-up, and other adornments – to conform to media-derived images of success.

In Shanghai, this may also be linked to the burgeoning discourses of individualism and self-fulfilment. Shanghainese undoubtedly now have available many new styles they can use to present to the world. Typically, though, the particular products that people desire to consume, and the lifestyles they hope to achieve, are closely related to the category systems of consumers constructed by advertisers. Consumers may, for instance, seek to emulate patterns of consumption depicted in 'lifestyle format' advertising (Leiss *et al.* 1986: 210–15). However, this is also a reflexive, interactive process. Producers, for instance, engage in extensive market research; they are responding to as well as (in)forming 'consumer demands'.

The desire of young people to buy *mingpai* contributes to a perception of many elderly people that Chinese youth are losing the traditional value of thrift. In buying clothes, older people generally stress durability. Chinese viewers of Western soaps remarked on the way that Western middle-aged woman 'dress-up' and wear make-up. They contrasted this to the lack of such adornments among their Chinese contemporaries. However, this is beginning to change.

The lure of the West is especially strong for university students and they often adopt the status symbols of the West. Male university students, for instance, wear suits and ties on a regular basis – ironically modes of dress that many Western students actively avoid. Shanghai youth dress-up to be *xiaosa* – 'stylish' or 'trendy'. Through being *xiaosa*, young people adopt the packaging of success and hope that this will help them obtain the other accoutrements of success – a good job, wealth, and a suitable spouse. Style, appearance and 'packaging' have become crucial in searching for employment. The employment of students is no longer a 'blind marriage' where neither party sees the other. Instead students must now present a 'marketable self' and appeal, often in competition with other candidates, to employers who can choose to accept or reject them.

Businessmen too wear expensive clothes to display their social status (*shenjia* – literally 'the value of their body', but also 'the selling price of a slave') and to facilitate their commercial activities. In the absence of personal ties, businessmen can most readily be judged by the cost of the clothing they wear. As one informant noted, 'they must have this face in order to do business.' In business, as in job hunting and mate selection, a good 'presentation' is extremely important.

The desire for *mingpai* provides evidence of a developing youth culture, and differentiation through consumption. Similar processes are at work in the Shanghai Christmas, and a final vignette illustrates how this recently imported consumer ritual can also incorporate resistance to the state.

Shanghai Christmas – a new ritual of consumerism

Shanghai is filling up with familiar retail outlets such as *McDonald's, Kentucky Fried Chicken, Pizza Hut* and *Häagen Daz* ice cream parlours. Does this mean that the city is losing its distinctiveness? A brief examination of the 'Shanghai Christmas', a recently imported ritual of consumption, indicates that convergence happens at only the most superficial of levels and that much is adapted and incorporated in unique ways. Christmas, like other forms of popular culture, 'offers a rich iconography, a set of symbols, objects and artefacts' (Hebdige 1988: 74) which people can reassemble to suit their own ends. Miller cites the Trinidadian Christmas as an example of the way 'consumption . . . takes the imported goods and gives them meaning in relation to local debates and symbolic struggles' (1994: 319, see also Miller 1993). This same process can be seen at work in the Shanghai Christmas.

The festival of Christmas re-emerged in Shanghai in the late 1980s and mainly involved university students organising their own festivities, they sent cards, gave presents, and held parties. In many respects this 'invocation of an exotic elsewhere' (Hebdige 1988: 9) had meanings very different from the places of its origin. In England, Christmas is a time for family gatherings at home. It is a ritual fully supported by the established church and the state. In Shanghai, by contrast, the appropriation of this Western festival provided Chinese youth with a space in which alternative (and, perhaps, oppositional) meanings to dominant cultural traditions could be negotiated and expressed.

Many young Shanghainese felt a sense of ennui for Spring Festival, a ritual promoted by the state and supported by their parents. This contrasted with their enthusiasm for the imported festival of Christmas. Their descriptions of Spring Festival resembled the dominant image of Christmas in England, both were dominated by the family and home, consumption of foods and television watching. For young Shanghainese, however, Christmas was a time to 'play' – to go out with friends, and for dancing parties.

The Shanghai Christmas contributed to a widening generation gap. It could also be oppositional to the state. The state has attempted to dampen enthusiasm for Christmas. Television stations were instructed to ignore Christmas because 'it is not a Chinese festival.' In work units, young workers were prevented from organising parties and taking time off. University students were told not to celebrate Christmas and threatened with punishment if they missed classes. Such restrictions were imposed in an attempt to restrict the influence of 'Westernisation' which had, in the view of the authorities, encouraged people to call for such 'bourgeois' ideas as greater democracy.

By 1993, Christmas had spread beyond the confines of universities. Across the city hotels staged expensive events, restaurants were decorated with coloured lights and imitation snow, and street stalls sold bundles of Christmas cards and pots of poinsettia plants described as *seng de ho/shengdanhua* – 'Christmas flowers'. Faced with these developments, a young joint venture employee complained that Christmas had become 'too commercialised' in Shanghai, a puzzling remark given that Christmas had no religious significance for her.

A small private restaurant I chanced upon in mid-December had just been refurbished and was ready to open. However, the manager explained that he was waiting until Christmas, a *renao* ('hot and noisy') time, to reopen. This deferment follows the 'traditional' belief that some days are more auspicious and lucky than others; 25 December had been slotted into this conception. The decor was a 'mix and match' of cultural forms with a statue of *Guanyin*, the Buddhist Goddess of Mercy, offerings of fresh oranges, little plastic models of Father Christmas and fir trees and, dominating the room, a large, brand new Japanese karaoke outfit. Here, as elsewhere in Shanghai, it is likely that the 'Christmas' decorations would remain on view throughout the year. Similarly, at parties to celebrate (the Western) New Year's Eve, the midnight hour is often marked by a karaoke rendition of 'Jingle Bells', a song associated with Christmas in Britain and America. This incorporation of Christmas into the local ritual and commercial calendar and the bricolage of cultural artefacts is a fine illustration of the way imported cultural forms are adapted and incorporated in unique ways.

CONCLUDING REMARKS

There is much to be welcomed in Shanghai's consumer revolution. As the city enters the new millennium, there is a degree of affluence and a multipareity of potentialities and opportunities that was unimaginable two decades ago. In daily media broadcasts, in the spirit of 'reporting only the good news and not the bad' (*baoxi bu baoyou*), the Party-state loudly trumpets the remarkable achievements of the reform era. In these concluding remarks, it is worth pondering some of the less positive aspects of the consumer revolution.

Consumerism in Shanghai is producing, facilitating, and marking out new divisions in society. These may involve potentially dangerous tensions. The Chinese revolution has long since ceased to be about revolutionary aims and ideals but about meeting the consumer demands of the masses. Deng Xiaoping held out the promise of a 'comfortable living standard' for all Shanghai citizens, and it is essential that his successors realise this goal. Raising expectations and aspirations is a dangerous business if they cannot be met.

At present Deng's objective appears attainable, incomes generally are higher, and the range and quality of consumer products is increasing. However, meeting consumer demands is inevitably a game of diminishing returns. Even if consumerism is an opium of the masses, it may take ever greater ingestion to reach the same high, and scary things can happen when the supply is denied. Somebody may remember when their family bought its first television set. They may, perhaps, recall when black-and-white was replaced with colour, although even this is surely less memorable. But acquisition of a second colour television or replacing the first set with a newer model is far less likely to leave a scratch on the memory. Expectations and desires, once fed, grow and their appetite is enlarged. Gratification is momentary, transient, and increasingly difficult to attain.

For much of the Maoist era people were stuck with ascribed, and largely immutable, class and political labels, and jobs they had probably not chosen; and egalitarian levels of consumption were strongly encouraged and, at times, enforced. Identities in Shanghai are, perhaps increasingly, contingent and contextual, there being a wide range of cross-cutting, possible identifications. Douglas Kellner (1992) contrasts 'modern' and 'post-modern' identities. He writes that '[w]hile the locus of modern identity revolved around one's occupation, one's function in the public sphere (or family), post-modern identity revolves around leisure, centred on looks, images, and consumption' (153). It is interesting to ask, according to these formulations, whether Shanghai is 'modern' or 'post-modern'?

The growth and proliferation of advertising, media images, and the stress upon consumption which has been so marked in the reform era have all provided material from which to forge and fashion a range of 'post-modern' identities. The availability of proliferating styles of clothing and personal decoration has opened up possibilities for the expression of many new kinds of identity. Shanghai's re-internationalisation has played an important part in this by providing local people with a plethora of alternative images and products from which to fashion identities. Social relationships and perceptions of self have become less bound to physical place, more fluid, and, perhaps, more ephemeral. The inflow of media images and products from exotic elsewheres spurs aspirational identities, identities which are asserted or recognised by or through the consumption of products. Imported cultural products can facilitate the development of deterritorialised consumer identities, they may also contribute to and cross-cut with notions of Shanghainese cosmopolitanism and sophistication enhancing senses of differentiation from China's rural poor and promoting identification with affluent overseas Chinese.

Inevitably the degree to which individuals are both able to and wish to 'buy' into such identities differs enormously. Additionally, 'modern' and 'post-modern' identities are not mutually exclusive, but often concurrent and inter-leaven. For many I met in Shanghai, their main preoccupations were their 'traditional' family roles as grandparents, parents, daughters or sons and as friends. These identities were, themselves, though being influenced and subtly redefined by proliferating media narratives which provide models and, at times, advise directly, for instance, on how to be a better mother or a more filial son.

For those with financial resources Shanghai's re-monetised economy offers much individual freedom. Some describe the reform process as China's 'second liberation'. But for the unemployed and impoverished this emancipation may well be chimeric; it is 'freedom *from* something, not liberty *to do* something' (Simmel 1990: 402). Even those on average incomes are faced with an ever upwardly spiralling list of consumer demands to meet, if not for themselves, then for their children or their grandchildren. The sense of injustice created by rising wealth inequalities never seems far away. Moreover, scratch the surface of consumer bliss and the scars of lives blighted and hopes dashed are revealed all too often.

In the event of a general economic downturn the newly emergent distinctions outlined in this chapter may rapidly become fractures and fissures along which frustrations and discontent flow. A new range of targets and scapegoats may serve as the focus for collective discontent amongst those denied access to popular consumerism or who lose their ability to participate in this consumption. Chief amongst these targets could be newly emergent strata of wealthy consumers, especially if they are considered to have achieved their wealth by unscrupulous means.

New forms of consumption undermine the state because they help to fashion identities beyond or at least less amenable to its reach. Governing China is, perhaps increasingly, like trying to pick up slippery mushrooms with chopsticks. The new sociological contours fostered by consumerism were almost certainly never anticipated by the Communist Party, and are likely to prove increasingly impervious to efforts to control and marshal them in directions of its choosing. The Chinese state's key resource to mobilise the populace remains an appeal to Chinese nationalism, a powerful but potentially volatile and uncontrollable force which surfaced most recently during the protests which followed the bombing of the Chinese embassy in Belgrade by NATO planes in May 1999.

If the fracturing of Chinese society into an ever greater range of market segments presents difficulties for Party-state control, it also undermines the scope for mass, collective resistance. During the demonstrations of Spring 1989 many participants acted under their work-place banners. The increasing fragmentation of the social fabric substantially precludes such solidarity. Moreover, the identities imbricated with consumer products and lifestyles are constructed on shifting sands; mobilisation built on mobile phone ownership or attachment to a brand label is clearly implausible. For better or worse, the genie is out of the consumer bottle and it cannot be forced back in.

5 Share dealers, trading places and new options in contemporary Shanghai

The comedy play 'OK Stock' performed in Shanghai in March 1993 portrayed many of the strands which were present and the changes which were taking place in that city in the early 1990s.[1] The protagonist was Ah Nai, a middle-aged factory worker who has been made redundant but who becomes increasingly involved in the newly resuscitated Shanghai share market. By the end of the play he has become a *dahu*, a rich man. Midway through the play Ah Nai delivers a short soliloquy which encapsulated much that I had heard and read about the lives of most Shanghai people before the 1980s. At this point in the play Ah Nai has just told his wife, Ding Yiying, that he has lost his job. She berates him and tells him that he should go to the factory and demand it back.

> **Ah Nai**: What would I go there for? To rebel? Since the higher authorities have already made a decision, I've just got to accept it.
>
> **Ding Yiying**: Accept, accept, accept! You only know how to accept. It's easy to bully you. People just piss on your head! Regulations are dead, people are alive!
> (Ah Nai moves to centre right stage and, illuminated by a single spotlight, sums up his life history)
>
> **Ah Nai**: Whether they are dead or alive, I carry them all out. In any case I've always lived according to regulations, I'm used to it... I was told which primary school I should go to, so I just went to that primary school; I was told which middle school to attend, so I just went to that middle school; when I was told where to go and work in the countryside, I went to that place to work in the countryside; when I was ordered to return to the city, I returned to the city; when I was ordered to go to a particular work unit, that was the work unit I went to. It even got to the point where I was told which hospital to go to, which rice store to buy rice in, where to buy special purchases for Spring Festival, and I just fell in line with each and every one of these orders. Now I'm told that I am made redundant (*xiagang*), so I just *xiagang*.

In the Preface, I recorded the comment of a prominent local writer that the changes he had witnessed since 1991–2 were 'of an extent that a person such as myself could never have imagined.' High among his list of unthinkable changes was the stock 'craze' or 'fever' (*gupiaore*) that took hold in the early 1990s. The re-introduction of a share market appears dramatically opposed to the policies and rhetoric which had gone before. How people reacted to this U-turn and what effect it had upon people's lifestyles and perceptions of society should tell us much about social relationships in contemporary urban China.

The resuscitation and exponential growth of a share market in Shanghai has played an important part in redrawing the social contours of the city. A review article described 'OK Stock' as 'so close to home that many Shanghai audiences feel that they are part of the story' (*SS* 5 March 1993: 15). Such assertions accorded with the comments of Shanghainese I attended the play with. Roy Dilley notes that a 'market' should not be seen as 'a transhistorical and acultural agent' but, rather, as a product of 'the participants' understanding and conception of their own social and economic activity' (1992: 14–15). It is just such an approach that this chapter takes. The focus is a 'share market with Chinese characteristics' – apparent even in the slang term *chao gupiao* – 'buying and selling shares' – which literally means to stir-fry stocks.

THE SHANGHAI SHARE MARKET: FROM COAGULATION TO SPECULATION[2]

Before 1949, Shanghai was a major banking and financial centre with a stock market similar in size to that of Tokyo and considerably larger than that of Hong Kong (see Karmel 1994: 1105–7). Fluctuations in the Shanghai stock exchange over the period 1919–49 exercised a significant influence over both these other markets. An official Chinese publication observed (with a note of irony?) that '[a]ll this disappeared with the founding of the People's Republic of China in 1949' (*BR* 1989a: 21). The new government regarded 'stock ownership as a kind of capitalist exploitation of workers' (cited in Engle 1986: 36).

In 1992, China's central government declared a national aim to create a 'socialist market economy'. As a crucial adjunct to this, Shanghai was earmarked to become an international financial and commercial centre. The fledgling Shanghai share market has been a key beneficiary of this new emphasis. One Shanghai textile factory is recorded as having 'quietly' issued stock in 1981 (Engle 1986: 36). However, it was not until November 1984 that shares were first sold officially to the Shanghai public when the collectively owned *Feile Audio Company* issued 10,000 shares at 50 *yuan* each. Two months later *Yanzhong Industrial Company* issued shares to the public.

In August 1986, the People's Bank of China established an over-the-counter market in Shanghai (another was set up in Shenyang). At this time *Feile* and *Yanzhong* were the only stocks traded on this market. During this 'experimental phase' transactions were carried out in eight offices (*China Newsletter* 1987). Prices were relatively static and most transactions completed by hand with little in the way of electronic equipment. Lack of communication facilities meant that sometimes the same stock had different prices at different trading centres. Little over five years later, the Shanghai Stock Exchange (SSE) had moved to paperless trading and real-time trading via satellite across China. Despite this, a distinct Chinese characteristic was that the SSE still closed for lunch from 11.30 a.m. until 1 p.m.

The SSE was officially opened on 19 December 1990, just over six months before China's other official stock exchange in Shenzhen.[3] By 1994, on an active day, its daily turnover rivalled that of the Hong Kong stock exchange (Karmel 1994: 1111). The SSE uses a real-time dealing system – Securities Trading Automated Quotations System (STAQS) – based on the US NASDAQ. As early as the closing months of 1990, some 400,000 of Shanghai's residents had already taken part in securities trading activities (*BR* 1989a: 22). However, it was in 1992 that 'share fever' really first took hold. In that year trading volume increased tenfold and the SSE index quadrupled in the space of a few months (*World Business Report* 25 March 1993). Until late 1991 only eight companies were listed on the SSE with a combined capitalisation of around 1 billion *yuan*. By the first half of 1993 there were 67 stocks with a capitalisation of 200 billion *yuan*. By the end of 1993 there were about 100 listed stocks, with manufacturing firms forming the majority. By mid-1997 there were 287 A-shares and 42 B-shares.[4]

In one year (to November 1993) the number of trading centres where one could buy and sell shares increased from 25 to over 300. The manager of one centre told me these 'now outnumber state rice-selling depots in the city.' Trading volume on the SSE increased at an incredible rate – in 1992 turnover was $11.17 billion, six times the figure for 1991. By 1994, dealing on a single day could be greater than for the whole of 1991. Between January–June 1994 turnover was 563 billion *yuan* ($64.7 billion) 14 per cent more than the total for 1993 (*SS* 12 July 1994: 7). By May 1994, Shanghai listed stocks had a market capitalisation of over $25 billion (*Economist* 14 May 1994: 111–12).

By mid-1993, the number of Shanghainese registered on the SSE rose to over one million and 60,000 new stock exchange accounts were being opened each week (*World Business Report* 24 June 1993). In late 1993, a Chinese source gave the number of Shanghai investors as two million (*XMWB* 5 December 1993: 5). Even taking the lower figure of one million, if each registration represents one family and each family has four members then the stock market touches the lives of about four million people, roughly one-third of Shanghai's population, in a significantly direct fashion.

The Shanghai 'stock craze' was sparked off by the issuing of share purchase certificates (*rengouzheng*) in February 1992. These certificates were a form of lottery system, in which winning tickets gave the holder the right to buy shares at their issue price. Whether by design or accident the proportion of winning coupons was far higher than originally expected. On the black market, coupons with a face value of 30 *yuan* were soon being sold for as much as 1,400 *yuan*. One tragi-comic motif in the play 'OK Stock' concerns an uneducated elderly man who unwittingly buys 3,000 *yuan* of *rengouzheng* whilst trying to deposit his life savings in the bank. Once he realises his mistake, he desperately tries to get a refund for this 'waste paper'. He finally manages to off-load the coupons, at a discount, on a sympathetic neighbour. Only then does the value of these coupons become apparent... An initial outlay of 3,000 *yuan* could ultimately translate into shares worth 300,000–500,000 *yuan* – in the space of a few weeks a new wealthy group was created in Shanghai. These certificates have passed into Shanghai popular mythology with stories of people who bought them by mistake and unexpectedly became wealthy overnight. One informant remarked to me that they had become like a child's fairy tale which people hope will be repeated.

'Socialist shares can only go up!'[5]

The Shanghai stock index is characterised by sharp fluctuations. The first big crash was in 1992 when the price index, which had reached over 1,300 in May, plummeted to 300 at the end of the year. Then, after reaching over 1,500 in early 1993, the A-share index fell for 18 months, losing around 80 per cent of its value, to a low of 328.9 at the end of July 1994. On one day alone, 21 April 1994, the market fell by 5.8 per cent to 552.5. In August, the government announced a series of 'market rescue measures' including a freeze on new issues for the rest of the year (*SS* 9 August 1994: 7). Investors reacted with 'volcanic enthusiasm' (*CD* 5 August 1994: 1). In the week 29 July–5 August 1994, the SSE index rose by 104 per cent, up from 349 to 683 with a weekly turnover of $3.9 billion and 5.7 billion shares traded. Just over one month later, by 7 September, the SSE had exceeded the 1,000 level. A rise of this magnitude would take several years on the London or New York stock exchanges. By mid-October the index had fallen back to 650. Individual shares can be even more volatile. In October 1993, the *Yanzhong Company* was subject to a take-over attempt and its share price fluctuated dramatically – at one point the price quadrupled in the space of a few hours.

Unlike Western share markets, which are dominated by pension funds and other institutional investors, on the Shanghai market individuals accounted for 90 per cent of the dealing in 'publicly issued individual shares' (*shehui geren gu*).[6] In work places, homes, buses, and restaurants all over the city, shares became a main topic of conversation. A vogue expression asserted that *quanguo jiegu* – 'the whole country likes shares.' A scientific research worker told me that 'in Shanghai everyone buys shares, from elderly housewives who normally just stay at home doing the housework to high-level cadres and intellectuals, from teenagers to old people in their seventies and eighties.'[7] In 1992–4, every day, on television, after the early evening news the latest share prices of all the increasing number of listed companies were read out to the sound of a piped version of *A Whiter Shade of Pale*. These bulletins and numerous newspaper, television, and radio references to shares all contributed to widespread awareness of and an active involvement in the share market.

Many Shanghainese could hardly believe the changes taking place in their city. A retired teacher noted how some people could now make millions from shares, and described how his neighbour's house had been searched by Red Guards during the Cultural Revolution. The neighbour had been dragged from his house, beaten, paraded through the streets, and abused as a 'capitalist'. His 'crime' was that a few dozen *yuan* of worthless, pre-1949 share certificates had been found. Faced with this incongruity the retired teacher remarked that along with many other people he had not yet 'changed his thinking' (*huan naodai*) in the way official rhetoric now exhorts citizens to do.

Chinese characteristics

The expression *chao gupiao*, literally to 'stir-fry' shares, refers to the rapid buying and selling of shares. The verb here is taken from the action used in stir-frying food in a wok. Following Lakoff and Johnson's (1980) contention that metaphor may be both expressive and constitutive of meaning, I will use the indigenous term rather than the English 'buying and selling shares' which lacks the pungency and sense of rapid motion implicit in the Chinese term. In Chinese cookery timing is often crucial, with fierce heat and a short cooking time. An expert share dealer told me that one should 'stir-fry' stocks until they are very hot, that is buy and sell them very rapidly, and thereby cook-up a profit. The way shares were often bought on a short-term basis was paralleled by a more general short-termism, a sense that one had better make money whilst it was still possible. Some of my informants described the current apparent economic boom in Shanghai as just *paomo*, a 'bubble'. Many people feared that unrest might follow the death of Deng Xiaoping. One *dahu* commented that on the day Deng dies Shanghai stocks would fall by 80 per cent. Although he added that, if you held your nerve, this could be an ideal buying point.[8]

One trading centre manager, a man in his early forties, provided some fascinating remarks which highlighted the 'Chineseness' of the Shanghai share market. In one of several discussions, I asked him if any people had their own computer software and could buy and sell shares from home. He estimated that about one hundred people in Shanghai had a home computer loaded with market analysis software. However, he considered it unlikely that many people would deal from home because of the nature of the Shanghai share market. In his estimation, if they were so isolated they would be unable to deal successfully, since Shanghai has an 'irrational and highly emotional share market' in which the *shiqi* ('market mood') and *renqi* ('popular mood') are extremely important. These terms defy simple translation. *Shi* means 'market', *ren* has various meanings including 'person, human being, people' but also 'personality, character' and 'state of one's health, how one feels.' *Qi*, he explained, was used here in the sense it is used in Chinese medicine – the dictionary definition for *qi* is 'vital energy, energy of life' – and that it includes, for example, 'people's feeling or mood' (*ren de qingxu*). He noted that because the share market has this character it is necessary to hear the 'talk of the masses' in order to pick up on the *renqi*. He added that the share market is affected by 'a climate created by everybody' and that even factors such as the weather can affect it. The way in which he described the share market as affected by 'feelings' (*ganqing*) ties in with wider indigenous notions of China as a 'feelings country' (*renqing guojia*).

Official reasons for reintroducing a share market

In Britain in the 1980s, Margaret Thatcher attempted to extend share ownership as part of her ideological attempt to foster 'popular capitalism'. Arriving in Shanghai in September 1992, I was struck by the extent to which this facet of popular capitalism had taken hold in a nominally socialist state. Why had Chinese planners embarked upon this experiment?

An article in *China Daily* on the stock system noted that initially 'some people rejected it as a capitalist practice' but added that this belief has 'faded' (*CD* 21 September 1992: 4). A prime motive for issuing stocks and bonds was to raise funds for investment and construction. In 1992, issuing stocks to the public raised 11.8 billion *yuan* ($2 billion) for construction in the city (*CD* 13 January 1993: 1). Another Chinese newspaper article suggested following the example of countries like Britain where shares of government-owned monopolies were sold to the public to 'get rid of the financial burdens posed by subsidies to these enterprises' (*CD* 4 February 1993: 4). Stock holding was claimed to promote decentralisation and promote efficiency, making enterprises answerable to stock holders rather than government ministries. It was also intended to consolidate companies' decision-making power and enhance employees' participation and motivation by making them share-holders in their companies, thereby strengthening 'enterprises' vitality' (*BR* 1989b: 22–3). The government also regarded huge personal bank deposits as a 'caged tiger' which, if released, would cause havoc in the consumer market-place (Xie 1990: 18). Issuing shares would be a positive way to use this money. In addition, the state receives tax revenue from share transactions – 3/1000 of each deal is earmarked for the government and the exchange receives 4/1000.

Proponents of the stock exchange experiment argued that issuing shares would 'enliven' the 'dead' economy and lead to increased efficiency and better-quality products. However, I heard contesting views in Shanghai. In local slang some shares were referred to as 'rubbish shares' (*lajigu*) – these included stocks in companies which produced unmarketable goods and issued shares primarily as a means for staving off bankruptcy. A similar term was 'mistress shares' (*qingfugu*). It was explained to me that such shares could be profitable if 'fooled around with' for a short time but definitely should not be held long-term. It was also said that workers who had now become shareholders in their companies had a more positive attitude towards their work. I did not research this specific topic but a television comedy sketch I watched hinted at potential problems. In the sketch a female shop assistant has just become a shareholder in her company. The comedy dwells on her repeated and unsuccessful attempts to be polite to customers now that she will benefit, indirectly, from the profits of the company.

'SHARE PEOPLE': SHANGHAI PUNTERS

Share dealers in Shanghai were collectively referred to as *gumin* – 'share people'. They were divided into three categories: *xiaohu* or *sanhu* (small or 'dispersed' *hu*), *zhonghu* (middle *hu*) and *dahu* (big *hu*).[9] The crowded ground floor of each securities trading centre was where 'small *hu*' *chao gupiao*, unheated in the freezing winter, stifling in the hot, humid summers. The latest share prices were displayed on a large black electronic screen, the audience peering anxiously at the constantly changing red figures, making careful notes and computations. Shares were bought and sold over a counter. These places had all the noise, bustle and excitement (*renao*) of more traditional markets. Individuals who wished to buy and sell shares had to first register and make an initial deposit of 5,000 *yuan*. They were then issued with a plastic magnetic card on which details were kept of their account balance, deals and share holdings.

The vast majority of share buyers were 'small *hu*' with no more than several thousand *yuan*.[10] However, the Shanghai stock market has made a significant contribution to the formation of a new wealthy stratum. I met one *dahu* in the coffee lounge of the city's five star Garden Hotel. I asked him about the impact of the share market and other reforms on Shanghai. He motioned to the luxurious surroundings and told me, 'five years ago the guests here were all foreigners, now look, they are mainly Chinese.' Rich share dealers I interviewed had appropriated a dialect term *mamaha/momohei* ('inky black') to describe a large amount of money. The image is of so much money that it cannot be clearly seen: it conveys a sense of uncountable, unimaginable riches.

Each of Shanghai's three hundred-plus securities trading centres had a special dealing room or rooms, *dahushi*. These were 'special spaces' for the sole use of those *dahu* who paid a monthly membership fee (*MZWYB* 17–23 May 1993: 4). One medium-sized centre I visited had 6,000–7,000 registered 'small *hu*' and three *dahushi*. Typically, these rooms had comfortable seating, air conditioning, individual computer terminals loaded with systems to analyse and track share movements and a receptionist who used a 'hot line' to phone direct to the SSE to buy and sell shares for members. In slack periods *dahu* chatted or played mah-jong. Many trading centres also had a separate room for 'middle *hu*'. These provided a lower level of service than the *dahushi*. The entrance requirement for a 'middle-*hu* room' was around 300,000 *yuan*. To put this in perspective, the monthly wage of most Shanghainese was between 300–1,000 *yuan*.

Dahu, the successful dealers

There were no statistics on the number of *dahu* nor was there a strict definition of who could be called a *dahu*. In the early years of the agricultural reforms propaganda praised 'ten thousand *yuan* households'. A local Shanghai rhyme adapted this and, exaggerating somewhat, asserted that – 'ten thousand *yuan* households are not even worth considering, one hundred thousand is just a first step, one million can be considered small fry, ten million is a *dahu*.' A trading centre manager estimated that there were between 10,000 and 20,000 *dahu* in Shanghai. This estimate, which seems reasonable, was based upon the assumption that each centre had an average of 30 *dahu*. The funds required to be entitled to use *dahushi* varied – some centres required half a million, others one million, even two million

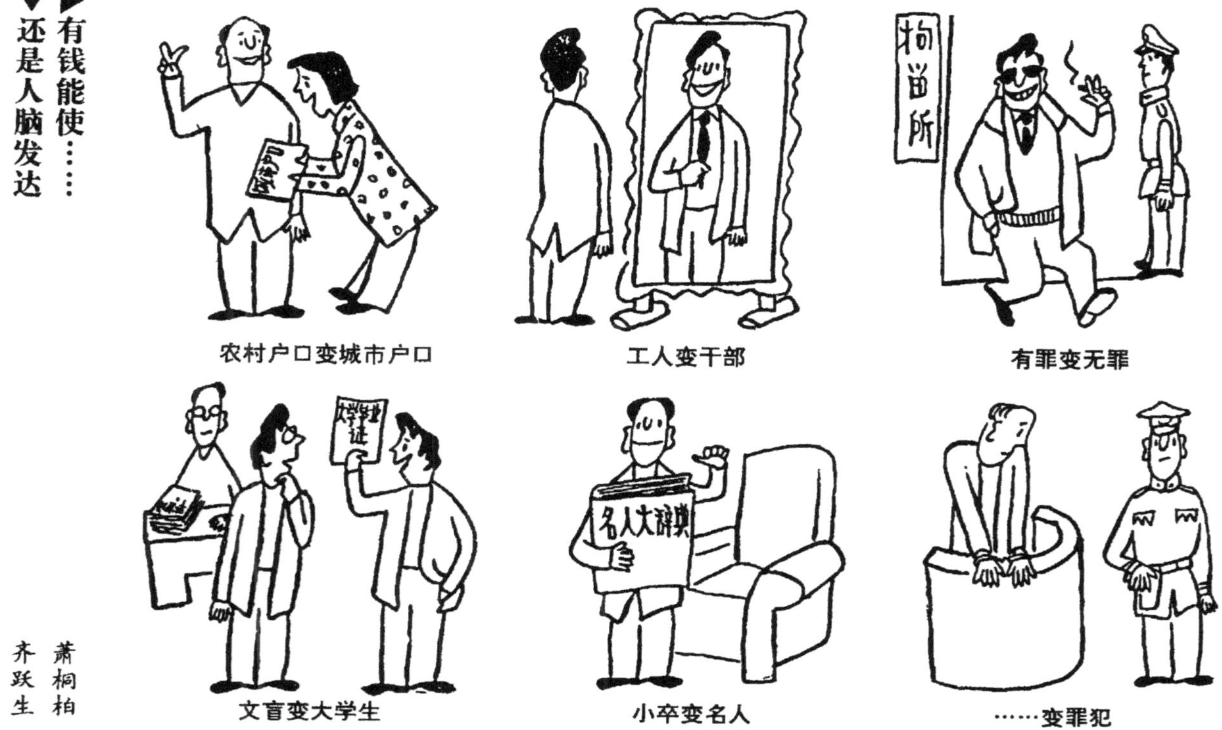

Cartoon 5.1 ‘Money can make . . .’ [From left to right, top to bottom] ‘a rural household registration into an urban one, a workers into a cadre, a guilty person into an innocent one, an illiterate person into a university student, a nobody into a famous person . . . into a crook.’

Source: *Manhua Shijie* (The World of Cartoons), 1994: 16.

yuan. During the extended 18-month bear market – described as a 'cold' (*leng*) period in the market – the requirement in some centres was lowered to 200,000 *yuan*. Some *dahu* used funds of friends and colleagues or acted on behalf of *danwei*. Not all share dealers who might be eligible wished to use a *dahushi*. Certainly the *dahu* constituted only a tiny percentage in a city of over 13 million people, an exceptional elite.

Some of the new indigenous terms concerning share dealing indicated that not all participants made a profit. One such term was *ge rou* – to cut or slice a piece of meat (from one's own body). This referred to selling shares at a loss, in the expectation that they would fall further still. Another term was *taozhu* ('stuck fast'), which occurred when shares fell below the price they were bought for and the owner waits in the hope that their value will rise again. A problem for those with such negative equity was that Shanghai shares were extremely volatile – they 'turn somersaults' (*fan gentou*). It was difficult to gauge when prices had reached their lowest point or, in picturesque local slang, when the market had 'shat itself clean' (*gusi sa qingzang/gushi la qingchu*). Another term was *tiaolou*, which has two meanings. One is to commit suicide by jumping out of a tall building – for several decades Shanghai was the only city in China with tall enough buildings to make this a feasible means of suicide. The second meaning is of shares falling rapidly in value.

A mythology of anecdotes and stories propagated by magazines, cheap novels, and endless gossip surrounded *dahu*. An early hero of this sort (from c.1989) was Yang Baiwan, 'Millions' Yang, a former warehouse worker who started with just 2,000–3,000 *yuan* in capital and became the first person to publicly make a million on the share market. A trading centre manager mused that 'Yang Baiwan is no big deal now. There are people with far more money than him but they keep quiet about it.'

Aside from celebrities such as 'Millions' Yang, *dahu* tended to maintain a low profile. A trading centre manager considered that many *dahu* live 'very simple, hard lives.' He suggested that they might be afraid to reveal their wealth as people might harm them or try to borrow money from them. He added that while many Chinese people seek fame and wealth (*jiang mingli*), *dahu* mostly want only wealth and not fame. I share this impression. A particularly striking example was the home of one female *dahu* I visited. Single and just under forty, she displayed no evidence of her wealth. Her tiny one-room flat, where she lived alone, had no television, no new furniture, and no heating. In style-conscious Shanghai she still wore the deeply unfashionable black canvas shoes one now only sees worn in the countryside. Some *dahu* wore the latest imported brand name fashions. However, like this woman, some showed no outward signs of wealth. One *dahu* remarked that wealthy businessmen were more likely to wear famous brand names since they needed to display their status to foster their business activities whilst 'share dealers only interact with a computer.' Entrances to *dahushi* often appeared to be deliberately discreet. One I visited was reached through a narrow passage, past overflowing rubbish bins and up a flight of stairs and into an unmarked door.

How did *dahu* use their new wealth? In popular perceptions those who rapidly made a fortune (*baofahu*) spent money lavishly and wastefully, especially on restaurant meals and leisure pursuits such as karaoke. *Dahu* I spoke with agreed that some spent a portion of their wealth in this way, but were keen to stress that further investment was more common. They bought more shares, and/or moved into other 'craze' sectors, opening restaurants, or investing in real estate or futures. Some would '*chao*' anything from golf club membership cards to a tiny plot of land in the US. One young *dahu*, a 26-year old man, spent part of his cash on compact discs of British heavy rock music. Another *dahu* had bought three houses in the nearby city of Suzhou. Each house had cost between $30,000–40,000 and he described them as long-term investments. He also owned a restaurant and had set up a small factory. When we discussed his plans for the future he talked about his hopes for his daughter. He suggested that he may arrange for her to study at Oxford or Harvard. These were long-term plans indeed, for his daughter was only three months old.

Since 1949 the Chinese state has promoted a series of selfless models for emulation. Most famous of these is Lei Feng (see page 60). In the early 1990s some successful share dealers were joining this august pantheon, and press articles reported on examples of *dahu* who used their money in a socially useful way. For example, *Nanfang Zhoumo* carried the story of a woman who came to Shanghai as a domestic maid but made a fortune share dealing (18 June 1993: 1). She was praised for not staying in Shanghai but, instead, returning to her home village and setting up a factory. In a similar way, newspaper articles commended 'Millions' Yang for giving money to a poor rural school and taking up an unpaid university post (*SWHYSB* 4–10 June 1993: 4). He was also praised for not moving from Shanghai's 'lower quarter' where he grew up.

More Chinese characteristics

Perceptions of who was successful and who failed in the share market engaged with indigenous notions about the characteristics of different categories of person. For instance, gender-based stereotypes were evident in explanations for the predominance of male *dahu* – only about one in eight of the *dahu* was female.[11] One female *dahu* felt that men are 'bolder' and 'more decisive' than women. Women, she characterised as 'irresolute and hesitant'. She added that often if a husband and wife embark upon share dealing, one of them retains a job in a *danwei* in order to keep benefits such as free medical treatment for themselves and their children. Families who adopt this type of strategy were described as *yi jia, liang zhi* ('one family, two systems'), a play upon the 'one nation, two systems' policy officially adopted for the administration of Hong Kong after its return to Chinese rule in 1997. In such cases the one who stayed at home was generally the female, since, in my informant's view, they are 'domestic-natured' (*jiatingxing*), whilst men are 'naturally inclined to gamble.'

A younger woman who did not feel attracted to buy shares felt that standing around outside a securities trading centre was inappropriate for women. A young teacher believed that men and women *chao gupiao* in different ways. Men he considered as having 'greater courage and blacker hearts' whilst women were 'less courageous and more flexible'.

One *dahu* commented that the way people buy shares depends upon such factors as their 'cultural/educational level' (*wenhua cengci*), amount of capital, and their 'personality'. Regional stereotypes also entered the share discourse. Shanghainese expressed pride in the orderly way in which shares were issued in their city. They compared this to the situation in Shenzhen in August 1992 when up to one million people tried to buy share application forms. In the ensuing chaos, and amidst allegations of official corruption over share allocations, there were demonstrations in which riot police fired tear gas (*FT* 11 August 1992: 14).

There were two main views about the kind of people who were *dahu*. Sometimes there was a sense of injustice, that 'fools' did well where experts lost out. A young teacher who bought shares himself suggested that those who most successfully *chao gupiao* tended to be 'people without much *wenhua* and of rather low quality'. He considered that few intellectuals successfully *chao gupiao* because they read too many books which left them 'lacking in courage'. The contrary and, I gauge, dominant view was that *dahu* were people who 'have great ability' and good connections. A young television worker said that the rich in general were 'sharp-witted' and could 'exploit loopholes'. A cotton mill worker in her mid-forties felt that *dahu* were *lao zu* who knew to buy the share purchase certificates mentioned above. *Lao zu* is the dialect term for *lao gui* – literally 'old devil'. She explained that a *lao zu* is somebody who is 'experienced' and 'extremely sharp' and can analyse shares. Some regarded the *nouveaux riches* as 'upstarts' (*baofahu*). However, a female office worker told me that Shanghai share dealers who got rich quick were not *baofahu* and that this term was more appropriately used of Cantonese who became rich quickly. She reasoned that Cantonese are 'without ability' while to be a *dahu* requires 'ability'. In her estimation '*dahu* are not like ordinary people.' She seemed to consider them as possessing almost superhuman powers.

Criticisms and problems of the market

It is inevitable that a phenomenon as novel as a socialist share market should have its critics. Participants in the market also attributed a range of problems to the 'childish' and 'immature' nature of the market, which was frequently described as being at the 'infant' (*yinger*) stage. Shanghai's share experiment has exacerbated social inequalities within the city and also made possible a whole new range of scams and criminal activities. A highly visible and potentially divisive development in Shanghai in the early 1990s was the increasing gap between rich and poor, a gap which the share market has widened significantly. The ambiguous nature of the newly rich was brought home to me in a chance meeting with a university student. This young man, from Hunan province, had made money by buying and selling televisions and then by *chao gupiao*. Like other Chinese students, he lived in a dormitory with six other students. I asked if his room mates knew about his activities. He said they did not and that they would be jealous if they knew. The exclusivity of space was notable. I met him in a comparatively expensive restaurant little over 100 metres from the main entrance to his university. I asked how he would explain being able to eat in such a place if his room mates should chance upon him. He did not anticipate this happening, since the restaurant was so expensive for them 'they would not even dream of coming near here.' His other leisure-time activities also placed him in spaces where his fellow students would not contemplate going, such as expensive karaoke bars and the dance floors of expensive international hotels.

On the occasion I met a *dahu* in the Garden Hotel, the coffee and small cakes eaten by us that afternoon cost the equivalent of two weeks' salary for most Shanghai workers. This is symptomatic of the rapidly growing inequality within China, an inequality which often bred resentment. The cotton mill worker complained to me that 'those of us who have to work miss out. We cannot spend all our time at the securities trading centre, we can only scrabble to pick up the crumbs left behind by the *dahu.*' She added that *dahu* get to eat the 'big meat' and small *hu* only the 'small meat'. In part, she believed, like many others, that *dahu* may act together to deliberately push a share's price up or down, for example, by spreading rumours.[12] She also stressed the necessity in *chao gupiao* of having quick access to information, feeling that *dahu* had information, which people such as herself lacked. Communication technology (see page 135–7) was increasingly important in Shanghai and the degree of access or lack of access to it an important factor in redefining the social contours of Shanghai. This factory worker complained that 'small *hu*' were 'put at a disadvantage' by *dahu* who could act much more rapidly. Whilst 'small *hu*' had to queue at the trading counters and wait to buy or sell shares, *dahu* could deal over the phone. Some people also had a pager which could show the latest share prices and other messages.

Dahu, however, also had their complaints. All shares listed on the SSE are at least 51 per cent owned by the state. Add to this the tight grip, the state still retained over information and it takes little imagination to realise that the state could be the ultimate 'insider trader'. One *dahu* told me that 'the *laobaixing* can tell from the volume of turnover in a share whether the government is buying or selling them.' There was a widespread belief that the market was frequently manipulated by this hidden hand to the advantage of those in positions of power and their sons and daughters. For instance, their special privileges (*tequan*) enabled them to obtain shares at their low issue price. A retired worker expressed the view that those with access to information could become rich but that 'the *laobaixing* cannot get into this circle.' This sense of unfairness and exclusion was common in Shanghai. Equally typical was the way in which the *laobaixing* are depicted as an entity acted upon. Legal regulation over the market was minimal and there was often no fair means of enforcing such laws as did exist. For instance, laws were introduced to stop senior officials buying shares but this did not prevent relatives buying them on their behalf.[13] Foreign commentators also consider the Shanghai share market an 'insider's market' with insider trading rampant, a highly confused regulatory framework, lack of disclosure and dubious use of flotation proceeds (see *FEER* 16 July 1992: 48–54; *FEER* 23 June 1994: 54–6).

The disruptive effect of the share market upon work units included not only unsanctioned absences from work but also the impact of the craving for information. Shanghai radio stations recited the latest share prices every hour. In many work places, workers were forbidden to listen to the radio during work hours since they paid more attention to stock prices than their jobs. Some work units forbade workers from carrying pagers for the same reason. A worker at the giant *Baogang* steel plant commented that there, not only were pagers prohibited but workers were not allowed to discuss shares whilst at work. I watched a short play, a black comedy, called 'Three Minutes Late', put on by a neighbourhood drama group which illustrated, melodramatically, popular perceptions of this problem. It featured a young girl who was injured and taken to hospital. The doctor is busy on the phone checking the latest share prices impervious to the frantic demands of the girl's distraught father. The inevitable outcome is that the girl is dead by the time he has finished his dealing. Actual experience may be just as cruel. Following the first big market crash of October 1992 there were reports of suicides of people who had lost their life savings and often money they had borrowed from friends and relatives.[14]

The share market also provided new scope for criminal activities. Shanghai newspapers had begun to report the first crop of court cases of people caught using their company's funds to buy shares in the hope of making a quick profit and replacing the 'borrowed' money before anyone noticed. In one case a 24-year-old accountant used 840,000 *yuan* of company money to set himself up as a *dahu* (*XMWB* 6 December 1993: 3). In another case four securities workers were jailed because they had misappropriated company funds to finance their own stock trading (*CDBW* 5–11 September 1993: 2). One of them, a 20-year-old computer operator, used 4.8 million *yuan* ($842,000) to trade shares. He was given a 20-year jail sentence for this.

Even securities company officials I met in Shanghai rarely described share buying as investment. Instead they invariably said that the Shanghai share market was speculative and, unlike markets in other countries, did not follow economic laws. More antipathetic views described it as 'abnormal' (*bu zhengchang*). Some dealers considered *chao gupiao* as akin to gambling. One informant described his feeling on entering a share trading centre as just like 'entering a casino.' It should be borne in mind that gambling is still illegal in China. A man in his nineties who characterised his outlook on life as predominantly Confucian commented that when he was 40–50 years old in Shanghai money made on shares was considered *bu yi zhi cai* (ill-gotten gains). He added that it was what the Communist Party had called *touji daoba* ('speculation and profiteering'), to abuse capitalists. He considered it 'extremely dangerous' that 'China is becoming a gambling nation where everyone is doing business.'

Similarly an academic of nearly seventy who stressed his Confucian outlook condemned shares as 'speculation', as not 'dependent upon labour', and as 'reaping without sowing' (*bu lao er huo*).[15] He stressed that it is 'not honourable' for intellectuals to discuss money or to buy shares. What is striking here is the degree of correspondence between the Confucian views of these two men and the rhetoric of the Maoist period. There is particular piquancy in this regard since both these men had been extremely critical of the Communist Party since the early 1950s. It also highlights the extent to which certain traditional morals, which are now being undermined, were upheld and promoted during the Maoist era under another 'label'.

WIDENING THE MARGINS

The share market has touched the lives of millions of Shanghainese and has made a significant contribution to expanding what Martin Whyte (1992) has called the 'zone of indifference'. I take this zone to be spaces, both physical and social, in which activities seemingly contrary to official rhetoric may be pursued with limited state interference. In keeping with the topic of this chapter, a more appropriate metaphor may be to say that the share market has contributed to 'widening the margins', that is, to enlarging the borders of the possible and the permissible and to further blurring the frontiers between the morally reprehensible and the socially desirable.[16]

The share market has furthered the loosening of the reliance of the populace upon the state and provided a new space for individual initiative and creativity. As a local newspaper commented, 'in the turbulent wave of the commodity economy, everyone faces opportunities and choices' (*SWHYSB* 5 March 1993: 2). A local sociologist remarked to me that 'previously everything was arranged by the government, but now the market plays a much greater role.' In his view, the self (*ziji, ziwo*) now had more power and the government less. A similar view was conveyed in the often heard expression that China now had a 'small government and a large society' (see page 42). An important site to examine such changes is the work unit (*danwei*).

During the reform period the functions of *danwei* have, to an extent, been eroded (see page 120–2). The introduction of the share market has hastened this erosion. A case in point is the degree to which people could take time off work, officially or unofficially, to *chao gupiao*. Some *dahu* resigned from their state *danwei* jobs and may be called *gupiaozhe*, that is, people whose profession is shares. Such people were entirely free of *danwei* restrictions (and benefits). By contrast, 'middle *hu*' generally regarded their share dealing as a subsidiary activity, a 'second job'. Those who retained the security of a *danwei* place but did not work there in practice were said to *gua*, literally 'to hang' (in the sense of 'hang a shop sign'), a *danwei*. The business card one *dahu* proffered to me showed that he was a clerk in a state transport unit. It soon transpired that he had not been anywhere near the unit for months but continued to '*gua*' this *danwei*. He observed that those at his *danwei* were jealous (*yanhong* – literally 'red eyes') of his wealth. On his rare visits he did his best to avoid the topic of shares, for fear of arousing the resentment of former colleagues who only earned about 400 *yuan* a month when he could make 10,000 *yuan* on a good day.

I asked a young *dahu* who had recently resigned from his state job whether he was concerned about the associated loss of social welfare benefits. He agreed that some fear a loss of this guarantee but that he was young and expected that by the time he retired there would be no benefits. He expected that, in future, welfare provision would be covered by insurance systems and would 'not be a matter for *danwei*.'

Share dealing provided opportunities for the emergence of new forms of association and interest groups. Those who became friends through meeting at the share market may be called *guyou* – 'share friends'. Some share dealers suggested to me that those whose shares had fallen in value and 'await liberation' may be called *taoyou* – 'stuck-fast friends'. A newspaper article described how several 'small *hu*' may combine to form a 'joint naval force' (*lianhe jiandui*) (*Dadi* 1993: 25). These small groups may be of three kinds: friends and relatives; work colleagues; and those who meet by chance in the securities trading centre. Most of these combined 'naval forces' have a single person who acts as 'helmsman' (*duoshou*). Ironically, Mao Zedong had formerly been referred to as 'the great helmsman'. In the early 1990s, these watery metaphors indicated that individuals might now chart their own course in the stormy waters of the 'share sea' (*guhai*).

Another article discussed a different type of 'warship captain' (*jianzhang*) (*MZWYB* 17–23 May 1993: 4). These were 'fake *dahu*' who operated using *danwei* funds. Although this activity was illegal, the article observed that 'above there is a strategy, below a counter-strategy.' It added that these 'fake *dahu*' may be acting with the full support of their *danwei* heads. Informants told me that it was especially *danwei* in financial straits which delegated an employee to buy and sell shares in this way. In the play 'OK Stock' the factory in which Ah Nai works closes and its manager visits Ah Nai with a proposal that they 'set up a company'. In practice this amounts to Ah Nai acting as a *dahu* on behalf of the *danwei*. A local magazine reported a young female *dahu*, a former teacher, who paid 500 *yuan* to a doctor to sign a sick note so that she did not have to work at the school (*Dadi* 1993: 24). She was called into the school expecting a reprimand, but instead the department head told her that the other teachers had pooled together 100,000 *yuan* and wanted her to trade shares on their behalf. An almost identical request was made to one of my informants. She refused this role for exactly the same reason as Ah Nai, saying 'if I make money that is fine, but what if I lose money?'

The Party-state – the view from the dealing floor

The share market discourse provided insights into the ways Shanghainese thought about the state and its actions. A middle-aged Party member, a local government cadre, told me that workers in his *danwei* were not allowed to buy shares. However, he was aware that colleagues nonetheless bought them stealthily, and he tacitly connived in this action. He noted, using the same expression as the newspaper article mentioned above, that 'the higher levels have a strategy, the lower levels have a counter-strategy.' This phrase was used often in

Shanghai. I would suggest that it conveys the sense ordinary Shanghainese had that they could, *en masse*, affect the way things are done. There is a sense that the *laobaixing* is not always just acted upon, but can constitute a kind of composite agent. This expression demonstrates the degree of space that many ordinary Shanghainese considered they now had. Such a phrase, were it uttered during the Maoist era, would have been taken as evidence of counter-revolutionary thought.

The generally declining role of the Communist Party was evident in *chao gupiao*. Party membership appeared to be irrelevant in the *dahushi*. I asked one *dahu* if others in his *dahushi* were party members. He claimed not to know, but added that he met party members in his other business activities and that he found many of them 'useless and lazy'. His portrayal was similar to the way a self-made businessman might talk about an hereditary aristocracy; that is, as a class at least unhelpful and, perhaps, inimical to his own interests.

In a long freewheeling discussion the *dahu* from the state transportation *danwei* elaborated on his views on life. He remarked that:

> The government tells us that money is not omnipotent, but if I have money I can do many things. For example, when I go travelling tickets are often sold out, but if you pay more you can always get a ticket. Being a share dealer I can give full vent to my talents. There is nothing which restrains or binds me, I am free, unrestrained. There is no one to tell me what to do.

This man's comments make clear the way in which the share market and success in it allowed individuals a new realm of freedom. Until a couple of years ago his main hope, like countless others in Shanghai, had been to study in America. But this had changed. 'I no longer want to go to America' he told me, 'I feel that it is easier for me make money here in China.'

Many kinds of slang and new expressions appeared with the share market. Some of these terms cast an ironic light on the state. I noted earlier the term *taozhu* – 'stuck fast' – when shares are at a level below the price paid for them. When shares rise back above their original level some *dahu* called this *jiefang* – liberation – the same term as is used for the Communist takeover in 1949. At one *dahu* dealing room I visited, several *dahu* grouped around a computer terminal likened the events on the screen to the 1946–9 civil war. A block graph coloured red and green showed the volume of shares being traded – red being shares bought and green those sold. They called the red the People's Liberation Army and the green the Nationalist Army, and used expressions such as 'the red army are coming' and 'Mao Zedong has reached Beijing'.

Inevitably a desire to make money was the key motive to *chao gupiao*. Sometimes this was described, using an expression learnt from Marxism, as *yuanshi jilei*, 'primitive accumulation'. However, other reasons people gave indicated a strong sense of an increased scope for individual agency and individualism. For instance, an unmarried female *dahu* who had recently resigned from her *danwei* told me, 'I *chao gupiao* to test my ability' and to attain 'self-fulfilment'. She added that now she worked for herself the 'feeling of oppression' (*yayigan*) she had felt when at her *danwei* had gone. A young *dahu* of 26 said *chao gupiao* gave him a 'feeling of newness' (*xinxiangan*). He stressed that in *chao gupiao* one should have 'one's own characteristics' and added that he 'relied upon feelings' and his 'own judgement'. Since resigning from his bank job a few months earlier he had felt more relaxed and, above all, appreciated being able to arrange his own time. On another occasion I asked a group of *dahu* what they derived most from *chao gupiao*. There was a common agreement that it was 'excitement'.

It would be a mistake to overemphasise the new degree of agency and individual choice. Many people in Shanghai undoubtedly still felt that their fate was largely beyond their hands. I spoke with a low-ranking local government worker in his early fifties soon after there had been an announcement that the number of government cadres was to be reduced. His attitude echoed almost word for word the soliloquy delivered by Ah Nai. He commented that even if he lost his present job he would not worry since 'the state will always arrange things.' The *dahu* who retained his place in a transportation *danwei* felt that nothing had changed there: as before employees spent all day 'reading newspapers and drinking tea.'

Change from the top?

It is possible to view the widening of the margins outlined above as a direct consequence of state-led reforms. However, economic policies adopted by the state often appeared to be reactive and *ad hoc*, in many instances legitimising what was already happening on the ground. The Shanghai share market provides a good instance of this.[17]

Much evidence suggests that companies began issuing shares counter to state wishes. I noted above the Shanghai textile factory which 'quietly' issued stock in 1981. Across China, between 1981–8, some 98 billion *yuan* in various stocks and bonds were issued, many of them centred in Shanghai (*BR* 1989a: 19). By the end of 1989, 2,700 Shanghai companies had issued stocks and bonds (Xie 1990: 24). It appears that it was especially from 1984–5 onwards that many enterprises issued shares. According to Engle, this was primarily in response to measures introduced by the central authorities to restrict enterprises' finance during 1984 (1986: 37). Similarly, another researcher on Chinese capital markets concludes that their emergence was primarily 'driven by the rising investment demands of economic agents who tried to circumvent various financial restrictions and barriers' (Tam 1991: 525).

Initially most stocks were sold to employees of the issuing enterprises. Engle notes that in some instances enterprises could only 'sell' stock by coercing employees to buy it (1986: 38). However, stocks were increasingly traded unofficially, especially in large kerb markets in Shanghai, Sichuan, and Shandong. In Shanghai, stocks were traded by 'yellow oxen' (*huangniu*), a local term for black market traders.[18] I asked a man in his early thirties who had engaged in this trade in Shanghai about its legality. He admitted that it was a black market but added that 'it seems to be permitted.' The official SSE grew out of and has replaced this black market. In other parts of China many semi-official kerb markets continue.[19] My informant now bought and sold unlisted stock all over China. He travelled by plane, and claimed that his suitcases were stuffed with wads of *renminbi*. An official publication makes clear that one reason for the establishment of stock markets in 1986 was 'so as to eliminate the black market which has already appeared' (*BR* 1989a: 21). It is, of course, moot how far the state permitted such black markets as an experiment, leaving open the option to crush or legalise them at a later date. However, the sense of events moving much faster than the Party expects is evident in comments made by former Shanghai mayor, now State premier, Zhu Rongji at a Beijing performance of 'OK Stock'. After watching the play, Zhu is reported to have commented that when he left Shanghai two years before he would never have envisaged the city's share market developing in the way it had (*XMWB* 5 December 1993: 5). Since this time, state control has further eroded as corporate and state shares in enterprises have increasingly found their way into private hands (You 1998: 186–90).

Blurring the margins

At the same time as the share market has promoted wealth inequalities, the opportunities it provides can also re-configure social contours in unexpected ways. For example, at a trading centre I visited, a woman of about 35, who looked like a poor peasant, retrieved from an old battered handbag a crumpled bag for dried milk. Inside were 500,000 *yuan* of Chinese government bonds. This woman's father had pulled a cart from which he sold water-melons. At the same time in this room was a man in his early seventies dressed in a smart suit, complete with a gold watch and dark glasses. He lived in the exclusive Portman Hotel. As a child he had been escorted to school by two White Russian bodyguards. From 1945 he had begun to speculate on shares, gold, and other commodities. He once again deals on the share market. It is ironic that in the non-egalitarian 1990s, these two people from very different backgrounds had now attained a level of equality, at least in the economic sphere, not achieved in the Maoist era. This man advised me that 'now is the best time to make money in Shanghai as it is chaotic. With stability there are fewer opportunities to get rich.'

By providing a new arena in which to make and, of course, lose money, the stock market has significantly contributed to a generally increasing degree of ambiguity over people's incomes. The share market can also affect family relationships. In many Shanghai families, husbands (occasionally these roles were reversed) turn over their monthly salary to their wives who control the family income. The wife returns a portion of this to the husband for him to buy cigarettes and other small daily items. In one family where the husband had made money on shares, he continued to hand over his salary as before. However, his daughter-in-law remarked that he retained this '*waikuai*' (see page 55) and did not disclose how much it was to the rest of the family. Although wealthy share dealers tended to be male, there was also the chance for women to prosper. Women who play the stock market successfully may be accorded greater social standing commensurate with their financial status. As a local saying asserts, 'it is the drawer [i.e. where family money is kept] which controls the family' (*chouti dangjia*).

Once somebody became a *dahu* they had some license to re-create their past in the light of what they had now become. One 36-year-old *dahu* had been unable to study at university when he left school because of the Cultural Revolution. Instead he had worked in a factory doing heavy manual work for seven years before going to university. He stressed that he had always possessed a 'will to struggle'. To my questions about his years in the factory he responded, 'then there was no choice... Although the job involved great hardship all I could do was endure (*renshou*). Now there is an opportunity to earn money and I seize this opportunity.' His words closely echo those of Deng Xiaoping who said that people should 'seize the opportunity'. My informant followed these comments by expressing his dislike for traditional family relationships. He felt that people must struggle for themselves. He gave the impression that he had had to fend off requests from family members for financial assistance. His retelling of his life story was like a dramatic account, with himself cast in the starring role.

A new need to know

One share trader advised me that 'choosing shares is harder than choosing a wife.' In opening up the share market the government created a new need for individuals to have access to information. This may lead them to search for information not readily available in the official media. Moreover, if individuals are to be successful traders, it is vital for them to critically assess information; they may well make interpretations and reach conclusions which differ markedly from those provided in official statements. Informants suggested to me that the burgeoning number of magazines, tip sheets and newspapers devoted to the share market were amongst the most 'democratic' of publications. In 1994 several stock market tip sheets such as *Shanghai Stock Express* and *Shanghai Stock Information* were banned. The official explanation was that these sheets 'lacked proper authorisation and spread unfounded rumours' (*FEER* 2 June 1994: 63).

A young teacher who dealt in shares explained to me the factors he considered in deciding which company's shares to buy, these included the sector in which the company operates, their products and the market for them, the government policy towards each sector, the character and skills of the head of the company, and his own expectations on future development in Shanghai. His preference was for companies which had diversified and become involved in the 'hot' sectors such as taxis and restaurants. Similarly, he favoured 'concept' shares – these were for companies involved in Pudong construction projects which were still at the 'concept' stage but had central government support.

One *dahu* remarked upon the accuracy of Bacon's dictum that 'knowledge is power'. She commented that initially she had relied upon feelings (*pin ganjue*) when she bought shares. However, after resigning from her *danwei* and devoting all her energies to *chao gupiao*, she now used technical analysis. She proudly showed me a selection of carefully drawn graphs and charts, her own meticulous analysis of market trends. She commented that this kind of analysis was only partial and must be combined with analysis of 'the general social situation', including state policy and politics.[20] The main sources of information she used in her 'analysis of society' were published and broadcast media and personal contacts. The latter appeared to be especially important. She remarked that *dahu*, 'small *hu*', and friends who worked in newspaper offices often phoned her with various news items. She stressed that the *dahushi* was the best place to hear the latest news and rumours. In her tiny flat there was a stream of visitors and telephone calls. All hinged on the latest news in the share market.

Another *dahu* who believed that share traders' success depended upon their extensive networks of social contacts and sources of information added that 'even false news may affect the market.' When I asked about rumours of the death of Deng Xiaoping he noted that Deng had already been killed off and revived by the share market seven or eight times! Every day he studied five newspapers and several of the pamphlets devoted to stocks. He explained that he did this because what politicians do and say affects the price of shares. However, he considered the 'grapevine' (*xiaodao xiaoxi*) to be the most rapid source of news, followed by broadcast media. Television and the telephone were his main sources of information and he carried both a pager and a mobile phone. The mobile phone was an important symbol of, and means for attaining, success (see page 157–8).

Some of Shanghai's *dahu* belonged to share salons, where people met and discussed the share market (see Hertz 1998: 166–8). One salon was reported to charge a monthly membership fee of 1,000 *yuan* (*Dadi* 1993: 24). Salons of this type indicate the 'solidifying' of an economic interest group. However, in a state where one Party asserts its inalienable right to govern, any suggestion that these groupings assert political power would be swiftly quashed. It might be for this reason that amongst dealers I met there was a preference for more informal meetings and social interaction.

That the need to exchange information was not restricted to *dahu* was evident in the rapid proliferation of magazines and news sheets devoted to the stock market. There did not appear to be professional advisors on shares. However, there were adult education classes on shares (see Hertz 1998: 164–6). One trading centre I visited organised a share market salon and regularly invited speakers. There were also informal salons. When the securities trading centres closed at 3 p.m., small groups of people clustered outside their doors discussing shares. Outside at least two especially highly rated centres these informal information exchange groups continued their discussions until past midnight even on freezing winter nights. Hertz (155–9) describes these gatherings as 'crowd clusters' and stresses the way that they are composed of strangers, and their openness which allows participants to enter or leave at will.

The importance of information was exemplified during an interview with a *dahu* which took place in a local government office. Once word got out that there was a *dahu* in the building my interview was soon taken over by an assortment of people who came in and began discussing market trends with him and asking his advice on specific stocks. Our conversation took place in the office of the man who had introduced me and he was present throughout. When we were alone again he commented that many of those who had joined the conversation were not supposed to buy shares because of their rank.

BACK TO THE FUTURE?

A key aim of promoting the market is to redefine Shanghai's role by developing the city as a national and international financial centre. Since 1992 an increasing number of non-Shanghai companies have been listed on the SSE. In September 1993, the exchange began to transmit real-time stock information via satellite to 12 Chinese cities including Fuzhou, Guangzhou, Haikou, and Hefei (*CD* 20 September 1993: 2). By early 2000, these links covered most of China and served over 45 million share holders across the country. A SSE spokesperson expressed the hope that by the year 2000 the Shanghai exchange would be ranked with those of London, New York, and Tokyo (*SYB* 18 January 1993: 1). This may have been overly-optimistic. However, foreign banks and brokerages have already begun to return to Shanghai (see *Economist* 14 May 1994: 111–12), and the market capitalisation of Shanghai A-shares has risen substantially from $29.3 billion in 1995 to $174.4 billion in 1999 (*SS* 29 August 2000: 10).

The consequences of Shanghai's redefined role and its reinscription into global financial markets remain to be seen. Communist Party rhetoric formerly criticised pre-1949 Shanghai as an 'adventurers' paradise' (see page 202). Many Shanghainese I spoke with seemed nostalgic for this lost past, and some at least hoped that the development of the SSE was a step towards a more adventurous future for their city. The SSE is currently still extremely insular, with Politburo policies having the most important effect. Even the Shenzhen and Hong Kong markets appear to have little influence on its fluctuations. If Shanghai's current re-internationalisation is to be more deeply rooted it is difficult to see how local traders can be successful in a global market without free access to information. As information flows become less constrained and as the range of legal activities, loopholes, and niches for shady dealings expands, so Shanghai's populace is becoming less amenable to direct control by the Party-state.

New options and dilemmas

Local commentators often used a metaphor drawn from computing to talk about changes in their city. Changes in 'software' refer to alterations of people's way of thinking and lifestyle, that is, 'culture' in the two senses of symbolic expression and organisational practices. It is evident that the share market has facilitated a redefinition of individuals' relationships both with other people and towards the state.

Share dealing provides individuals with a forum for market exchanges. If they wish, individuals may engage in these activities away from family and the work unit, disembedded from the dense network of human relations, obligations, and dependencies of these spheres. Participants in this market can exercise their agency *as* individuals and can choose to avoid or engage other dealers in relatively 'free-floating' relationships. In a city as lacking in privacy as Shanghai, share dealing is an important new arena in which to act as an individual operator. Such involvement offers the possibility for the development of new senses of self. Successful dealers I met tended to project themselves as entrepreneurial, self-made men and women, self-images imbricated with notions of Shanghainese sophistication and financial adroitness.

Share dealers can exercise agency in decisions which will affect their financial standing. They may join the wealthy elite or lose everything in the fluctuations of the market. Failure may bring severe repercussions for themselves and, most likely, their family and friends too. Success will permit a radically different lifestyle with access to the full panoply of consumer luxuries now readily available in Shanghai. In a city with rapidly growing inequalities of wealth, differential consumption patterns serve to produce, facilitate, and mark out new divisions in society.

What is the share market's role in Shanghai's emergent civil society, now that stock-holding is no longer just an experiment and 'shares have already formed an indissoluble bond with Shanghainese'? (*Dadi* 1993: 22). It would be tempting to portray the attention to politics and economic affairs by share dealers described above as indicative of a nascent civil society. However, it would be a mistake to infer from this an interest in politics by citizens *as* citizens. The *dahu* mentioned earlier who daily read five newspapers assured me that he had 'no interest' in politics, describing it as 'nothing to do with the common people.' This attitude was shared by other *dahu* I interviewed.

Nonetheless, it was clear that new interest groups were beginning to coalesce around the share market. At one level were the securities companies themselves. These often have highly complex organisational links and ambiguous interconnections with state departments. Then there were the share dealers. The social status of Shanghai's share dealing *nouveaux riches* is generally dependent neither upon the Communist Party or the work unit; these people have the makings of an economic interest group. Many share dealers met, exchanged information, and may form the 'joint naval forces' mentioned above. One article described these groups as composed of people with a common will and purpose (*zhitong daohezhe*) – the expression from which the term 'comrade' (*tongzhi*) derived (*Dadi* 1993: 25). It is also conceivable that *taoyou*, fellow holders of shares 'stuck fast' in a bear market, could form an interest group based upon mutual engagement. It will be interesting to observe the extent to which emergent interest groups press for recognition of their own interests.[21] Should this occur, they will face pressure from the Party-state. In the event of any significant economic downturn, the *nouveaux riches* may also become targets for the dispossessed and resentful. As it is, some Shanghainese consider their wealth to have derived from morally suspect speculation and gambling.

The state is currently promoting corporatisation as a means to rescue loss-making state enterprises. State control is also eroding as state shares and corporate shares increasingly find their way into private hands. Further extension of stock-holding and 'the market' generally poses many problems. For instance, replacing state directives by the profit motive brings the distinct danger of far higher levels of unemployment, which could be a source of instability. The share market has also revealed the weakness of the Party-state. Hertz describes a situation in September and October 1992 when the government spent millions of *yuan* attempting to prop up the market. She describes how investors throughout Shanghai had 'watched spellbound while the government repeatedly failed to manipulate the market to suit its needs' (1998: 184). Despite this, the government's involvement in the market led some to 'curse the state' when share prices fell. It appears that the Party-state retains sufficient power to influence market trends, and enough of a heavy hand to receive the blame when things go wrong, but has insufficient control to bend these economic forces wholly to its will.

The Shanghai share market is both indicative and constitutive of the dramatic pace of change in Shanghai. The various share discourses provide evidence of the widening and blurring of 'margins' in Shanghai, whilst the practices of participants in the market have widened faultlines in the social fabric and propagated tenacious new growths in the increasingly spacious and fertile borderlines between official rhetoric and daily life. The share market contains and is fostering many ambiguities and actual or potential points of tension. In all these respects the share experiment is a fascinating microcosm of the wider project of 'reform and the open door' of which it forms a part. The forces and trends unleashed by reform, whether those planned by the Party-state or those which result from citizens everyday actions, are remaking the social landscape of Shanghai. The Party-state often takes the blame when problems arise, but holding back the 'tides' may be beyond its power.

6 Concluding impressions

China's dominant political figure since 1976, Deng Xiaoping, described the process of reform in China as *mozhe shitou guohe* – crossing the stream, by feeling the boulders. This term has the dual merit of being an apposite and vivid metaphor both of Shanghai's transition away from rigid state planning and for my own practices of research and writing. This ethnographic account of China's largest city has sought to highlight the degree of flux and diversity in this metropolis, and to sketch some of the boulders, tides and shifting currents. Ethnography tends to fix in aspic cultural phenomena which are in process, in flux. There is an inevitable attrition in the reduction of diverse activities, everyday situations, and a plurality of voices, to the two-dimensionality of the written page. The activity of undertaking ethnographic research in a city where the state promotes policies deliberately designed to produce 'some change every year and a great change every three years', highlights the limitations of this anthropological *fiction*. In this final chapter, I summarise the main findings of this study. I then explore further some of the trends which have been traced and conclude by speculating on future developments in Shanghai.

In *Chapter 1*, I outlined Shanghai residents' descriptions of pre-reform Shanghai and the socio-spatial and watery/irrigation metaphors which permeated discourses on *gaige kaifang*. A predominant view was that pre-reform Shanghai had been like a woman with bound feet, made into a 'lame city' (*bojiao chengshi*) by the central government's expropriations of the wealth created in the city (*DW* 1992: 43). The city was portrayed to me as having been 'stuck in a frame' and as having 'solidified'; lack of change in the city's physical structure was frequently presented as paralleled by a similar fixity and immutability in people's daily lives, careers and expectations. A long-term lack of investment in the city's infrastructure had saddled the residents of Shanghai with a huge debt. Above all, a dilapidated housing stock and a groaning transport network were 'millstones around the neck of the city' (ibid.: 44) and strenuous efforts are being made to 'shed' these burdens of the past.

The sluice gate metaphor seems especially appropriate since it suggests a build-up of pressure, with a powerful inflow, followed, perhaps, by some backwash. In Shanghai, with the opening of the 'sluice gate', the contours of the Maoist period have already been, or are in the process of being, reconfigured. Where politics had once been in command, and the hand of the Party-state had weighed heavily on the shoulder of each citizen, informants now characterised Shanghai as having a 'small government and a large society'. Much more 'space' has opened up for many citizens.

From the first and subsequent chapters, it should be evident that my informants often depicted a social landscape composed of binary oppositions. These contrasts, which informants used to describe the world around them, were generally asserted with a degree of certainty and explicitness which was remarkable in itself, even though in practice the dichotomies were readily modified, shifted, and even, contradicted. Frequent 'sharp-edged' contrasts were drawn between a range of inside (*nei*) and outside (*wai*) dichotomies. Particularly pervasive spatial and territorial contrasts were those made between Chinese and non-Chinese – with overseas Chinese as an intermediate category; between Shanghainese and non-Shanghainese; between urban and rural; between work unit and 'society'; between work unit and home; and between home and 'outside'.

When discussing changes in Shanghai and in their own lives, informants frequently had recourse to a number of chronological dichotomies. The main chronological contours they referred to were: pre-Opium War or feudalism/post-Opium War, pre-Liberation/after Liberation, pre-*gaige kaifang* or Cultural Revolution/after *gaige kaifang* or 'now'. Informants often contrasted the present to 'before'. Sometimes the 'before' referred to was specified, as in the routinely used expressions 'before Liberation' and 'after Liberation'. On other occasions, the 'before' referred to was dependent upon the context. I frequently had to follow up informants' comments which included this term by asking 'when was "before"?'[1]

When the Communist Party took power in 1949 it actively sought to draw a clear line between 'Old' and 'New' China – between 'before Liberation' and 'after Liberation'. In contemporary Shanghai and with, it seemed, the encouragement of the Party, the populace often drew a distinct line between the present and the Maoist past. Fixed expressions that have come into everyday use, and which parallel 'before Liberation' and 'after Liberation', are 'before *gaige kaifang*' and 'after *gaige kaifang*'. The term *gaige kaifang* appeared to be used in two rather distinct ways. Often informants spoke of 'after *gaige kaifang*' – this depicts *gaige kaifang* as something that had happened in the past, a stream that had already been crossed. For instance, a share dealer in his early forties told me that people such as himself could compare pre-*gaige kaifang* to the present since they had 'crossed over from that time.' To use a Chinese proverb, the river had been crossed and the bridge demolished (*guohe chaiqiao*) – there could be no turning back. Informants would also say 'now is *gaige kaifang*'. In this second sense, *gaige kaifang* seems akin to a *zeitgeist* and to have a more processual meaning, as an evolving set of policies and developments of which there may be more or less in the future.

In *Chapter 2*, I explored the increasing porousness of Shanghai's boundaries with regard to both intra-national and global flows. Before the 1980s Shanghai could be depicted as vertically integrated, cellular, and relatively closed to both global and intra-national flows. With this 'closed door' Shanghai's *laobaixing* were depicted as having been 'blind', 'unable to see', and 'unable to hear' what the 'outside' was like. Like the proverbial frog 'looking at the sky from the bottom of a well', they had only a very narrow and circumscribed view of the world. Since the mid-1980s this pattern had altered significantly with Shanghai's increasing reintegration into the global economy, a greater stress upon horizontal linkages, and extensive global and intra-national flows. The 'information landscape' (Wark 1993: 141) of the city has changed dramatically. In contemporary Shanghai, global events are no longer extraneous but an unavoidable ingredient of people's daily lives.

I examined the consequences of various flows for 'Chinese' and 'Shanghainese' identities in Shanghai. The conclusions I reached were ambiguous. There was evidence that these flows might help to sustain 'Chinese' and 'Shanghainese' identities, but also that they might redefine, fracture, or deconstruct these imagined communities. I found considerable vitality to identifications by residents as both 'Chinese' and as 'Shanghainese'. Since 'ethnic' boundaries of this type are generally of most significance when they are breached, then these identifications may have acquired greater valency in the reform era. Shanghai is regaining its attraction – lost since the 1950s – as a 'paradise of adventurers'. Once again, migrants flood into the city from all over China and the rest of the world. A substantial proportion of the Chinese migrants swell a burgeoning 'second class' or 'underclass' who are denied urban household registration status. Identification as 'Shanghainese' was most conspicuously asserted in contrast to these rural migrants. My informants invariably formulated relations between 'Shanghainese' and developed countries as homologous to those between rural migrants and Shanghai.

With rising regional autonomy, long-term central government expropriations, and the post-Mao influx of rural migrants who have breached Shanghai's 'wall'; I had anticipated the beginnings at least of a more overtly political assertion of regional 'voices', even of Shanghai 'nationalism'. However, I found little evidence of such an assertion. When I asked informants if there was any conflict between 'being Shanghainese' and 'being Chinese', such questions were regarded as nonsensical. China, and most especially its heartland, is significantly different from, say, the former Soviet Union, in terms of its relative ethnic homogeneity. Appropriate analogies for the relationship between identification as 'Chinese' and as 'Shanghainese' were derived from the comments of informants. Thus 'being Shanghainese' could be described as a 'different flavour' of Chineseness. Similarly, in the same way as regional operas differ greatly in style but tend to stick to a range of common basic plots, so regional identities constitute variations on the theme of 'being Chinese'. Even though much of the seed corn exists for an assertive localism there was scant evidence of this happening.

Shanghai's reinscription into global cultural flows provides residents with many more 'contemporaries'. Where once there was little alternative to the state's monologic voice and its interpretations of how things were or should be, in contemporary Shanghai there is a proliferation of alternative images, rationalisations, and explanations. For Shanghainese, who frequently assert their urban sophistication and superiority, the 'others' with whom they tend to identify, or seek to emulate, are those with wealthy metropolitan lifestyles. As I observe, this cosmopolitan identity, to which they both aspire and feel entitled, neglects and fails to include the poor of rural China, hundreds of thousands of whom are industriously engaged upon building a city which fitted this vision.

Joshua Meyrowitz (1985) rightly argues that electronic media have profound effects in altering the significance of time and space. However, I do not accept his view that electronic media have 'homogenised places and experiences' (viii). Homogenisation takes place only at the most superficial of levels. Rather, global cultural flows and rising prosperity are increasing the repertoire of possible identities and communities to which Shanghai citizens may belong. Shanghainese residents, like ourselves, now 'live in a world of fluid, blurred, overlapping cultural identities' (Jenner 1992: 209). Not only has the city become a vast physical construction site, but Shanghai's re-internationalisation also provides many new deterritorialised sites for the construction of identities. Included amongst the new range of 'aspirational identities' are various consumer 'lifestyles' and youth subcultures which can cross-cut with territorial identifications.

In *Chapter 3*, I unravelled further strands of complexity in senses of being 'Shanghainese' by exploring the differential attribution of qualities and identities which residents made of places and people in, or from, different parts of Shanghai. The persistence and apparent reinforcing of representations of 'upper' and 'lower' quarters during the Maoist era demonstrates the way in which socio-economic policies of that time often operated to produce consequences in direct opposition to the ideals espoused.

In this chapter, I also investigated aspects of the rapidly altering cityscape of Shanghai. Many physical boundaries are being dismantled or transformed and new 'walls' created. I concentrated upon trends by which *danwei* have lost their all-encompassing functions, and become less enclosed and bounded. Concurrently homes are increasingly privatised and cloissonéed. Under the Maoist model, workers were clustered in all-encompassing work units, often inside walled compounds. The ideal was for such units to be cellular, functionally autarkic and answerable to superiors in a vertically ordered structure of command which reached, ultimately, to a government department in Beijing. In the reform era, these vertical links have been loosened and each *danwei* encouraged to finance its own running costs. To achieve this, many units have turned their component service segments 'inside out': that is, they turn their activities into outward-facing commercial entities. Processes within *danwei* are often paralleled by the rupture and reconfiguration of their physical boundaries. The cityscape is being directly altered by the logic of commercialism as *danwei* physically open their perimeter walls onto the street.

Home styles are also changing, in ways which are often a mirror image of the trends affecting work units. Shanghai is rapidly becoming a city with a substantial proportion of private homeowners. By early 2000, over 400,000 local residents had used housing loans to buy their own homes (*SS* 11 January 2000: 10). The privatisation of housing would, on its own, increase the home's separateness and closure from the world outside. This process is further reinforced by a combination of factors, including the impact of past political campaigns, the rehousing and relocation of residents in suburban high-rise housing, a fear of rising crime, and the spread of new technologies such as television, video-players and air-conditioning. Alongside changes at home and work, I also noted the proliferation and diversification of leisure activities which provide alternative sites and whose vitality and variety indicate the space that has opened beyond direct state intervention. However, in leisure pursuits, as in many other aspects of life in contemporary Shanghai, access and opportunities to these sites often depend very largely upon one's status or ability to pay.

I also suggested ways in which communication technologies might be regarded as indicative of social status. In the first half of the 1990s, before mobile phones became widely available, a term which Chinese newspapers used, for instance, was 'mobile phone stratum'. Those with cellular phones were perceived to be quite distinct from those enclosed within the cellular walls of *danwei*. The mobile phone owner was marked out as a successful person. At the same time a mobile phone provided access to opportunities denied to those with inadequate, immobile communication facilities. This is an instance of the way, in contemporary society, consumption of products can be used to ascribe identities. Such instances also demonstrate how electronic media can both facilitate 'connections' but also create new boundaries and types of exclusion.

In *Chapter 4*, I investigated various notions surrounding consumption in Shanghai. I explored ways in which terminology taken from the literal consumption of food serves, through metaphors and analogies, to describe many aspects of life. Particularly interesting aspects of this are depictions of the state as a consumer of Shanghai's wealth, and of individuals' consumption of the state or the *laobaixing*'s wealth. The ideal propagated during the Maoist period was for *danwei* to be 'iron rice bowls'. In contemporary Shanghai this notion conveys a sense of dependency and idleness. Moreover, it is felt that with *gaige kaifang* many people have refined the ability to consume and parasitically live off the state.

Differential patterns of consumption can serve to produce, facilitate, and mark out new divisions in society. The inflow of foreign images and products has played an important part in this by providing local people with a plethora of new resources from which to fashion identities. However, as was shown in both this chapter and Chapter 2, this influx does not enter into a vacuum, rather it 'enters into various kinds of interaction with already existing meanings and meaningful forms' (Hannerz 1992: 262). In Shanghai, for instance, imported cultural festivals such as Christmas have become important, but with quite distinctive 'Shanghainese characteristics'. Other cultural imports, such as 'democracy' and 'freedom', are similarly understood in 'Chinese' local contexts and subject to subtle redefinitions. In some instances, imported cultural products can facilitate the development of deterritorialised consumer identities. However, such identities may also contribute to and cross-cut with notions of Shanghainese cosmopolitanism and sophistication.

Modernity with Chinese characteristics now translates into the ability to consume at an appropriate, and ever increasing, level. The expectations of young people are especially high; unlike their parents they take the benefits brought by *gaige kaifang* for granted and expect much more in the future. Some actively seek to be able to enjoy high class consumption, their desires fuelled by peer pressure, media images, and advertising. Young people are both forced and encouraged to 'look towards money', not least as the security once provided by state *danwei* is steadily eroded, with a general expectation that this process will only hasten and become more ubiquitous.

Changing spending patterns indicate the shifting concerns of Shanghai residents. A survey in early 2000 indicated that Shanghainese now put providing for old age, the education of their children, and home buying at the top of their list for spending savings (*SS* 4 February 2000: 2). Just a few years before, residents had saved for specific consumer goods. Nowadays, they must accommodate themselves to the more fundamental, long-term needs created by the state's increasing withdrawal from welfare and social provision.

My informants generally felt a greater degree of personal freedom in the monetising economy. The increasing significance of money payment for labour allowed (some) workers to engage in a wider range of more contractual, less embedded, associations than before. At the turn of the millennium, for instance, Shanghai entrepreneurs and the young and talented participated in the global trend for Internet start-ups and extensive job-hopping to dotcoms (*SS* 15 August 2000: 11). The power of money might indeed 'lend to the individual a new independence from group interests' (Simmel 1990: 342). However, increased monetisation could also produce new forms of dependency. For instance, the increased cost of wedding arrangements may have made young couples more reliant upon parents than during the Maoist era. There are also new dangers such as the fear of inflation and the sense of injustice created by rising wealth inequalities. Many informants described the reform process – with its attendant monetisation of the economy – as China's second 'liberation' (*jiefang*).[2] For those with financial resources the monetised economy of contemporary Shanghai offers much individual freedom. But in the case of the unemployed and impoverished this emancipation may well be chimeric, and even threatening and oppressive.

In *Chapter 5*, I outlined the emergent discourse on stocks and shares. If the recently completed Shanghai Radio and Television Tower in Pudong is a physical icon of change,[3] then the stock market is a parallel institutional icon. The changes constituted, and encouraged, by the rapid development of the share market provide a microcosm of the forces and trends unleashed by *gaige kaifang* including inflated expectations, hopes, dangers, risks, and unpredictability.

The share market has hastened and played an important part in redefining the relationship of the individual to society. It has increased the scope for individual agency, contributed to 'widening the margins', and to the rapid social differentiation in the city. The share market has directly created a substantial number of *nouveaux riches* and contributed to the wider development of the rise of wealth as both indicative and constituent of social status. At the same time, perhaps especially because of the inherently speculative nature of this wealth creation, it has fuelled the sense of injustice many Shanghainese feel over rising wealth inequalities. The share market has also encouraged and provided an environment for civil society to emerge. Access to information is vital for traders and various formal and many more informal interest groups have already begun to coalesce around the share market. The extent to which such emergent interest groups press for recognition of their own interests remains to be seen.

A satellite net already links the SSE to punters across China and the intention is that this currently very insular market will be integral to and help leverage Shanghai's ambition to become a world financial centre. Foreign banks and brokerages have begun to return to Shanghai; and in December 2001 China became a member of the World Trade Organisation. In early 2000, there were indications that the roughly 1,050 companies listed on China's two stock exchanges, in Shenzhen and Shanghai, would combine to form a single bourse in Shanghai (*FT Survey* 2000: 10). In mid-2000, it was announced that the distinction between the A- and B-share categories would eventually be abolished. At the same time, the Anglo-Dutch conglomerate Unilever has indicated that it may seek to become the first foreign company to list its China business on the A-share market. These developments indicate progress towards the achievement of Shanghai's long-term goal.

It does not seem too far-fetched to draw a parallel between Shanghai's changing status and that of changing family structures in the city. Pre-reform Shanghai was like a 'traditional' daughter-in-law thrust into an arranged marriage, bound to a previously unseen groom, at the mercy of a tyrannical mother-in-law. The body of Shanghai was penetrated by the patriarch, her dowry used up, and her former good looks withered. With atrophying bound feet, and scarcely able to stand, this daughter-in-law was expected and commanded both to 'stand erect on two legs' and to 'hold up half the sky'.

By the time the old Patriarch died, outlived by his now emaciated bride, family life had already begun to change. The 'modern' woman marries whom she chooses, goes out to work, and is an equal (at least) of her husband. A popular stereotype is that Shanghainese men suffer from *qiguanyan* – tracheitis. A homonym of this term is 'the wife controls strictly'. In Shanghai, men shop, knit, look after babies, and their incomes are controlled by their wives. They enjoy sexual favours only if they 'kneel beside the bed' (*chuangtou gui* – a pun on 'bedside cupboard'). The situation of the modern daughter-in-law is quite different in relation to the mother-in-law. The 'traditional' stereotype of the subservient, exploited daughter-in-law has largely been replaced with one where it is the mother-in-law who is exploited. If Shanghai is construed as a newly assertive daughter-in-law in the context of China it is interesting to recall, and ponder upon, Olga Lang's description of the situation of mothers-in-law with such daughters-in-law. Lang's assessment on the basis of research carried out in 1930s Shanghai was that '[t]he fate of these old women with modern daughters-in-law is tragic indeed' (1946: 237).

In addition to the inside/outside spatial dichotomies and the before/after chronological dichotomies mentioned above, informants also made a series of contrasts between various sociological inside/outside categories. During the Maoist period the following categories appear to have predominated: Party members/non-Party members, the 'people' (or the good classes)/enemies of the people (or the bad classes), and state and collective/private. I examine here ways in which these categories have been blurred and new contours are emerging.

During Mao Zedong's time a crucial distinction was between 'the people' and 'enemies of the people'.[4] A less severe, but still significant dichotomy was also drawn between Communist Party and non-Party members. Party members were extolled as 'special material' and moral exemplars. To be 'in' the Party was a mark of social approval. During the 1990s the Party member versus non-Party member distinction, though still important, appears to have become increasingly hazy, especially at the level of ordinary Party members. Informants told me that generally they no longer felt any need to exercise caution in their conversations when low-level Party members were present. Despite this, the latter still receive some extra benefits, and one common complaint was that *danwei* cadres have better access to housing.

Informants drew a much clearer distinction between themselves and high-ranking Party officials. The latter were described as a stratum or, more controversially, a *class* with special power (*tequan jieceng/jieji*) quite distinct from ordinary people (*laobaixing*). Any notion that Party members 'served the people' had, it appeared, long since evaporated. Joining the Communist Party was overwhelmingly viewed by my informants as a route to career advancement – Party officials served themselves and their families first. Although *gaige kaifang* has opened up more 'routes' to success, Party membership remains the sole route to political power. Additionally, the distinction between merchant and bureaucrat has blurred. A popular view is that this blurring involves considerable unfairness and, often, corruption. As an observer in Shanghai during Spring 1989, I gauge that official sleaze (*guandao*) was *the* main focus of protesters' anger.

Since the late 1970s the Party has ceased using class labels and abandoned the rhetoric of 'class struggle' in which 'the people' were sharply distinguished from 'the enemies of the people'. This latter category included, for example, former capitalists and landlords. The only time I heard language of this type used was by politically dissatisfied individuals who described, with acerbic irony, the Communist Party itself as the 'enemy of the people'.

During much of the Maoist period there appears to have been little official acceptance of *any* notion of a positive 'private' domain. From the mid-1950s until the late 1970s, official rhetoric generally condemned private enterprise as morally bad. Even between the two 'good' types of enterprise – collective and state – a distinct hierarchy was maintained. The highest prestige was accorded to state work units which could provide the full range of socialist-style benefits. During the reform era the distinctions between state, collective and private enterprise have blurred. It has become easier to move from collective to state *danwei*, and private enterprises are now permitted and even encouraged as a means to provide jobs for those laid-off from state enterprises. Indeed, by 1998, state-ownership of industries in Shanghai had decreased to less than 60 per cent of the total number. By 1999, the city had 94,000 private firms with 750,000 employees (*SS* 22 January 1999: 1). By early 2000, the city had 109,974 private enterprises (*SS* 15 February 2000: 10). In addition, as I have shown, new forms of enterprise have been established such as share-issuing companies and arrangements whereby state or collective enterprises are contracted-out to business people. There has also been a reintroduction of various forms of foreign-funded ventures and a proliferation of brokers – including latter day 'compradors' – who operate along the interstices of these entities.

A distinction which appeared to be of growing significance is that between young and old. Significantly, an imported term – *daigou* ('generation gap') – is used to describe this widening gulf. Those under the age of about forty spoke a rather different language, both in a rhetorical and a literal sense, to those socialised in the Maoist period. Amongst young Shanghainese I met, the 'insistency, repetitiveness, and monotony of Chinese [state] propaganda' (Nathan 1986: 172) had no appeal at all. Their most frequent reaction to this 'thin discourse of control' (Weller 1994: 206) was boredom and disinterest. Increasingly, government propagandists can only get their message across by competing in the cultural market place (see Barmé 1999). In competition with the lure of the widely available *gangtai* popular songs, disco-dancing, karaoke, romantic novels, kung-fu fiction, and melodramatic soap operas the Communist Party's univocal 'drone' has little chance, not least because many informants assumed that Party officials had, themselves, long since ceased to believe their own rhetoric.

Another significant contour which appears to be solidifying is an increasing assertion of self. A common refrain of the Maoist past is that people then had no 'mind', no 'self'. Denial of agency was typical of the collective amnesia which seemed to surround much of the Maoist past. The depoliticisation of everyday life has played a part in the emergence of a rhetoric of individualism. During the Maoist era, political education and the communal activities it involved were designed to promote a sense of common purpose and to link each citizen to the Party-state. In the reform era these activities – which had in any case become subject to considerable cynicism – have diminished both in scale and intensity. At the same time, trends such as work units becoming less inclusive and for a labour market to develop place the onus on individuals to make decisions and pursue their own goals. Belief in the self, with an increased stress upon individual desires and a search for self-fulfilment, is likely to become even more pronounced amongst the one-child generation. Few of the current generation of teenagers has a brother or a sister and many have grown up not only with the undivided and close attention of two parents but also two sets of grandparents. It will be intriguing to observe the sociological and psychological contours which emerge as this uniquely cosseted cohort reaches maturity.

Two particularly striking and emotionally charged categories which were brought to my attention in daily conversations were those between *laobaixing* and non-*laobaixing* and between poor and rich. During the 1990s the newly re-emergent differentiation between rich and poor was a fault line which seemed daily to widen. This distinction overlaps with that between *laobaixing*/non-*laobaixing*. A common way to depict wealth inequalities is as a contrast between those with 'ways' or 'roads', including those who take 'crooked roads', and those without 'ways' or 'roads'. High Party members are amongst those with 'ways' and 'roads' since their official posts give them contacts and the power to allocate resources. *Getihu* are also routinely cited as wealthy. However, although this is the dominant (expressed) view, a 'sub-text' sometimes appears; if questioned further on this topic informants often acknowledged that many *getihu* are also poor. The rich/poor divide is often portrayed in terms of consumption styles. For instance, the wealthy are those who eat the best food, are car owners or in a mobile phone-owning 'stratum'.

In the Preface, I noted the discursive creation of the '*laobaixing*' as a discrete category of persons in the everyday conversations of Shanghainese. Its components accord with John Fiske's comments on 'the people' which he describes as a:

> Shifting set of social allegiances, which are described better in terms of people's felt collectivity than in terms of external sociological factors such as class, gender, age, race, region, or what have you. Such allegiances may coincide with class and other social categories, but they don't necessarily: they can often cut across these categories, or often ignore them (1989: 24).

The *laobaixing* were discursively present in thousands of comments. Typically the *laobaixing* were personified in remarks such as: 'in 1949 the Shanghai *laobaixing* welcomed the Communist Party', 'the *laobaixing* are honest and hard working', 'the *laobaixing* would not accept great inequalities of wealth', and 'the *laobaixing* are made angry by official corruption.'

With the exception of high Party members, who were always excluded, membership of the category *laobaixing* was sometimes contested. The wealthy and intellectuals were ambiguous members of this shifting category. The category *laobaixing* generally concorded with those who 'relied on their salaries to eat'. The *laobaixing* were portrayed as morally good, honest, and hard-working. In the case of *getihu*, many of my informants excluded them from the category because they were considered to be rich and also morally suspect. For their part, *getihu* were keen to assert that they were *laobaixing*.

Intellectuals' inclusion as *laobaixing* was rather ambivalent. If asked directly whether they were *laobaixing*, intellectuals affirmed this, but in their conversations they would differentiate themselves from *laobaixing*, portraying the latter as a category separate, separated by education, from themselves. Above all, they depicted '*laobaixing*' as being 'without *wenhua*', a definition which, logically, would exclude themselves from being *laobaixing*.

The term *laobaixing* (literally 'old one hundred names') was so common and seemingly innocuous it would be easy to ignore it. Early in my research when I asked one elderly man to explain who the *laobaixing* were, he summed up his exposition with the statement that 'the *laobaixing* are always the victims.' However, as has been shown in this study, and in the examples given above, the *laobaixing* could also be represented in other ways. They were a long-suffering mass ('the masses') and could indeed be victims. Being *laoshi* – a term which means 'honest' but also conveys a sense of naiveté, even gullibility – they were potential victims of slick fraudsters or a pathological emperor. However, they could not all be fooled for all of the time. In a term favoured, for quite different motives, by both nineteenth-century European Orientalists and many of my informants, there would come a time when they would 'wake-up'. As such, risen from their slumbers, they would be a force to be reckoned with. Imbued with an innate sense of right and wrong, capable of multiple resistances, they could thwart the ambitions of false prophets (or those who accrued undeserved profits). The way in which informants would say, for instance, that 'the *laobaixing* will not accept great inequalities of wealth', hinted at just such a potentiality for resistance and agency.

Analysts who have examined the potential for 'civil society' in China, and my own findings indicate, as yet, a lack of institutional bases of sociality. In part this is because the Party-state actively seeks to prevent the growth of, and to eradicate the shoots of, any form of organisation which could threaten its own place. Additionally, the lack of trust between strangers, between those who do not 'know' each other, seems likely to exercise a powerful constraint on the development of associations. As Chamberlain comments 'Chinese civil society seems not so clearly in evidence. Individual and parochial interests typically take precedence over the common good' (1993: 210–11). However, in the same way as Chamberlain suggests that Sinologists have wrongly focused their attention on intellectual elites and that, for instance, sites such as the industrial workplace may be more fruitful, so it may be that the nebulous category '*laobaixing*' requires further attention.

As I note, the *laobaixing* were often personified. Statements made on behalf of 'the *laobaixing*' would usually make perfectly good sense if the speaker used 'I' in its place. The displacement of what were, presumably, the speakers' own views and feelings (and their potential agency) onto this category is not surprising. Traditional Chinese philosophy has tended to stress the collective good. Moreover, open personal statements of defiance have been dangerous at many times in Chinese history – a traditional proverb states: fame portends trouble for men just as fattening does for pigs. From a more positive perspective, however, the ways in which the term *laobaixing* is used do seem to indicate a moral economy of sorts, involving a sense of shared feeling, of collectivity, of the potentiality for forms of association that cross-cut everyday boundaries.

A theme of this study has been to show ways in which identities in Shanghai are, perhaps increasingly, contingent and contextual, there being a wide range of cross-cutting, possible identifications.[5] Ulf Hannerz writes that 'post-modern culture is characterised by a multiplicity of perspectives and voices. It is a thing of shreds and patches. Juxtaposition becomes the prevalent experience' (1992: 34). With its increasing degree of 'imported cultural heterogeneity' (201) and 'availability of cultural interfaces' (203), one may describe contemporary Shanghai as increasingly post-modern. However, I am sceptical of those who consider global cultural flow as solely a contemporary phenomenon. Thus, when compared to accounts of the city in the 1930s, early 1990s Shanghai at least was still a rather insular place. Indeed, it is hard to imagine a place of *more* juxtapositions and *more* cultural heterogeneity than inter-war Shanghai with its Qing dynasty wooden houses, art deco experiments, classical style public buildings, mock Tudor cottages, and the assemblages of migrants from all over China, White Russians, prostitutes, missionaries, Jewish refugees, 'underground' Communist activists, British 'Shanghailanders', Sikh and Annamese policemen, and Japanese soldiers.

Along with the need to interrogate ethnocentric biases anthropologists also need to be alert to what may be called a chrono-centrism: that is, the notion that *all* contemporary phenomena are unique. What is novel since the late twentieth century is the ease and sheer speed with which cultural phenomena may now ricochet back and forth across the planet. The impact of electronic media has been a significant theme of this study. Their impact, like so many of the findings of this study, has been multi-faceted and ambiguous.

Comments made by the human rights activist Harry Wu (1995) during a lecture delivered at London University were illuminating on this account. Wu described how he had been arrested as he tried to cross into China from Kazakhstan a few weeks before. His intention had been to use micro-cameras to film secret labour camps, places hidden in 'dark corners'. In his estimation, his arrest at this remote border post could be attributed to the successes of *gaige kaifang* which had brought in funds for China's Public Security Bureau, thereby allowing them to computerise their activities. He was caught in this new electronic web. This example demonstrates the ambiguity of electronic media – it would be mistaken to focus only upon and to overemphasise their 'de-territorialising' effects. Such devices may be 'technologies without boundaries' (Noam 1990), but they can also facilitate vastly improved means of surveillance and control, and seal boundaries much more effectively. The aim of Harry Wu, whose current career and activities could be described as consisting of and embodying a 'global positive feedback loop' (Wark 1993: 140), was to show images of prison camps on the Western media and thereby bring pressure to bear on both the American and Chinese governments. As he discovered, electronic media can contemporaneously illuminate China's interstitial places and close gaps in the 'wall'.

In Shanghai, as elsewhere in the world, electronic messages 'steal into places like thieves in the night' (Meyrowitz 1985: 117). The Party-state is busily trying to ensure that these 'thieves' are kept out or, at least, do not steal anything of value. The city government has recently engaged upon a large-scale project to install a cable system. The motive appears to be to pre-empt citizens acquiring satellite dishes which are less susceptible to state controls. Cable systems have the great advantage that they can be more readily filtered and, if need be, cut off. Similarly, reports describe how 'China has laid the foundations of an electronic Great Wall to fend off invaders on the information superhighway' (*Guardian* 4 September 1995: 9). A Hong Kong-based subsidiary of China's *Xinhua* News Agency has developed 'a politically correct version of the Internet. Purged of pornography, political dissent and other forms of "spiritual pollution"' (ibid.). A cartoon in the *Financial Times* refers to this China Internet as 'a kind of information superhighway without the information' (*FT* 10 July 1995: 13). Nonetheless, the former of these articles adds that 'this new barrier is already in danger of being overrun. In June [1995], its defences lowered by the profit motive, China allowed citizens of Beijing and Shanghai to buy time on the real Internet.'

Since the mid-1990s, annual growth in Internet use in China has been meteoric, from 620,000 users in 1997 to 8.9 million at the end of 1999 (*SS* 1 February 2000: 6). By mid-2000, Shanghai was said to have 1.48 million Internet surfers (*SS* 25 July 2000: 11). The city also has several thousand Internet cafés, many of them reported to be operated by laid-off workers (*SS* 13 July 1999: 4). China's integration into global information flows looks unstoppable. China's national planners are, in any event, determined that the country should develop a high-tech industrial base, with Shanghai playing a major role as a producer of communications equipment. Pursuing this ambition, while warding off what the Party-state deems 'unwelcome' influences, may become increasingly difficult. In 1999 and 2000, for instance, followers of the *falungong* sect used e-mail to organise their activities, including protest demonstrations around *zhongnanhai*, the Communist Party leaders' compound in Beijing.

> China matters because it was until 1850 the world's largest economic power... It is reasonable to assume that within our lifetime this will once again be the world's largest economy, the world's, perhaps, most powerful state, certainly the most dominant state in the most economically booming area of the world, in East Asia. Therefore, it matters economically... strategically... and in terms of spreading its culture and values.
>
> (Gerald Segal 1996)

> Viewed as a place of trade, I fear that Hong Kong will be a failure.
>
> (Robert Fortune 1853: Vol. 1, 13)

If China is 'crossing the stream' one is tempted to ask what lies on the other side? The long-term consequences of the far-reaching socio-economic changes now in motion in Shanghai can only be guessed at. Moreover, as Robert Fortune's words demonstrate, and his assessment was shared by many contemporaries, China 'experts' have often been proved spectacularly wrong.

In speculating on the future contours of Shanghai it is interesting to compare the following two comments. The first, from the introduction to an edited volume on urban China, states that '[a] sense of the incompleteness of change emerged strongly... from all the essays in this volume'. The second, from a study on Shanghai, states that the '[o]ld things are passing away and the new order is not yet firmly established.' These remarkably similar assessments are separated by almost 80 years, the first from Naughton's (1995a: 26) introductory comments to Davis *et al.*'s *Urban Spaces in Contemporary China*; the second is from the conclusion to Mary Gamewell's *The Gateway to China: Pictures of Shanghai* published in 1916. It seems that while the present always consists of flux and indeterminacy, certainty and clarity are *always* anticipated to lie just around the corner. I deliberately avoid calling this chapter a conclusion for just this reason.

In democratic nations political imperatives often limit future planning to no more than a couple of years ahead. In Shanghai it is striking to hear so many media reports on plans for projects which are only expected to reach their full fruition decades hence. When I asked an elderly informant, born a citizen of the Qing empire, how he envisaged Shanghai's future he mentioned the plans which are being made. Then he remarked that during the Cultural Revolution one could never have imagined Shanghai would be the way it is now. So, he added, 'the decades ahead may be equally beyond our imaginations . . . '

When Deng Xiaoping spoke of China 'crossing the stream' he envisioned, presumably, that what lay on the other bank would be a rich, powerful nation-state, with the Communist Party firmly in control. Continued social stability and the Communist Party's legitimacy now appears dependent upon continued rising living standards for the majority of the population. There appear to be good grounds for the fulfilment of Deng's prophecy. In the five years following his advocating Shanghai to take 'faster steps in reform' in 1992, the city's GDP averaged annual growth of more than 14 per cent (*SS* 15 August 1997: 3). By 2000, with an average of $3,400 per head, Shanghai's GDP was on a par with that of South Africa or Turkey. This figure was substantially lower than that of Hong Kong ($22,990), but far higher than that of the poorest province in China, Guizhou ($280) (*Economist* 8 April 2000: 5). The goal for the first decade of the twenty-first century, announced by President Jiang Zemin in September 1997, is for China's GNP to double (*FT Survey* 1997: I). Shanghai's economic growth is expected to exceed this ambitious target. Moreover, my informants were mostly optimistic, believing in a bright prosperous and glorious future for their city.

As I have mentioned, Shanghai achieved notoriety as a 'paradise of adventurers', this description seems to have been subject to shifting meanings. This appellation was, perhaps, derived from the title of G.E. Miller's (1937) novel *Shanghai, The Paradise of Adventurers*. In August 1949, a *Jingji Zhoubao* (*Economic Weekly*) article described Shanghai as 'a non-productive city . . . a parasitic city . . . a criminal city . . . It is the paradise of adventurers . . . a city where waste is even greater than consumption' (cited in Gaulton 1981: 46). Shanghainese now commonly use this term to express both a positive nostalgia for a lost past and a hope for the future. Even the official media seem to support the notion of the desirability of Shanghai once again becoming more like it once was. A front-page *Shanghai Star* report on a meeting orchestrated by Shanghai's then mayor, Huang Ju, on the topic of the future of Shanghai, described it as part of 'the city government's efforts to revive the past glories of Shanghai' (2 July 1993).

In the 1950s Shanghai's citizens began to learn the language of class struggle. Since the early 1990s a new vocabulary of 'markets', 'opportunities', 'competition', 'redundancy' and 'bankruptcy' has begun to infiltrate into daily life. Shanghai's commercialising economy is loosening and remaking the fabric of the society. This offers novel opportunities and possibilities. At the same time it creates new reasons to be fearful and mistrustful, new sources of risk, uncertainty and danger to replace the old. As I mentioned in the Preface, those for whom *gaige kaifang* has brought the fewest benefits and, above all, those whose livelihoods have been undermined, were the most reluctant to speak with a foreign researcher. However, even amongst the majority of my informants who considered their living standards to be improving I found many simmering discontents and resentments. For some of my informants Shanghai was a city in which each passing day brought change (*rixin yueyi*), a development they responded to positively. However, there were others for whom daily life continued as before, or for whom change was unwelcome. For instance, a state *danwei* worker in her late twenties complained to me that:

> Most of the benefits from *gaige kaifang* go to foreigners whilst many problems, such as pollution, are left behind for the *laobaixing*. It increases the weight of Chinese people's burden. Shanghai's environment is increasingly bad. There is no fresh air, no clean water. Everything is done for short-term benefit, for money. People are alienated by material goods, people serve money.[6]

For much of the 1990s, Shanghai's sociological landscape displayed all the volatility and unpredictability of the city's stock market. However, trends which may create serious tensions in the future, have begun to distil into discernible contours. Issues which cause particular concern include rising inequalities of wealth, corruption by officials, and crime – the latter often blamed upon migrant workers, 'outsiders'. These phenomena are already making Shanghai a less ordered, a less safe place.[7] Deeper undercurrents of discontent include resentments over past mistreatment or a sense of a youth 'lost' in the countryside. For the time being these jagged reefs of resentment have been submerged by generally increasing prosperity and the opiate of plentiful and affordable consumer goods. Real dangers will lie ahead if this growth is not sustained. Additionally, a potentially hazardous feature of the reform era has been the raising of expectations and aspirations. Expectations are extremely high; for instance, many of my informants anticipated that Shanghai would soon surpass the economic development attained by Hong Kong and Singapore. Social stability and the future of the Communist Party would appear to be largely entwined with the provision of constantly rising living standards, an ambitious target for any nation.

A strong consensus of my informants was that the sluice gate which had been opened could not be closed again. Nevertheless concerns were expressed over the near to mid-term future. A commonly expressed fear was that in the event of economic recession or political instability the fractures and fissures which emerged in 1990s Shanghai would widen and become the courses along which frustrations and discontent flow. It is interesting to speculate on where future protesters will look for inspiration in future protests. In the future, popular aspirations may once again extend to imported cultural products such as 'democracy' and 'freedom', understood, inevitably in local contexts and subject to subtle redefinitions. Although in Spring 1989 protesters tended to look to Western cultural symbols, this need not necessarily be the case in the future. Western analysts' preoccupation with 'democracy' tends to overlook the quite different cultural background in China. The dominant view amongst my informants was that Communist Party rhetoric on, for example, controlling crime and corruption was correct. However, some informants considered the Party too entangled in these activities to control them, while another common perception (see page 41–3), was that it had become *too* weak, *too* lacking in authority to control them. They perceived this weakness in their daily lives, for instance, in the inability of the Party-state to collect tax, control crime, prostitution, and the influx of rural migrants, or even to provide free education and health care. The Party-state's weakness was believed, largely, to have been a product of *gaige kaifang* and its attendant dilution of Communist Party power. For most of my informants, press freedom and parliamentary democracy were not the solution. Rather, the Confucian ideal of an honest, upright official (*qingguan*) seemed more appropriate.

At a superficial level many Shanghainese decry the Maoist past. However, alongside this denigration of the past – which serves the interests of the Communist Party if kept within bounds – there were also more positive assessments of the past. In rural China, Anagnost (1989) found that egalitarianism although officially repudiated remains an important element of popular peasant values. She concluded that 'the fear of polarisation is based on a memory of the old society recreated in local histories' (215). In Shanghai, too, many of my informants harked back to the early 1950s as a time with little corruption, good order, equality, comradeship, and a sense of shared goals. The certainties of this past, a collective memory, rarefied, embellished and cleansed by the passage of time, and facilitated by 'politically enforced amnesia' (Schwarcz 1991: 98) were a basis for considerable nostalgia. This nostalgia could extend to those born after the 1950s, a nostalgia untrammeled by experience. In the face of uncertainty and risk, the dispossessed and disenchanted may seek the welcome embrace and security of a nostalgia increasingly cut lose from memory. Of course, nostalgia may remain as just that, but these 'memories' do provide a latent, and potentially fertile, source for the creation of a powerful political agenda.

I found that young people's knowledge of the Cultural Revolution, let alone the 1950s, was generally extremely limited.[8] It may be, therefore, that symbols from this era will become particularly malleable and capable of incorporation into new demands. Is it too fanciful to suppose that in future protests, for participants who find themselves in a present which is confused, incoherent and disturbing, the 'memories' of a stable, well-ordered period may be particularly appealing? At a time when state officials appear to be busily re-inventing Shanghai's pre-1949 past as a desirable future, is it possible that 'Maoist' emblems of egalitarianism and class struggle could become the focus, the rallying call, for participants in protest movements?

In the face of potential deep-rooted difficulties, it is an encouraging sign that discussion of the city's problems has become rather more open. For instance, a recent front-page article in the *Shanghai Star* explored the difficulties faced by 160,000 laid-off workers, who subsist on a monthly income of around 300 *yuan* ($36) (1 February 2000: 1). Similarly, city planners have begun to consider the implications of the developed world demographic profile that Shanghai will soon face. A recent estimate stated that the family planning policies adopted in the city since 1963 have decreased population growth by an estimated 7 million babies (*SS* 9 April 1999: 1). As a result of these policies, along with improved health care, the city has an ageing population, by 2003 it is expected that 37 per cent of its citizens will be over 60.

In December 2001, after 15 years of negotiations, China finally acceded to the World Trade Organisation. Shanghai has a strong pro-WTO lobby, anticipating that the city will benefit from membership. For instance, there are hopes that accession will bring a surge of foreign investment. Demand for imports is also likely to be fuelled by WTO entry; a local newspaper article anticipates that with WTO accession Shanghai 'will open up the sluice gates to hundreds and thousands more imported goods' (*SS* 23 November 1999: 7). Although WTO accession is generally welcomed in Shanghai, it will present a challenge not only to many state-owned enterprises but also to joint ventures such as Shanghai General Motors and Shanghai Volkswagen. At present, tariffs on imported autos range from 80–110 per cent, these will be drastically reduced once WTO rules come into operation, thereby fuelling competition between importers and domestic producers.

National and international developments will have a major impact on Shanghai's future development. There is considerable potential for the state to initiate and mobilise the forces of nationalism, for instance, in the event of conflict over the sovereignty of Taiwan. By contrast to this centralising impulse there are centrifugal forces which may foster the development of a truly assertive Shanghainese 'nationalism'. Between these two extremes, Shanghai is likely to continue to become more deeply integrated into the global economy and to play an increasingly vital and vibrant role within it. WTO membership will play a part in this by binding and integrating both Shanghai and China generally closer to the world economy. There can be little doubt that Shanghai has the potential to become one of the world's major economic and cultural centres in the twenty-first century. Let us hope that all Shanghai's citizens will benefit from the fruits of this development.

Notes

Preface: ethnography of a city

1 There are numerous problems with statistics in China. In 1999, for instance, China's finance ministry uncovered widespread accounting abuses among state-owned enterprises. An auditing probe of 100 state companies showed that 81 had falsified their accounts. Of these, 69 reported 2.75 billion *yuan* (£206 million) in profits that did not exist. Auditors also found off-book business, unlawful money-lending, false reports of assets and liabilities and improper use of funds raised from share issues. Chinese economists concluded that if the sample was representative of the 300,000 strong state sector, this rendered official state statistics virtually meaningless (*FT* 24–5 December 1999: 7).

2 White (1994: 67–8) gives figures for Shanghai's population for every year from 1950–92. These include: 1950 – 4.9 m, 1955 – 6.4 m, 1960 – 10.4 m, 1965 – 10.9 m, 1970 – 10.8 m, 1975 – 10.7 m, 1980 – 11.4 m, 1985 – 12.1 m, 1990 – 12.8 m, 1992 – 12.8 m.

3 Dictionaries of the Shanghai dialect include Creamer (1991); Min *et al.* (1991); Pott (1924); Qian (1987); Silsby (1911).

4 This perception is so deeply ingrained that Chinese migrants in England routinely refer to all residents of non-Chinese descent as *waiguoren* – 'foreigners'.

5 People would often discuss 'foreigners' – including 'English people' – in my presence, imputing to them ways of behaving, characteristics, or world views they knew I did not possess. Such disjunctures rarely seemed to impinge upon the stereotypes.

6 People I met for the first time and, for instance, market traders would often intersperse their conversation with the assertion 'we are all friends'. In the former case, this seemed designed to create a basis of fraternity and equality, whilst in the latter traders appeared to imply that they would treat customers as though they were friends – with the implication that I could trust them not to cheat me.

Introduction

1 This section draws upon Bergère (1981, 1989); *Chinese Repository*; Ch'en (1979); Clifford (1991); Darwent (1904); Davidson-Houston (1962); De Jesus (1909); Honig (1986, 1992); Howe (1981); Johnson (1993a, 1995); Lanning and Couling (1921); Lu (1999); MacLellan (1889); Murphey (1953, 1974); Perry (1993, 1994); Pott (1928); Sutherland (1984); Wakeman and Yeh (1992); Wasserstrom (1991); White (1978, 1981, 1994); White and Cheng (1993).

2 Historians and geographers of China (e.g. Appleton 1951; Dawson 1967; Mackerras 1989; March 1974) have shown how representations of China by Western writers have changed over the years in response to shifting cultural trends within Europe.

3 There is an evocative and closely observed account of everyday life in Republican era (1911–49) Shanghai in Lu (1999).

4 On *danwei* see Lü and Perry (1997), Walder (1986) and You (1998).

5 Shanghainese migrants to Hong Kong played a vital role in the post-war development of the Crown Colony (see Wong 1988).
6 A general overview of the period 1979–89 is presented in Saich (1992).
7 In 1988, larger private enterprises (*siying qiye*) which could employ over eight people were permitted.
8 On events in Shanghai during Spring 1989 see Forward (1991) and Warner (1991).

1 Opening the door, crossing the stream: representations and metaphors of reform in contemporary Shanghai

1 This is an adaptation of the phrase: *gua yangtou, mai gourou* – 'hang up a sheep's head and sell dog meat' – try to palm-off something inferior to what it purports to be.
2 The controversial six-part television documentary series *Heshang* (River Elegy) was transmitted in China in 1988. Many of its makers were criticised in the aftermath of 4 June 1989.
3 Although replaced in some contexts and diluted by a proliferation of terms, some military metaphors persist. Examples include *nanxun* ('southern patrol') the name given to Deng Xiaoping's Spring Festival 1992 visit to southern China, and *xiagang* ('come or go off sentry duty') which entered civilian life in the 1990s to describe a worker who has been laid off.
4 'Transparency' (*toumingdu*) is the Chinese equivalent of the Russian *glasnost* ('openness') (Su and Wang 1991: 219–20, Note 59).
5 An intriguing aspect of *River Elegy* is the similarity in its ideology to that of the dominant early nineteenth-century colonial discourse on China. Lanning and Couling, for instance, wrote of the pre-Opium War 'stagnation . . . in China's progress' and described it as due to 'the lack of suitable stimulation from without' (1921: 15). With their idealised, even romantic, portrayal of 'the West', the makers of *River Elegy* appear to desire just such a 'stimulation'.
6 The component characters of the term *jiefang*, officially used of the Communist Party's take-over of power in 1949, are worth noting: *jie* – undo, untie; *fang* – let go, set free, release.
7 A statement Deng first made as early as March 1961 (Li 1994: 376).
8 In 2000, a government official admitted that the municipal government was considering building a racecourse (*SS* 26 May 2000: 3).
9 In late 2000, Rong Yiren was estimated to be worth $1.9 billion (*FT* 10 November 2000: 14).
10 The introduction of the rural household responsibility system in the late 1970s and early 1980s was another instance of this. In many parts of China peasants spontaneously divided up land before the state policy was announced (see Vogel 1989: 96).
11 That there *was* scope for individuals to adopt various strategies and counter-strategies is evident in Shirk (1982). See also Walder (1986: 181–5) on the use of particularistic relationships (*guanxi*) to circumvent bureaucratic and egalitarian norms.
12 In 1987, per capita GNP in Shanghai was $1,174 and in Hong Kong $7,673 (Wong 1996: 27).
13 In 1988, the annual wage of salaried staff and workers in Shanghai was estimated to be 1,747 *yuan*. The income of private entrepreneurs was estimated to average over 5,000 *yuan* with some 10 per cent having an annual income in excess of 10,000 *yuan* (Wilson 1990: 58).
14 The term *wenhua* presents great difficulties in translation. Generally translated as 'culture', *wenhua* also means 'education, schooling, literacy' (CED 1988: 721–2). As this definition suggests, and as its use makes apparent in everyday contexts, a clear linkage, even a conflation, is often made between the English concepts of 'culture' and 'education' – education *per se* is usually referred to as *jiaoyu*. I suggest that this indicates the priority which has traditionally been accorded to the written

word in China. Since '*wenhua*' defies easy translation, the Chinese term is used throughout this book.

15 In 1980, 64 per cent of Shanghai's retail sales were conducted in state stores; by 1996 only 39 per cent (Shanghai 1997: 21).

16 This report added that in 1996 a further 150,000 people were unemployed.

17 Between 1994–6 there were 58 bankruptcies in Shanghai. It was expected that a further 50 companies would go bankrupt in 1997 (*FT Survey* 1997: VII)

18 Neighbourhood Residents' Committees are the lowest level of organisation, each includes 500–1,300 households. Their main functions are mediation in quarrels between neighbours, to organise participation in elections for People's Representatives, the maintenance of cleanliness and sanitation, dissemination of propaganda and information, and liaison with local police stations (see Parish and Whyte 1984: 22–5).

19 In Shanghai in 1946, the KMT set up a public security system through the grouping of households and streets (see White 1981: 51). This was, itself, a revived version of the traditional *baojia* system.

20 There was some evidence of this after 4 June 1989 when families and neighbours were encouraged to turn in 'counter-revolutionary elements'.

21 *Shehui fengqi* is not easily translated into English – note the problems outlined above (see page 29) in translating *feng*. It encompasses prevailing norms, morals, standards of behaviour and, more generally, the 'spirit of the age' or *zeitgeist*.

22 This is an ironic play upon Deng Xiaoping's famous aphorism of the early 1980s: 'it does not matter if the cat is black or white so long as it catches mice.' This statement was understood as implying that ideology is less important than economic development.

23 For a far more negative view of personal relations in pre-Cultural Revolution China see Vogel (1965).

24 Note, however, that strong friendships could also be forged at this time, see the example of rusticated youth mentioned above in 'Making contacts' in the Preface.

25 This new ethos is by no means limited to Shanghai. Madsen writes of the new generation of leaders in a Cantonese village in the 1970s that 'a common term used to characterise their private lives was selfishness; these people did not care about anything outside the circle of their own small families' (1984: 218).

26 However, comparing income levels is problematic since most of the latter two types of enterprise would not provide housing and have less extensive welfare benefits.

27 On the *nouveaux riches* in China generally see Goodman (1996) and Buckley (1999).

28 Official rhetoric also accepts this as a problem (see, for instance, *CD* '"*Fanpai* companies" must sever their former ties', 23 November 1993: 4).

29 It should be borne in mind that many of the generation now in their twenties received much of their early socialisation from grandparents who reached maturity before 1949.

30 This is an ironic use of the verb *zhipei* which is generally used for the allocation of materials and labour.

2 Global and intra-national cultural flows: renegotiating boundaries and identities in contemporary Shanghai

1 In 1949 there were some 4,000 Britons in Shanghai (Clifford 1991: 277).

2 In early 1949, 75 per cent of the audience patronised American films. By June 1950, this figure was down to 28.3 per cent, falling to zero with the start of the Korean War (Gaulton 1981: 50).

3 An exception to this were the underground hand-copied volumes of entertainment fiction which circulated in urban China during the Cultural Revolution (see Link 1989). These texts were frequently 'set in foreign countries or otherwise involved with foreign countries' (28–9).

4 See, for instance, Nien Cheng's account of her experiences during the Cultural Revolution. Because of her contact with foreigners – she had been employed by the *Shell International Petroleum Company* – she was suspected of being a spy and still working for the 'imperialists' (1986: 19–22, 161–8).

5 I realise the problem of 'over-Maoising' the years 1949–76 and ignoring significant shifts in policies over these years. However, I am providing a Weberian 'ideal type' model which, whilst it may gloss over certain nuances, is faithful to the portrayals I was provided with by local residents.

6 These comments apply equally, of course, to the foreign residents of Shanghai.

7 For further examples of links between native-place and employment in Shanghai see Bergère (1989: 141–52); Ch'en (1979: 221–4); Goodman (1995: 29–38); Johnson 1993b: (158–68); White 1978: (100–1).

8 See Leung (1982) on the rivalry between Cantonese and Ningboese in Shanghai during the second half of the nineteenth century.

9 However, although Maoist era policies may have hastened cultural divergence, there is evidence that the cultural bifurcation of urban and rural forms predated the Maoist era. The iconoclastic 'civilised weddings' (*wenming hunli*) of 1930s Shanghai, which copied Western models, are an instance of this.

10 By the term 'orientalising' I indicate the essentialising and stereotypical defining of other ethnic groups.

11 This did not preclude people retaining personal memories of contact with foreigners or their cultural artefacts which contrasted with the official line. However, the effects of state propaganda should not be underestimated; a strong-willed individual who had undergone 'thought reform' in the early 1950s told me that in this process he had begun to sincerely doubt his own judgement and, in the words of a slogan of that time, to 'follow the Communist Party'.

12 According to Nathan (1986: 163) there were some 141 million loudspeakers in use in China in 1974.

13 Note He Di's comment that Mao Zedong 'deliberately shaped a distorted image of the United States for consumption by the Chinese people' (1994: 148), even though he himself 'saw the American people positively' (155).

14 It is interesting to note the extent to which early British travellers and residents in China also engaged in a discourse on regional stereotypes. Visitors to Shanghai often favourably contrasted the 'peaceable and hospitable community' at Shanghai to the 'furious and ignorant mob' of Canton (Forbes 1848: 13). Similarly, Fortune – whose comments on 'northern Chinese' refer to Shanghainese – remarks on the friendliness of 'the northern Chinese, who differ widely from their haughty and insolent countrymen in the south' (1853: Vol. I, 108). Conflicts in the city were often attributed to outsiders, especially Cantonese and Fujianese. For example, an 1848 report mentions that 'murderous affrays are very common here among the people from Fukhien' (*CR*: 17(9), 473). Lt-Colonel Fisher, in Shanghai in the late 1850s, described how 'the Cantonese swagger about the streets, and give themselves great airs as being far superior to the people of the place. They are generally considered a braver but somewhat lawless race' (1863: 345). In comparison to Fujianese and Cantonese, Ningboese were said to be 'more numerous, and far more tractable' (*CR* 1850: 19(2), 107). Decades later, Ross wrote that '[i]n the South people are smaller, yellower, less manly and less courageous. The ugly, wrinkled, cat-like wily Chinaman of dime-novel fiction come from the South. They are quicker of wit than the Northerners but harder for us to understand or trust. Upon the Canton type is built the cherished literary legend of the unfathomableness and superhuman craftiness of the Oriental' (1911: 29). A striking feature is the degree to which these historical Westerners' comments match stereotypes I heard contemporary Shanghainese express (see also Lin 1935: 17–23). It is interesting to speculate on the degree to which the 'Orientalist' stereotypes of Western writers might have originated in indigenous discourses rather than vice-versa.

15 Hong Kong's Cantonese used 'Shanghainese' as a catch-all term for most northern Chinese (Vogel 1989: 48).

16 On *wenhua* see Chapter 1, Note 14.

17 Many people I spoke with accepted a eugenic view that the children of parents from different population groups (including different provinces of China) are more intelligent. Dikötter (1992) describes how such ideas were popularised in China during the late nineteenth century. He comments that some saw 'interracial marriage... as a means of strengthening the people of the empire' (87).

18 Generally *paiwai* (anti-foreign; exclusive – literally 'exclude the outside') refers to foreigners, but this man was clearly referring to other Chinese.

19 Note how closely these contrasts between 'Beijing' and 'Shanghai' parallel those made in *River Elegy* between the enclosed, stagnant, and insular mentality of 'yellow culture' (China) and the open, dynamic, and exploratory spirit of the 'blue ocean' (the West).

20 In a more general sense, *all* things coming from 'outside' are regarded as potentially destructive. Within families, for instance, incoming wives may be regarded as sources of disharmony until thoroughly absorbed by the 'inner' circle. Another example concerns the children of 'rusticated' Shanghainese who went to the border regions in the 1950s. Since the late 1970s some of these youngsters have been permitted to migrate to Shanghai. These newcomers were often described to me as disruptive and as figuring highly among the ranks of child offenders.

21 These characteristics are similar to representations of black people – the most 'other' of China's others (see Dikötter 1992: 12). However, in popular perceptions rural Chinese are generally seen, unlike black people, as morally good.

22 This latter perception appears to be backed up by statistics. In 1983, 7 per cent of crime was committed by non-registered people, by 1989 this figure had risen to 31 per cent (White 1994: 90). A Shanghai radio report (cited in FBIS CHI-95–118, 20 June 1995: 62) reported that in the three months March, April and May 1995, there had been 2,956 arrests in the city and that 57.85 per cent of these were of people from other provinces.

23 Shanghai dialect belongs to the Wu dialect family which is spoken in the Yangtze delta and coastal region around Shanghai and has some 80,750,000 speakers (Ramsey 1987: 87–95).

24 Grillo defines 'dominant language' as 'a variety characteristically employed by those occupying superordinate positions' (1989: 12).

25 My attempts to study Shanghai dialect with a private teacher illustrate the agentive role an anthropologist can play whether wittingly or unwittingly. As we progressed he told me that he was discovering ever more vocabulary items and realising that Shanghai dialect is very 'colourful' and 'rich'. After several weeks he confided that he had originally considered the dialect as only involving pronunciation differences from *putonghua*, and had anticipated that these could easily be taught within five or six weeks. Now, however, he realised that there was far more to it than this and that 'when one speaks it all the day one pays no attention and does not realise this.' He became increasingly aware of, and to relish, the distinctiveness of the dialect. In this interaction, at the same time as I was learning, I was also being instrumental in altering my teacher's perceptions and understanding of the language he spoke every day. In facilitating this shift of his non-discursive knowledge to the realm of discursive awareness, it could even be that I was helping to foster his (new) sense of Shanghainese identity.

26 On the diverse range of meanings of *feng* see page 208, note 21.

27 When foreigners were first allowed to visit China in any numbers a dual currency system was introduced. Chinese citizens used *renminbi* (RMB) – 'people's money'. Foreigners were issued with *Foreign Exchange Certificates* (FEC) which they had to use to pay for purchases including imported goods, accommodation, and transportation. Conversely, Chinese citizens were excluded from making certain purchases and

staying in certain hotels by their lack of FEC. This dual currency system gradually diminished, not least, as the currency black market became ever more extensive.

28 Foreign students are generally subject to far fewer restrictions than their Chinese counterparts. Ironically, this laxity paralleled the pre-1949 extra-territoriality which foreign residents in China claimed for themselves. It also seems to parallel the indulgence typically shown to small children in China.

29 In 2000, it was announced that China's first express railway, linking Shanghai and Beijing, was expected to start construction in 2001. This will shorten the journey time to seven hours (*SS* 2 June 2000: 1).

30 In 1995, Deng failed to appear, fostering speculation over his failing health.

31 According to Li (1991: 345), *China Central Television Station* first used a live satellite broadcast for the 1978 football World Cup. From April 1980, CCTV began to receive daily foreign news by satellite.

32 As Wark points out, this 'global positive feedback loop' included the state's close scrutiny of broadcasts shown in the West during its collection of evidence in the post-4 June round-up of participants (1993: 140).

33 This 20 episode series was based on the book of the same name, *Beijingren Zai Niuyue* (Glen Cao 1993). The author migrated to the United States in 1981.

34 This does not diminish the notion of the imagined community. People may violently disagree with official statements just because they are incompatible with their own conception of the relevant imagined community.

35 Even before this, Mary Gamewell described how '[y]oung men back from years of study in America or Europe, and there are many of them in Shanghai, wear foreign clothes and look well in them' (1916: 160).

3 The walls within: Shanghai inside out

1 The following contrasts are drawn from a typical text of the imperial era (Wilson 1887: 20–5):

Chinese native city	*Foreign settlement*
Past/middle ages	Present/future
Isolation/arrested development	Progressive ideas/hope
Fever and filth	Well paved
Struggling and sordid multitude	Well-selected population
Sordid struggle of life, sloth	Industry, thrift, enterprise
Decrepitude and decay, squalor	Luxury and comfort

2 '*Subeiren*' (Subei person) may be used in a similar fashion. A bundle of notions seemed to overlap – poverty, chaos, bad taste, low-status, *xiazhijiao*, *Subeiren*.

3 In Shanghai, I often heard people describe having many children as an indication of lack of *wenhua*.

4 In an interview with the share dealer 'Millions Yang' the interviewer found it strange that Yang had not moved from his native Zhabei to Xuhui, Jing'an, or Hongqiao districts. Yang agreed that these areas were 'extremely good', but remarked that 'it would not feel right for an emancipated "poor peasant" like myself to move there' (*SWHYSB* 4–10 June 1993: 4).

5 Physically Nanshi had changed very little. The narrow streets, densely packed low-level housing, and extremely high population density present enormous problems for redevelopment.

6 The way in which 'bad elements' were given such work as a punishment would have reinforced these views.
7 For the purposes of analysis I am depicting an 'ideal type' model of *danwei*. Even during the peak of collectivisation many work places never achieved the ideal model. The full range of benefits and security applied only to permanent workers in larger state enterprises, about 42 per cent of the industrial workforce in 1981 (Walder 1987: 59).
8 Jinshan is a county of Shanghai 70 kilometres from the city centre. The plant is one of China's six largest enterprises. It has some 60,000 employees, around 30,000 of whom commute from urban Shanghai. It contributes about 10 per cent of Shanghai's tax to the central government.
9 *Danwei* are also internally spatially differentiated. Rofel describes how in Hangzhou silk weaving factories the main offices of the party secretary and factory director are 'set in a separate building well apart from the workshops ... completely walled off from the shop floor ... [by] thick concrete walls' (1992: 101).
10 This statement requires some qualification. For certain sections of the population the Cultural Revolution provided significant spatial (and social) mobility. Rofel (1992) describes instances of this in Hangzhou silk weaving factories. Some workers there physically walked away from their work position to engage in politics and others 'mix[ed] the space of the factory with "domestic" space by doing their laundry, shopping, and washing bicycles at the factory or during work hours' (97).
11 A teacher pointed out that originally schoolchildren had engaged in labour as a part of their 'thought education'. Only later did profit become the main motive for such activities.
12 The school's entry into commercial affairs was highly controversial and it had to mobilise various alumni on its behalf. These included former students now employed in the media who published articles on its behalf. Subsequently, the school became engaged in a court case with a client and once again it sought the aid of alumni to campaign on its behalf. This involved not only a publicity campaign but also backstage connection pulling, gift-giving, and meal invitations.
13 From the day before New Year's Eve until the fifth day of the new lunar month people reverted to the traditional lunar calendar. In a sense, for these few days people are both physically and temporally in a different place to the state.
14 Studies by Davis (1989) on household interiors in Shanghai and Laing (1989) on furniture arrangement and decoration indicate the potential for such an ethnography.
15 Accommodation may be acquired in five basic ways – *danwei* allocation, city housing authority allocation, purchase, private rental, and inheritance.
16 For example, see 'Increase rents to sell homes says newspaper' (*CD* 10 September 1993: 4). This article suggested that rents should be raised at least sixfold to promote the sale of residential housing.
17 This price did not convey full freehold rights.

4 Consuming Shanghai: hairy crabs, ghosts, and Christmas trees

1 See Penelope Prime (1989) on the relationship between 'curtailed consumption and leisure' and the Maoist policies of self-reliance and emphasis on heavy industry.
2 This comment provides evidence of the flux in Maoist China – the implication here is that one *could* assess 'a man's station in life by his clothes' before the Cultural Revolution. Even during the Cultural Revolution, when 'the virtue of austerity reached its pinnacle' (Prime 1989: 146), subtle distinctions in dress persisted. For instance, the number of pens in a person's pocket could display their status. I also noticed that informants could readily distinguish Chinese officials by recognisable physical mannerisms such as bodily posture and gestures – this was presumably also true during the Cultural Revolution.

3 Nien Cheng also records this practice, and that of women having permed hair cut off (1986: 65–6). However, I would add that both these incidents have become 'myth-stories' in Shanghai – everybody seemed to know of them, but few had personally witnessed them.
4 According to Stross (1990: 486), advertising made its first major reappearance in China at Chinese New Year in 1979, when Shanghai's *Liberation Daily* carried a series of advertisements for consumer products.
5 By 1997, there were 101 refrigerators and over 113 colour televisions per hundred households in Shanghai (*FT Survey* 1998: 19).
6 Given the global nature of the manufacturing and assembly of television sets and their components, actual differences in set quality are likely to be minimal.
7 On courtship generally see Honig and Hershatter (1988: 81–136).
8 This may constitute over one-third of a person's monthly salary. Wedding attendance could be a great financial burden especially if several friends married at around the same time.
9 Parish and Whyte (1984: 137, Note 34) report that in the mid-1970s, expenditure by the groom's side averaged 500–800 *yuan*, around three to five months income for the average urban family, with the bride's side contributing around 300–500 *yuan*.
10 This term is a re-ordering of the Chinese name for Canada – *Jianada*.
11 An informant also suggested that the Chinese authorities show foreigners on Chinese television to demonstrate that China has 'foreign friends' and international prestige.
12 This is not a new phenomenon. Bergère comments that in early twentieth-century Shanghai '[m]odernism was equated with Westernism' (1989: 48).
13 See, for example, Parish and Whyte (1978: 273–97); Thompson (1994); Wolf (1974).
14 In contemporary Shanghai, some fashionable restaurants now serve such dishes; an instance of the way '[t]he past is raided . . . for commoditisable nostalgias' (Hannerz 1992: 35).
15 The Party tried to discredit the Beijing hunger strike by showing film of a prominent student leader and hunger striker, Wu'er Kaixi, apparently enjoying a luxurious meal at this time.
16 In a more extended investigation of fashion, gender would play a significant part. For instance, the sexually undifferentiated style of dress and manner urged on women during the Cultural Revolution has been rejected. Instead magazines and other media 'educate' women in how to be 'feminine', including advice on posture, make-up, fashion, and bodily shape (see, for example, Evans 1996).

5 Share dealers, trading places, and new options in contemporary Shanghai

1 This play was written by the Shanghai playwright Zhao Nanhua in 1992. It was sponsored by *Shanghai Shenyin Securities* and such listed firms as *Yanzhong Industrial, Feile Audio*, and *Vacuum Electron*. It was performed in Shanghai during early 1993 and received both official and popular support.
2 The main sources for the information in this section are *BR* (1989a,b); Brayshaw and Teng (1995); Engle (1986: 35–8); Karmel (1994); Xia *et al.* (1992).
3 China's second stock exchange in Shenzhen was set up on 3 July 1991.
4 There are three main classes of share: state shares, corporate shares, and individual shares. Of these only the latter can be traded by individuals on the stock exchange. Stocks are also divided into A- and B-shares. A-shares, which I focus upon in this chapter, are priced in Chinese *yuan* and can only be bought by Chinese citizens. B-shares, first issued in Shanghai in early 1992, must be paid for using hard currency and are intended for foreigners or Chinese bringing in money from overseas. By the end of 1993 there were about a dozen B-shares.
5 A line spoken by one of the characters in 'OK Stock'. Later in the play this character attempts suicide after losing all his money and the savings of his best friend.

6 In the UK less than 20 per cent of shares traded on the London Stock Exchange are held by individuals. China is considering whether to allow pension funds and other institutions to trade in shares.

7 A report in early 2000 recorded how a 101-year old woman had just become a day trader on the Shanghai stock market! (*SS* 22 February 2000: 1).

8 On 20 February 1997, the first trading day after Deng's death, the SSE A-share index initially dropped by 10 per cent, but by the end of the day had risen 0.28 per cent to 1007.731 points.

9 The categories of *dahu* and *sanhu* are discussed in detail in Hertz (1998: 129–73).

10 A survey in Shanghai found that 90.7 per cent of investors' share-holdings totalled less than 50,000 *yuan*, with 26.49 per cent having holdings under 5,000 *yuan* (see *XMWB* 22 March 1993: 12).

11 A Chinese article disagrees with the view that 'shares are a male hobby'. It points out that 'of course' most *dahu* are men but that there are also female *dahu* (*Dadi* 1993: 22–3).

12 This may have been possible in the early days of the share market. Hertz (1998: 148) notes similar sentiments, although she found no evidence of *dahu* acting in cartels in order to manipulate the market. By the time of my research, the increased capitalisation value of Shanghai's share market would have made such manipulation less likely.

13 An article described how when the Shenzhen stock market had just opened, the secretary of the Municipal Committee of the Communist Party had 'taken the lead' in subscribing for stocks, in order to 'encourage the masses'. But once local officials owning stocks became 'a sensitive and explosive problem in Shenzhen', it was clearly stipulated that municipal government cadres were not allowed to hold stocks (*Women of China* 1992: 32–3).

14 In March 1994, in the first court case over such a suicide, the widow of a factory worker was awarded a 50,000 *yuan* 'humanitarian settlement' (*FEER* 5 May 1994: 82).

15 Share dealing is also described as '*wan gupiao*'. The verb *wan* is often translated as 'play' but has a wider range of meanings than this. The most salient point is that it is used for leisure activities and in opposition to work.

16 This term derives from a remark made by the playwright Zhang Xian in a discussion on his play 'The Karaoke Upstairs'. The play stars 'a Taiwanese ex-hippie-turned-futures-trader' who falls in love with a bar girl. Zhang suggests that its punchline could be 'we're all margin traders now' (*FEER* 14 April 1994: 51).

17 Several other Chinese cities including Wuhan, Beijing, and Tianjin all prepared facilities for a third stock exchange. Wuhan was reported to have 400 operating terminals all ready and plans a 40 storey financial centre. In each instance the local authorities hoped to present the central government with a *fait accompli* (*FEER* 17 February 1994: 60).

18 In the 1970s and 1980s *huangniu* specialised in trading ration coupons. With the elimination of rationing their main activities are now as touts for theatre, cinema and other types of tickets, currency dealing, and trading in tax exemption certificates for imported goods.

19 At times the state has moved to prevent the unauthorised issuing of stocks and bonds. The State Council halted the Urumqi state-owned *Hongyuan Investment Trust* from issuing 56 million *yuan* ($9.9 m) of shares. Tens of thousands of Urumqi investors were already involved in a kerb market dealing in share purchase certificates and exchanging information on this company (*FEER* 20 May 1993: 58–9).

20 Contrast this need to know about key current events to a wealthy business woman I interviewed the same day who told me that she rarely read newspapers or watched the television news.

21 An article in the *South China Morning Post* described a manifestation of '*gumin* power' in autumn 1996, in the wake of collapses in the Shanghai and Shenzhen bourses. According to this report, 'Investors... held demonstrations in several cities

during which the offices of government departments and stock-brokers were vandalised' (Lam 1997: 17).

6 Concluding impressions

1 'Fixing' when events had occurred could be problematic since grammatical structures to create tenses are more limited in the Chinese language compared to English. For instance, the Chinese verb *shi*, to be, also means 'was, were, are, is.' Jenner comments, too, on the tendency in Chinese to blur past and present and for images of history and the present to 'coexist timelessly' (1992: 7).

2 It is interesting to bear in mind comments made by Anita Chan. Chan records that in researching a book on the Cultural Revolution 'again and again people remembered having felt that same heady sense of "liberation" in 1966–7 when they had first joined colleagues in casting free from subservience to their work-unit leadership' (1991: 126). It should be added that occasionally informants referred to the downfall of the Qing empire in 1911 as the 'first liberation', thereby effectively dismissing and downgrading the importance of the Communist Party's coming to power in 1949, which it, of course, emphatically describes as 'liberation'.

3 This 460-metre high tower (see page 30) is located directly across the Huangpu River from (and a symbolic retort to?) the colonial built Bund.

4 I cannot resist recounting a story told me by a Chinese professor. On an occasion during the Cultural Revolution he was treated in an off-hand way by a store assistant. He pointed out the slogan above the counter '*wei renmin fuwu*' (serve the people), and indicated that her behaviour fell short of this sentiment. Unabashed she replied, 'how do I know that you are "the people"?'!

5 My own identities in Shanghai as 'foreign' and 'English' are an obvious instance of this. Both of these identities were 'imagined' on my behalf by people I encountered. In London, 'being English' is usually a non-discursive, dormant identification. In Shanghai, by contrast, I was daily made aware of 'being English' as others constantly referred to it. When I listened to Shanghainese residents' depictions of Englishness, they generally bore so little relation to my own understandings of this category that I felt myself, by turns, a voyeur, an impostor, and a trespasser on people's fondly held stereotypes. However, even when my presentation of self differed markedly from the ascribed characteristics the stereotype seemed unaffected.

6 The final comment is a play on the Maoist slogan 'serve the people'.

7 In 2000, the UK security consultancy Control Risks Group, advised travellers in Shanghai to 'take the same precautions as in any other city.' Just four years earlier CRG had seen 'no problems' in Shanghai, and described the city as 'safer than most urban centres in Europe' (cited in *FT* 21 November 2000: 24).

8 In 1988, Su Xiaokang wrote that '[t]hough less than twenty years have passed, the children of today are as ignorant of the Cultural Revolution as if it belonged to another century; they find it extremely strange as well as inconceivable' (cited in Su and Wang 1991: 291).

Glossary of Chinese Terms

This glossary is ordered alphabetically. Shanghai dialect terms are located after the Mandarian equivalent.

aiguo yu	爱国鱼	'patriotic fish'
baofahu	暴发户	upstart, suddenly rich person
baoxi bu baoyou	报喜不报忧	reporting only good news and not the bad
baozhuang	包装	packaging
bazi	巴子	bumpkin
Beijingren aiguo, Guangzhouren maiguo, Shanghairen chuguo	北京人爱国,广州人卖国,上海人出国	Beijingers love the country, Guangzhou people sell the country, Shanghainese leave the country
biguan zishou	闭关自守	close the country to international intercourse
bojiao chengshi	跛脚城市	lame city
bu huan pin, zhi huan bu jun	不患贫,只患不均	do not fear poverty, only fear inequality
bu lao er huo	不劳而获	to reap without sowing
bu yao Pudong yi zhuang lou, zhi yao Puxi yi zhang chuang	不要浦东一幢楼,只要浦西一张床	prefer a bed in Puxi, to a whole house in Pudong
bu yi zhi cai	不益之财	ill-gotten gains
bu zhengchang	不正常	abnormal
bu zheng zhi feng	不正之风	an unhealthy trend
Cai Shen	财神	God of Wealth
chadui luohu xiongdi	插队落户兄弟	sent down to the countryside brothers
chamei	插妹	sent down to the countryside sisters
chao gupiao	抄股票	'stir-fry' stocks
chao youyu/tso hiu hu	抄鱿鱼	be given the sack

chaxiong	插兄	friends made when sent down the countryside
chengshu/bu chengshu	成熟/不成熟	mature/immature
chi daguofan	吃大锅饭	eat from the national pot
chi gongkuan	吃公款	eating public funds
chi guojia de	吃国家的	eating/living off the state
chi laogong	吃老共	eating/living off the Communist Party
chi lixi	吃利息	live off interest
chi waihui de ren	吃外汇的人	people who live off income from abroad
chouti dangjia	抽屉当家	the drawer is the household head
chu fengtou/tse fongdü	出风头	show off
chu ke/tse ku xiongdi	出棵兄弟	brothers from the same nest
Chuan jun	川军	Sichuan army
chuangtou gui	床头跪/床头柜	kneel beside the bed/bedside cupboard
chugong bu chuli	出工不出力	go to work, but not expend energy
chuguo dujin	出国镀金	the gold plating which comes from having been abroad
chuguore	出国热	leaving the country fever
chulu	出路	way/means out
congming	聪明	intelligent, clever
da ca bian qiu	打擦边球	(in ping-pong) hit an edge ball, (figuratively) sail close to the edge
da di	搭的	call a taxi
da paidang	大排档	food stall
dabing	大饼	kind of local bread
dageda jieceng	大哥大阶层	mobile phone stratum
dahu	大户	big player
dahushi	大户室	big players room at stock brokerage
daigou	代沟	generation gap
dajia na/jianada	大家拿/加拿大	everybody grabs/Canada
dakai shuizha	打开水闸	open the sluice gate
dangan	档案	personal file, dossier
danwei	单位	work unit, unit
dao bu xing, cheng cha fu yu hai	道不行, 乘槎浮于海	when the way is not upheld, take to the seas
di shui chuan shi	滴水穿石	dripping water wears holes in stone
douzheng	斗争	struggle, combat

duanlian	锻炼	tempering
duo yige pengyou, duo yitiao lu	多一个朋友, 多一条路	one more friend is one more route
duo zuo, duo cuo	多做,多错	the more one does, the more mistakes one makes
duoshou	舵手	helmsman
fahui	发挥	give free rein to
fan gentou	翻跟头	'turn somersaults', (of shares) increase rapidly in value
fangong	反攻	counterattack
fanpai gongsi	反派公司	flipped-plate companies
fashaoyou	发烧友	'fevered-friends', fans
fazhi	法制	rule by law
feng	风	wind, style, practice
fengqi	风气	social atmosphere, prevailing norms, morals, and standards of behaviour
fuza	复杂	complicated, complex
gaige kaifang	改革开放	Open Door policy
gangtai	港台	Hong Kong and Taiwan (style)
ganqing nong de gushi	感情浓的股市	a stock market rich in feelings
ganqing touzi	感情投资	invest in feelings
ge ren guan ge ren	个人管个人	each person looks out for themselves
ge rou	割肉	'cut flesh', cut one's losses
gerenhua	个人化	individualistic
getihu	个体户	small-scale entrepreneur or enterprise
gongxian	贡献	contribution
gua	挂	to hang
gua yangtou, mai gourou	挂羊头,卖狗肉	hang up a sheep's head, but sell dog meat – try to palm-off something inferior to what it purports to be
guaibin	怪宾	strange guests
guan paitou/gue padü	惯派头	display a rich and arrogant manner to show off one's wealth or status
guan–shang bu fen	官商不分	unable to distinguish between officials and merchants
guandao	官倒	official corruption
guanxi	关系	relationship, personal connection, connections

guanxi wang	关系网	network
guhai	股海	share 'sea'
guibin	贵宾	distinguished guest
guizu	贵族	aristocrat
gumin	股民	'stock people', investors
gundilong	滚地龙	'rolling along the ground dragons' – temporary shacks
guo you qiye	国有企业	state-held enterprises
guohe chaiqiao	过河拆桥	demolish the bridge after crossing the river
guojia	国家	country, nation-state
guoying qiye	国营企业	state-managed enterprises
gupiaore	股票热	stock fever
gupiaozhe	股票者	share-holder
gushi la qingchu/gusi sa qingzang	股市拉清楚	the market has shat itself clean
guyou	股友	share/stock-friends
hai ren zhi xin bu ke you, fang ren zhi xin bu ke wu	害人之心不可有，防人之心不可无	do not have a heart which harms others, but do not lack a heart which defends oneself against others
haipai wenxue	海派文学	coastal-style literature
haiwai guanxi	海外关系	overseas connections
haiwai qitan	海外奇谈	strange tales from over the seas
hongbao	红包	red envelope (containing money)
huajixi	滑稽戏	Shanghai comic play
huan naodai/naozi	还 脑袋/脑子	change one's way of thinking
huangniu	黄牛	'yellow oxen', black market trader
huise shouru	灰色收入	'grey' income
huisu wangshi	回溯往时	recall past events
huju	沪剧	Shanghai opera
hukou	户口	household registration
hun fan chi/hun ve tci	混饭吃	get a meal just by muddling through – put the minimum effort required into one's job
jia	家	family, home
jia chou bu ke wai yang	家丑不可外扬	domestic shame should not be made public
jiang mingli	讲名利	stress fame and fortune
jianzhang	舰长	warship captain
jiatingxing	家庭性	domestic-natured

jie Caishen	接财神	greet the God of Wealth
jieceng	阶层	stratum
jiefang sixiang	解放思想	liberate (one's) thinking
jiegui	结轨	to connect or join tracks, converge with
jieji	阶级	(social) class
jinbu	进步	progress
jingji guilu	经济规律	economic laws
jingming	精明	sharp, astute, shrewd
jiti	集体	collective
jiurou pengyou	酒肉朋友	'wine-and-meat' friends, fair-weather friends
jixing	畸形	deformed
kai houmen	开后门	use the 'backdoor', get something done through pull
kaifang	开放	open, Open Door (policy), lift a ban or restriction etc.
kaisuo	开锁	open a lock, come loose
kao gongzi chifan	靠工资吃饭	rely on salary to eat
la guanxi	拉关系	to 'pull' *guanxi*, to call on personal connections for help
lao huangniu	老黄牛	'old oxen', elderly parents who still support their children
lao Shanghai	老上海	'old Shanghai', Shanghainese
laobaixing	老百姓	ordinary people, common people
lao gui/lao zu	老鬼	old devil
laojia	老家	native-place
laoshi	老实	honest
lao xiang	老乡	people of one's native-place
leng	冷	cold
lianluoyuan	联络员	liaison personnel
liang dian yi xian	两点一线	two points and a line
liang lei cha dao	两肋插刀	cut out one's ribs
lianhe jiandui	联合舰队	joint naval force
li-hai guanxi	利害关系	relationship of mutual benefit
liu zai shehui	流在社会	remain in society
liudong renkou	流动人口	floating population
liushou nushi	留守女士	women left at home
liuxing	流行	popular, flow, prevail, be current

liuxuesheng	留学生	student studying (or who has studied) abroad
luan	乱	chaos, disorder
lü deng	绿灯	green light
luzi	路子	roads, paths, routes to get something done
luzi hen cu	路子很粗	thick roads
luzi hen tong	路子很通	open roads
madasaodaiban	马大嫂代办/买打扫带办	buying, washing, cleaning, looking after, arranging
maiban	买办	comprador
maide bu chi, chide bu mai/ma ge va tci, tci ge va ma	买的不吃,吃的不买	those who buy it don't eat it, those who eat it don't buy it
man tian guo hai	瞒天过海	cross the sea by a trick, practice deception
maojiao nüxu	毛脚女婿	'hairy-legged' son-in-law, prospective son-in-law
men	闷	depressed
menkanjing/men ke jing	门槛精	sharp, astute, shrewd
menlu	门路	social connections
mianzi	面子	face
mianzi hen da	面子很大	big or large face
mingong	民工	migrant worker
mingpai	名牌	famous brand
mohu gongzi	模糊工资	'blurred' or 'indistinct' salary
momohei/mamaha	墨墨黑	inky black
moqi	默契	tacit agreement
mozhe shitou guohe	摸着石头过河	crossing the river, by feeling the boulders
nanxun	南训	southern tour
nei-wai you bie	内外有别	distinguish between inside and outside
ninggu	凝固	coagulated, congealed
niugui sheshen	牛鬼蛇神	forces of evil, class enemies of all descriptions
pai mapi	拍马屁	'pat the horse's backside', flattery
paomo jingji	泡沫经济	bubble economy
piaoyou xiahai	票友下海	amateur enthusiast of Peking opera who becomes a professional actor
pin ganjue	凭感觉	rely on feelings

poqiang kaidian	破墙开店	break down the walls and set up a store
pulu	铺路	spread the path
pusa	菩萨	bodhissatva
putonghua	普通话	common speech, standard Chinese, Mandarin
qianke/dzi ka	掮客	broker
qiguanyan/qi guan yan	气管炎/妻管严	tracheitis/the wife controls strictly
qingfugu	情夫股	'mistress' shares
qingguan	清官	honest, upright official
qinqigan	亲戚感	feeling of being related
quan guo chi Shanghai	全国吃上海	the whole country lives off Shanghai
quanguo jiegu	全国皆股	the whole country loves shares
quanmin jingshang	全民经商	all the people go into business
quanzi	圈子	circles
ren cai ren	人踩人	people trample on each other
ren chi ren	人吃人	people eat each other
ren de qingxu	人的情绪	people's mood
riben guizi	日本鬼子	Japanese devil
ren wang gaochu zou, shui xiang dichu liu	人往高处走 水向低处流	people go toward high places, water runs to low places
rechao	热潮	great mass fervour, upsurge
ren wu huang, cai wu fa	人无慌,财无发	if a person does no wrong, they will not become wealthy
ren zuo le, cha liang le	人走了, 茶凉了	when the person leaves, the tea goes cold
rencai liudong	人才流动	flow of talent
rengouzheng	认购证	share purchase certificates
renminbi	人民币	RMB, *yuan*, unit of Chinese currency
renqi	人气	popular mood
renqing guojia	人情国家	human feeling country
renshou	忍受	endure, bear, stand
renzhi	人制	rule by man
rixin yueyi	日新月异	change with each passing day
rudang zuoguan	入党做官	join the Party and become an official

sanhu	散户	small or scattered players on the stock market
san shi liu kuai, wansui!	三十六块万岁	long live 36 yuan!
shangtai	上台	appear on stage, assume power
shangmian you zhengce, xiamian you duice	上面有政策，下面有对策	above there is a strategy, below there is a counter-strategy
shangzhijiao/zang tsa ko	上只角	upper quarter
shaoxiang	烧香	burn incense, give a bribe
shehui fengqi	社会风气	social trend
shehui geren gu	社会个人股	publicly issued individual shares
shengdanhua/seng de ho	圣诞花	poinsettia
shenme ren fu le/sa nin fu la?	什么人福了	who is rich?
shi kumen	石库门	traditional Shanghai alleyway houses
shi li yangchang	十里洋场	'ten-mile foreign square', a term for pre-liberation Shanghai
shi mianzi/te de	失面子	lose face
shijingyu	市井语	'city well' language
shiqi	市气	market mood
shiye	失业	be unemployed
shui neng zai zhou, yi neng fu zhou	水能载舟，亦能覆舟	water can support a boat, it can also turn it over
shui zhang chuan gao	水涨船高	when the river rises the boat goes up – particular things improve with the improvement of the general situation
shui zhi qing, ze wu yu	水至清，则无鱼	when the water is clear, there are no fish
shuidao qucheng	水到渠成	where water flows, a channel is formed
shuiluo shichu	水落石出	when the water subsides the rocks emerge
shunshui tui zhou	顺水推舟	push the boat along with the current, make use of an opportunity to gain one's end
shuren	熟人	familiar person
sibuqi	死不起	be unable to afford to die
silu	思路	train of thought, thinking
silu yi tiao	死路一条	dead end

sixiang	思想	thought, thinking, idea
Su jun	苏军	Subei army
Taibao	台胞	Taiwan compatriots
Taibazi	台巴子	Taiwan bumpkins
tang si ling	汤司令	'order of the soup'
Tang siling	唐司令	General Tang
taoyou	套友	stuck-fast friends (i.e. those who's shares are all *taozhu*)
taozhu	套住	stuck-fast, caught (when price of shares on the market falls below the value paid for them
tatai/te de	塌台	'collapsing stage', lose face
tengfei	腾飞	galloping ahead
tequan jieji	特权阶级	class with special power
tiaocao	跳槽	change jobs
tiaolou	跳楼	sudden drop in share prices, commit suicide by jumping from a tall building
tongzhi youyi	同志友谊	comradely friendship
touji daoba	投机倒把	speculation and profiteering
toumingdu	透明度	transparency
touru le guhai	投入了股海	throw oneself into the share 'sea'
tu boshi	土博士	PhD from China
wai luzi	外路子	irregular means
waidi mingong chao	外地民工潮	'tide' of migrant workers from other provinces
waidiren/nadinin	外地人	outsider (from another province)
waiguoren/nakunin	外国人	foreigner
waikuai/na kua	外块	'outside' money (money earned from sources apart from one's ordinary job)
Wan jun	皖军	Anhui army
wang qian kan	往前看/往钱看	look to the future/look to money
wei renmin fuwu	为人民服务	serve the people
wenhua/ven ho	文化	culture, education
wenren xiangqing	文人相轻	intellectuals despise each other
women Shanghairen/ a la Sang he nin	我们上海人	we Shanghainese

women zijia ren/ala ziga nin	我们自家人	one of us, one of our own
wu shi niandai ren bang ren, liu shi niandai ren dou ren, qi shi niandai ren pian ren	五十年代人帮人, 六十年代人斗人, 七十年代人骗人	in the 1950s people helped each other, in the 1960s they struggled against each other, in the 1970s they cheated each other
xia zhi jiao/o tsa ko	下只角	lower quarter
xiagang	下岗	laid-off (worker)
xiahai	下海	'set out to sea', go into business
xialiu	下流	the lower reaches (of a river), low-down, mean, obscene, dirty
xiandai, xiandaihua	现代, 现代化	modern, modernity
Xiang jun	湘军	Hunan army
xiangbalao	乡巴老	country bumpkin
xiangxiaren/xiang o nin	乡下人	country person
xiao hu	小户	small player
xiao xiongdi	小兄弟	'little brother'
xiao congming	小聪明	cleverness in petty things
xiao zhengfu, da shehui	小政府, 大社会	small government, large society
xiaodao xiaoxi	小道消息	gossip, news through the grapevine
xiaosa	潇洒	carefree, stylish
xiashui	下水	enter the water – take to evil doing
xiatai	下台	step down from a stage, leave office
xifang	西方	the West
xin de ganjue	新的感觉	a feeling of newness
xin zhong you shu	心中有数	to know in one's heart
xinfu jieceng	新福阶层	new wealthy stratum
xincun	新村	new village
xinxiangan	新鲜感	feeling of newness
xuechao	学潮	student movement
yamen bazi dakai, you li wu qian mo jin lai	衙门八字打开, 有理无钱莫近来	the yamen gate is wide open, with right but no money do not enter
yan duo cai bu huai, li duo ren bu guai	盐多菜不坏, 礼多人不怪	too much salt does not ruin food, nobody will be blamed for giving too many gifts
yang boshi	洋博士	PhD from overseas

yang zhuang biesan, ziji shaofan	洋装瘪三, 自己烧饭	western-suited trash, cook one's own food
yanhong	眼红	'red eyes', jealousy
yanjiu	研究/烟酒	research, investigation/ cigarettes and alcohol
yapishi	雅皮士	yuppie
yayigan	压抑感	feeling of oppression
yezonghui	夜总会	nightclub
yi pan san sha	一盘散沙	a tray of loose sand
yikufan	忆苦饭	a poor meal made up of twigs, grass, and soil
ying	硬	hard, (of a connection) reliable
yinger	婴儿	baby, infant
yiqi	义气	personal loyalty
youshui meiyou le/hiusi ma la	油水没有了	fat (i.e. money) all gone
youtiao	油条	fried bread stick
yu hu mou pi	与虎谋皮	ask a tiger for its skin
yuanshi jilei	原始积累	primitive accumulation
zai jiali kao qinqi, zai waimian kao pengyou bangmang	在家里靠亲戚, 在外面靠朋友帮忙	at home rely on relatives, outside rely on the help of friends
zenme zuoren	怎么做人	how to be a person
zhan/tse	斩	'cut', rip-off
zheng lu	正路	the right way, the correct path
zhige ren shi xiazhijiao laide/dige nin si ho sa ko leige	这个人是下只角来的	this person is from the lower quarter
zhitong daohezhe	志同道合者	people with a common will and purpose
zhixin pengyou	知心朋友	intimate friends
zhonghu	中户	middle player (on the stock market)
ziji, ziwo	自己, 自我	self
ziji zhao chulu	自己找出路	find one's own way out
zili gengsheng	自力更生	self-reliance
zou houmen	走后门	go through/use the backdoor
zuiba yao jin, koudai yao song	嘴巴要紧, 口袋要松	keep mouth tight shut and pockets loose
zuo jing guan tian	坐井观天	look at the world from the bottom of a well
zuoguan facai	做官发财	get rich by being an official

Bibliography

Abu-Lughod, Janet. 1991. 'Going beyond global babble', pp. 131–7 in A.K. King (ed.), *Culture Globalization and the World System: Contemporary Conditions for the Representation of Identity*. London: Macmillan.

Anagnost, Ann. 1989. 'Prosperity and counterprosperity: the moral discourse on wealth in post-Mao China', pp. 210–34 in A. Dirlik and M. Meisner (eds), *Marxism and the Chinese Experience*. New York: M.E. Sharpe.

Anderson, Eugene N. 1988. *The Food of China*. London: Yale University Press.

Anderson, Benedict. 1983. *Imagined Communities: Reflections on the Origin and Spread of Nationalism*. London: Verso.

Appadurai, Arjun. 1990. 'Disjuncture and difference in the global cultural economy', *Public Culture* 2(2): 1–24.

Appadurai, Arjun. 1991. 'Global ethnoscapes: notes and queries for a transnational anthropology', pp. 191–210 in R.G. Fox (ed.), *Recapturing Anthropology: Working in the Present*. Santa Fe: School of American Research Press.

Appleton, William. 1951. *A Cycle of Cathay: The Chinese Vogue in England During the Seventeenth and Eighteenth Centuries*. New York: Columbia University Press.

Bachman, David M. 1985. *Chen Yun and the Chinese Political System*. Berkeley: Institute of East Asian Studies.

Barmé, Geremie. 1992. 'The greying of Chinese culture', pp. 13.1–13.53 in H-C. Kuan and M. Brosseau (eds), *China Review*. Hong Kong: The Chinese University Press.

Barmé, Geremie. 1999. 'CCP™ & ADCULT PRC', *The China Journal* 41: 1–23.

Barth, Frederik. 1970. 'Introduction', pp. 9–38 in F. Barth (ed.), *Ethnic Groups and Boundaries: The Social Organization of Culture Difference*. London: George Allen & Unwin.

BBC2. 1995. 'The whole world in his hands: a speculative report on the future of Rupert Murdoch', broadcast 20 February.

BBC2. 1995. 'Cities of the future', broadcast 29 November.

Beijing Review 1989a. 'Shanghai: stock market re-established', 32(18): 19–23.

Beijing Review 1989b. 'China's stock and bond market', 32(44): 22–3.

Bergère, Marie-Claire. 1981. '"The other China": Shanghai from 1919 to 1949', pp. 1–34 in C. Howe (ed.), *Shanghai, Revolution and Development in an Asian Metropolis*. Cambridge: Cambridge University Press.

Bergère, Marie-Claire. 1989. *The Golden Age of the Chinese Bourgeoisie, 1911–1937*, Cambridge: Cambridge University Press.

Bigham, Clive. 1901. *A Year in China, 1899–1900 With Some Account of Admiral Sir E. Seymour's Expedition*. London: Macmillan & Co.

Bin, Zhao. 1997. 'Consumerism, Confucianism, Communism: making sense of China today', *New Left Review* 222: 43–59.

Bishop, J.F. 1899. *The Yangtze Valley and Beyond: An Account of Journeys in China, Chiefly in the Province of Sze Chuan and Among the Man-tze of the Somo Territory*. London: John Murray.

Bocock, Robert. 1993. *Consumption*. London: Routledge.

Bodman, Richard W. 1991. 'From history to allegory to art: a personal search for interpretation', pp. 1–61 in Su Xiaokang and Wang Luxiang (eds), *Deathsong of the River: A Reader's Guide to the Chinese TV Series Heshang*. New York: Cornell East Asia Papers.

Bourdieu, Pierre. 1984. *Distinction: A Social Critique of the Judgement of Taste*. London: Routledge.

Brayshaw, R. and Z. Teng 1995. 'Re-emergence of the Chinese stock market', pp. 85–129 in J. Blake and S. Gao (eds), *Perspectives on Accounting and Finance in China*. London: Routledge.

Buckley, Christopher. 1999. 'How a revolution becomes a dinner party: stratification, mobility and the new rich in urban China', pp. 208–29 in M. Pinches (ed.), *Culture and Privilege in Capitalist Asia*. London: Routledge.

Burgess, M. Elaine. 1978. 'The resurgence of ethnicity: myth or reality?', *Ethnic and Racial Studies* 1(3): 265–85.

Butler, Steven B. 1983. 'Field research in China's communes: views of a "guest"', pp. 99–121 in A.F. Thurston and B. Pasternak (eds), *The Social Sciences and Fieldwork in China: Views from the Field*. Boulder: Westview Press.

Carter, Erica., Donald, James and Judith, Squires. 1993. 'Introduction', pp. vii–xv in E. Carter, J. Donald and J. Squires (eds), *Space and Place: Theories of Identity and Location*. London: Laurence & Wishart.

CED. 1988. *A Chinese-English Dictionary*. Beijing: Shangwu Yinshuguan.

Chamberlain, Heath B. 1993. 'On the search for civil society in China', *Modern China* 19(2): 199–215.

Chan, Anita. 1991. 'The social origins and consequences of the Tiananmen crisis', pp. 105–30 in D.S.G. Goodman and G. Segal (eds), *China in the Nineties: Crisis Management and Beyond*. Oxford: Clarendon Press.

Chan, Anita., Madsen, Richard and Jonathon, Unger. 1992. *Chen Village Under Mao and Deng: Expanded and Updated Edition*. Berkeley: University of California.

Chan, Kam Wing. 1994. *Cities With Invisible Walls: Reinterpreting Urbanization in Post-1949 China*. New York: Oxford University Press.

Chang, K.C. (ed.). 1977. *Food in Chinese Culture: Anthropological and Historical Perspectives*. London: Yale University Press.

Chang, Sen-dou. 1977. 'The morphology of walled capitals', pp. 75–100 in G.W. Skinner (ed.), *The City in Late Imperial China*. Stanford: Stanford University Press.

Chao, Linda and Ramon H. Myers. 1998. 'China's consumer revolution: the 1990s and beyond', *Journal of Contemporary China* 7(18): 351–68.

Chapman, Malcolm. 1982. '"Semantics" and the "Celt"', pp. 123–43 in D. Parkin (ed.), *Semantic Anthropology*. London: Academic Press.

Ch'en, Jerome. 1979. *China and the West: Society and Culture 1815–1937*. London: Hutchinson.

Cheng, Nien. 1986. *Life and Death in Shanghai*. New York: Grove Press.

China Daily 1992. 'Companies face major reform in share-holding', 21 September: 4.

China Daily 1993. 'Shanghai cashes in on reform and opening', 13 January: 1.

China Daily 1993. 'Stock market problems require ironing out', 4 February: 4.
China Daily 1993. 'Big cities go shopping mad', 22 February: 6.
China Daily 1993. '"Second job fever" not a crippling disease', 8 March: 4.
China Daily 1993. 'Chinese pay dearly to have phones installed in homes', 13 March: 3.
China Daily 1993. 'Schooling aimed at moneyed classes', 18 May: 3.
China Daily 1993. 'China vogue for fashion', 20 May: 5.
China Daily 1993. 'Reform bringing about profound social changes', 27 May: 4.
China Daily 1993. 'Money fever becomes epidemic in China', 15 July: 4.
China Daily 1993. 'Market will help resolve the brain drain', 17 July: 4.
China Daily 1993. 'Increase rents to sell homes says newspaper', 10 September: 4.
China Daily 1993. 'Stock news sent by satellite', 20 September: 2.
China Daily 1993. 'Deng puts development at top of agenda', 12 November: 4.
China Daily 1993. 'Radio and TV tower termed Shanghai pearl', 15 November: 5.
China Daily 1993. '"*Fanpai* companies" must sever their former ties', 23 November: 4.
China Daily Business Weekly 1993. 'Consuming passion hits the populous', 14–20 February: 8.
China Daily Business Weekly 1993. 'Gold king', 16–22 May: 8.
China Daily Business Weekly 1993. 'Four securities workers jailed for corruption', 5–11 September: 2.
China Daily Business Weekly 1993. 'Support for Pudong not expected to waver', 26 September–2 October: 4.
China Daily Business Weekly 1993. 'New service is attack on black mart', 7–13 November: 3.
China Newsletter 1987. 'Reforms in the Shanghai financial system', 71: 19–21.
Chinese Repository. 1840–51 (journal published monthly in Canton).
Chu, David S.K. 1985. 'Introduction: the study of social problems in socialist China', *Chinese Sociology and Anthropology* 17(3): 3–27.
Chu, G. 1985. 'The changing concept of self in contemporary China', pp. 252–77 in G. De Vos, A. Marsella and F. Hsu (eds), *Culture and Self: Asian and Western Perspectives*. New York: Tavistock.
Clifford, Nicholas R. 1991. *Spoilt Children of Empire: Westerners in Shanghai and the Chinese Revolution of the 1920s*. Hanover: Middlebury College Press.
Cohen, Abner. 1974. 'Introduction: the lesson of ethnicity', pp. ix–xxiv in A. Cohen (ed.), *Urban Ethnicity*. London: Tavistock.
Cohen, Anthony P. 1982. 'Belonging: the experience of culture', pp. 1–17 in A.P. Cohen (ed.), *Belonging: Identity and Social Organization in British Rural Cultures*. Manchester: Manchester University Press.
Cohen, Anthony P. 1985. *The Symbolic Construction of Community*. London: Tavistock Publications.
Cohen, Myron L. 1991. 'Being Chinese: the peripheralization of traditional identity', *Daedalus* 120(2): 113–34.
Comaroff, John L. 1987. 'Of totemism and ethnicity: consciousness, practice and the signs of inequality', *Ethnos* 3–4: 301–23.
Creamer, Thomas. 1991. *A Chinese-English Dictionary of the Wu Dialect*. Kensington, MD: Dunwoody Press.
Crissman, L.W. 1967. 'The segmentary structure of urban overseas Chinese communities', *Man* 2(2): 185–204.
Croll, Elisabeth J. 1994. *From Heaven to Earth: Images and Experiences of Development in China*. London: Routledge.

Cumming, C.F. 1886. *Wanderings in China* (Volume 2). Edinburgh: William Blackwood & Sons.

Dadi. 1993. '*Shanghai tan de nu gumin*' (Female share dealers in Shanghai), *Dadi Monthly* 6(18): 22–8.

Dahlgren, Peter. 1988. 'What's the meaning of this? viewers' plural sense-making of TV news', *Media, Culture and Society* 10(3): 285–301.

Darwent, C.E. 1904. *Shanghai: A Handbook for Travellers and Residents*. Shanghai: Kelly & Walsh.

Davidson-Houston, J.V. 1962. *Yellow Creek: The Story of Shanghai*. London: Putnam & Co.

Davis, Deborah S. 1989. 'My mother's house', pp. 88–100 in P. Link, R. Madsen and P.G. Pickowicz (eds), *Unofficial China: Popular Culture and Thought in the PRC*. Boulder: Westview Press.

Davis, Deborah S. 1990. 'Urban job mobility', pp. 85–108 in D. Davis and E.F. Vogel (eds), *Chinese Society on the Eve of Tiananmen*. Harvard University: The Council on East Asian Studies.

Davis, Deborah S., Kraus, Richard., Naughton, Barry and Elizabeth J. Perry (eds), *Urban Spaces in Contemporary China: The Potential for Autonomy and Community in Post-Mao China*. Cambridge: Cambridge University Press.

Dawson, Raymond. 1967. *The Chinese Chameleon: An Analysis of European Conceptions of Chinese Civilisation*. London: Oxford University Press.

De Certeau, Michel. 1984. *The Practice of Everyday Life*. London: University of California Press.

De Glopper, Donald R. 1972. 'Doing business in Lukang', pp. 297–326 in W.E. Willmott (ed.), *Economic Organization in Chinese Society*. Stanford: Stanford University Press.

De Jesus, C.A. Montalto. 1909. *Historical Shanghai*. Shanghai: Shanghai Mercury.

Deng Xiaoping. 1983. *Deng Xiaoping Wenxuan: Di Er Juan* (Deng Xiaoping Selected Works: Volume 2). Beijing: Renmin Chubanshe.

Deng Xiaoping. 1993. *Deng Xiaoping Wenxuan: Di San Juan* (Deng Xiaoping Selected Works: Volume 3). Beijing: Renmin Chubanshe.

Deng Jian. 1993. *Zhongguo Zhiqing Meng* (The Dream of China's Sent-Down Educated Youth). Beijing: Renmin Wenxue Chubanshe.

Diamond, Norma. 1983. 'Taitou revisited: prospects for community restudies', pp. 123–42 in A.F. Thurston and B. Pasternak (eds), *The Social Sciences and Fieldwork in China: Views from the Field*. Boulder: Westview Press.

Dickens, Charles J.H. 1960 [1859]. *A Tale of Two Cities*. London: Oxford University Press.

Dickens, Charles J.H. 1971 [1853]. *Bleak House*. Aylesbury: Penguin Books.

Dikötter, Frank. 1992. *The Discourse of Race in Modern China*. London: Hurst & Co.

Dilley, Roy. 1992. 'Contesting markets: a general introduction to market ideology, imagery and discourse', pp. 1–34 in R. Dilley (ed.), *Contesting Markets: Analyses of Ideology, Discourse and Practice*. Edinburgh: Edinburgh University Press.

Douglas, Mary. 1992. *Risk and Blame: Essays in Cultural Theory*. London: Routledge.

Douglas, Mary and Baron Isherwood. 1978. *The World of Goods: Towards an Anthropology of Consumption*. Harmondsworth: Penguin Books.

Drummond, Lee. 1980. 'The cultural continuum: a theory of intersystems', *Man* 15(2): 352–74.

Dutton, Michael. 1992. 'A mass-line without politics: community policing and economic reform', pp. 200–27 in A. Watson (ed.), *Economic Reform and Social Change in China*. London: Routledge.

Duzhe Wenzhai (Readers' Digest) 1992. '*Da Shanghai, ni hai beideqi zhongguo ma*?' (Great Shanghai, can you still carry China), (9): 42–7.

Dyce, Charles M. 1906. *Personal Reminiscences of Thirty Years' Residence in the Model Settlement Shanghai, 1870–1900*. London: Chapman & Hall.

Eberhard, W. 1965. 'Chinese regional stereotypes', *Asian Survey* 5(12): 596–608.

Economist, The 1994. 'Bears in a china shop', 14 May: 111–12.

Economist, The 1997. *A Survey of China*, 8 March.

Economist, The 1999. 'Clouds over Hong Kong', 14 August: 63–4.

Economist, The 2000. *A Survey of China*, 8 April.

Elvin, Mark. 1974. 'The administration of Shanghai, 1905–1914', pp. 239–62 in M. Elvin and G.W. Skinner (eds), *The Chinese City Between Two Worlds*. California: Stanford University Press.

Elvin, Mark. 1977. 'Market towns and waterways: the county of Shang-hai from 1480 to 1910', pp. 441–73 in G.W. Skinner (ed.), *The City in Late Imperial China*. Stanford: Stanford University Press.

Elvin, Mark. 1991. 'The inner world of 1830', *Daedalus* 120(2): 33–61.

Engle, Tom. 1986. 'Stocks: new domestic financial tool', *The China Business Review* January–February: 35–8.

Evans, Harriet. 1996. *Women and Sexuality in China: Dominant Discourses of Female Sexuality and Gender Since 1949*. Oxford: Polity Press.

Ewen, Stuart. 1990. 'Marketing dreams: the political elements of style', pp. 41–56 in A. Tomlinson (ed.), *Consumption, Identity, and Style: Marketing, Meanings, and the Packaging of Pleasure*. London: Routledge.

Ewen, Stuart and Elizabeth Ewen. 1982. *Channels of Desire: Mass Images and the Shaping of American Consciousness*. New York: McGraw-Hill.

Faison, Seth. 1990. 'The changing role of the Chinese media', pp. 145–63 in T. Saich (ed.), *The Chinese People's Movement: Perspectives on Spring 1989*. London: M.E. Sharp.

Fan, Xiangda. 1992. *Shanghai Xin Guizu* (Shanghai's New Aristocrats). Shanghai: Shanghai Young People's Press.

Far Eastern Economic Review 1992. 'Babes in the bourse', 16 July: 48–54.

Far Eastern Economic Review 1993. 'Share float torpedoed', 20 May: 58–9.

Far Eastern Economic Review 1994. 'All dressed up', 17 February: 60.

Far Eastern Economic Review 1994. 'Shanghai fables', 14 April: 50–1.

Far Eastern Economic Review 1994. 'Bond allure', 5 May: 82.

Far Eastern Economic Review 1994. 'Stock sheets banned', 2 June: 63.

Far Eastern Economic Review 1994. 'Shanghai: capital of China's get-rich-quick capitalism, 23 June: 54–6.

Fardon, Richard. 1987. '"African ethnogenesis": limits to the comparability of ethnic phenomena', pp. 168–88 in L. Holy (ed.), *Comparative Anthropology*. Oxford: Basil Blackwell.

Featherstone, Mike. 1991. 'The body in consumer culture', pp. 170–96 in M. Featherstone, M. Hepworth and B.S. Turner (eds), *The Body: Social Process and Cultural Theory*. London: Sage Publications.

Feetham, Richard. 1931. *Shanghai Municipal Council Report Volume I*. Shanghai: North China Daily News.

Fei, Xiaotong. 1992. *From the Soil: The Foundations of Chinese Society* (translated by G.C. Hamilton and W. Zheng). Berkeley: University of California Press.

Financial Times 1992. 'Chinese speculators riot over shares chaos', 11 August: 14.

Financial Times 1995. 'Net for China: no smut, no politics, no decadent culture', 10 July: 13.
Financial Times 1995. 'China is "risking collapse" from fiscal weakness', 16 June: 6.
Financial Times 1998. 'Pacific century goes online in Asia', 13 March: 29.
Financial Times 1998. 'China's premier pledges a nation of homeowners', 20 March: 1.
Financial Times 1998. 'China plans to channel funds into housing', 26 May: 4.
Financial Times 1999. 'China uncovers mass fraud in state companies', 24–5 December: 7.
Financial Times 2000. 'China rich list features new entrepreneurs', 10 November: 14.
Financial Times 2000. 'Unhealthy rise in dangerous destinations', 21 November: 24.
Financial Times Survey 1997. 'Financial Times Survey: China', 8 December.
Financial Times Survey 1998. 'Financial Times Survey: Shanghai', 19 May.
Financial Times Survey 2000. 'Financial Times Survey: China', 13 November.
Finkelstein, Joanne. 1991. *The Fashioned Self.* Cambridge: Polity Press.
Fisher, Lt-Col. 1863. *Three Years Service in China.* London: Richard Bentley.
Fiske, J. 1989. *Understanding Popular Culture.* London: Routledge.
Fitzgerald, T.K. 1991. 'Media and changing metaphors of ethnicity and identity', *Media, Culture and Society* 13(2): 193–214.
Forbes, F.E. 1848. *Five Years in China: From 1842 to 1847.* London: Richard Bentley.
Fortune, Robert. 1853. *Two Visits to the Tea Countries of China and the British Tea Plantations in the Himalaya* (two volumes). London: John Murray.
Forward, Roy. 1991. 'Letter from Shanghai', pp. 187–203 in J. Unger (ed.), *The Pro-Democracy Protests in China: Reports from the Provinces.* London: M.E. Sharp.
Fung, Ka-iu. 1981. 'The spatial development of Shanghai', pp. 269–300 in C. Howe (ed.), *Shanghai, Revolution and Development in an Asian Metropolis.* Cambridge: Cambridge University Press.
Gamble, Jos. 1991. 'Mis/representing the Chinese: an ethnography of representations of self and other', MA dissertation. SOAS.
Gamewell, Mary N. 1916. *The Gateway to China: Pictures of Shanghai.* New York: Fleming H. Revell Company.
Gaubatz, Piper Rae. 1995. 'Urban transformation in post-Mao China: impacts of the reform era on China's urban form', pp. 28–60 in D.S. Davis, R. Kraus, B. Naughton and E.J. Perry (eds), *Urban Spaces in Contemporary China: The Potential for Autonomy and Community in Post-Mao China.* Cambridge: Cambridge University Press.
Gaulton, Richard. 1981. 'Political mobilization in Shanghai, 1949–1951', pp. 35–65 in C. Howe (ed.), *Shanghai, Revolution and Development in an Asian Metropolis.* Cambridge: Cambridge University Press.
Geertz, Clifford. 1973. 'Thick description: toward an interpretative theory of culture', pp. 3–30 in *The Interpretation of Culture: Selected Essays by Clifford Geertz.* London: Hutchinson.
Geertz, Clifford. 1995. *After the Fact: Two Countries, Four Decades, One Anthropologist.* Cambridge, Massachusetts: Harvard University Press.
Gell, Alfred. 1986. 'Newcomers to the world of goods: consumption among Muria Gonds', pp. 110–38 in A. Appadurai (ed.), *The Social Life of Things: Commodities in Cultural Perspective.* Cambridge: Cambridge University Press.
Giddens, Anthony. 1990. *The Consequences of Modernity.* Cambridge: Polity Press.
Giddens, Anthony. 1991. *Modernity and Self-Identity: Self and Society in the Late Modern Age.* Cambridge: Polity Press.
Gold, Thomas B. 1985. 'After comradeship: personal relations in China since the Cultural Revolution', *The China Quarterly* 104: 657–75.

Gold, Thomas B. 1989. 'Guerrilla interviewing among the *getihu*', pp. 175–92 in P. Link, R. Madsen and P.G. Pickowicz (eds), *Unofficial China: Popular Culture and Thought in the PRC*. Boulder: Westview Press.

Gold, Thomas B. 1990. 'Urban private business and social change', pp. 157–78 in D. Davis and E.F. Vogel (eds), *Chinese Society on the Eve of Tiananmen*. Harvard University: The Council on East Asian Studies.

Gold, Thomas B. 1993. 'Go with your feelings: Hong Kong and Taiwan popular culture in greater China', *The China Quarterly* 136: 907–25.

Goodman, David S.G. 1991. 'Introduction: the authoritarian outlook', pp. 1–18 in D.S.G. Goodman and G. Segal (eds), *China in the Nineties: Crisis Management and Beyond*. Oxford: Clarendon Press.

Goodman, David S.G. 1994. 'The politics of regionalism: economic development, conflict and negotiation', pp. 1–20 in D.S.G. Goodman and G. Segal (eds), *China Deconstructs: Politics, Trade and Regionalism*. London: Routledge.

Goodman, David S.G. 1996. 'The People's Republic of China: the party-state, capitalist revolution and new entrepreneurs', pp. 225–42 in R. Robison and D.S.G. Goodman (eds), *The New Rich in Asia: Mobile Phones, McDonald's and Middle Class Revolution*. London: Routledge.

Goodman, David S.G. and George Segal (eds). 1989. *China at Forty: Mid-Life Crisis?* Oxford: Clarendon Paperbacks.

Goodman, David S.G. and Gerald Segal (eds). 1994. *China Deconstructs: Politics, Trade and Regionalism*. London: Routledge.

Goodman, Bryna. 1992. 'New culture, old habits: native-place organization and the May Fourth movement', pp. 76–107 in F.E. Wakeman and W. Yeh (eds), *Shanghai Sojourners*. Berkeley: Institute of East Asian Studies.

Goodman, Bryna. 1995. *Native Place, City, and Nation: Regional Networks and Identities in Shanghai, 1853–1937*. Berkeley: University of California Press.

Graham, E.D. 1983. 'The "imaginative geography" of China', pp. 31–43 in W.I. Cohen (ed.), *Reflections on Orientalism*. Michigan: Asian Studies Centre.

Green, O.M. 1942. *The Foreigner in China*. London: Hutchinson.

Grillo, R.D. 1989. *Dominant Languages: Language and Hierarchy in Britain and France*. Cambridge: Cambridge University Press.

Grub, Philip and Sudweeks, Bryan L. 1988. 'Securities markets and the People's Republic of China', *China Newsletter* 74: 11–16.

Guardian, The 1995. 'China tries to shut out internet anarchy', 4 September: 9.

Gupta, Akhil and James, Ferguson. 1992. 'Beyond "culture": space, identity, and the politics of difference', *Cultural Anthropology* 7(1): 6–23.

Gutzlaff, Rev. Charles. 1833. 'Gutzlaff's journal', *Chinese Repository* 2(1): 20–32.

Hall, Stuart. 1991. 'The local and the global: globalization and ethnicity', pp. 19–39 in A.K. King (ed.), *Culture Globalization and the World System: Contemporary Conditions for the Representation of Identity*. London: Macmillan.

Hannerz, Ulf. 1980. *Exploring the City: Inquiries Toward an Urban Anthropology*. New York: Columbia University Press.

Hannerz, Ulf. 1992. *Cultural Complexity: Studies in the Social Organization of Meaning*. New York: Columbia University Press.

Hardy, Edward J. 1907. *John Chinaman at Home: Sketches of Men, Manners and Things in China*. London: T. Fisher Unwin.

Hartley, John. 1987. 'Invisible fictions: television audiences, paedocracy, pleasure', *Textual Practice* 1(2): 121–38.

Harvey, David. 1989. *The Urban Experience*. Oxford: Basil Blackwell.
Hauser, Ernest O. 1940. *Shanghai: City For Sale*. New York: Harcourt, Brace & Co.
Hebdige, Dick. 1988. *Hiding in the Light: On Images and Things*. London: Routledge.
Henderson, Gail E. and Myron S. Cohen. 1984. *The Chinese Hospital: A Socialist Work Unit*. New Haven: Yale University Press.
Hepple, Leslie W. 1992. 'Metaphor, geopolitical discourse and the military in South America', pp. 136–54 in T.J. Barnes and J.S. Duncan (eds), *Writing Worlds: Discourse, Text and Metaphor in the Representation of Landscape*. London: Routledge.
Hershatter, Gail. 1989. 'The hierarchy of Shanghai prostitution, 1870–1949', *Modern China* 15(4): 463–98.
Hershatter, Gail. 1992. 'Regulating sex in Shanghai: the reform of prostitution in 1920 and 1951', pp. 145–85 in F.E. Wakeman and W. Yeh (eds), *Shanghai Sojourners*. Berkeley: Institute of East Asian Studies.
Hertz, Ellen L. 1998. *The Trading Crowd: An Ethnography of the Shanghai Stock Market*. Cambridge: Cambridge University Press.
Ho, David and Nancy, Leigh. 1994. 'A retail revolution', *The China Business Review* 21(1): 22–8.
HKTDC. 1999. 'Market profiles on Chinese cities and provinces, Shanghai municipality', Hong Kong Trade Development Council, http://www.tdc.org.hk/main/china/htm, 16 June.
HKTDC. 2000. 'Market profiles on Chinese cities and provinces, Shanghai municipality', Hong Kong Trade Development Council, http://www.tdctrade.com/mktprof/china/mpshh.htm, 19 October.
Honig, Emily. 1986. *Sisters and Strangers: Women in the Shanghai Cotton Mills, 1919–49*. Stanford: Stanford University Press.
Honig, Emily. 1989a. 'Pride and prejudice: Subei people in contemporary Shanghai', pp. 138–55 in P. Link, R. Madsen and P.G. Pickowicz (eds), *Unofficial China: Popular Culture and Thought in the PRC*. Boulder: Westview Press.
Honig, Emily. 1989b. 'The politics of prejudice: Subei people in republican era Shanghai', *Modern China* 15(3): 242–73.
Honig, Emily. 1990. 'Invisible inequalities: the status of Subei people in contemporary Shanghai', *The China Quarterly* 122: 273–92.
Honig, Emily. 1992. *Creating Chinese Ethnicity: Subei People in Shanghai, 1850–1980*. Michigan: Yale University Press.
Honig, Emily and Gail, Hershatter. 1988. *Personal Voices. Chinese Women in the 1980s*. Stanford: Stanford University Press.
Howe, Christopher. 1968. 'The supply and administration of urban housing in mainland China: the case of Shanghai', *The China Quarterly* 33: 73–97.
Howe, Christopher. (ed.). 1981. *Shanghai, Revolution and Development in an Asian Metropolis*. Cambridge: Cambridge University Press.
Hu, Hsien-chin. 1944. 'The Chinese concept of "face"', *American Anthropologist* 46(1): 45–64.
Hu, Yaobang. 1986. 'On the party's journalism work (1985)', *Chinese Sociology and Anthropology* 18: 174–98.
Hughes, E.R. 1937. *The Invasion of China by the Western World*. London: Adam & Charles Black.
Inden, Ronald B. 1990. *Imagining India*. Oxford: Blackwell.
Jacobs, J. Bruce. 1997. 'Shanghai: an alternative centre?', pp. 163–93 in D.S.G. Goodman (ed.), *China's Provinces in Reform: Class, Community and Political Culture*. London: Routledge.

Jacobs, J. Bruce and Hong, Lijian. 1994. 'Shanghai and the lower Yangzi valley', pp. 224–52 in D.S.G. Goodman and G. Segal (eds), *China Deconstructs: Politics, Trade and Regionalism*. London: Routledge.

Jankowiak, William R. 1993. *Sex, Death, and Hierarchy in a Chinese City: An Anthropological Account*. New York: Columbia University Press.

Jenner, William J.F. 1992. *The Tyranny of History: The Roots of China's Crisis*. London: Allen Lane.

Jiefang Ribao 1993. '*Qingshaonian "guduzheng" zhide guanzhu*' (Youngsters' 'loneliness disease' merits attention), 13 June: 10.

Jiefang Ribao 1993. '"*Chuguore*" *jiang wen le*!' ('Going abroad craze' cools!), 29 October: 3.

Jiefang Ribao 1993. '*Yi jianshe you zhongguo tese shehuizhuyi lilun zhidao Shanghai gongzuo*' (Let Shanghai's work be led by the theory of establishing socialism with Chinese characteristics), 3 July: 1.

Johnson, Linda C. (ed.). 1993a. *Cities of Jiangnan in Late Imperial China*. New York: State University of New York Press.

Johnson, Linda C. (ed.). 1993b. 'Shanghai: an emerging Jiangnan port, 1683–1840', pp. 151–81 in L.C. Johnson (ed.), *Cities of Jiangnan in Late Imperial China*. New York: State University of New York Press.

Johnson, Linda C. 1995. *Shanghai: From Market Town to Treaty Port, 1074–1858*. Stanford: Stanford University Press.

Jones, Susan M. 1974. 'The Ningpo *pang* and financial power at Shanghai', pp. 73–96 in M. Elvin and G.W. Skinner (eds), *The Chinese City Between Two Worlds*. California: Stanford University Press.

Karmel, Solomon M. 1994. 'Emerging securities markets in China: capitalism with Chinese characteristics', *The China Quarterly* 140: 1105–20.

Kellner, Douglas. 1992. 'Popular culture and the construction of postmodern identities', pp. 141–77 in S. Lash and J. Friedman (eds), *Modernity and Identity*. Oxford: Blackwell.

King, Ambrose Y. 1991. '*Kuan-hsi* and network building: a sociological interpretation', *Daedalus* 120(2): 63–84.

Kirkby, Richard J.R. 1985. *Urbanisation in China: Town and Country in a Developing Economy 1949–2000 AD*. London: Croom Helm.

Kraus, Richard C. 1995. 'China's artists between plan and market', pp. 173–92 in D.S. Davis, R. Kraus, B. Naughton and E.J. Perry (eds), *Urban Spaces in Contemporary China: The Potential for Autonomy and Community in Post-Mao China*. Cambridge: Cambridge University Press.

Laing, E.J. 1989. 'The persistence of propriety in the 1980s', pp. 156–71 in P. Link, R. Madsen and P.G. Pickowicz (eds), *Unofficial China: Popular Culture and Thought in the PRC*. Boulder: Westview Press.

Lakoff, George. 1993. 'The contemporary theory of metaphor', pp. 202–51 in A. Ortony (ed.), *Metaphor and Thought (Second Edition)*. Cambridge: Cambridge University Press.

Lakoff, George and Mark, Johnson. 1980. *Metaphors We Live By*. London: University of Chicago Press.

Lam, Willy Wo-Lap. 1997. 'Signs of peaceful evolution', *South China Morning Post* 23 April: 17.

Lang, Olga. 1946. *Chinese Family and Society*. New Haven: Yale University Press.

Lanning, G. and S. Couling. 1921. *The History of Shanghai*. Shanghai: Kelly & Walsh.

Lay, G.T. 1843. 'Remarks on Chinese character and customs', *Chinese Repository* XII(3): 135–42.

Leiss, William, Stephen Kline and Sut Jhally. 1986. *Social Communication in Advertising: Persons, Products, and Images of Well-Being*. London: Methuen.
Leung, Yuen-sang. 1982. 'Regional rivalry in mid-nineteenth century Shanghai: Cantonese vs. Ningpo men', *Ch'ing Shih Wen-T'i* 4(8): 29–50.
Li Zhisui. 1994. *The Private Life of Chairman Mao*. London: Chatto & Windus.
Li Xiaoping. 1991. 'The Chinese television system and television news', *The China Quarterly* 126: 340–55.
Lin Yutang. 1935. *My Country and My People*. New York: John Day.
Link, Perry. 1989. 'Hand-copied entertainment fiction from the Cultural Revolution', pp. 17–36 in P. Link, R. Madsen and P.G. Pickowicz (eds), *Unofficial China: Popular Culture and Thought in the PRC*. Boulder: Westview Press.
Link, Perry. 1993. 'China's "core" problem', *Daedalus* 122(2): 189–205.
Little, Archibald. 1899. *Intimate China: The Chinese as I have seen Them*. London: Hutchinson & Co.
Lu Hanchao. 1999. *Beyond the Neon Lights: Everyday Shanghai in the Early Twentieth Century*. Berkeley: University of California Press.
Lü Xiaobao and Elizabeth J. Perry (eds). 1997. *Danwei: The Changing Chinese Workplace in Historical and Comparative Perspective*. New York: M.E. Sharpe.
Lü Xiaobao. 1997. 'Minor public economy: the revolutionary origins of the danwei', pp. 21–41 in X. Lü and E.J. Perry (eds), *Danwei: The Changing Chinese Workplace in Historical and Comparative Perspective*. New York: M.E. Sharpe
Lull, James, 1990. 'China's new star: the reformation on prime-time television', pp. 96–145 in J. Lull (ed.), *Inside Family Viewing: Ethnographic Research on Television Audiences*. London: Routledge.
Lull, James. 1991. *China Turned On: Television, Reform, and Resistance*. London: Routledge.
Lull, James and Se-Wen Sun. 1988. 'Agent of modernization: television and urban Chinese families', pp. 193–236 in J. Lull (ed.), *World Families Watch Television*. London: Sage.
MacGowan, John. 1897. *Pictures of Southern China*. London: The Religious Tract Society.
MacLellan, J.W. 1889. *The Story of Shanghai: From the Opening of the Port to Foreign Trade*. Shanghai: North China Herald.
Madsen, Richard. 1984. *Morality and Power in a Chinese Village*. London: University of California Press.
Madsen, Richard. 1993. 'The academic China specialists', pp. 163–75 in D. Shambaugh (ed.), *American Studies of Contemporary China*. New York: M.E. Sharpe.
March, A.L. 1974. *The Idea of China: Myth and Theory in Geographic Thought*. Vancouver: David & Charles.
Mackerras, Colin. 1989. *Western Images of China*. Oxford: Oxford University Press.
Martin, Brian G. 1992. '"The pact with the devil": the relationship between the green gang and the Shanghai French concession authorities, 1925–1935', pp. 266–304 in F.E. Wakeman and W. Yeh (eds), *Shanghai Sojourners*. Berkeley: Institute of East Asian Studies.
Meizhou Wenyi Bao 1993. '*Gupiao dahushi*' (Big time share dealers' room), 17–23 May: 4.
Meyrowitz, J. 1985. *No Sense of Place: The Impact of Electronic Media on Social Behavior*. Oxford: Oxford University Press.
Miller, Daniel. 1987. *Material Culture and Mass Consumption*. Blackwell: Oxford.
Miller, Daniel. (ed.). 1993. *Unwrapping Christmas*. Oxford: Clarendon Press.

Miller, Daniel. 1994. *Modernity. An Ethnographic Approach: Dualism and Mass Consumption in Trinidad*. Oxford: Berg.

Miller, G.E. 1937. *Shanghai, The Paradise of Adventurers*. New York: Orsay Publishing House.

Min Jiaji, Fan Xiao, Zhu Chuan and Zhang Song Yue. 1986. *Jianming Wu Fangyan Cidian* (Concise Dictionary of the Wu Dialect). Shanghai: Shanghai Cidian Chubanshe.

Morley, David. 1991. 'Where the global meets the local: notes from the sitting room', *Screen* 32(1): 1–15.

Morley, David and Kevin Robins. 1989. 'Spaces of identity: communications technologies and the reconfiguration of Europe', *Screen* 30(4): 10–34.

Morley, David and Roger, Silverstone. 1990. 'Domestic communication – technologies and meanings', *Media, Culture and Society* 12(1): 31–55.

Mote, Frederick W. 1977. 'The transformation of Nanking, 1350–1400', pp. 101–54 in G.W. Skinner (ed.), *The City in Late Imperial China*. Stanford: Stanford University Press.

Moule, Arthur E. 1911. *Half a Century in China: Recollections and Observations*. London: Hodder & Stoughton.

Murphey, Rhoads. 1953. *Shanghai, Key to Modern China*. Cambridge: Harvard University Press.

Murphey, Rhoads. 1974. 'The treaty ports and China's modernization', pp. 17–71 in M. Elvin and G.W. Skinner (eds), *The Chinese City Between Two Worlds*. California: Stanford University Press.

Nanfang Zhoumo 1993. '*Yongjin guchao de nurenmen*' (The women who surge into the share wave), 18 June: 1.

Nathan, Andrew J. 1986. *Chinese Democracy*. London: I.B. Tarsus & Co.

Naughton, Barry. 1995a. 'Urban space: introduction', pp. 23–7 in D.S. Davis, R. Kraus, B. Naughton and E.J. Perry (eds), *Urban Spaces in Contemporary China: The Potential for Autonomy and Community in Post-Mao China*. Cambridge: Cambridge University Press.

Naughton, Barry. 1995b. 'Cities in the Chinese economic system: changing roles and conditions for autonomy', pp. 61–89 in D.S. Davis, R. Kraus, B. Naughton and E.J. Perry (eds), *Urban Spaces in Contemporary China: The Potential for Autonomy and Community in Post-Mao China*. Cambridge: Cambridge University Press.

Noam, Eli M. (ed.). 1990. *Technologies Without Boundaries: On Telecommunications in a Global Age*. Cambridge, Massachusetts: Harvard University Press.

Pan Ling. 1984. *Old Shanghai: Gangsters in Paradise*. Hong Kong: Heinemann.

Pannell, Clifton W. 1981. 'Recent growth and change in China's urban system', pp. 91–113 in L.J.C. Ma and E.W. Hanten (eds), *Urban Development in Modern China*. Boulder: Westview Press.

Parish, William L. and Martin K. Whyte. 1978. *Village and Family in Contemporary China*. Chicago: University of Chicago Press.

Parish, William L. and Martin K. Whyte. 1984. *Urban Life in Contemporary China*. Chicago: University of Chicago Press.

Parker, R.A. 1923. *Lessons in the Shanghai Dialect*. Shanghai: Shanghai Municipal Council.

Parkin, David. 1987. 'Comparison as the search for continuity', pp. 52–69 in L. Holy (ed.), *Comparative Anthropology*. Oxford: Basil Blackwell.

Parkin, David. 1993. '*Nemi* in the modern world: return of the exotic?', *Man* 28(1): 79–99.

Pellow, D. 1993. 'No place to live, no place to love: coping in Shanghai', pp. 396–424 in G.E. Guldin and A. Southall (eds), *Urban Anthropology in China*. Leiden: E.J. Brill.

Perry, Elizabeth J. 1989. 'State and society in contemporary China', *World Politics* XLI(4): 579–91.

Perry, Elizabeth J. 1992. 'Introduction: Chinese political culture revisited', pp. 1–13 in J.N. Wasserstrom and E.J. Perry (eds), *Popular Protest and Political Culture in Modern China: Learning from 1989*. Oxford: Westview Press.

Perry, Elizabeth J. 1993. *Shanghai On Strike: The Politics of Chinese Labor*. Stanford: Stanford University Press.

Perry, Elizabeth J. 1994. 'Shanghai's strike wave of 1957', *The China Quarterly* 137: 1–27.

Perry, Elizabeth J. 1995. 'Urban associations: introduction', pp. 297–301 in D.S. Davis, R. Kraus, B. Naughton and E.J. Perry (eds), *Urban Spaces in Contemporary China: The Potential for Autonomy and Community in Post-Mao China*. Cambridge: Cambridge University Press.

Pickowicz, Paul G. 1995. 'Velvet prisons and the political economy of Chinese filmmaking', pp. 193–220 in D.S. Davis, R. Kraus, B. Naughton and E.J. Perry (eds), *Urban Spaces in Contemporary China: The Potential for Autonomy and Community in Post-Mao China*. Cambridge: Cambridge University Press.

Pieke, Frank N. 1996. *The Ordinary and the Extraordinary: An Anthropological Study of Chinese Reform and the 1989 People's Movement in Beijing*. London: Kegan Paul International.

Pott, F.L. Hawks. 1924. *Lessons in the Shanghai Dialect*. Shanghai: Commercial Press.

Pott, F.L. Hawks. 1928. *A Short History of Shanghai*. Shanghai: Kelly & Walsh.

Potter, Sulamith H. and Jack M. Potter. 1990. *China's Peasants. The Anthropology of a Revolution*. Cambridge: Cambridge University Press.

Prime, Penelope B. 1989. 'Socialism and economic development: the politics of accumulation in China', pp. 136–51 in A. Dirlik and M. Meisner (eds), *Marxism and the Chinese Experience*. New York: M.E. Sharpe.

Pye, Lucian W. 1981. 'Foreword', pp. xi–xvi in C. Howe (ed.), *Shanghai, Revolution and Development in an Asian Metropolis*. Cambridge: Cambridge University Press.

Pye, Lucian W. 1993. 'An introductory profile: Deng Xiaoping and China's political culture', *The China Quarterly* 135: 412–43.

Qian Zhongshu. 1991 [1947]. *Wei Cheng* (Fortress Besieged). Beijing: Renmin Wenxue Chubanshe.

Rai, Shirin. 1991. *Resistance and Reaction: University Politics in Post-Mao China*. Hemmel Hempstead: Harvester Wheatsheaf.

Ramsey, S. Robert. 1987. *The Languages of China*. Princeton: Princeton University Press.

Redding, S. Gordon. 1993. *The Spirit of Chinese Capitalism*. Berlin: Walter de Gruyter.

Rofel, Lisa. 1989. 'Hegemony and productivity: workers in post-Mao China', pp. 235–52 in A. Dirlik and M. Meisner (eds), *Marxism and the Chinese Experience*. New York: M.E. Sharpe.

Rofel, Lisa. 1992. 'Rethinking modernity: space and factory discipline in China', *Cultural Anthropology* 7(1): 93–114.

Ross, Edward A. 1911. *The Changing Chinese: The Conflict of Oriental and Western Cultures in China*. London: T. Fisher Unwin.

Sahin, H. and J.P. Robinson. 1981. 'Beyond the realm of necessity: television and the colonization of leisure', *Media, Culture and Society* 3(1): 85–95.

Saich, Tony. 1992. 'The reform decade in China: the limits to revolution from above', pp. 10–73 in T. Saich and M. Dassù (eds), *The Reform Decade in China: From Hope to Dismay*. London: Kegan Paul.

Said, Edward W. 1978. *Orientalism*. London: Routledge & Kegan Paul.

Scannell, Paddy. 1988. 'Radio times: the temporal arrangements of broadcasting in the modern world', pp. 15–31 in P. Drummond and R. Paterson (eds), *Television and Its Audiences: International Research Perspectives*. London: British Film Institute.

Schwarcz, Vera. 1991. 'No solace from lethe: history, memory, and cultural identity in twentieth-century China', *Daedalus* 120(2): 85–112.

Scott, James C. 1990 [1985]. *Weapons of the Weak: Everyday Forms of Peasant Resistance*. Delhi: Oxford University Press.

Segal, Gerald. 1996. 'Asia Gold' *BBC Radio 4*, broadcast 4 January.

Shambaugh, David. 1993. 'Deng Xiaoping: the politician', *The China Quarterly* 132: 457–90.

Shanghai. 1997. *Shanghai Basic Facts*. Beijing: China Intercontinental Press.

Shanghai Star 1992. 'Housing plan ahead of schedule', 18 December: 2.

Shanghai Star 1993. 'New drama plays to the markets', 5 March: 15.

Shanghai Star 1993. 'City of future', 2 July: 1.

Shanghai Star 1993. 'Network wires economic news', 19 November: 3.

Shanghai Star 1993. 'Milestone for mobile phones', 18 December: 2.

Shanghai Star 1994. 'Stock exchange expands', 12 July: 7.

Shanghai Star 1994. 'A rockets 104% in week', 9 August: 7.

Shanghai Star 1997. '$36 million to finance growth in the provinces', 9 May: 6.

Shanghai Star 1997. 'No more new paging stations', 16 May: 3.

Shanghai Star 1997. 'Creating new jobs', 27 May: 1.

Shanghai Star 1997. 'Income gap widens', 6 June: 2.

Shanghai Star 1997. 'Airlinks proliferate', 6 June: 4.

Shanghai Star 1997. 'Untangling gridlock', 10 June: 3.

Shanghai Star 1997. 'Insurance sales grow', 17 June: 6.

Shanghai Star 1997. 'Foreign ventures vital', 27 June: 2.

Shanghai Star 1997. 'Private sector blossoms', 22 July: 1.

Shanghai Star 1997. 'Call phones wars rising in sales', 1 August: 4.

Shanghai Star 1997. 'Deng's vision a blessing', 15 August: 3.

Shanghai Star 1997. 'Students return to work in Shanghai', 26 August: 4.

Shanghai Star 1997. 'More local people marrying foreigners', 29 August: 3.

Shanghai Star 1997. 'Living standards rise', 9 September: 3.

Shanghai Star 1999. 'Auto giants race to grip China's market', 5 January: 6.

Shanghai Star 1999. 'Buildings provide relief', 12 January: 4.

Shanghai Star 1999. 'Clean firms' management', 22 January: 1.

Shanghai Star 1999. 'Housing sales remain vigorous', 29 January: 6.

Shanghai Star 1999. 'Families in need', 1 February: 1.

Shanghai Star 1999. 'Efforts to regulate signs', 2 March: 2.

Shanghai Star 1999. 'Final work on airport', 19 March: 1.

Shanghai Star 1999. 'Low birth rate focus', 9 April: 1.

Shanghai Star 1999. 'Pitfalls on road to WTO', 25 May: 1.

Shanghai Star 1999. 'Youth claim, "money matters"', 25 May: 9.

Shanghai Star 1999. 'Crack down on surfing the net illegally', 13 July: 4.

Shanghai Star 1999. 'Talent pool to be channelled into city', 13 August: 3.

Shanghai Star 1999. 'Number of mobile phone users soars', 21 September: 3.

Shanghai Star 1999. 'Good opportunity for retail sector', 23 November: 7.

Shanghai Star 2000. 'Foreign influx', 7 January: 1.

Shanghai Star 2000. 'Better house loan outlook', 11 January: 10.

Shanghai Star 2000. 'Shanghai eases its car market protectionism', 28 January: 4.
Shanghai Star 2000. 'Internet age to evolve gradually', 1 February: 6.
Shanghai Star 2000. 'Survey shows shift in attitudes', 4 February: 2.
Shanghai Star 2000. 'Entrepreneurs hit the big time', 15 February: 10.
Shanghai Star 2000. 'Bridging the gap', 22 February: 1.
Shanghai Star 2000. 'How the city will look in 2020', 22 February: 4.
Shanghai Star 2000. 'Centenarian plays the markets', 22 February: 9.
Shanghai Star 2000. 'Fight for justice', 7 March: 1.
Shanghai Star 2000. 'Housing sales in 15% yearly gain', 11 April: 11.
Shanghai Star 2000. 'Hi-tech mover', 18 April: 1.
Shanghai Star 2000. 'Speculation heats up over racecourse', 26 May: 3.
Shanghai Star 2000. 'Beijing express', 2 June: 1.
Shanghai Star 2000. 'Survey: bias, lower pay rife', 7 July: 3
Shanghai Star 2000. 'Spread in sex aids outlets', 11 July: 4.
Shanghai Star 2000. 'Internet to total 30 million users in 2002', 25 July: 11.
Shanghai Star 2000. 'Till the divorce court do us part', 1 August: 4.
Shanghai Star 2000. 'Entertainment places offer "unlawful services"', 11 August: 4.
Shanghai Star 2000. 'Dotcoms vie for talent', 15 August: 11.
Shanghai Star 2000. 'Reforms to fuel economy', 29 August: 10.
Shanghai Star 2000. 'Major changes coming in property market', 12 September: 10.
Shanghai Today. 2000. 'Economic development', http://china-window.com/shanghai1/english/index1.html, accessed 16 November.
Shanghai Wenhua Yishu Bao 1993. '*Kan huaju "OK gupiao"*' (Watching the play 'OK Stock'), 5 March: 2.
Shanghai Wenhua Yishu Bao 1993. '*Yang baiwan*' (Millions Yang), 4–10 June: 4.
Shanghai Wenyi Bao 1993. '*Dushi liuxing da zhanwang*' (Forecasting metropolitan fashions), 5 March: 2.
Shanghai Yibao 1993. '*Shanghai gushi jiakuai fazhan sudu*' (Shanghai share market speeds up its pace of development), 18 January: 1.
Shiba, Yoshinobu. 1977. 'Ningpo and its hinterland', pp. 391–440 in G.W. Skinner (ed.), *The City in Late Imperial China*. Stanford: Stanford University Press.
Shirk, Susan L. 1982. *Competitive Comrades: Career Incentives and Student Strategies in China*. Berkeley: University of California Press.
Shue, Vivienne. 1988. *The Reach of the State: Sketches of the Chinese Body Politic*. Stanford: Stanford University Press.
Silsby, J.A. 1911. *Introduction to the Study of the Shanghai Vernacular*. Shanghai: American Presbyterian Mission Press.
Simmel, Georg. 1990 [1900]. *The Philosophy of Money* (edited by D. Frisby and T. Bottomore). London: Routledge.
Siu, Helen F. 1993. 'Cultural identity and the politics of difference in South China', *Daedalus* 122(2): 19–42.
Skinner, G. William. 1977a. 'Introduction: urban and rural in Chinese society', pp. 253–73 in G.W. Skinner (ed.), *The City in Late Imperial China*. Stanford: Stanford University Press.
Skinner, G. William. 1977b. 'Introduction: urban social structure in Ch'ing China', pp. 521–53 in G.W. Skinner (ed.), *The City in Late Imperial China*. Stanford: Stanford University Press.
Smart, A. 1993. 'Gifts, bribes, and *guanxi*: a reconsideration of Bourdieu's social capital', *Cultural Anthropology* 8(3): 388–408.

Solinger, Dorothy J. 1992. 'Urban entrepreneurs and the state: the merger of state and society', pp. 121–41 in A.L. Rosenbaum (ed.), *State and Society in China: The Consequences of Reform*. Boulder: Westview Press.

Solinger, Dorothy J. 1995. 'The floating population in the cities: chances for assimilation?', pp. 113–39 in D.S. Davis, R. Kraus, B. Naughton and E.J. Perry (eds), *Urban Spaces in Contemporary China: The Potential for Autonomy and Community in Post-Mao China*. Cambridge: Cambridge University Press.

Statistical Yearbook. 1996. *Statistical Yearbook of Shanghai*. Shanghai Municipal Statistics Bureau. China Statistical Publishing House.

Stross, Randall. 1990. 'The return of advertising in China: a survey of the ideological reversal', *The China Quarterly* 123: 485–502.

Su, Xiaokang. 1991. 'The distress of a dragon year – notes on *Heshang*', pp. 271–99 in X. Su and L. Wang (eds), *Deathsong of the River: A Reader's Guide to the Chinese TV Series Heshang*. New York: Cornell East Asia Papers.

Su, Xiaokang and Wang, Luxiang (eds). 1991. *Deathsong of the River: A Reader's Guide to the Chinese TV Series Heshang*. Translated by R. Bodman and P.P. Wang. New York: Cornell East Asia Papers.

Sutherland, Christopher F. 1985. *Urban Change in Revolutionary China: Shanghai 1949–1982*. Ann Arbor: University Microfilms International.

SWB. 1996. Summary of World Broadcasts, FEW/0418 WG/22, 17 January.

Tam, On Kit. 1991. 'Capital market development in China', *World Development* 19(5): 511–32.

Taylor, William. 1984. 'Metaphors of educational discourse', pp. 4–20 in W. Taylor (ed.), *Metaphors of Education*. London: Heinemann Educational Books.

Thompson, John B. 1990. *Ideology and Modern Culture: Critical Social Theory in the Era of Mass Communication*. Oxford: Polity Press.

Thompson, Stuart E. 1990. 'Metaphors the Chinese age by', pp. 102–20 in P. Spencer (ed.), *Anthropology and the Riddle of the Sphinx*. London: Routledge.

Thompson, Stuart E. 1994. '*Riz* de passage: life bytes and alimentary practices', *China Now* 149: 10–12.

Thurston, Anne F. 1983. 'The social sciences and fieldwork in China: an overview', pp. 3–36 in A.F. Thurston and B. Pasternak (eds), *The Social Sciences and Fieldwork in China: Views from the Field*. Boulder: Westview Press.

Tomlinson, Alan. 1990a. 'Introduction. Consumer culture and the aura of the commodity', pp. 1–38 in A. Tomlinson (ed.), *Consumption, Identity, and Style: Marketing, Meanings, and the Packaging of Pleasure*. London: Routledge.

Tomlinson, Alan. 1990b. 'Home fixtures: doing-it-yourself in a privatized world', pp. 57–73 in A. Tomlinson (ed.), *Consumption, Identity, and Style: Marketing, Meanings, and the Packaging of Pleasure*. London: Routledge.

Tu Wei-ming. 1991. 'Cultural China: the periphery as the center', *Daedalus* 120(2): 1–32.

Tu Wei-ming. 1992. 'Intellectual effervescence in China', *Daedalus* 121(2): 251–92.

Vogel, Ezra F. 1965. 'From friendship to comradeship', *The China Quarterly* 21: 455–60.

Vogel, Ezra F. 1989. *One Step Ahead in China: Guangdong Under Reform*. Cambridge, Massachusetts: Harvard University Press.

Wakeman, Frederic E. and Wen-hsin Yeh (eds). 1992. *Shanghai Sojourners*. Berkeley: Institute of East Asian Studies.

Walder, Andrew G. 1986. *Communist Neo-Traditionalism: Work and Authority in Chinese Industry*. Berkeley: University of California Press.

Walder, Andrew G. 1987. 'Communist social structure and workers' politics in China', pp. 45–89 in V.C. Falkenheim (ed.), *Citizens and Groups in Contemporary China*. Ann Arbor: University of Michigan.

Walder, Andrew G. 1989. 'The political sociology of the Beijing upheaval of 1989', *Problems of Communism* 38: 30–48.

Walder, Andrew G. 1990. 'Economic reform and income distribution in Tianjin, 1976–1986', pp. 135–56 in D. Davis and E.F. Vogel (eds), *Chinese Society on the Eve of Tiananmen*. Harvard University: The Council on East Asian Studies.

Walder, Andrew G. 1992. 'Urban industrial workers: some observations on the 1980s', pp. 103–20 in A.L. Rosenbaum (ed.), *State and Society in China: The Consequences of Reform*. Boulder: Westview Press.

Wallerstein, Immanuel. 1979. *The Capitalist World-Economy: Essays by Immanuel Wallerstein*. Cambridge: Cambridge University Press.

Wang, Shaoguang. 1995. 'The politics of private time: changing leisure patterns in urban China', pp. 149–72 in D.S. Davis, R. Kraus, B. Naughton and E.J. Perry (eds), *Urban Spaces in Contemporary China: The Potential for Autonomy and Community in Post-Mao China*. Cambridge: Cambridge University Press.

Ward, Barbara. 1985. *Through Other Eyes*. Hong Kong: The Chinese University Press.

Wark, Mckenzie. 1993. 'Vectors of memory . . . seeds of fire: the Western media and the Beijing demonstrations', pp. 129–42 in E. Carter, J. Donald and J. Squires (eds), *Space and Place: Theories of Identity and Location*. London: Laurence & Wishart.

Warner, Shelley. 1991. 'Shanghai's response to the deluge', pp. 215–31 in J. Unger (ed.), *The Pro-Democracy Protests in China: Reports from the Provinces*. London: M.E. Sharp.

Wasserstrom, Jeffrey N. 1991. *Student Protests in Twentieth Century China: The View from Shanghai*. Stanford: Stanford University Press.

Watson, James L. 1992. 'The renegotiation of Chinese cultural identity in the post-Mao era', pp. 67–84 in J.N. Wasserstrom and E.J. Perry (eds), *Popular Protest and Political Culture in Modern China: Learning from 1989*. Oxford: Westview Press.

Watson, James L. (ed.). 1997a. *Golden Arches East: McDonald's in East Asia*. Stanford: Stanford University Press.

Watson, James L. 1997b. 'Transnationalism, localization, and fast foods in East Asia', pp. 1–38 in J.L. Watson (ed.), *Golden Arches East: McDonald's in East Asia*. Stanford: Stanford University Press.

Weller, Robert P. 1994. *Resistance, Chaos and Control in China: Taiping Rebels, Taiwanese Ghost and Tiananmen*. London: Macmillan.

Wenhui Bao 1993. '"*Mingpai*" *xiaofeichao nengfou chijiu*?' (Can the flood of consuming 'famous brand names' endure?), 13 May: 7.

Wenhui Bao 1993. '*Shanghai changkai damen huanying touzizhe*' (Shanghai opens wide its great door and welcomes investors), 26 May: 1.

Wenhui Dianying Shibao 1993. '*Jiushi niandai xiaofeichao toushi*' (Perspectives on the consumer flood in the nineties), 5 June: 7.

White III, Lynn T. 1978. *Careers in Shanghai: The Social Guidance of Personal Energies in a Developing Chinese City, 1949–1966*. Berkeley: University of California Press.

White III, Lynn T. 1981. 'Non-governmentalism in the historical development of Shanghai', pp. 19–57 in L.J.C. Ma and E.W. Hanten (eds), *Urban Development in Modern China*. Boulder: Westview Press.

White III, Lynn T. 1994. 'Migration and politics on the Shanghai delta', *Issues and Studies* 30(9): 63–94.

White III, Lynn T. and Li, Cheng. 1993. 'China coast identities: regional, national, and global', pp. 154–93 in L. Dittmer and S.S. Kim (eds), *China's Quest for National Identity*. Ithaca: Cornell University Press.

White, Gordon. 1987. 'Riding the tiger: grass-roots rural politics in the wake of the Chinese economic reforms', pp. 250–69 in A. Saith (ed.), *The Re-emergence of the Chinese Peasantry: Aspects of Rural Decollectivization*. London: Croom Helm.

White, Gordon. (ed.). 1991. *The Chinese State in the Era of Economic Reform: The Road to Crisis*. London: Macmillan.

White, Gordon. 1993. *Riding the Tiger: The Politics of Economic Reform in Post-Mao China*. London: Macmillan.

Whyte, Martin K. 1988. 'Death in the People's Republic of China', pp. 289–316 in J.L. Watson and E.S. Rawski (eds), *Death Ritual in Late Imperial and Modern China*. London: University of California Press.

Whyte, Martin K. 1992. 'China's Social Future'. Talk given as part of *The China Quarterly* 'China After Deng' conference. School of Oriental and African Studies, University of London, 8 May.

Wilson, James H. 1887. *China: Travels and Investigations in the 'Middle Kingdom'*. New York: D. Appleton & Co.

Wilson, Jeanne L. 1990. 'Labor policy in China: reform and retrogression', *Problems of Communism* 39: 44–65.

Wolf, Arthur P. 1974. 'Gods, ghosts, and ancestors', pp. 131–82 in A.P. Wolf (ed.), *Religion and Ritual in Chinese Society*. Stanford: Stanford University Press.

Womack, Brantly and Guangzhi, Zhao. 1994. 'The many worlds of China's provinces: foreign trade and diversification', pp. 131–76 in D.S.G. Goodman and G. Segal (eds), *China Deconstructs: Politics, Trade and Regionalism*. London: Routledge.

Women of China 1992. 'Rising stocks', 10: 32–3.

Wong, Siu-lun. 1988. *Emigrant Entrepreneurs: Shanghai Industrialists in Hong Kong*. Hong Kong: Oxford University Press.

Wong, Siu-lun. 1996. 'The entrepreneurial spirit: Shanghai and Hong Kong compared', pp. 25–48 in Y.M. Yeung and S. Yun-wing (eds), *Shanghai: Transformation and Modernization Under China's Open Policy*. Hong Kong: The Chinese University Press.

World Bank. 1990. *China: Macroeconomic Stability and Industrial Growth Under Decentralized Socialism*. Washington, DC: The World Bank.

World Business Report 1993. BBC World Service, 25 March.

World Business Report 1993. BBC World Service, 24 June.

Wu, David Yen-ho. 1991. 'The construction of Chinese and non-Chinese identities', *Daedalus* 120(2): 159–79.

Wu, Harry. 1995. 'Human rights in China', SOAS Centre of Chinese Studies Special Seminar, 15 November.

Wu, Lijiang and Lan, Chendong. 1985. 'A stumbling block to the establishment of a new system of social relations: a summary of interviews concerning discrimination against natives of northern Jiangsu', *Chinese Sociology and Anthropology* 17(3): 74–81.

Wu Lijiang, Ying Tingjia, Xu Zhiyuan and Chen Zhongya. 1985. 'An investigation into the circumstances of discrimination against natives of northern Jiangsu', *Chinese Sociology and Anthropology* 17(3): 62–73.

Xia Mei, Jian Lin Hai and Philip D. Grub. 1992. *The Re-Emerging Securities Market in China*. Westport, Connecticut: Quorum Books.

Xia Yan. 1959. *Baoshen Gong* (Indentured Labourer). Beijing: Gongren Chubanshe.

Xie, Simin. 1990. 'China's stock market: problems and future development', *China Newsletter* 89: 18–25.

Xinmin Wanbao 1992. '*Shanghaitan chuxian "yapishi"*' ('Yuppies' appear in Shanghai), 26 October: 2.

Xinmin Wanbao 1993. '*Hushang "dageda" jiazu kewang zisun mantang*' (Shanghai's mobile phones increase the pace of meeting the desire to seek advice), 16 January: 2.

Xinmin Wanbao 1993. '*Xunmi xie wang*' (Searching for the king of the crabs), 17 January: 1.

Xinmin Wanbao 1993. '*Deng Xiaoping tongzhi yu Shanghai gejie xiying xinchun*' (Comrade Deng Xiaoping welcomes the days after Chinese New Year with Shanghainese from all walks of life), 23 January: 1.

Xinmin Wanbao 1993. '*Zhongguo gumin reng zai "yinger qi"*' (Chinese share buyers still at 'infant stage'), 22 March: 12.

Xinmin Wanbao 1993. '*Ye chuan KTV*' (Night-time visit to KTV), 9 July: 13.

Xinmin Wanbao 1993. '*"Youjidui" qiaoqiaode jin chang*' ('Guerilla force' quietly entering factories), 22 July: 12.

Xinmin Wanbao 1993. '*Hushang jindian duo haishi midian duo*' (Are there more gold stores or more rice stores in Shanghai), 5 November: 14.

Xinmin Wanbao 1993. '*Fangfu chonghui Shanghai shiguang*' (Just like returning to Shanghai), 5 December: 5.

Xinmin Wanbao 1993. '*Chaogu dahu yuanshi tanwu dahu*' (Share dealing rich man originally was a corrupt rich man), 6 December: 3.

Xu, Xunchu. 1993. 'A look into Shanghai's 21st century passenger transport', the Institute of Urban Planning and Architecture of Tongji University. Unpublished paper from the International Workshop on the Planning and Development of Metropolitan Regions, Shanghai 11–14 October. 19 pages.

Xu, Pinli. nd (early 1990s). *Zuotian de Guiyuan Shu* (Yesterday's Longan Tree). Shanghai: Shanghai Xiju Xueyuan.

Yan, Yunxiang. 1997. 'McDonald's in Beijing: the localization of Americana', pp. 39–76 in J.L. Watson (ed.), *Golden Arches East: McDonald's in East Asia*. Stanford: Stanford University Press.

Yan, Zhongmin. 1985. 'Shanghai: the growth and shifting emphasis of China's largest city', pp. 94–127 in V.F.S. Sit (ed.), *Chinese Cities: The Growth of the Metropolis Since 1949*. Hong Kong: Oxford University Press.

Yang, Mayfair M. 1986. 'The art of social relationships and exchange in China', PhD thesis, Berkeley: University of California.

Yang, Mayfair M. 1989a. 'The gift economy and state power in China', *Comparative Studies in Society and History* 31: 25–54.

Yang, Mayfair M. 1989b. 'Between state and society: the construction of corporateness in a Chinese socialist factory', *Australian Journal of Chinese Affairs* 22: 31–60.

Yang, Mayfair M. 1994. *Gifts, Favors and Banquets: The Art of Social Relationships in China*. Ithaca: Cornell University Press.

Yang, Mayfair M. 1997. 'Mass media and transnational subjectivity in Shanghai: notes on (re)cosmopolitanism in a Chinese metropolis', pp. 287–319 in A. Ong and D.M. Nonini (eds), *Ungrounded Empires: The Cultural Politics of Modern Chinese Transnationalism*. London: Routledge.

Yi, Gang. 1994. *Money, Banking, and Financial Markets in China*. Boulder: Westview Press.

Young, Susan. 1991. 'Wealth but not security: attitudes towards private business in China in the 1980s', *Australian Journal of Chinese Affairs* 25: 115–37.

You, Ji. 1998. *China's Enterprise Reform: Changing State/Society Relations after Mao.* Routledge: London.

Zhao, Min. 1993. 'Economic growth and urban development in Shanghai – environmental considerations', unpublished paper from the International Workshop on the Planning and Development of Metropolitan Regions, Shanghai, 11–14 October. 27 pages.

Index

For Product Safety Concerns and Information please contact our EU
representative GPSR@taylorandfrancis.com
Taylor & Francis Verlag GmbH, Kaufingerstraße 24, 80331 München, Germany

www.ingramcontent.com/pod-product-compliance
Ingram Content Group UK Ltd.
Pitfield, Milton Keynes, MK11 3LW, UK
UKHW020013200926
475702UK00014B/1856

* 9 7 8 0 4 1 5 8 6 1 6 2 5 *